Algorithmic
Problem Solving

Algorithmic Problem Solving

Roland Backhouse

University of Nottingham

A John Wiley & Sons, Ltd., Publication

This edition first published 2011
© 2011 John Wiley & Sons Ltd.

Registered office
John Wiley & Sons Ltd., The Atrium, Southern Gate, Chichester, West Sussex, PO19 8SQ, United Kingdom

For details of our global editorial offices, for customer services and for information about how to apply for permission to reuse the copyright material in this book please see our website at www.wiley.com.

Library of Congress Cataloging-in-Publication Data

Backhouse, Roland C., 1948-
   Algorithmic problem solving / Roland Backhouse.
      p. cm.
   Includes bibliographical references and index.
   ISBN 978-0-470-68453-5 (pbk. : alk. paper)
   1. Computer algorithms. 2. Problem solving. I. Title.
   QA76.9.A43B34 2011
   005.1 – dc23

                       2011022716

A catalogue record for this book is available from the British Library.

Set in 9/12 Sabon by Laserwords Private Ltd., Chennai, India.
Printed in Great Britain by TJ International, Padstow, Cornwall

Contents

Preface

In the modern, developed world our lifestyles, our livelihoods and even our lives have become highly dependent on computer technology in a way that would have been unimaginable fifty years ago. Underpinning the developments that have made this possible has been a fundamental change in the nature of our problem-solving skills: in many cases, the solution to a difficult and challenging problem has to be formulated as a computer program to be executed by a dumb machine. Not only have the size and complexity of the problems we tackle changed beyond measure, the precision and accuracy with which our solutions need to be formulated have undergone a revolution. Algorithmic problem solving is about the skills that are needed to meet the new challenges that we face.

This book is based on a first-year, first-semester module that was first introduced at the University of Nottingham in September 2003. Initially the module was optional but, in 2006, it was made compulsory for all first-year Computer Science and Software Engineering students (as well as still being optional for students on other degree programmes) and has remained so ever since. The module is taught at each of the University's three campuses in China, Malaysia and the UK.

The aim of the book is to instill good problem-solving skills, particularly but not exclusively in cases where the solution to a problem involves the design of an algorithm. The approach is problem-driven: the main part of the book consists of a series of examples that introduce the principles of algorithmic problem solving in a systematic fashion. The use of a problem-driven approach is crucial to exciting students' natural propensity to take on a challenge; however, examples without theory are meaningless, so the second part of the book is about the mathematics that underpins the principles. Boxes within the text point the reader to the mathematics that is relevant to a particular example.

The presentation deviates from traditional mathematical practice in a number of ways. The treatment of boolean algebra and logic, for example, is non-standard and some notation is also non-standard. These deviations are, however, based on developments in algorithmic problem solving that have been well understood for at least twenty years. (Although twenty years is a very short time-span in the development of mathematics, it is a relatively long period in the modern computer age.) Potential teachers who are not already convinced or unfamiliar with the material are asked to approach it with an open mind.

The majority of the book is class-tested but not all, and not all at the level of the first year, first semester of an undergraduate degree. For three years I taught the mathematical techniques (Part II of the book) in a module that was given in the same semester as the module on algorithmic problem solving (Part I), but that is no longer the case. Also, both parts of the book cover more material than I am able to cover in any one year. Some topics (such as boolean algebra) could be presented at pre-university level but some (in the later chapters) are better postponed to later years.

Having an excess of example problems has the advantage of offering a choice. My own practice is to base assessment firmly on coursework that involves the students in active problem solving and which I vary from year to year so that no two years are the same. Model solutions to all exercises, which I have given to students for feedback purposes, are included at the end of the text. Solutions are omitted, however, for some exercises that I call "projects" and some projects that I set have not been included in the text. (Model solutions to the projects are given to the students in hard-copy form in order to be able to reuse them without the risk of plagiarism.)

When teaching a topic such as this, it is very important that the examples are challenging but within the grasp of the students. The problems I have chosen are most often ones that the reader should be able to solve in a brute-force fashion without any mathematical knowledge but which can be solved much more effectively with the knowledge. The hidden agenda in the book is to engage the reader in the process of doing mathematics: the process of modelling and calculating the solutions to problems even when mathematics does not seem to be directly relevant.

The presentation here is very strongly influenced by the writings of Edsger W. Dijkstra (1930–2002). Dijkstra is renowned for his contributions to algorithm design. In addition, throughout his career he put much effort into trying to articulate and, by so doing, improve mathematical method. My own view is that his contribution to mathematical method is yet greater than his (phenomenal) contribution to computing science. Occasionally I have used his words (or paraphrases of his words) without direct acknowledgement; like true proverbs, they deserve the acceptance that only comes with anonymity. One such is Dijkstra's definition of mathematics as "the art of effective reasoning" (see Chapter 12). I will never be able to emulate his problem-solving skills but I do hope that by trying to continue his work on mathematical method, I might encourage others to think more critically about and deliberately articulate good and bad problem-solving skills.

I have received a lot of support from colleagues in the preparation of the book and I would like to thank them all. I would particularly like to thank Diethard Michaelis and David Gries, both of whom have given very detailed criticism and suggestions for improvement. Particular thanks also go to those who have helped with the teaching of the module: Siang Yew Chong and John Woodward have taught the module in Malaysia and China, respectively, for several years. João Ferreira also taught the module in Nottingham for one year when I was on sabbatical and has assisted me for many years with classes and with marking coursework and examinations, as have Wei Chen and

Alexandra Mendes. I am very grateful to them all for the way that they have engaged so positively with the challenges of an unconventional teaching method. Thanks go to the publishers John Wiley & Sons, in particular Georgia King and Jonathan Shipley for their patience and cooperation, and to the ten (mostly anonymous) reviewers for their comments and feedback. Finally, my thanks to the students who have successfully completed the course and rewarded me with their enthusiasm. The best feedback I have had was the student (whom I can still picture but whose name I do not recollect) who said: "This is the most challenging module, but I like a challenge."

Roland Backhouse
March 2011

Part I

Algorithmic Problem Solving

Chapter

Introduction

1

In 1964 the word "algorithm" was not included in the newly published fifth edition of the *Concise Oxford Dictionary*. Today it is commonplace for ordinary people to read about "algorithms", for example algorithms for detecting inappropriate or unusual use of the Internet, algorithms for improving car safety and algorithms for identifying and responding to gestures. The notion of an algorithm hardly needs any introduction in our modern computerised society.

It is not that algorithms have only recently come into existence. On the contrary, algorithms have been used for millennia. Algorithms are used, for example, in building and in measurement: an algorithm is used when tunnelling through a mountain to ensure that the two ends meet in the middle, and cartographers use algorithms to determine the height of mountains without having to climb up them. But, before the computer age, it does not seem to have been considered important or relevant to emphasise the algorithm being used.

1.1 ALGORITHMS

An algorithm is a well-defined procedure, consisting of a number of instructions that are executed in turn. In the past, algorithms were almost always executed by human beings, which may explain the earlier lack of emphasis on algorithms. After all, human beings are intelligent and cope well with imprecise or incomplete instructions. Nowadays, however, algorithms are being automated more and more often and so are typically executed by computers,[1] which can at best be described as "dumb" machines. As a consequence, the instructions need to be both precise and very detailed. This has led to major new challenges that tax our problem-solving ability and to major changes in what

---

[1] Long ago a "computer" was understood to be a person, so we should really say "electronic digital computer". However, we now take it for granted that this is the sole meaning of the word "computer".

we understand as the solution to a problem. The computer age has revolutionised not just our way of life, but also our way of thinking.

1.2 ALGORITHMIC PROBLEM SOLVING

Human beings are quite good at executing algorithms. For example, children are taught at an early age how to execute long division in order to evaluate, say, 123456 divided by 78 and its remainder, and most soon become quite good at it. However, human beings are liable to make mistakes, and computers are much better than us at executing algorithms, at least so long as the algorithm is formulated precisely and correctly. The use of a computer to perform routine calculations is very effective.

Formulating algorithms is a different matter. This is a task that few human beings practise and so we cannot claim to be good at it. But human beings are creative; computers, on the other hand, are incapable of formulating algorithms and even so-called "intelligent" systems rely on a human being to formulate the algorithm that is then executed by the computer. Algorithmic problem solving is about formulating the algorithms to solve a collection of problems. Improving our skills in algorithmic problem solving is a major challenge of the computer age.

This book is introductory and so the problems discussed are inevitably "toy" problems. The problem below is typical of the sort of problems we discuss. It is sometimes known as the "flashlight" problem and sometimes as the "U2" problem and is reputed to have been used by at least one major software company in interviews for new employees (although it is now considered to be too well known for such purposes).

> Four people wish to cross a bridge. It is dark, and it is necessary to use a torch when crossing the bridge, but they have only one torch between them. The bridge is narrow, and only two people can be on it at any one time. The four people take different amounts of time to cross the bridge; when two cross together they proceed at the speed of the slowest. The first person takes 1 minute to cross, the second 2 minutes, the third 5 minutes and the fourth 10 minutes. The torch must be ferried back and forth across the bridge, so that it is always carried when the bridge is crossed.
>
> Show that all four can cross the bridge within 17 minutes.

The solution to this problem is clearly a sequence of instructions about how to get all four people across the bridge. A typical instruction will be: "persons x and y cross the bridge" or "person z crosses the bridge". The sequence of instructions solves the problem if the total time taken to execute the instructions is (at most) 17 minutes.

An algorithm is typically more general than this. Normally, an algorithm will have certain *inputs*; for each input, the algorithm should compute an *output* that is related to the input by a certain so-called *input–output relation*. In the case of the bridge-crossing problem, an algorithm might input four numbers, the crossing time for each person, and output the total time needed to get all four across the bridge. For example, if the input is the numbers 1, 3, 19, 20, the output should be 30 and if the input is the numbers 1, 4, 5, 6 the output should be 17. The input values are called the *parameters* of the algorithm. (An algorithm to solve the bridge problem is derived in Section 3.5. The presentation takes the form of a hypothetical dialogue between an interviewer and an interviewee in order to illustrate how the problem might be tackled in a systematic fashion.)

A second example is the chicken-chasing problem in Chapter 9. The problem, which is about catching chickens on a farm, was formulated by the famous puzzle-maker Sam Loyd in 1914. Briefly summarised, Loyd's problem is a very simple game played on a chessboard according to very simple rules (much simpler than the rules for chess). The game can be played on the Internet, and it is a very easy game to win. Most players will be able to do so within a short time. But it is likely that very few players would be able to formulate the *algorithm* that is needed to win the game on a board of arbitrary size in the smallest number of moves. Loyd, in fact, formulated the problem as determining the number of moves needed to win the game, but his solution gives only the number and not the algorithm. Our modern-day reliance on computers to execute algorithms for us means the notion of problem solving has shifted from determining solutions to particular problems to formulating algorithms to solve classes of problems. This is what algorithmic problem solving is about.

Formulating an algorithm makes problem solving decidedly harder, because it is necessary to formulate very clearly and precisely the procedure for solving the problem. The more general the problem, the harder it gets. (For instance, the bridge-crossing problem can be generalised by allowing the number of people to be variable.) The advantage, however, is a much greater understanding of the solution. The process of formulating an algorithm demands a full understanding of *why* the algorithm is correct.

1.3 OVERVIEW

The key to effective problem solving is economy of thought and of expression: the avoidance of unnecessary detail and complexity. The mastery of complexity is especially important in the computer age because of the unprecedented size of computer programs: a typical computer program will have hundreds, thousands or even millions of lines of code. Coupled with the unforgiving nature of digital computers, whereby a single error can cause an entire system to abruptly "crash", it is perhaps not so surprising that the challenges of algorithm design have had an immense impact on our problem-solving skills.

This book aims to impart these new skills and insights using an *example-driven* approach. It aims to demonstrate the importance of mathematical calculation, but the examples chosen are typically not mathematical; instead, like the chicken-chasing and bridge-crossing problems, they are problems that are readily understood by a lay person, with only elementary mathematical knowledge. The book also aims to challenge; most of the problems are quite difficult, at least to the untrained or poorly trained practitioner.

The book is divided into two parts. The first part is a succession of small-scale but nevertheless challenging problems. The second part is about the mathematical techniques that link the problems together and aid in their solution. In the first part of the book, pointers to the relevant mathematical techniques are given in boxes alongside the text.

Many of the problems are well known from recreational mathematics, but here the focus is on "algorithmics", which is a new sort of mathematics. The problems are presented in an order designed to facilitate a systematic introduction of the principles of algorithmics. Even well-established areas of mathematics deserve and get a different focus.

The book begins in Chapter 2 with "invariants", a notion that is central to all non-trivial algorithms. Algorithms are expressed using a combination of different sorts of "statements"; the statement types and ways of combining statements (assignment statements, sequential decomposition, case analysis and, finally, induction and loops) are introduced one by one via a series of examples. For this reason, it is recommended that Chapters 2–7 are read in order, with the exception of Chapter 5 which can be read independently of the earlier chapters. Later chapters can be read in an arbitrary order; they apply the principles introduced earlier to harder problems.

A danger of an example-driven approach is that the examples themselves are perceived as being the subject matter of the book, whereas that is not the case. The primary aim of the book is to impart the skills that are central to algorithmic problem solving: how to analyse problems and model them mathematically and how to then calculate algorithmic solutions. The book is thus primarily about *method* as opposed to facts. Read on if that is your interest and you are ready for a challenge.

1.4 BIBLIOGRAPHIC REMARKS

The observation that the word "algorithm" did not appear in popular dictionaries in the 1960s is due to Donald Knuth [Knu68]. (Actually his observation was about the 1950s. The word appears to have begun to be regularly included in popular dictionaries in the 1980s.) Knuth has written many highly influential and encyclopaedic books on algorithms and computing mathematics which are highly recommended for further study.

I first found the bridge problem in [Lev03] which is also where I first encountered the phrase "algorithmic problem solving". An introductory text that takes a problem-based approach similar to this one (but with implicit rather than explicit emphasis on algorithms) is [MM08].

Chapter
Invariants

"Invariant" means "not changing". An invariant of some process is some attribute or property of the process that does not change. Other names for "invariant" are "constant" and "pattern".

The recognition of invariants is an important problem-solving skill, possibly the most important. This chapter introduces the notion of an invariant and discusses a number of examples of its use.

We first present a number of problems for you to tackle. Some you may find easy, but others you may find difficult or even impossible to solve. If you cannot solve one, move on to the next. To gain full benefit, however, it is better that you try the problems first before reading further.

We then return to each of the problems individually. The first problem we discuss in detail, showing how an invariant is used to solve the problem. Along the way, we introduce some basic skills related to computer programming – the use of assignment statements and how to reason about assignments. The problem is followed by an exercise which can be solved using very similar techniques.

The second problem develops the techniques further. It is followed by a discussion of good and bad problem-solving techniques. The third problem is quite easy, but it involves a new concept, which we discuss in detail. Then, it is your turn again. From a proper understanding of the solution to these initial problems, you should be able to solve the next couple of problems. This process is repeated as the problems get harder; we demonstrate how to solve one problem, and then leave you to solve some more. You should find them much easier to solve.

1. **Chocolate Bars**   A rectangular chocolate bar is divided into squares by horizontal and vertical grooves, in the usual way. It is to be cut into individual squares. A cut is

made by choosing a piece and cutting along one of its grooves. (Thus each cut splits one piece into two pieces.)

Figure 2.1 shows a 4×3 chocolate bar that has been cut into five pieces. The cuts are indicated by solid lines.

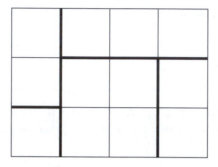

Figure 2.1: Chocolate-bar problem.

How many cuts are needed to completely cut the chocolate into all its squares?

2. **Empty Boxes**   Eleven large empty boxes are placed on a table. An unknown number of the boxes is selected and, into each one, eight medium boxes are placed. An unknown number of the medium boxes is selected and, into each one, eight small boxes are placed.

At the end of this process there are 102 empty boxes. How many boxes are there in total?

3. **Tumblers**   Several tumblers are placed on a table. Some tumblers are upside down, some are upside up. (See Figure 2.2.) It is required to turn all the tumblers upside up. However, the tumblers may not be turned individually; an allowed move is to turn any *two* tumblers simultaneously.

Figure 2.2: Tumbler problem.

From which initial states of the tumblers is it possible to turn all the tumblers upside up?

4. **Black and White Balls**   Consider an urn filled with a number of balls each of which is either black or white. There are also enough balls outside the urn to play the

following game. We want to reduce the number of balls in the urn to one by repeating the following process as often as necessary.

Take any two balls out of the urn. If both have the same colour, throw them away but put another black ball into the urn; if they have different colours, return the white one to the urn and throw the black one away.

Each execution of the above process reduces the number of balls in the urn by one; when only one ball is left the game is over.

What, if anything, can be said about the colour of the final ball in the urn in relation to the original number of black balls and white balls?

5. **Dominoes**   A chessboard has had its top-right and bottom-left squares removed so that 62 squares remain (see Figure 2.3). An unlimited supply of dominoes has been provided; each domino will cover exactly two squares of the chessboard.

Is it possible to cover all 62 squares of the chessboard with the dominoes without any domino overlapping another domino or sticking out beyond the edges of the board?

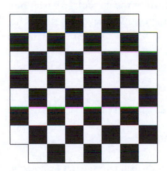

○ Figure 2.3: Mutilated chess board.

6. **Tetrominoes**   A *tetromino* is a figure made from 4 squares of the same size. There are five different tetrominoes, called the O-, Z-, L-, T- and I-tetrominoes. (See Figure 2.4.)

The following exercises concern covering a rectangular board with tetrominoes. Assume that the board is made up of squares of the same size as the ones used to make the tetrominoes. Overlapping tetrominoes or tetrominoes that stick out from the sides of the board are not allowed.

(a) Suppose a rectangular board is covered with tetrominoes. Show that at least one side of the rectangle has an even number of squares.

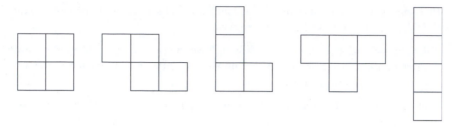

○ **Figure 2.4:** O-, Z-, L-, T- and I-tetromino.

(b) Suppose a rectangular board can be covered with T-tetrominoes. Show that the number of squares is a multiple of 8.
(c) Suppose a rectangular board can be covered with L-tetrominoes. Show that the number of squares is a multiple of 8.
(d) An 8×8 board cannot be covered with one O-tetromino and fifteen L-tetrominoes. Why not?

Note that all of these problems involve an *algorithm*. In each case, the algorithm involves repeating a simple process (cutting the chocolate bar, filling a box, turning two tumblers, etc.). This is not difficult to spot. Whenever an algorithm has this form, the first task is to identify the "invariants" of the algorithm. This important skill is the focus of this chapter.

2.1 CHOCOLATE BARS

Recall the problem statement:

A rectangular chocolate bar is divided into squares by horizontal and vertical grooves, in the usual way. It is to be cut into individual squares. A cut is made by choosing a piece and cutting along one of its grooves. (Thus each cut splits one piece into two pieces.)

How many cuts are needed to completely cut the chocolate into all its squares?

2.1.1 The Solution

Here is a solution to the chocolate-bar problem. Whenever a cut is made, the number of cuts increases by one and the number of pieces increases by one. Thus, the number of cuts and the number of pieces both change. What *does not* change, however, is the *difference* between the number of cuts and the number of pieces. This is an "invariant", or a "constant", of the process of cutting the chocolate bar.

We begin with one piece and zero cuts. So, the difference between the number of pieces and the number of cuts, at the outset, is one. It being a constant means that it will always be one, no matter how many cuts have been made. That is, the number of pieces will always be one more than the number of cuts. Equivalently, the number of cuts will always be one less than the number of pieces.

We conclude that to cut the chocolate bar into all its individual squares, the number of cuts needed is one less than the number of squares.

2.1.2 The Mathematical Solution

Once the skill of identifying invariants has been mastered, this is an easy problem to solve. For this reason, we have used English to describe the solution, rather than formulating the solution in a mathematical notation. For more complex problems, mathematical notation helps considerably, because it is more succinct and more precise. Let us use this problem to illustrate what we mean.

 Throughout the text we use the language of mathematics to make things precise. For example, we use words like "function" and "set" with their mathematical meaning, sometimes without introduction. Part II of this book, on mathematical techniques, provides the necessary background. Chapter 12 introduces much of the vocabulary. Consult this chapter if unfamiliar terms are used.

Abstraction   The mathematical solution begins by introducing two *variables*. We let variable p be the number of pieces and c be the number of cuts. The values of these variables describe the *state* of the chocolate bar.

This first step is called *abstraction*. We "abstract" from the problem a collection of variables (or "parameters") that completely characterise the essential elements of the problem. In this step, inessential details are eliminated.

One of the inessential details is that the problem has anything to do with chocolate bars! This is totally irrelevant and, accordingly, has been eliminated. The problem could equally well have been about cutting postage stamps from a sheet of stamps. The problem has become a "mathematical" problem, because it is about properties of numbers, rather than a "real-world" problem. Real-world problems can be very hard, if not impossible, to solve; in contrast, problems that succumb to mathematical analysis are relatively easy.

Other inessential details that have been eliminated are the sequence of cuts that have been made and the shapes and sizes of the resulting pieces. That is, the variables p and c do not completely characterise the state of the chocolate bar or the sequence of cuts that have been made to reach that state. Knowing that, say, four cuts have been made, making five pieces, does not allow us to reconstruct the sizes of the individual pieces. That is irrelevant to solving the problem.

The abstraction step is often the hardest step to make. It is very easy to fall into the trap of including unnecessary detail, making the problem and its solution over-complicated. Conversely, deciding what is essential is far from easy: there is no algorithm for making such decisions! The best problem-solvers are probably the ones most skilled in abstraction.

(Texts on problem solving often advise drawing a figure. This may help to clarify the problem statement – for example, we included Figure 2.1 in order to clarify what is meant by a cut – but it can also be a handicap! There are two reasons. The first is that extreme cases are often difficult to capture in a figure. This is something we return to later. The second is that figures often contain much unnecessary detail, as exemplified by Figure 2.1. Our advice is to use figures with the utmost caution; mathematical formulae are often far more effective.)

Assignments   The next step in the problem's solution is to model the process of cutting the chocolate bar. We do so by means of the *assignment statement*

$$p,c \ := \ p+1,c+1.$$

An assignment statement has two sides, a *left* side and a *right* side. The two sides are separated by the *assignment symbol* ":=", pronounced "becomes". The left side is a comma-separated list of variables (in this case, p,c). No variable may occur more than once on the left side. The right side is a comma-separated list of expressions (in this case, p+1,c+1). The list must have length equal to the number of variables on the left side.

An assignment effects a change of state. To execute an assignment statement, first evaluate, in the current state, each expression on the right side and then replace the value of each variable on the left side by the value of the corresponding expression on the right side. In our example, the state – the number of pieces and the number of cuts – is changed by evaluating p+1 and c+1 and then replacing the values of p and c by these values, respectively. In words, p "becomes" p + 1, and c "becomes" c+1. This is how the assignment statement models the process of making a single cut of the chocolate bar.

⚠️ A word of warning *(for those who have already learnt to program in a language like Java or C). We use what is called a* simultaneous *assignment because several variables are allowed on the left side, their values being* updated simultaneously *once the right side has been evaluated. Most programming languages restrict the left side of an assignment to a* single *variable. Java is an example. Instead of a simultaneous assignment, one has to write a sequence of assignments. This is a nuisance, but only that. Much worse is that the equality symbol, "=", is used instead of the assignment symbol, Java again being an example. This is a major problem because it causes confusion between assignments and equalities, which are two quite different things. Most novice programmers frequently confuse the two, and even experienced programmers sometimes do, leading to errors that are difficult to find. If you do write Java or C programs, always remember to pronounce an assignment as "left side becomes right side" and not "left side equals right side", even if your teachers do not do so. Also, write the assignment with no blank between the left side variable and the "=" symbol, as in* p= p+1, *so that it does not look symmetric.*

An *invariant* of an assignment is some function of the state whose value remains constant under execution of the assignment. For example, $p-c$ is an invariant of the assignment $p,c := p+1,c+1$.

Suppose expression E depends on the values of the state variables. (For example, expression $p-c$ depends on variables p and c.) We can check that E is an invariant simply by checking for equality between the value of E and the value of E after replacing all variables as prescribed by the assignment. For example, the equality

$$p-c = (p+1)-(c+1)$$

simplifies to true whatever the values of p and c. This checks that $p-c$ is an invariant of the assignment $p,c := p+1,c+1$. The left side of this equality is the expression E and the right side is the expression E after replacing all variables as prescribed by the assignment.

⚠ *Here is a detailed calculation showing how* $(p+1)-(c+1)$ *is simplified to* $p-c$. *The calculation illustrates the style we will be using throughout the text. The style is discussed in detail in Chapter 12, in particular in Section 12.8. This example provides a simple introduction.*

$$(p+1)-(c+1)$$

$$= \qquad \{ \qquad [\, x-y = x+(-y)\,] \text{ with } x,y := p+1,c+1 \quad \}$$

$$(p+1) + (-(c+1))$$

$$= \qquad \{ \qquad \text{negation distributes through addition} \quad \}$$

$$(p+1)+((-c)+(-1))$$

=   {   addition is associative and symmetric   }

$$p+(-c)+1+(-1)$$

=   {   [x−y = x+(−y)]

with x,y := p,c and with x,y := 1,−1,

[x−x = 0] with x := 1   }

$$p-c.$$

The calculation consists of four steps. Each step relates two arithmetic expressions. The relation between each expression in this calculation is equality (of numbers). Sometimes other relations occur in calculations (for example, the "at-most" relation).

Each step asserts that the relation holds between the two expressions "everywhere" – that is, for all possible values of the variables in the two expressions. For example, the final step asserts that, no matter what values variables p and c have, the value of the expression p+(−c)+1+(−1) equals the value of expression p−c.

Each step is justified by a hint. *Sometimes the hint states one or more laws together with how the law is instantiated. This is the case for the first and last steps. Laws are recognised by the square "everywhere" brackets. For example, "[x−x = 0]" means that x−x is 0 "everywhere", that is, for all possible values of variable x. Sometimes a law is given in words, as in the two middle steps.*

If you are not familiar with the terminology used in a hint – for example, if you do not know what "distributes" means – consult the appropriate section in Part II of the book.

As another example, consider two variables m and n and the assignment

$$m,n := m+3,n-1.$$

We check that $m+3\times n$ is invariant by checking that

$$m+3\times n = (m+3)+3\times(n-1)$$

simplifies to true whatever the values of m and n. Simple algebra shows that this is indeed the case. So, increasing m by 3, simultaneously decreasing n by 1, does not change the value of $m + 3 \times n$.

Given an expression E and an assignment ls := rs,

$$E[\text{ls} := \text{rs}]$$

is used to denote the expression obtained by replacing all occurrences of the variables in E listed in ls by the corresponding expression in the list of expressions rs. Here are some examples:

$$(p-c)[p,c := p+1,c+1] = (p+1) - (c+1),$$

$$(m+3 \times n)[m,n := m+3,n-1] = (m+3) + 3 \times (n-1),$$

$$(m+n+p)[m,n,p := 3 \times n,m+3,n-1] = (3 \times n) + (m+3) + (n-1).$$

The invariant rule for assignments is then the following: E is an *invariant* of the assignment ls := rs if, for all instances of the variables in E,

$$E[\text{ls} := \text{rs}] = E.$$

The examples we saw above of this rule are, first, $p-c$ is an invariant of the assignment $p,c := p+1,c+1$ because

$$(p-c)[p,c := p+1,c+1] = p-c$$

for all instances of variables p and c, and, second, $m+3 \times n$ is an invariant of the assignment $m,n := m+3,n-1$ because

$$(m+3 \times n)[m,n := m+3,n-1] = m+3 \times n$$

for all instances of variables m and n.

Induction   The final step in the solution of the chocolate-bar problem is to exploit the invariance of $p-c$.

Initially, $p=1$ and $c=0$. So, initially, $p-c=1$. But, $p-c$ is invariant. So, $p-c=1$ no matter how many cuts have been made. When the bar has been cut into all its squares, $p=s$, where s is the number of squares. So, at that time, the number of cuts, c, satisfies $s-c=1$. That is, $c=s-1$. The number of cuts is one less than the number of squares.

An important principle is being used here, called the *principle of mathematical induction*. The principle is simple. It is that, if the value of an expression is unchanged by some assignment to its variables, the value will be unchanged no matter how many times the assignment is applied. That is, if the assignment is applied zero times, the value of the expression is unchanged (obviously, because applying the assignment zero times means doing nothing). If the assignment is applied once, the value of the expression is unchanged, by assumption. Applying the assignment twice means applying it once and then once again. Both times, the value of the expression remains unchanged, so the end result is also no change. And so on, for three times, four times, etc.

Note that the case of *zero* times is included here. Do not forget zero! In the case of the chocolate-bar problem, it is vital to solving the problem in the case where the chocolate bar has exactly one square (in which case zero cuts are required).

Summary   This completes our discussion of the chocolate-bar problem. A number of important problem-solving principles have been introduced: abstraction, invariants and induction. We will see these principles again and again.

> **Exercise 2.1**   A *knockout tournament* is a series of games. Two players compete in each game; the loser is knocked out (i.e. does not play any more), the winner carries on. The winner of the tournament is the player that is left after all other players have been knocked out.
>
> Suppose there are 1234 players in a tournament. How many games are played before the tournament winner is decided? (Hint: choose suitable variables, and seek an invariant.)

2.2 EMPTY BOXES

Recall the empty-box problem:

> Eleven large empty boxes are placed on a table. An unknown number of the boxes is selected and into each eight medium boxes are placed. An unknown number of the medium boxes is selected and into each eight small boxes are placed.

> **At the end of this process there are 102 empty boxes. How many boxes are there in total?**

This problem is very much like the chocolate-bar problem in Section 2.1 and the knockout-tournament problem in Exercise 2.1. The core of the problem is a simple algorithm that is repeatedly applied to change the state. Given the initial state and some incomplete information about the final state, we are required to completely characterise the final state. The strategy we use to solve the problem is the following.

> ⚠️ *George Pólya (1887–1985) was an eminent mathematician who wrote pro-lifically on problem solving. In his classic book* How To Solve It, *he offered simple but very wise advice on how to approach new problems in mathematics. His step-by-step guide is roughly summarised in the following three steps.*
>
> 1. *Familiarise yourself with the problem. Identify the unknown. Identify what is given.*
>
> 2. *Devise and then execute a plan, checking each step carefully.*
>
> 3. *Review your solution.*
>
> *Problem solving is, of course, never straightforward. Even so, Pólya's rough guide is remarkably pertinent to many problems. It is worthwhile thinking consciously about each of the steps each time you encounter a new problem.*

1. Identify what is unknown about the final state and what is known.

2. Introduce variables that together represent the state at an arbitrary point in time.

3. Model the process of filling boxes as an assignment to the state variables.

4. Identify an invariant of the assignment.

5. Combine the previous steps to deduce the final state.

The first step is easy. The unknown is the number of boxes in the final state; what is known is the number of empty boxes. This suggests we introduce (in the second step) variables b and e for the number of boxes and the number of empty boxes, respectively, at an arbitrary point in time.

These first two steps are particularly important. Note that they are goal-directed. We are guided by the goal – determine the number of boxes given the number of empty boxes – to the introduction of variables b and e. A common mistake is to try to count the number of medium boxes or the number of small boxes. These are irrelevant, and a solution that introduces variables representing these quantities is over-complicated. This is a key to effective problem solving: keep it simple!

Let us proceed with the final three steps of our solution plan. The problem statement describes a process of filling boxes. When a box is filled, the number of boxes increases by 8; the number of empty boxes increases by 8−1 since 8 empty boxes are added and 1 is filled. We can therefore model the process by the assignment:

$$b,e \ := \ b+8,e+7.$$

We now seek to identify an invariant of this assignment.

Until now, the assignments have been simple, and it has not been too hard to identify an invariant. This assignment is more complicated and the inexperienced problem-solver may have difficulty carrying out the task. Traditionally, the advice given might be to guess. But we do not want to rely on guesswork. Another tactic is to introduce a new variable, n say, to count the number of times boxes are filled. For the boxes problem, this is quite a natural thing to do but we reject it here because we want to illustrate a more general methodology by which guesswork can be turned into calculation when seeking invariants. (We return to the tactic of introducing a count in Section 2.2.1.)

We do have to perform some guesswork. Look at the individual assignments to b and to e. The assignment to b is $b := b+8$. Thus 8 is repeatedly added to b, and b takes on the values b_0 (its initial value – which happens to be 11, but that is not important at this stage), b_0+8, $b_0+2\times8$, $b_0+3\times8$, etc. Similarly, the values of e are e_0, e_0+7, $e_0+2\times7$, $e_0+3\times7$, etc. In mathematical parlance, the successive values of e are called *linear combinations* of e_0 and 7. Similarly, the successive values of b are linear combinations of b_0 and 8. The guess we make is that an invariant is some linear combination of b and e. Now we formulate the guess and proceed to calculate.

We guess that, for some numbers M and N, the number $M\times b + N\times e$ is an invariant of the assignment, and we try to calculate values for M and N as follows:

$$M\times b + N\times e \quad \text{is an invariant of} \quad b,e \ := \ b+8,e+7$$

$$= \qquad \{ \qquad \text{definition of invariant} \ \}$$

$$(M\times b + N\times e)[b,e \ := \ b+8,e+7] \ = \ M\times b + N\times e$$

$$= \qquad \{ \qquad \text{definition of substitution} \ \}$$

$$M\times(b+8) + N\times(e+7) \ = \ M\times b + N\times e$$

$$= \qquad \{ \qquad \text{arithmetic} \ \}$$

$$(M\times b + N\times e) + (M\times 8 + N\times 7) \ = \ M\times b + N\times e$$

$$= \qquad \{ \qquad \text{cancellation} \ \}$$

$$M\times 8 + N\times 7 \ = \ 0$$

$$\Leftarrow \qquad \{ \qquad \text{arithmetic} \ \}$$

$$M = 7 \ \wedge \ N = -8.$$

Success! Our calculation has concluded that $7\times b - 8\times e$ is an invariant of the assignment. We now have the information we need to solve the boxes problem.

Initially, both of b and e are 11. So the initial value of $7\times b - 8\times e$ is -11. This remains constant throughout the process of filling boxes. In the final state we are given that e is

102; so in the final state, the number of boxes, b, is given by the equation

$$-11 \;=\; 7 \times b - 8 \times 102.$$

Solving this equation, we deduce that $115 = b$; the number of boxes in the final state is 115.

2.2.1 Review

One of the best ways of learning effective problem solving is to compare different solution methods. This is, perhaps, the only way to identify the "mistakes" that are often made. By "mistakes" we do not mean factual errors, but choices and tracks that make the solution more difficult or impossible to find.

We have already commented that it is a mistake to introduce variables for the number of small boxes, the number of medium boxes and the number of large boxes. Doing so will not necessarily prevent a solution being found, but the solution method becomes more awkward. The mistake is nevertheless commonly made; it can be avoided by adopting a goal-directed approach to problem solving. The first question to ask is: what is the unknown? Then work backwards to determine what information is needed to determine the unknown.

Goal-directed reasoning is evident in our calculation of M and N. The calculation begins with the defining property and ends with values that satisfy that property. The final step is an if step – the linear combination $M \times b + N \times e$ is an invariant *if* M is 7 and N is -8. Other values of M and N also give invariants, for example, when M is -7 and N is 8. (The extreme case is when both M and N are 0. In this case, we deduce that 0 is an invariant of the assignment. But the constant 0 is an invariant of all assignments, so that observation does not help to solve the problem!)

The use of if steps in calculations is a relatively recent innovation, and almost unknown in traditional mathematical texts. Mathematicians will typically postulate the solution and then *verify* that it is correct. This is shorter but hides the discovery process. We occasionally do the same but only when the techniques for constructing the solution are already clear.

 The calculation of M *and* N *is another example of the style of calculation we use in this text. The calculation consists of five steps. Each step relates two boolean expressions. For example, the third step relates the expressions*

$$M \times (b+8) + N \times (e+7) \;=\; M \times b + N \times e \qquad (2.2)$$

and

$$(M \times b + N \times e) + (M \times 8 + N \times 7) \quad = \quad M \times b + N \times e. \tag{2.3}$$

In all but the last step, the relation is (boolean) equality. In the last step, the relation is "⇐" (pronounced "if"). A boolean expression may evaluate to true *or to* false *depending on the values of the variables in the expression. For example, if the values of M and N are both zero, the value of the expression* $M \times 8 + N \times 7 = 0$ *is* true *while the value of* $M = 7 \wedge N = -8$ *is* false*. The symbol "∧" is pronounced "and".*

Each step asserts that the relation holds between the two expressions "everywhere" – that is, for all possible values of the variables in the two expressions. For example, the third step asserts that no matter what value variables M, N, b and e have, the value of the expression (2.2) equals the value of expression (2.3). (For example, if the variables M, N, b and e all have the value 0, the values of (2.2) and (2.3) are both true*; if all the variables have the value 1 the values of (2.2) and (2.3) are both* false*.) The assertion is justified by a hint, enclosed in curly brackets.*

The calculation uses three boolean operators – "=", "⇐" and "∧". See Section 12.6 for how to evaluate expressions involving these operators. The final step in the calculation is an if step and not an equality step because it is the case that whenever $M = 7 \wedge N = -8$ *evaluates to* true *then so too does* $M \times 8 + N \times 7 = 0$*. However, when M and N are both 0, the former expression evaluates to* false *while the latter evaluates to* true*. The expressions are thus not equal everywhere.*

Note that we use the equality symbol "=" both for equality of boolean values (as in the first four steps) and for equality of numbers (as in "M = 7"). This so-called "overloading" of the operator is discussed in Chapter 12.

Another solution method for this problem is to introduce a variable, n say, for the number of times eight boxes are filled. The number of boxes and the number of empty boxes at time n are then denoted using a subscript – b_0, b_1, b_2, etc. and e_0, e_1, e_2, etc. Instead of an assignment, we then have equalities:

$$b_{n+1} = b_n + 8 \quad \wedge \quad e_{n+1} = e_n + 7.$$

This solution method works for this problem but at the expense of the increased complexity of subscripted variables. We can avoid the complexity if we accept that change of state caused by an assignment is an inescapable feature of algorithmic problem solving; we must therefore learn how to reason about assignments directly rather than work around them.

Such a solution is one that is intermediate between our solution and the solution with subscripted variables: a count is introduced but the variables are not subscripted. The problem then becomes to identify invariants of the assignment

$$b,e,n := b+8,e+7,n+1.$$

The variable n, which counts the number of times the assignment is executed, is called an *auxiliary* variable; its role is to assist in the reasoning. Auxiliary variables are, indeed, sometimes useful for more complex problems. In this case, it is perhaps easier to spot that $b-8\times n$ and $e-7\times n$ are both invariants of the assignment. Moroever, if E and F are both invariants of the assignment, any combination $E \oplus F$ will also be invariant. So $7\times(b-8\times n)-8\times(e-7\times n)$ is also invariant, and this expression simplifies to $7\times b-8\times e$. When an assignment involves three or more variables, it can be a useful strategy to seek invariant combinations of subsets of the variables and then combine the invariants into one.

A third way of utilising an auxiliary variable is to consider the effect of executing the assignment

$$b,e := b+8,e+7$$

n times in succession. This is equivalent to one execution of the assignment

$$b,e := b+n\times 8, e+n\times 7.$$

Starting from a state where e has the value 11 and ending in a state where e is 102 is only possible if $n=13$. The final value of b must then be $11+13\times 8$. This solution appears to avoid the use of invariants altogether, but that is not the case: a fuller argument would use invariants to justify the initial claim about n executions of the assignment.

> **Exercise 2.4** Can you generalise the boxes problem? Suppose there are initially m boxes and then repeatedly k smaller boxes are inserted into one empty box. Suppose there are ultimately n empty boxes. You are asked to calculate the number of boxes when this process is complete. Determine a condition on m, k and n that guarantees that the problem is well-formulated and give the solution.
>
> You should find that the problem is not well formulated when k equals 1. Explain in words why this is the case.

2.3 THE TUMBLER PROBLEM

Recall the statement of the tumbler problem.

> Several tumblers are placed on a table. Some tumblers are upside down, some are upside up. It is required to turn all the tumblers upside up. However, the tumblers may not be turned individually; an allowed move is to turn any *two* tumblers simultaneously.

From which initial states of the tumblers is it possible to turn all the tumblers upside up?

It is not difficult to discover that all the tumblers can be turned upside up if the number of upside-down tumblers is even. The algorithm is to repeatedly choose two upside-down tumblers and turn these; the number of upside-down tumblers is thus repeatedly decreased and will eventually become zero. The more difficult problem is to consider all possibilities and not just this special case.

The algorithm suggests that we introduce just one variable, namely the number of tumblers that are upside down. Let us call it u.

There are three possible effects of turning two of the tumblers. Two tumblers that are both upside up are turned upside down. This is modelled by the assignment

$$u \ := \ u+2.$$

Turning two tumblers that are both upside down has the opposite effect: u decreases by two. This is modelled by the assignment

$$u \ := \ u-2.$$

Finally, turning two tumblers that are the opposite way up (i.e. one upside down, the other upside up) has no effect on u. In programming terms, this is modelled by a so-called *skip* statement. "Skip" means "do nothing" or "having no effect". In this example, it is equivalent to the assignment

$$u \ := \ u,$$

but it is better to have a name for the statement that does not depend on any variables. We use the name skip. So, the third possibility is to execute

skip.

The choice of which of these three statements is executed is left unspecified. An invariant of the turning process must therefore be an invariant of each of the three.

Everything is an invariant of skip. So, we can discount skip. We therefore seek an invariant of the two assignments u := u+2 and u := u−2. What does not change if we add or subtract two from u?

The answer is the so-called *parity* of u. The parity of u is a *boolean* value: it is either true or false. It is true if u is even $(0, 2, 4, 6, 8,$ etc.), and it is false if u is odd $(1, 3, 5, 7,$ etc.). Let us write even(u) for this boolean quantity. Then,

$$\text{even}(u)[u := u+2] = \text{even}(u+2) = \text{even}(u).$$

That is, even(u) is an invariant of the assignment u := u+2. Also,

$$\text{even}(u)[u := u-2] = \text{even}(u-2) = \text{even}(u).$$

That is, even(u) is also an invariant of the assignment u := u−2.

> ⚠ *An expression of the form* $E = F = G$ *is called a* continued equality *and is read* conjunctionally. *That is, it means* $E = F$ *and* $F = G$. *Because equality is a* transitive relation, *the conjunct* $E = G$ *can be added too. See Section 12.7.4 for further discussion of these concepts.*

We conclude that, no matter how many times we turn two tumblers over, the parity of the number of upside-down tumblers will not change. If there is an even number at the outset, there will always be an even number; if there is an odd number at the outset, there will always be an odd number.

The goal is to repeat the turning process until there are zero upside-down tumblers. Zero is an even number, so the answer to the question is that there must be an even number of upside-down tumblers at the outset.

2.3.1 Non-deterministic Choice

In order to solve the tumblers problem, we had to reason about a combination of three different statements. The combination is called the *non-deterministic choice* of the statements and is denoted using the infix "□" symbol (pronounced "choose"). The statement

    u := u+2 □ skip □ u := u−2

is executed by choosing arbitrarily ("non-deterministically") one of the three statements. An expression is an invariant of a non-deterministic choice when it is an invariant of each statement forming the choice.

Non-deterministic statements are not usually allowed in programming languages. Programmers are usually required to instruct the computer what action to take in all circumstances. Programmers do, however, need to understand and be able to reason about non-determinism because the actions of a user of a computer system are typically non-deterministic: the user is free to choose from a selection of actions. For the same reason, we exploit non-determinism in this book, in particular when we consider two-person games. Each player in such a game has no control over the opponent's actions and so must model the actions as a non-deterministic choice.

> **Exercise 2.5**   Solve the problem of the black and white balls and the chessboard problem (problems 4 and 5 at the beginning of this chapter). For the ball problem, apply the method of introducing appropriate variables to describe the state of the balls in the urn. Then express the process of removing and/or replacing balls by a choice among a number of assignment statements. Identify an invariant, and draw the appropriate conclusion.
>
> The chessboard problem is a little harder, but it can be solved in the same way. (Hint: use the colouring of the squares on the chessboard.)
>
> You are also in a position to solve problem 6(a).

2.4 TETROMINOES

In this section, we present the solution of problem 6(b). This gives us the opportunity to illustrate in more detail our style of mathematical calculation.

Recall the problem:

> Suppose a rectangular board can be covered with T-tetrominoes. Show that the number of squares is a multiple of 8.

A brief analysis of this problem reveals an obvious invariant. Suppose c denotes the number of covered squares. Then, placing a tetromino on the board is modelled by

$$c \ := \ c{+}4.$$

Thus, $c \bmod 4$ is invariant. ($c \bmod 4$ is the remainder after dividing c by 4. For example, $7 \bmod 4$ is 3 and $16 \bmod 4$ is 0.) Initially c is 0, so $c \bmod 4$ is $0 \bmod 4$, which is 0. So, $c \bmod 4$ is always 0. In words, we say that "c is a multiple of 4 is an invariant property". More often, the words "is an invariant property" are omitted, and we say "c is a multiple of 4".

⚠ c mod 4 *is an example of what is called a "modulus". So-called "modular arithmetic" is a form of arithmetic in which values are always reduced to remainder values. For example, counting "modulo" 2 goes 0, 1, 0, 1, 0, 1, 0, etc. instead of 0, 1, 2, 3, 4, 5, 6, etc. At each step, the number is reduced to its remainder after dividing by 2. Similarly, counting "modulo" 3 goes 0, 1, 2, 0, 1, 2, 0, etc. At each step the number is reduced to its remainder after dividing by 3. Modular arithmetic is surprisingly useful. See Section 15.4 for a full account.*

Now, suppose the tetrominoes cover an $m \times n$ board. (That is, the number of squares along one side is m and the number along the other side is n.) Then $c = m \times n$, so $m \times n$ is a multiple of 4. For the product $m \times n$ of two numbers m and n to be a multiple of 4, either m or n (or both) is a multiple of 2.

Note that, so far, the argument has been about tetrominoes in general, and not particularly about T-tetrominoes. What we have just shown is, in fact, the solution to problem 6(a): if a rectangular board is covered by tetrominoes, at least one of the sides of the rectangle must have even length.

The discovery of a solution to problem 6(a), in this way, illustrates a general phenomenon in solving problems. The process of solving more difficult problems typically involves formulating and solving simpler subproblems. In fact, many "difficult" problems are solved by putting together the solution to several simpler problems. Looked at this way, "difficult" problems become a lot more manageable. Just keep on solving simple problems until you have reached your goal!

At this point, we want to replace the verbose arguments we have been using by mathematical calculation. Here is the above argument in a calculational style:

> an $m \times n$ board is covered with tetrominoes

$\Rightarrow$ {   invariant: c is a multiple of 4, $c = m \times n$ }

> $m \times n$ is a multiple of 4

$\Rightarrow$ {   property of multiples   }

> m is a multiple of 2 $\lor$ n is a multiple of 2.

This is a two-step calculation. The first step is a so-called "implication" step, as indicated by the "$\Rightarrow$" symbol. The step is read as

> an $m \times n$ board is covered with tetrominoes *only if* $m \times n$ is a multiple of 4.

(Alternatively, "an m×n board is covered with tetrominoes *implies* m×n is a multiple of 4" or "*if* an m×n board is covered with tetrominoes, m×n is a multiple of 4.")

The text between curly brackets, following the "⇒" symbol, is a hint why the statement is true. Here the hint is the combination of the fact, proved earlier, that the number of covered squares is always a multiple of 4 (whatever the shape of the area covered) together with the fact that, if an m×n board has been covered, the number of covered squares is m×n.

The second step is read as:

  m×n is a multiple of 4 only if m is a multiple of 2 or n is a multiple of 2.

Again, the "⇒" symbol signifies an implication. The symbol "∨" means "or". Note that by "or" we mean so-called "inclusive-or": the possibility that both m and n are multiples of 2 is included. A so-called "exclusive-or" would mean that m is a multiple of 2 or n is a multiple of 2, but not both – that is, it would exclude this possibility.

The hint in this case is less specific. The property that is being alluded to has to do with expressing numbers as multiples of prime numbers. You may or may not be familiar with the general theorem, but you should have sufficient knowledge of multiplying numbers by 4 to accept that the step is valid.

The conclusion of the calculation is also an "only if" statement. It is:

  An m×n board is covered with tetrominoes only if m is a multiple of 2 or n is a multiple of 2.

(Equivalently, if an m×n board is covered with tetrominoes, m is a multiple of 2 or n is a multiple of 2.)

This style of presenting a mathematical calculation reverses the normal style: mathematical expressions are interspersed with text, rather than the other way around. Including hints within curly brackets between two expressions means that the hints may be as long as we like; they may even include other subcalculations. Including the symbol "⇒" makes clear the relation between the expressions it connects. More importantly, it allows us to use other relations. As we have already seen, some calculations use "⇐" as the connecting relation. Such calculations work backwards from a goal to what has been given, which is often the most effective way to reason.

 Our use of "⇒" in a calculation has a formal mathematical meaning. It does not mean "and the next step is"! Implication is a boolean connective. Section 12.6 explains how to evaluate an expression p⇒q, where p and q

denote booleans. When we use "⇒" in a calculation step like

E

⇒   {   *hint*   }

F

it means that E⇒F evaluates to true *"everywhere", that is, for all instances of the variables on which expressions E and F depend.*

It can be very important to know whether a step is an implication step or an equality step. An implication step is called a "weakening" step because the proposition F is weaker than E. Sometimes an implication can make a proposition too weak, leading to a dead end in a calculation. If this happens, the implication steps are the first to review.

Conversely, if ("⇐") steps are strengthening steps, and sometimes the strengthening can be overdone. The two types of steps should never be combined in one calculation. See Section 12.8 for more discussion.

Let us now tackle problem 6(b). Clearly, the solution must take account of the shape of a T-tetromino. (It is not true for I-tetrominoes. A 4×1 board can be covered with 1 I-tetromino, and 4 is not a multiple of 8.)

What distinguishes a T-tetromino is that it has one square that is adjacent to the other three squares. Colouring this one square differently from the other three suggests colouring the squares of the rectangle in the way a chessboard is coloured.

Suppose we indeed colour the rectangle with black and white squares, as on a chessboard. The T-tetrominoes should be coloured in the same way. This gives us two types, one with three black squares and one white square, and one with three white squares and one black square. We call them *dark* and *light* T-tetrominoes. (See Figure 2.5.) Placing the tetrominoes on the board now involves choosing the appropriate type so that the colours of the covered squares match the colours of the tetrominoes.

○ **Figure 2.5: Dark and light T-tetrominoes.**

We introduce four variables to describe the state of the board. Variable b records the number of covered black squares, while w records the number of covered white squares. In addition, d records the number of dark T-tetrominoes that have been used, and ℓ records the number of light tetrominoes.

Placing a dark tetromino on the board is modelled by the assignment

$$d, b, w := d+1, b+3, w+1.$$

Placing a light tetromino on the board is modelled by the assignment

$$\ell, b, w := \ell+1, b+1, w+3.$$

An invariant of both assignments is

$$b - 3 \times d - \ell,$$

since

$$(b - 3 \times d - \ell)[d, b, w := d+1, b+3, w+1]$$

$$= \qquad \{ \qquad \text{definition of substitution} \quad \}$$

$$(b+3) - 3 \times (d+1) - \ell$$

$$= \qquad \{ \qquad \text{arithmetic} \quad \}$$

$$b - 3 \times d - \ell$$

and

$$(b - 3 \times d - \ell)[\ell, b, w := \ell+1, b+1, w+3]$$

$$= \qquad \{ \qquad \text{definition of substitution} \quad \}$$

$$(b+1) - 3 \times d - (\ell+1)$$

$$= \qquad \{ \qquad \text{arithmetic} \quad \}$$

$$b - 3 \times d - \ell.$$

Similarly, another invariant of both assignments is

$$w - 3 \times \ell - d.$$

Now, the initial value of $b - 3 \times d - \ell$ is zero, so it is always zero, no matter how many T-tetrominoes are placed on the board. Similarly, the value of $w - 3 \times \ell - d$ is always zero.

⚠️ *In order not to interrupt the flow of the argument, we have verified that*
$b - 3 \times d - \ell$ *is an invariant of both assignments rather than constructed it.*
This gives the impression that it is pulled out of a hat, which is not the case.
The invariants of the two assignments can be constructed using the technique
discussed in Section 2.2: postulate that some linear combination of the variables is
an invariant and then construct the coefficients. See Exercise 2.9. The motivation
for seeking an invariant combination of b, d and ℓ and of w, d and ℓ is the
equation b = w in the calculation below.

We can now solve the given problem.

a rectangular board is covered by T-tetrominoes

$\Rightarrow$ {   from problem 6(a) we know that at least one

side of the board has an even number of squares,

which means that the number of black squares

equals the number of white squares   }

$b = w$

$=$ { $b - 3 \times d - \ell = 0$

$w - 3 \times \ell - d = 0$ }

$(b = w) \wedge (3 \times d + \ell = 3 \times \ell + d)$

$=$ {   arithmetic   }

$(b = w) \wedge (\ell = d)$

$=$ { $b - 3 \times d - \ell = 0$

$w - 3 \times \ell - d = 0$ }

$b = w = 4 \times d = 4 \times \ell$

$\Rightarrow$ {   arithmetic   }

$b + w = 8 \times d$

$\Rightarrow$ { $b + w$ is the number of covered squares   }

the number of covered squares is a multiple of 8.

We conclude that

If a rectangular board is covered by T-tetrominoes, the number of covered squares is divisible
by 8.

You can now tackle problem 6(c). The problem looks very much like problem 6(b), which suggests that it can be solved in a similar way. Indeed, it can. Look at other ways of colouring the squares black and white. Having found a suitable way, you should be able to repeat the same argument as above. Be careful to check that all steps remain valid.

(How easily you can adapt the solution to one problem in order to solve another is a good measure of the effectiveness of your solution method. It should not be too difficult to solve problem 6(c) because the solution to problem 6(b), above, takes care to clearly identify those steps where a property or properties of T-tetrominoes are used. Similarly, the solution also clearly identifies where the fact that the area covered is rectangular is exploited. Badly presented calculations do not make clear which properties are being used. As a result, they are difficult to adapt to new circumstances.)

Problem 6(d) is relatively easy, once problem 6(c) has been solved. Good luck!

2.5 SUMMARY

This chapter has been about algorithms that involve a simple repetitive process, like the algorithm used in a knockout tournament to eliminate competitors one by one. The concept of an invariant is central to reasoning about such algorithms. The concept is arguably the most important concept of all in algorithmic problem solving, which is why we have chosen to begin the book in this way. For the moment, we have used the concept primarily to establish conditions that must hold for an algorithmic problem to be solvable; later we see how the concept is central to the construction of algorithms as well.

In mathematical terms, the use of invariants corresponds to what is called the *principle of mathematical induction*. The principle is straightforward: if a value is invariant under a single execution of some process then it is invariant under an arbitrary finite number (including zero) of executions of the process.

Along the way we have also introduced simultaneous assignments and non-deterministic choice. These are important components in the construction of computer programs.

Elements of problem solving that we have introduced are (goal-directed) *abstraction* and *calculation*.

Abstraction is the process of identifying what is relevant to a problem's solution and discarding what is not. Abstraction is often the key to success in problem solving. It is not easy, and it requires practice. As you gain experience with problem solving, examine carefully the abstractions you have made to see whether they can be bettered.

Mathematical calculation is fundamental to algorithmic problem solving. If we can reduce a problem to calculation, we are a long way towards its solution. Calculation avoids guessing. Of course, some element of creativity is inherent in problem solving, and we cannot avoid guessing completely. The key to success is to limit the amount of guessing to a minimum. We saw how this was done for the boxes problem: we guessed that the invariant was a linear combination of the state variables, then we calculated the coefficients. This sort of technique will be used again and again.

Abstraction and calculation are two components of a commonly occurring pattern in real-world problem solving. The third component is *interpretation*. The pattern is summarised in Figure 2.6. Given a real-world problem, the first step is to *abstract* a problem that can be expressed in mathematical terms and is amenable to calculation. Mathematical *calculation* – without reference to the original real-world problem – is then applied to determine a solution to the mathematical problem. The final step is to *interpret* the results back to the context of the real-world problem. This three-step process is typically repeated many times over before the real-world problem is properly understood and considered to be "solved".

Note that mathematics is about all three components of the abstraction–calculation–interpretation cycle; a common misunderstanding is that it is just about calculation.

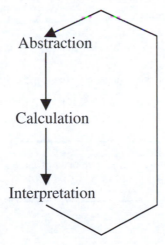

Abstraction

Calculation

Interpretation

○ **Figure 2.6: The abstraction–calculation–interpretation cycle.**

Exercise 2.6   The assignment

> x,y := y,x

swaps the values of x and y. (Variables x and y can have any type so long as it is the same for both.) Suppose f is a binary function of the appropriate type. Name the property that f should have in order that f(x,y) is an invariant of the assignment.

 If you are unable to answer this question, read Section 12.5 on algebraic properties of binary operators.

Exercise 2.7

(a) Identify an invariant of the non-deterministic choice

> m := m+6 ☐ m := m+15.

   (Recall that an expression is an invariant of a non-deterministic choice exactly when it is an invariant of all components of the choice.)

(b) Generalise your answer to

> m := m+j ☐ m := m+k

   where j and k are arbitrary integers. Give a formal verification of your claim.

(c) Is your answer valid when j and/or k is 0 (i.e. one or both of the assignments is equivalent to skip)? What other extreme cases can you identify?

 To anwer this question, review Section 15.4. Only elementary properties are needed.

Exercise 2.8   When an assignment involves several variables, we can seek invariants that combine different subsets of the set of variables. For example, the assignment

m,n := m+2,n+3

has invariants $m \bmod 2$, $n \bmod 3$ and $3{\times}m - 2{\times}n$. This is what we did in Section 2.4 when we disregarded the variable w and considered only the variables b, d and ℓ.

Consider the following non-deterministic choice:

m,n := m+1,n+2 □ n,p := n+1,p+3.

Identify as many (non-trivial) invariants as you can. (Begin by listing invariants of the individual assignments.)

Exercise 2.9   Consider the non-deterministic choice discussed in Section 2.4:

d,b,w := d+1,b+3,w+1 □ ℓ,b,w := ℓ+1,b+1,w+3.

There we *verified* that $b - 3{\times}d - \ell$ is an invariant of the choice. This exercise is about *constructing* invariants that are linear combinations of subsets of the variables. Apply the technique discussed in Section 2.2: postulate that some linear combination of the variables is an invariant and then construct the coefficients. Because there are two assignments, you will get two equations in the unknowns.

(a) Determine whether a linear combination of *two* of the variables is an invariant of both assignments. (The answer is yes, but in an unhelpful way.)

(b) For each set of three variables, construct a (non-trivial) linear combination of the variables that is invariant under both assignments. (In this way, for b, d and ℓ, the linear combination $b - 3{\times}d - \ell$ can be constructed. Similarly, an invariant linear combination of b, ℓ and w can be constructed, and likewise for b, d and w.

(c) What happens when you apply the technique to try to determine a linear combination of all four variables that is invariant?

2.6 BIBLIOGRAPHIC REMARKS

The empty-box problem was given to me by Wim Feijen. The problem of the black and white balls is from [Gri81]. The tetromino problems are from the 1999 *Vierkant Voor Wiskunde* calendar (see `http://www.vierkantvoorwiskunde.nl/puzzels/`). Vierkant Voor Wiskunde – foursquare for mathematics – is a foundation that promotes mathematics in Dutch schools. Their publications contain many examples of mathematical puzzles, both new and old. I have made grateful use of them throughout this text. Thanks go to Jeremy Weissman for suggestions on how to improve the presentation of the tetromino problems, some of which I have used. The domino and tumbler problems are old chestnuts. I do not know their origin.

Chapter
Crossing a River

3

The examples in this chapter all involve getting a number of people or things across a river under certain constraints. We use them as simple illustrations of "brute-force" search and problem decomposition.

Brute-force search means systematically trying all possibilities. Brute force does not require any skill, but it does require a lot of careful and accurate work. Using brute force is not something human beings are good at; lots of careful, accurate work is something more suited to computers. But brute force is not even practical for implementation on a computer. The amount of work involved explodes as the problem size gets bigger, making it impractical for all but toy problems. Nevertheless, it is useful to know what brute force entails, because it helps to understand the nature of problem solving.

Problem decomposition is something we humans are much better at. Problem decomposition involves exploiting the structure of a problem to break it down into smaller, more manageable problems. Once a problem has been broken down in this way, brute force may be applicable. Indeed, it is often the case that, ultimately, brute force is the only solution method, so we cannot dispense with it. But it is better to explore problem decomposition first, postponing the use of a brute-force search for as long as possible.

All river-crossing problems have an obvious structural property, namely the symmetry between the two banks of the river. The exploitation of symmetry is an important problem-solving technique, but is often overlooked, particularly when using brute force. You may already have seen the problems, or similar ones, elsewhere. As illustrations of brute-force search – which is how their solutions are often presented – they are extremely uninteresting! However, as illustrations of the use of symmetry, combined with problem decomposition, they have startling, hidden beauty.

An important issue that emerges in this chapter is *naming* the elements of a problem. Deciding on what and how names should be introduced can be crucial to success. We shall see how inappropriate or unnecessary naming can increase the complexity of a problem, making it impossible to solve even with the aid of a very powerful computer.

3.1 PROBLEMS

As in Chapter 2, we begin the chapter by listing a number of problems that will be discussed later. Tackling the problems first before reading on is an aid to a better understanding of their solutions.

1. **Goat, Cabbage and Wolf**   A farmer wishes to ferry a goat, a cabbage and a wolf across a river. However, his boat is only large enough to take one of them at a time, making several trips across the river necessary. The goat should not be left alone with the cabbage (otherwise, the goat would eat the cabbage), and the wolf should not be left alone with the goat (otherwise, the wolf would eat the goat).

   How can the farmer achieve the task?

2. **The Nervous Couples**   Three couples (president and bodyguard) wish to cross a river. They have one boat that can carry at most two people, making several trips across the river necessary. The presidents are nervous of the other presidents' bodyguards so that none is willing to be on a bank or in the boat with another president's bodyguard unless their own bodyguard is also present.

   How can all three couples get across the river?

3. **Adults and Children**   A group of adults and children are on one side of a river. They have one boat that is only big enough to accommodate one adult or two children.

   How can all the adults and all the children cross the river? Make clear any assumptions you are obliged to make.

4. **Overweight**   Ann, Bob, Col and Dee are on one side of a river. They have one rowing boat that can carry at most 100 kilos. Ann weighs 46 kilos; Bob, 49; Col, 52; Dee, 100. Bob cannot row.

   How can they all get to the other side?

3.2 BRUTE FORCE

3.2.1 Goat, Cabbage and Wolf

The goat–cabbage–wolf problem is often used to illustrate brute-force search. Our main purpose in showing the brute-force solution is to illustrate the pitfalls of *poor* problem-solving skills. Additionally, we introduce some terminology that is useful when discussing the efficiency of a particular solution to a problem.

> A farmer wishes to ferry a goat, a cabbage and a wolf across a river. However, his boat is only large enough to take one of them at a time, making several trips across the river necessary. The goat should not be left alone with the cabbage (otherwise, the goat would eat the cabbage), and the wolf should not be left alone with the goat (otherwise, the wolf would eat the goat).

> How can the farmer achieve the task?

The problem involves four individuals, and each is at one of the two river banks. This means that we can represent a state by four variables, each of which has one of two values. We call the variables f (for farmer), g (for goat), c (for cabbage) and w (for wolf), and we call their possible values L (for left) and R (for right). A value of R means "at the right bank". A value of L means "at the left bank". Note that the boat is always where the farmer is, so we do not need to introduce a variable to represent its position.

A *brute-force search* involves constructing a *state-transition graph* that models all possible *states*, and ways of changing from one state to another – the *state transitions*. In the goat–cabbage–wolf problem, a state describes on which bank each of the four individuals can be found. A state transition is a change of state that is allowed by the problem specification. For example, two states between which there is a valid state transition are:

1. All four are at the left bank.

2. The farmer and goat are at the right bank, while the cabbage and wolf are at the left bank.

For the simplest problems, a diagram can be drawn depicting a state-transition graph. The states are drawn as circles, and the state transitions are drawn as lines connecting the circles. The lines have arrows on them if some state transitions are not reversible; if so, the diagram is called a *directed graph*. If all state transitions are reversible, the arrows are not necessary and the diagram is called an *undirected graph*. We draw a state-transition graph to demonstrate the brute-force solution to this problem.

If four variables can each have one of two values, there are 2^4 (i.e. 16) different combinations of values. However, in this problem some of these combinations are excluded. The requirement that the goat cannot be left alone with the cabbage is

expressed by the *system invariant*

$$f = g = c \ \lor \ g \neq c.$$

 Read Chapter 16 for detailed definitions of directed and undirected graphs. The problems discussed here are all path-finding problems. Chapter 16 formulates such problems algebraically.

That is, either the farmer, the goat and the cabbage are all on the same bank ($f = g = c$), or the goat and cabbage are on different banks ($g \neq c$). This excludes cases where g and c are equal, but different from f. Similarly, the requirement that the goat cannot be left alone with the wolf is expressed by the system invariant

$$f = g = w \ \lor \ g \neq w.$$

If we list all states, eliminating the ones that are not allowed, the total reduces to 10. Table 3.1 shows the ten different combinations. (Notice that when f and g are equal all combinations of c and w are allowed; when f and g are different, c and w are required to be equal.)

f	g	c	w
L	L	L	L
L	L	L	R
L	L	R	L
L	L	R	R
L	R	L	L
R	L	R	R
R	R	L	L
R	R	L	R
R	R	R	L
R	R	R	R

Table 3.1: Goat–cabbage–wolf problem: allowed states.

Now, we enumerate all the possible transitions between these states. The graph in Figure 3.1 does just this. The *nodes* of the graph – the boxes – represent states, and the *edges* of the graph – the lines connecting the boxes – represent transitions. There are no arrows on the edges because each transition can be reversed.

At the left, the node labelled "LLLL" represents the state where all four are on the left bank. The only allowed transition from this state is to the state where the farmer

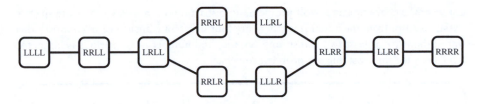

○ **Figure 3.1: Goat–cabbage–wolf problem.**

and goat are at the right bank, and the cabbage and wolf are at the left bank. This is represented by the line connecting LLLL to RRLL.

From the graph, it is clear that there are two (minimal) solutions to the problem. Each solution is given by a *path* through the graph from LLLL to RRRR. The upper path gives the following solution:

1. The farmer takes the goat to the right bank and returns alone. This is the path from LLLL to LRLL.

2. The farmer takes the cabbage to the right bank and returns with the goat. This is the path from LRLL to LLRL.

3. The farmer takes the wolf to the right bank and returns alone. This is the path from LLRL to LLRR.

4. The farmer takes the goat to the right bank. This is the path from LLRR to RRRR.

The alternative solution, given by the lower path, interchanges "cabbage" and "wolf" in the second and third steps.

3.2.2 State–Space Explosion

There is often a tendency to apply brute force without thinking when faced with a new problem. However, it should be used only where it is unavoidable. Brute force is useful only for very simple problems. For other problems, the search space quickly becomes much too large. In the jargon used by computing scientists, brute force does not "scale up" to larger problems. The goat–cabbage–wolf problem is not representative; the above – thoughtless! – solution has a manageable number of states, and a manageable number of transitions.

We can see how quickly the search space can grow by analysing what is involved in using brute force to solve the remaining problems in Section 3.1.

In the "overweight" problem, there are four named individuals and no restrictions on their being together on the same side of the bank. So, there are 16 possible states;

unlike in the goat–cabbage–wolf problem, no restriction on the size of the state space is possible. Also, from the initial state there are four different transitions; from most other states, there are at least two transitions. So, the total number of transitions is large, too large even for the most diligent problem-solvers.

> ⚠ *The mathematical theory used to count the number of states is called* combinatorics. *Here we are only using very simple combinatorial reasoning. In the "overweight" problem, a state is a function giving, for each individual, which side of the bank that individual is on. Section 12.4.2 discusses how to count the number of functions of a given type.*

The situation in an unskilled solution of the "nervous-couples" problem is even worse. Six individuals are involved, each of whom can be on either side of the river bank. If we give each individual a distinct name, the number of states is 2^6 (i.e. 64). That is an impossible number for most human beings to cope with, and we have not begun to count the number of transitions. In another variation on the nervous-couples problem, there are five couples, and the boat can take three people at a time. That means, if all are named, there are are 2^{10} (i.e. 1024) different states, and a yet larger number of transitions. Take note: these are "toy" problems, not real problems.

The "adults-and-children" problem illustrates another failing of brute force, namely that it can be applied only in specific cases, and not in the general case. The number of adults and children is not specified in this problem. Yet, it is in fact the easiest of all to solve.

The use of a computer to perform a brute-force search shifts the meaning of what is a "small" problem and what is a "large" problem, but not as much as one might expect. The so-called "state-space explosion problem" gets in the way. The river-crossing problems illustrate state-space explosion well. If there are n individuals in such a problem, there are, in principle, 2^n different states to be considered. But, even for quite small n, 2^n is a very large number. We speak of an "exponential" growth in the number of states (n is the exponent in 2^n). Whenever the state space of a class of problems grows exponentially, it means that even the largest and fastest supercomputers can tackle only quite small instances.

Drawing state-transition diagrams is equally ineffective. A diagram can occasionally be used to illustrate the solution of a simple, well-chosen problem. But constructing a diagram is rarely helpful in problem solving. Instead, diagrams quickly become a problem in themselves: apart from the size of paper needed, how are the nodes to be placed on the paper so that the diagram becomes readable?

3.2.3 Abstraction

The state-space explosion is often caused by a failure to properly analyse a problem; a particularly frequent cause is unnecessary or inappropriate *naming*. The goat–cabbage–wolf problem is a good example.

In the goat–cabbage–wolf problem, distinct names are given to the "farmer", the "goat", the "cabbage" and the "wolf", but do we really need to distinguish between all four? In the discussion of the state space, we remarked on a "similarity" between the wolf and the cabbage. Specifically, the goat cannot be left with either the wolf or the cabbage. This "similarity" also emerged in the solution: two solutions were obtained, symmetrical in the interchange of "wolf" and "cabbage". Why, then, are the "wolf" and the "cabbage" distinguished by giving them different names?

Let us restate the problem, this time with a naming convention that omits the unnecessary distinction between the wolf and the cabbage. In the restated problem, we call the goat an "alpha" and the cabbage and the wolf "betas".

> A farmer wishes to ferry an alpha and two betas across a river. However, his boat is large enough to take only one of them at a time, making several trips across the river necessary. Also, an alpha should not be left alone with a beta.
>
> How can the farmer achieve the task?

Now the problem becomes much easier to solve. Indeed, there is only one solution: take the alpha across, and then one beta across, returning with the alpha. Then take the second beta across, followed by the alpha. Because there is only one solution, it is easy to discover, and it is unnecessary to construct a state-transition diagram for the problem.

The problem-solving principle that we learn from this example is worth emphasising: *avoid unnecessary or inappropriate naming*. When elements of a problem are given individual names, it distinguishes them from other elements of the problem, and adds to the size of the state space. The process of omitting unnecessary detail and reducing a problem to its essentials is called *abstraction*. Poor solutions to problems are ones that fail to "abstract" adequately, making the problem more complicated than it really is. We encounter the importance of appropriate naming time and again in the coming chapters. Bear it in mind as you read.

> ⚠ *The crux of this simplification is that the relation "not with" is symmetric. It is the so-called complement (negation) of the relation "with", which is also symmetric. Indeed, a relation is symmetric exactly when its complement is symmetric. See Section 12.7.2 for more on symmetric relations.*

We will see more examples where it is useful to spot that a crucial relation is symmetric.

3.3 NERVOUS COUPLES

Often, the inherent structure of a problem facilitates its decomposition into smaller problems. The smaller problems can then be further decomposed until they become sufficiently manageable to be solvable by other means, perhaps even by brute force. Their solutions are then put together to form a solution to the original problem.

The nervous-couples problem is an excellent example. It can be solved by brute force, making it decidedly boring, but it can be solved much more effectively, making use of general problem-solving principles.

Recall its statement:

> Three couples (president and bodyguard) wish to cross a river. They have one boat that can carry at most two people, making several trips across the river necessary. The presidents are nervous of the other presidents' bodyguards so that none is willing to be on a bank or in the boat with another president's bodyguard unless their own bodyguard is also present.

How can all three couples get across the river?

3.3.1 What Is the Problem?

Let us begin by determining the essence of the problem.

Suppose there is one boat that can carry two "things", and there are no other restrictions. Then, clearly, it is possible to get any number of "things" across the river: repeat the process of letting two cross from left to right, followed by one returning from right to left, until at most two remain on the left bank.

Now, by replacing "thing" by "couple", we infer that a boat that can carry two couples at one crossing can be used to ferry an arbitrary number of couples across the river. (After all, couples are not nervous of each other!) Since a couple is two people, this means that a boat that can carry four people is sufficient to ferry an arbitrary number of couples across the river.

This simple analysis gives us a different slant on the problem. Rather than tackle the problem as stated, we can tackle a related problem, namely, what is the minimum capacity needed to ferry three couples across the river? More generally, what is the minimum capacity needed to ferry n couples across the river? Obviously, the minimum capacity is at least two (since it is not possible to ferry more than one person across a river in a boat that can only carry one person at a time), and we have just shown that the minimum capacity is at most four.

Alternatively, we can specify the capacity of the boat and ask what is the maximum number of couples that can be ferried across with that capacity. If the capacity is one (or less) the maximum number of couples is zero, and if the capacity is four, there is no maximum. So, the question is how many couples can be ferried with a boat of capacity two and how many couples can be ferried with a boat of capacity three.

The new problems look more difficult than the original. In the original problem, we are given the answer – in the case of three couples, a boat with capacity two is needed – and we are required to give a constructive proof that this is the case. But there is often an advantage in not knowing the answer because we can sometimes gain insight by generalising and then first solving simpler instances of the general problem.

3.3.2 Problem Structure

The structure of this problem suggests several ways in which it might be decomposed. First, there are three couples. This suggests seeking a solution that gets each couple across in turn. That is, we decompose the problem into three subproblems: get the first couple across, get the second couple across, and get the third couple across.

Another decomposition is into presidents and bodyguards. We could try first getting all the presidents across, followed by all the bodyguards. Alternatively, we could try first getting all the bodyguards across, followed by all the presidents.

Getting all the presidents across while their bodyguards remain at the left bank turns out to be easy. The reason is that, if the bodyguards all stay in one place, there is no difficulty in transferring the presidents *away* from them. Getting all the bodyguards across first, while their presidents stay at the left bank, seems much harder. On the other hand, getting the bodyguards to join their presidents may prove to be harder than getting the presidents to join their bodyguards. It is not immediately clear that either strategy will work.

There is, however, one key structural property of the problem that we have not yet considered. It is the *symmetry* between the left and right banks. The process of getting a group of people from left to right can always be reversed; the result is a process for getting the same group of people from right to left. Perhaps a symmetric solution is possible. If that is the case, we halve our effort, and that is a major saving. This is indeed what we do.

(The state-transition diagram for the goat–cabbage–wolf problem exhibits the left–right symmetry well. The diagram also illustrates the symmetry between the cabbage and wolf. Both symmetries were to be expected from the problem statement; by ignoring them and using brute force, we lost the opportunity of a reduction in effort.)

3.3.3 Denoting States and Transitions

We begin by introducing some local notation to make the solution strategy precise. The introduction of notation involves *naming* the elements of the problem that we want to distinguish. As discussed earlier, this is a crucial step in finding a solution. Here, we use letters B, P and C to mean bodyguard, president and couple, respectively. These are preceded by a number; for example, 2B means two bodyguards, 3C means three couples and 1C,2B means one couple and two bodyguards. We exploit the notation to distinguish between couples and individuals; for example, 1B,1P means a bodyguard and president who do not form a couple, while 1C means a bodyguard and president who do form a couple. Note that we do *not* name the individual people as we do, for example, in the "overweight" problem. It is only the *numbers* of bodyguards, presidents and couples that is relevant to the problem's solution. Number is an extremely important mathematical abstraction.

We distinguish between *states* and *actions*.

A *state* describes a situation in which each individual (bodyguard or president) is at one of the banks. A state is denoted by two sequences separated by bars. An example is 3B || 3P, which denotes the state in which all three bodyguards are at the left bank, and all three presidents are at the right bank. A second example of a state is 1C,2B || 2P, which denotes the state in which one couple and two bodyguards are at the left bank and two presidents are at the right bank. The starting state is thus 3C || and the required finishing state is || 3C.

An *action* transports some individuals across the river. An example is 3B |2P| 1P; this denotes the action of transporting two presidents across the river, leaving three bodyguards at the left bank and one president at the right bank.

Note that the notation for states and actions does not specify the position or direction of the boat, and, taken out of context, could be ambiguous. Since the position of the boat must alternate between the left bank and the right bank, this ambiguity is easily resolved.

The notation allows valid and invalid states/actions to be easily identified. For example, 1C,1P || 1C,1B is invalid (because there is a president who is alone on the same side of the river as another president's bodyguard). Also, 3B |3P| is invalid because the boat can carry at most two people.

In general, a complete, detailed solution to the problem is a sequence, beginning with the state 3C || and ending with the state || 3C, that alternates between valid states and actions.

An action results in a change of state. (In the terminology of state-transition diagrams, an action effects a transition between states.) Additional notation helps to express the result of actions. If p and q denote states, and S denotes a sequence of actions,

$$\{ \ p \ \}$$

$$S$$

$$\{ \ q \ \}$$

is the property that execution of S beginning in state p results in state q. So, for example,

$$\{ \ 2C,1B \ || \ 1P \ \}$$

$$3B \ |2P| \ 1P$$

$$\{ \ 3B \ || \ 3P \ \}$$

is the property that, beginning in the state where two couples and one bodyguard are at the left bank, letting two presidents cross will result in a state in which all three bodyguards are at the left bank, while all three presidents are at the right bank.

Of course, we should always check the validity of such properties. It is easy to make a mistake and make an invalid claim. Care is needed, but the checks are straightforward.

3.3.4 Problem Decomposition

Using this notation we can express our strategy for decomposing the problem. The goal is to construct a sequence of actions S_0 satisfying

$$\{ \ 3C \ || \ \} \quad S_0 \quad \{ \ || \ 3C \ \}.$$

Our strategy can be summarised as exploiting two properties of the problem:

- the left–right symmetry;
- the fact that it is easy to get the presidents from one side to the other while their bodyguards remain on one bank.

This strategy is realised by decomposing S_0 into three sequences S_1, S_2 and S_3 such that

$$\{ \ 3C \ || \ \} \quad S_1 \quad \{ \ 3B \ || \ 3P \ \},$$

$$\{ \ 3B \ || \ 3P \ \} \quad S_2 \quad \{ \ 3P \ || \ 3B \ \},$$

$$\{ \ 3P \ || \ 3B \ \} \quad S_3 \quad \{ \ || \ 3C \ \}.$$

Sequence S_1 changes the state from the start state to the state where all the presidents are at the right bank and all the bodyguards are at the left bank. Sequence S_2 changes the end state of S_1 to the state where the positions of the presidents and bodyguards are reversed. Finally, sequence S_3 changes the end state of S_2 to the state where everyone is at the right bank. So, doing S_1 followed by S_2 followed by S_3, which we denote by S_1 ; S_2 ; S_3, will achieve the objective of changing the state from the start state (everyone is at the left bank) to the final state (everyone is at the right bank).

The decomposition is into *three* components because we want to exploit symmetry, but, clearly, an *odd* number of crossings will be necessary. Symmetry is captured by making the function of S_3 entirely symmetrical to the function of S_1. If we consider the reverse of S_3, its task is to transfer all the presidents from the right bank to the left bank. So, if we construct S_1, it is a simple task to construct S_3 directly from it.

We now have to tackle the problem of constructing S_1 and S_2.

As mentioned earlier, getting all the presidents across the river, leaving their bodyguards at the left bank is easy. Here is how it is achieved.

$$\{\ 3C\ ||\ \}$$
$$1C,2B\ |2P|$$
$$;\quad \{\ 1C,2B\ ||\ 2P\ \}$$
$$1C,2B\ |1P|\ 1P$$
$$;\quad \{\ 2C,1B\ ||\ 1P\ \}$$
$$3B\ |2P|\ 1P$$
$$\{\ 3B\ ||\ 3P\ \}.$$

That is,

$$\{\ 3C\ ||\ \}\quad 1C,2B\ |2P|\ ;\ 1C,2B\ |1P|\ 1P\ ;\ 3B\ |2P|\ 1P\quad \{\ 3B\ ||\ 3P\ \}.$$

As discussed above, the sequence S_3 is the reverse of S_1:

$$\{\ 3P\ ||\ 3B\ \}\quad 1P\ |2P|\ 3B\ ;\ 1P\ |1P|\ 1C,2B\ ;\ |2P|\ 1C,2B\quad \{\ ||\ 3C\ \}.$$

We are now faced with the harder task of constructing S_2. We seek a solution that is symmetrical about the middle.

Note that, for S_2, the starting position of the boat is the right bank, and its finishing position is the left bank. This is a requirement for S_2 to follow S_1 and be followed by S_3. The length of S_2 must also be odd.

Again, we look for a decomposition into three subsequences. If the solution is to remain symmetric, the middle action must be 1C |1C| 1C because this is the only action that is symmetric between left and right. That is, the solution must take the following form:

$$\{\ 3B \parallel 3P\ \}$$
$$T_1$$
$$;\qquad 1C\ |1C|\ 1C$$
$$;\qquad T_2$$
$$\{\ 3P \parallel 3B\ \}.$$

However, the middle action may be a left-to-right crossing or a right-to-left crossing; which is not immediately clear. The task is now to construct the symmetric sequences of actions T_1 and T_2.

If the middle action is from right to left, the action must be preceded by the state 1C || 2C and results in the state 2C || 1C. Vice versa, if the middle action is from left to right, the action must be preceded by the state 2C || 1C and results in the state 1C || 2C. There is little alternative but to use brute-force search to try to determine which can be achieved, but now the state space is relatively small.

Fortunately, T_1 is soon discovered. It consists of just two actions:

$$\{\ 3B \parallel 3P\ \}$$
$$3B\ |1P|\ 2P$$
$$;\qquad \{\ 1C,2B \parallel 2P\ \}$$
$$1C\ |2B|\ 2P$$
$$\{\ 1C \parallel 2C\ \}.$$

Symmetrically, for T_2 we have:

$$\{\ 2C \parallel 1C\ \}$$
$$2P\ |2B|\ 1C$$
$$;\qquad \{\ 2P \parallel 1C,2B\ \}$$
$$2P\ |1P|\ 3B$$
$$\{\ 3P \parallel 3B\ \}.$$

Finally, putting everything together, we have the complete solution to the nervous-couples problem:

$$\{ \ 3C \ || \ \}$$

1C,2B |2P| ; 1C,2B |1P| 1P ; 3B |2P| 1P

;   { 3B || 3P }

3B |1P| 2P ;   1C |2B| 2P

;   { 1C || 2C }

1C |1C| 1C

;   { 2C || 1C }

2P |2B| 1C ;   2P |1P| 3B

;   { 3P || 3B }

1P |2P| 3B ; 1P |1P| 1C,2B ; |2P| 1C,2B

{ || 3C }.

(In this solution, not all intermediate states are shown. This helps to document the solution, by recording the main steps, but not every step. Too much detail in program documentation can be a hindrance.)

3.3.5 A Review

Pause awhile to review the method used to solve the nervous-couples problem, so that you can fully appreciate how much more effective it is than brute-force search.

The construction seeks at each stage to exploit the symmetry between the left and right banks. Since the number of crossings will inevitably be odd, each decomposition is into *three* subsequences, where the first and last are "mirror images" in some sense. The middle crossing must be 1C |1C| 1C since this is the only symmetric action, but the direction of crossing is not immediately obvious. Naming the unknown sequences, and formally specifying their function using the { p } S { q } notation, helps to clarify what has to be achieved and to avoid error.

The final solution involves 11 crossings. That is too many to commit to memory. But, because the solution *method* is well structured, it is easy to remember, making a reconstruction of the solution straighforward. Moreover, the solution to the problem *cannot* be used in other contexts, but the solution method *can*. For the proof of the pudding, solve the following related problem:

Exercise 3.1 (Five-Couple Problem) There are five nervous couples, and their boat can carry a maximum of three individuals. Determine how to transport all the couples across the river.

Exercise 3.2 (Four-Couple Problem) Unfortunately, the symmetry between the left and right banks does not guarantee that every river-crossing problem has a symmetric solution. The case of four couples and a three-person boat has a solution, but it is not symmetric. Determine a solution to this problem.

The following hint may be helpful. Four is less than five, and, by now, you will have solved the problem of transporting five couples across the river (Exercise 3.1). Try to modify the solution for five couples to obtain a solution for four. You should be able to find two solutions in this way, one being obtained from the other by reversing left and right.

(In general, individual solutions need not be symmetric, but the set of solutions is symmetric. That is, there is a transformation from solutions to solutions based on reversing left and right. A solution is symmetric if this transformation maps the solution to itself.)

Exercise 3.3 (Project) The goal of this project is to give first-hand experience of the combinatorial explosion that occurs when using brute-force search. This is done by asking you to construct the state-transition diagrams for the three- and five-couple problems – this is feasible because they are not too large – and then asking you to calculate the number of states if all the individuals are named. (It would be entirely infeasible to draw the state diagram.) You are also asked to calculate the number of different ways of getting the couples across, first when individuals are not distinguished and then when they are distinguished. You will need to study Chapter 16, in particular Section 16.4.1, in order to tackle some parts of the project.

(a) How many states are there in the state-transition diagram for the problem of three couples?

How many states are there in the state-transition diagram for the problem of four couples?

How many states are there in the state-transition diagram for the problem of five couples?

(b) Construct the state-transition diagram for the problem of five couples with a boat of capacity three.

(c) How many different ways are there of getting three couples across the river in a boat of capacity two using the minimum number of crossings?

How many different ways are there of getting five couples across the river in a boat of capacity three using the minimum number of crossings?

(d) Suppose each president and each bodyguard is named (e.g. Ann and Bob, Con and Dan, etc.) and states are distinguished by the names of the individuals on each side of the river. How many states would there then be in the state-transition diagram for the problem of five couples with a boat of capacity three? How many different ways would there be of getting them all across the river in a boat of capacity three using the minimum number of crossings?

3.4 RULE OF SEQUENTIAL COMPOSITION

The { p } S { q } notation we used for solving the nervous-couples problem is the notation used for specifying and constructing computer programs. It is called a *Hoare triple*. (The British computing scientist Sir Tony Hoare introduced the notation in his pioneering work on techniques for formally verifying the correctness of computer programs.)

A computer program is specified by a relation between the input values and the output values. The allowed input values are specified by a so-called *precondition*, p, and the output values are specified by a *postcondition*, q. Preconditions and postconditions are properties of the program variables.

If S is a program and p and q are properties of the program variables,

$$\{ p \} S \{ q \}$$

means that execution of S begun in a state that satisfies property p is guaranteed to terminate in a state that satisfies property q. For example, a program to compute the remainder r and dividend d after dividing number M by number N would have precondition

$$N \neq 0$$

(since dividing by 0 is not allowed) and postcondition

$$M = N \times d + r \ \wedge \ 0 \leq r < N.$$

If the program is S, the specification of the program is thus

$$\{\,N\neq0\,\}\quad S\quad\{\,M=N\times d+r\ \wedge\ 0\leq r<N\,\}.$$

Programs are often composed by sequencing; the individual components are executed one after the other. A semicolon is usually used to denote sequencing. Thus, if S_1, S_2 and S_3 are programs, S_1 ; S_2 ; S_3 denotes the program that is executed by first executing S_1, then executing S_2, and then executing S_3. This is called the *sequential composition* of S_1, S_2 and S_3.

A sequential composition is introduced into a program when the problem it solves is decomposed into subproblems. In the case of a decomposition into two components, given a precondition p and a postcondition q, an intermediate condition r, say, is invented. The problem of constructing a program S satisfying the specification

$$\{\,p\,\}\,S\,\{\,q\,\}$$

is then resolved by letting S be S_1 ; S_2 and constructing S_1 and S_2 to satisfy the specifications

$$\{\,p\,\}\,S_1\,\{\,r\,\}$$

and

$$\{\,r\,\}\,S_2\,\{\,q\,\}.$$

The intermediate condition r thus acts as postcondition for S_1 and precondition for S_2.

If the problem is decomposed into three subproblems, two intermediate conditions are needed. This is what we did in solving the nervous-couples problem. The initial problem statement has precondition 3C || and postcondition || 3C. The intermediate conditions 3B || 3P and 3P || 3B were then introduced in order to make the first decomposition.

There are different ways of using the rule of sequential composition. The structure of the given problem may suggest an appropriate intermediate condition. Alternatively, the problem may suggest an appropriate initial computation S_1; the task is then to identify the intermediate condition and the final computation S_2. Conversely, the problem may suggest an appropriate final computation S_2; then the task becomes one of identifying the intermediate condition r and the initial computation S_1. The following exercises provide practice in the technique.

Exercise 3.4 This exercise is about a simple solitaire-like game on a one-dimensional board.

Suppose a long strip of paper has been divided into squares. A single coin is placed on one of the squares. The objective is to displace the coin six places to the right using a sequence of *moves*, which we now define. The moves are reversible; a move is to replace a single coin on one square by two coins, one on each of the two adjacent squares. The reverse move (which is also allowed) is to replace two coins on squares that are separated by just one square by one coin on the separating square. No other moves are possible, and there are no other restrictions on moves. (The number of coins on any one square is unlimited, and it is not necessary for the separating square in a reverse move to be empty.)

Figure 3.2 shows the starting position, the finishing position and the allowed moves. (The double arrow indicates that the move is reversible.)

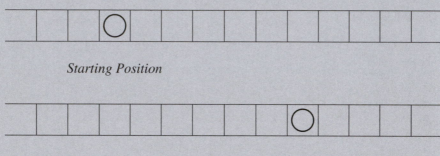

Starting Position

Finishing Position   *(6 places to the right)*

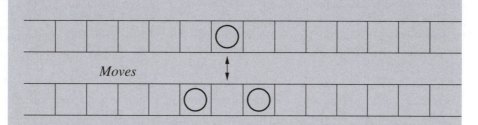

Moves

Figure 3.2: A one-dimensional game of solitaire.

Exploit the insights from this chapter. The moves exhibit a symmetry property, which you should exploit by considering (symmetrical) sequences of moves from the start and finish positions. Also, decompose the problem.

Exercise 3.5   This problem is like the one in Exercise 3.4 but the moves and goal are different. Figure 3.3 illustrates the start and finish positions and the allowed moves.

As in Exercise 3.4, a single coin is placed on one of the squares but this time the objective is to displace it four places to the right. The allowed moves are slightly different. If there is at least one coin on any square, two extra coins can be added in the two adjacent squares. The reverse move is also possible: if there are three adjacent coins, two outer coins can be removed leaving just the middle coin.

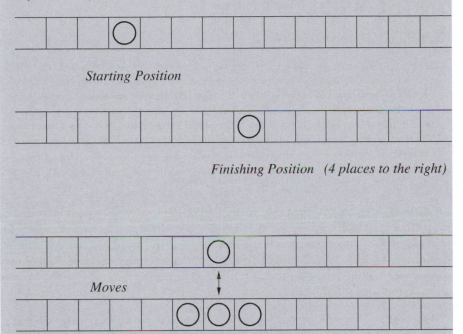

Figure 3.3: Another one-dimensional game of solitaire.

The same hint applies to this problem as for Exercise 3.4: exploit symmetry and decompose.

Exercise 3.6   This problem is like the ones in Exercises 3.4 and 3.5 but, again, the moves and goal are different.

As in those problems, a single coin is placed on one of the squares. The allowed moves are slightly different. If there is at least one coin on any square, three extra coins can be added, one in the square itself and one in each of the two adjacent squares. The reverse move is also possible: if there are three adjacent coins, and the middle square has at least two coins, three adjacent coins can be removed.

The question is to find the smallest number m such that it is possible to displace the coin by m spaces.

3.5 THE BRIDGE PROBLEM

Recall the bridge problem posed in Chapter 1:

Four people wish to cross a bridge. It is dark, and it is necessary to use a torch when crossing the bridge, but they have only one torch between them. The bridge is narrow, and only two people can be on it at any one time. The four people take different amounts of time to cross the bridge; when two cross together they proceed at the speed of the slowest. The first person takes 1 minute to cross, the second 2 minutes, the third 5 minutes and the fourth 10 minutes. The torch must be ferried back and forth across the bridge, so that it is always carried when the bridge is crossed.

Show that all four can cross the bridge within 17 minutes.

The problem is reputed to have been used by a major software manufacturer in interviews for software engineers; nowadays its solution is considered to be too well known for such use. In this section, we hypothesise how the interview might proceed assuming the candidate is well acquainted with algorithmic problem-solving techniques. Rather than consider the specific problem above, let us introduce input parameters for the crossing times. In this way, the problem becomes:

Four people wish to cross a bridge. It is dark, and it is necessary to use a torch when crossing the bridge, but they have only one torch between them. The bridge is narrow, and only two people can be on it at any one time. The four people take t.1, t.2, t.3 and t.4 minutes to cross the bridge; when two cross together they proceed at the speed of the slowest. The torch must be ferried back and forth across the bridge, so that it is always carried when the bridge is crossed.

Construct an algorithm that will get all four across the bridge in the shortest possible time.

 The notation "t.1" makes clear that t is a function from people to times. The infix dot denotes function application. It is a commonly used notation in computer programs: in a program to solve this problem we might write

time.person *or* person.time *(depending on the programming language and how the variables have been declared). Do not confuse it with multiplication. Other notations that could have been used are subscripts, t_1, or t(1). It is advisable to avoid subscripts where they can be complex expressions. The dot notation has been chosen here because the use of subscripts would have led to subscripts of subscripts and the traditional notation t(1) introduces unnecessary parentheses. See Section 12.3.1 for a discussion of the myriad of notations for function application.*

We present the interview as a hypothetical dialogue between the interviewer and the interviewee. The interviewer's questions are indicated by the letter Q and the interviewee's answers are indicated by the letter A. You might want to use a piece of paper to cover up each answer as the dialogue proceeds, revealing the answer only when you have formulated your own response. We take up the interview from the point at which the interviewee has indicated that he understands the statement of the problem.

Q: Let's start with an easy question. What is the minimum number of crossings required to get all four across?

A: That will be when, at each step, the maximum number cross and the minimum number return. That is, 2 cross, 1 returns, 2 cross, 1 returns and then 2 cross. That makes 3 forward trips and 2 return trips, 5 in total.

Q: Good. Now, will the shortest time be achieved with the minimum number of crossings?

A: [Thinks: this sounds like a trick question!] Hmm, seems like it but I'm not sure.

Q: It's good that you are not sure. That's not such an easy question to answer. Let's assume the answer is yes. We can return to the question later.

 See Exercise 3.15.

You said that two return trips are needed. What is the implication for the number of people who make a return trip?

A: At most two make a return trip. [Quickly adds:] And at least one, of course.

Q: Right. So either one or two people make a return trip. Let's call them "returners".

What implication does that have for the number of different ways it is possible to get all four across using the minimum number of crossings?

A: Can you explain what you mean by "different"? Do you want me to distinguish each of the four people or not? If you do, it's going to be a lot and I would need paper and pencil to work it out.

Q: Good question. I was hoping you would ask. The answer is no. Although the people are distinguished by their crossing times, I would like you to ignore that for the moment. You should not need paper and pencil.

 Exercise 3.14 asks you to determine the number when the people are all individually named.

A: OK. Then I guess you want me to do a case analysis on whether one or two people return.

[Pauses briefly.] If just one person returns, there is only one way to get all four across: the returner accompanies each of the other three across. All solutions of this form are indistinguishable in the sense that they correspond to permutations of the four people.

Q: Yes, that's right. We will need that for later. Can you write down the sequence of crossings? I would suggest you introduce π to denote a permutation of the set $\{1,2,3,4\}$ so that you can give the sequence in its most general form. Also, it might be useful to number the sequence so that we can refer to it later.

 Permutations are discussed in Section 16.8.2.

A: OK. The sequence is: [Writes, simultaneously explaining that "+" indicates a forward trip, "−" a return trip, and $\pi.i$ is person i in the permutation π.]

$$+\{\pi.1,\pi.2\} \; ; \; -\{\pi.1\} \; ; \; +\{\pi.1,\pi.3\} \; ; \; -\{\pi.1\} \; ; \; +\{\pi.1,\pi.4\}. \tag{3.7}$$

Q: That's correct. Every sequence of crossings in which there is just one returner is obtained by a suitable choice of the permutation π.

Now can you consider the case when two people return? How many different ways are there of this form?

A: Hm. That means that the two returners are $\pi.1$ and $\pi.2$, say. The issue is at what stage they cross. [Thinks hard for several minutes.] Yes! I think I know the answer. There are just *two* ways. Either the returners cross twice again immediately, or they do not. Let me write that down. The case where the returners cross again immediately has the form

$$+\{\pi.1,\pi.3\} \; ; \; -\{\pi.1\} \; ; \; +\{\pi.1,\pi.2\} \; ; \; -\{\pi.2\} \; ; \; +\{\pi.2,\pi.4\}, \tag{3.8}$$

and the case where they do not has the form

$$+\{\pi.1,\pi.2\} \; ; \; -\{\pi.1\} \; ; \; +\{\pi.3,\pi.4\} \; ; \; -\{\pi.2\} \; ; \; +\{\pi.1,\pi.2\}. \tag{3.9}$$

There is no other possibility because each returner must cross twice.

Q: Very good. That is indeed correct. There are just three different ways of getting everyone across: one way if there is one returner and two ways if there are two returners. Many of our candidates make the mistake of naming the individual people; usually they end up making everything grossly over-complicated.

Let's now take the crossing times into account. For each of the three ways, what is the time taken?

A: When there is one returner, [Writes, simultaneously explaining that "↑" means maximum.]

$$t.(\pi.1)\!\uparrow\!t.(\pi.2) + t.(\pi.1) + t.(\pi.1)\!\uparrow\!t.(\pi.3) + t.(\pi.1) + t.(\pi.1)\!\uparrow\!t.(\pi.4), \tag{3.10}$$

when there are two returners who cross again immediately,

$$t.(\pi.1)\!\uparrow\!t.(\pi.3) + t.(\pi.1) + t.(\pi.1)\!\uparrow\!t.(\pi.2) + t.(\pi.2) + t.(\pi.2)\!\uparrow\!t.(\pi.4), \tag{3.11}$$

and when there are two returners who do not cross again immediately,

$$t.(\pi.1)\!\uparrow\!t.(\pi.2) + t.(\pi.1) + t.(\pi.3)\!\uparrow\!t.(\pi.4) + t.(\pi.2) + t.(\pi.1)\!\uparrow\!t.(\pi.2). \tag{3.12}$$

Q: Good. Let's consider these in turn. In the case of (3.10) how would you choose the permutation π so as to minimise the time?

A: That's easy. Just choose person 1 to be the fastest person.

Q: Can you make that precise?

A: Yes. [Picks up paper and pencil again.] Let's suppose that the people are numbered so that person 1 is the fastest. So, let's assume that $t.1 \leq t.1 \!\downarrow\! t.2 \!\downarrow\! t.3 \!\downarrow\! t.4$ and π is any permutation of the people. Then [writes]

$$t.1\!\uparrow\!t.2 + t.1 + t.1\!\uparrow\!t.3 + t.1 + t.1\!\uparrow\!t.4$$
$$\leq \;\; t.(\pi.1)\!\uparrow\!t.(\pi.2) + t.(\pi.1) + t.(\pi.1)\!\uparrow\!t.(\pi.3) + t.(\pi.1) + t.(\pi.1)\!\uparrow\!t.(\pi.4)$$
$$\Leftarrow \quad \{ \qquad \text{monotonicity of addition} \quad \}$$
$$t.1\!\uparrow\!t.2 + t.1 + t.1\!\uparrow\!t.3 + t.1\!\uparrow\!t.4$$

$\leq$ $t.(\pi.1)\uparrow t.(\pi.2) + t.(\pi.1) + t.(\pi.1)\uparrow t.(\pi.3) + t.(\pi.1)\uparrow t.(\pi.4)$

$\wedge$ $t.1 \leq t.(\pi.1)$

$=$ {   assumption: $t.1 \leq t.1 \downarrow t.2 \downarrow t.3 \downarrow t.4$ }

   $t.2 + t.1 + t.3 + t.4$

$\leq$ $t.(\pi.1)\uparrow t.(\pi.2) + t.(\pi.1) + t.(\pi.1)\uparrow t.(\pi.3) + t.(\pi.1)\uparrow t.(\pi.4)$

$\wedge$ $t.1 \leq t.(\pi.1)$

$=$ {   the assumption implies that $t.1 \leq t.(\pi.1)$,

            rearranging }

   $t.1 + t.2 + t.3 + t.4$

$\leq$ $t.(\pi.1) + t.(\pi.1)\uparrow t.(\pi.2) + t.(\pi.1)\uparrow t.(\pi.3) + t.(\pi.1)\uparrow t.(\pi.4)$

$\Leftarrow$ {   transitivity of $\leq$ }

   $t.1 + t.2 + t.3 + t.4$

$\leq$ $t.(\pi.1) + t.(\pi.2) + t.(\pi.3) + t.(\pi.4)$

$\leq$ $t.(\pi.1) + t.(\pi.1)\uparrow t.(\pi.2) + t.(\pi.1)\uparrow t.(\pi.3) + t.(\pi.1)\uparrow t.(\pi.4)$

$=$ {   first inequality: π is a permutation,

            second inequality: $[\ x \leq x \uparrow y\ ]$ and monotonicity

            of addition }

   true.

⚠ *Expressions involving the at-most relation ("$\leq$") are called* inequalities. *The cancellation rule and other rules for manipulating inequalities are discussed in Section 15.1. Properties of maximum and minimum are discussed in Section 15.2.*

Phew! I didn't expect the calculation to be quite so long. I had to think hard about the first step. The use of monotonicity of addition seemed to be the obvious thing to do, but there are so many ways to split the five summands on each side of the inequality. Then it seemed obvious: I was aiming to use the fact that π is a permutation (since that is the only thing known about it); that dictated splitting five into four and one. I postponed other more obvious steps because I didn't want to make the mistake of combining two many steps into one.

> ⚠ *The use of the fact that π is a permutation in the final step is an instance of the range-translation rule for quantifications (14.8) discussed in Section 14.2.3. See Section 14.5 for its generalisation to operators other than addition.*

Q: Excellent! Although the calculation seems long, it leaves no room for doubt, and it's good that you document each step. Our company values careful, precise work.

Now let's look at how to optimise the times when there are two returners. First, compare (3.10) and (3.11); do you spot anything?

A: Oh, yes. The first three terms in each summand are the same. So they can be cancelled leaving the comparison of the last two terms:

$$t.(\pi.1) + t.(\pi.1){\uparrow}t.(\pi.4) \ ? \ t.(\pi.2) + t.(\pi.2){\uparrow}t.(\pi.4).$$

Obviously the former is at most the latter if $t.(\pi.1)$ is at most $t.(\pi.2)$.

Q: That's right. So, by choosing person 1 to be the fastest person, method (3.8) (two returners who cross again immediately) can be discounted. It always takes at least the time taken when just the fastest person returns.

What about the case of two returners who do not cross again immediately, method (3.9)? How would you choose π to optimise the time?

A: It looks like persons 1 and 2 should be the fastest and persons 3 and 4 the slowest, but it does not seem so obvious. Can I do the calculation?

Q: Yes, of course. Go ahead. [Hands pencil and paper over again.]

A: Let's assume $t.1{\uparrow}t.2 \leq t.3{\downarrow}t.4$. Then, for any permutation π, we have: [Writes.]

$$t.1{\uparrow}t.2 + t.1 + t.3{\uparrow}t.4 + t.2 + t.1{\uparrow}t.2$$

$$\leq \ t.(\pi.1){\uparrow}t.(\pi.2) + t.(\pi.1) + t.(\pi.3){\uparrow}t.(\pi.4) + t.(\pi.2) + t.(\pi.1){\uparrow}t.(\pi.2)$$

$$\Leftarrow \quad \{ \qquad \text{by assumption: } t.1{\uparrow}t.2 \leq t.(\pi.1){\uparrow}t.(\pi.2),$$

$$\text{monotonicity of addition} \quad \}$$

$$t.1 + t.3{\uparrow}t.4 + t.2$$

$$\leq \ t.(\pi.1) + t.(\pi.3){\uparrow}t.(\pi.4) + t.(\pi.2)$$

$$\Leftarrow \quad \{ \qquad \text{by assumption: } t.(\pi.3){\downarrow}t.(\pi.4) \leq t.3{\downarrow}t.4,$$

$$\text{monotonicity of addition} \quad \}$$

$$t.3 \downarrow t.4 + t.1 + t.3 \uparrow t.4 + t.2$$

$$\leq \quad t.(\pi.3) \downarrow t.(\pi.4) + t.(\pi.1) + t.(\pi.3) \uparrow t.(\pi.4) + t.(\pi.2)$$

$$\Leftarrow \quad \{ \qquad \pi \text{ is a permutation } \}$$

true.

Q: That's another beautiful calculation. I like the way you expanded three terms to four in the two summands, exploiting the symmetry between persons 1 and 2 (the two fastest) and persons 3 and 4 (the two slowest). We call that a "complification" step; it's clear that your priority is to simplify but sometimes – in the more interesting calculations – it is necessary to complify.

A: [Smiles.] I've heard of "simplification" but not of "complification". Complify: converse of simplify. That's neat! I wonder why it's not used elsewhere?

Q: [Tries to hide a smile.] Well, our company is at the forefront of innovation in many ways, but we can't claim that idea. The word has been in use for at least a quarter of a century among Dutch computing scientists, but the English-speaking world has yet to catch on. But let's move on. Can you summarise what you have determined so far?

A: Yes. We have determined that there are only two cases to consider. The first case is when the fastest person accompanies each other person across. If we assume that the people have been ordered in such a way that

$$t.1 \leq t.1 \downarrow t.2 \downarrow t.3 \downarrow t.4,$$

the time taken (after simplification) is

$$t.2 + t.1 + t.3 + t.1 + t.4.$$

The second case is when two people return and do not cross again immediately. If we assume that the people have been ordered in such a way that

$$t.1 \uparrow t.2 \leq t.3 \downarrow t.4,$$

the time taken is

$$t.1 \uparrow t.2 + t.1 + t.3 \uparrow t.4 + t.2 + t.1 \uparrow t.2.$$

Q: Yes, we are nearly there now. How do you choose between the two?

A: Well, the two conditions on the ordering can be strengthened to

$$t.1 \leq t.2 \leq t.3 \leq t.4.$$

Then, with this assumption, it's simply a matter of determining which (if any) of the two times is smaller.

Q: Can you simplify the comparison?

A: [Looks at what is written.] Looks like it. Is it OK for me to use the assumption to simplify the terms? The simplifications are very elementary.

Q: Yes, go ahead.

A: [Writes]

$$t.2+t.1+t.3+t.1+t.4 \ \leq \ t.2 + t.1 + t.4 + t.2 + t.2$$

$$= \qquad \{ \qquad \text{cancellation} \quad \}$$

$$t.3+t.1 \ \leq \ 2 \times t.2.$$

So one returner is chosen if $t.3+t.1 \leq 2 \times t.2$ and two returners is chosen if $2 \times t.2 \leq t.3+t.1$.

Q: Very good. I've noticed that you have connected steps in your calculations sometimes by the "if" symbol and sometimes by the equality symbol. Can you explain why you use the equality symbol here rather than the more conventional "if and only if" symbol?

A: That's simple to explain. The first rule of logic is the rule of substitution of equals for equals. The comparison between the two expressions is to be used in a program and if one boolean expression is to be replaced by another it is vital that they are everywhere equal.

> ⚠️ *Substitution of equals for equals is a rule that is ubiquitous in mathematical calculations but rarely made explicit. When calculating with boolean expressions, the rule is obscured by the traditional focus on implicational rather than equational reasoning and the use of "if and only if". See Chapters 5 and 13 for more explanation.*

Q: Very good. All that needs to be done now is to write down the algorithm. Can you do that for me?

A: No problem.

[Writes, recalling that "+" indicates a forward trip and "−" a return trip.]

order the people

; { $t.1 \leq t.2 \leq t.3 \leq t.4$ }

if $t.3+t.1 \leq 2 \times t.2 \ \rightarrow$ $+\{1,2\}$; $-\{1\}$; $+\{1,3\}$; $-\{1\}$; $+\{1,4\}$

□ $2 \times t.2 \leq t.3+t.1 \ \rightarrow$ $+\{1,2\}$; $-\{1\}$; $+\{3,4\}$; $-\{2\}$; $+\{1,2\}$

fi

{ all people are across in the shortest time }

Q: That's excellent.

We didn't resolve the issue of whether the optimal time is always achieved using the minumum number of crossings. We don't have time for that now but here are some exercises for you to think about later. [Hands over Exercises 3.13, 3.14 and 3.15.]

A: Do I need to complete these exercises before you decide whether or not to offer me a position?

Q: No, you have passed the interview with flying colours. And we will offer you a pay rise immediately. Congratulations!

Exercise 3.13   Construct a single expression that gives the minimal crossing time (assuming that the people are ordered in increasing order of crossing time).

Check that, if the crossing times are 1 minute, 2 minutes, 5 minutes and 10 minutes, the algorithm deduces that the minimal crossing time is 17 minutes.

Construct crossing times for the four people such that it is faster for person 1 to accompany each other person across the bridge rather than let the two slowest cross together.

Exercise 3.14   Suppose all four people are named and a brute-force search is used to solve the problem assuming that an optimal solution uses the minimum number of crossings. This would mean enumerating all the different ways of getting four (individually named) people across the bridge in five trips. How many ways are there?

 In the first crossing, two people are chosen from four; in the second step, one person is chosen from two to make the return crossing, and so on. See Section 16.8.2 for how to evaluate the number of such choices.

Exercise 3.15   Suppose there are five people with crossing times 1, 1, 4, 4 and 4 minutes and suppose that three people can cross the bridge together. What is the shortest time needed to get all five across?

What is the minimum number of crossings needed to get all five across, and what is the shortest time to get them across if the minimum number of crossings is used? (Your answer should demonstrate that getting the people across in the minimum number of crossings is not necessarily optimal.)

Show that, if just two people can cross together, it is the case that an optimal solution uses the minimal number of crossings.

Exercise 3.16 A 3×3 chessboard is to be coloured using at most four colours. Two squares on the board *touch* if they share a side or a corner point. The requirement is that touching squares should be coloured differently. How many different ways are there of colouring the board? Take care to make clear how you differentiate colourings. (Hint: first identify how many different squares there are. You do not need any knowledge of combinatorics.)

3.6 CONDITIONAL STATEMENTS

The solution to the bridge problem uses a so-called *conditional statement*. A conditional statement chooses between a number of different options according to the value of a number of boolean expressions, called "conditions". The conditional statement in the bridge problem is recognised by the "if–fi" brackets; one method of getting the four people across is chosen if the boolean expression $t.3+t.1 \leq 2 \times t.2$ has the value true and the second method is chosen if the boolean expression $2 \times t.2 \leq t.3+t.1$ has the value true. If both have the value true an arbitrary choice is made between the two methods.

In this book, conditional statements always have the form of a (possibly non-deterministic) choice – indicated by the "□" symbol – among a number of *guarded commands*, bracketed by "if" and "fi". A guarded command has the form $b \rightarrow S$, where b is a boolean expression called the *guard* and S is a statement called the *body*. The if–fi statement in the solution to the bridge problem has two guards, but there may be more. A concrete example of a conditional statement with three guards is the following:

$$\text{if } i < j \;\rightarrow\; i := i+1$$
$$\square \; i = j \;\rightarrow\; \text{skip}$$
$$\square \; j < i \;\rightarrow\; j := j+1$$
$$\text{fi}$$

(In this example, the choice is deterministic.)

Conditional statements are used to express *case analysis*. Case analysis is a commonly used problem-solving strategy. Suppose a problem is specified by a precondition P and postcondition Q. Case analysis involves splitting the problem's solution into several cases, specified by boolean expressions b_1 thru[1] b_k, for some k. The cases must be *exhaustive* in the sense that

$$[\ P \ \Rightarrow \ \langle \exists i : 1 \leq i \leq k : b_i \rangle \ ].$$

(In words, in every state satisfying the precondition P at least one of the boolean expressions must have the value true.) The problem then becomes to find, for each i, a solution S_i to the problem with precondition $P \wedge b_i$ and postcondition Q. That is, for each i, S_i is constructed so that

$$\{ P \wedge b_i \} \ S_i \ \{ Q \}.$$

 The expression "$\langle \exists i : 1 \leq i \leq k : b_i \rangle$" is a so-called "existential quantification". It is read as "there exists an i such that 1 is at most i is at most k such that b_i (is true)" or, more informally, "b_1 or b_2 or dotdotdot b_k (is true)". See Section 14.3.2.

These are then combined in a conditional statement to form a solution to the original problem. Specifically, the solution takes the following form:

$$\{ \ P \ \}$$
$$\text{if} \quad b_1 \ \rightarrow \ S_1$$
$$\square \ \ldots$$
$$\square \quad b_k \ \rightarrow \ S_k$$
$$\text{fi}$$
$$\{ \ Q \ \}$$

Starting in a given state, a conditional statement is executed by choosing a guarded command whose guard evaluates to true and then executing its body. If several guards

---

[1]We use "thru" when we want to specify an inclusive range of numbers. For example, "1 thru 4" means the numbers 1, 2, 3 and 4. The English expression "1 to 4" is ambiguous about whether the number 4 is included or not. In mathematical expressions, two dots are used as an abbreviation, as in 1..4; the dots are pronounced "thru".

evaluate to true, an arbitrary choice of command is made. If none of the guards evaluates to true, execution aborts.[2]

3.7 SUMMARY

In this chapter, we have contrasted brute-force search with problem decomposition. Brute-force search should be used only as a last resort. Modern computer technology means that some problems that are too large for human beings to solve do become solvable, but the state-space explosion makes the method impractical for realistic problems, even with the most powerful computers. Complexity theory, which is a topic of study in more advanced courses on algorithm design, lends greater force to this argument; no matter how much bigger and faster computers become, they can never compete with the increase in size of the state space caused by modest increases in problem size.

Problem decomposition seeks to exploit the inherent structure of the problem domain. In all river-crossing or similar problems, there is a symmetry between the left and right banks. This suggests tackling the problems by decomposing them into three components, the first and last being symmetrical in some way. This strategy has no guarantee of success, but, if the problems are tackled in this way, they become more manageable, and often have clear, easily remembered and easily reproduced solutions. Most importantly, the solution method can be applied repeatedly, in contrast to the solutions, which are relevant to just one particular problem.

Along the way, the issue of deciding what to name (and what not to name) has emerged as an important problem-solving skill that can have significant impact on the complexity of the problem. The process is called *abstraction*: from the myriad of details that surround any real-world description of a problem, we abstract the few that are relevant, introducing appropriate, clearly defined mathematical notation to assist in the problem's solution.

3.8 BIBLIOGRAPHIC REMARKS

The nervous-couples problem is from the 1999 *Vierkant Voor Wiskunde* calendar. (See Section 2.6 for further information.) For further information on the bridge problem, see

---

[2]If you are already familiar with a conventional programming language, you will be familiar with *deterministic* conditional statements: if−then−else statements. In such statements, the choice of which of the optional statements should be executed is completely determined by the state of the program variables. In a non-deterministic choice, as used here, the choice is not completely determined.

Section 10.8. Exercises 3.4 and 3.5 are from the website `http://mathlesstraveled.com` where they are called the "nuclear pennies game" and the "thermonuclear pennies game", respectively. Underlying solitaire-like games is the theory of "polynomials", which is outside the scope of this text. See [BCaF10] for further information.

The goat–cabbage–wolf problem is reputed to be thousands of years old and is discussed in a great many books. Surprisingly, the symmetry between the cabbage and wolf never seems to be mentioned. The symmetry, and how to exploit it, was pointed out by E.W. Dijkstra (who was a very accomplished problem-solver and a pioneer in mathematical methodology and the formal development of algorithms). Netty van Gasteren [vG90] emphasises the importance of naming in problem solving, using a number of more advanced algorithmic problems as examples.

Chapter
Games

4

This chapter is about how to win some simple two-person games. The goal is to have some method (i.e. "algorithm") for deciding what to do so that the eventual outcome is a win.

The key to developing a winning strategy is the recognition of invariants. So, in essence, this chapter is a continuation of Chapter 2. The chapter is also about trying to identify and exploit structure in problems. In this sense, it introduces the importance of algebra in problem solving.

The next section introduces a number of games with matchsticks, in order to give the flavour of the games that we consider. Following it, we develop a method of systematically identifying winning and losing positions in a game (assuming a number of simplifying constraints on the rules of the game). A *winning strategy* is then what we call "maintaining an invariant". "Maintaining an invariant" is an important technique in algorithm development. Here, it will mean ensuring that the opponent is always placed in a position from which losing is inevitable.

4.1 MATCHSTICK GAMES

A *matchstick game* is played with one or more piles of matches. Two players take turns to make a move. Moves involve removing one or more matches from one of the piles, according to a given rule. The game *ends* when it is no longer possible to make a move. The player whose turn it is to move is the *loser*, and the other player is the *winner*.

A matchstick game is an example of an *impartial, two-person* game with *complete information*. "Impartial" means that rules for moving apply equally to both players. (Chess, for example, is not impartial, because white can move only white pieces, and black can move only black pieces.) "Complete information" means that both players know the complete state of the game. In contrast, in card games like poker, each player does not know the cards held by the other player; the players have incomplete information about the state of the game.

A *winning position* is one from which a perfect player is always assured of a win. A *losing position* is one from which a player can never win, when playing against a perfect player. A *winning strategy* is an algorithm for choosing moves from winning positions that guarantees a win.

As an example, suppose there is one pile of matches, and an allowed move is to remove 1 or 2 matches. The losing positions are the positions where the number of matches is a multiple of 3 (i.e. the number of matches is 0, 3, 6, 9, etc.). The remaining positions are the winning positions. If n is the number of matches in such a position (i.e. n is not a multiple of 3), the strategy is to remove $n \bmod 3$ matches.[1] This is either 1 or 2, so the move is valid. The opponent is then put in a position where the number of matches is a multiple of 3. This means that there are either 0 matches left, in which case the opponent loses, or any move they make will result in there again being a number of matches remaining that is not a multiple of 3.

In an impartial game that is guaranteed to terminate no matter how the players choose their moves (i.e. the possibility of stalemate is excluded), it is always possible to characterise the positions as either winning or losing positions. The following exercises ask you to do this in specific cases.

1. There is one pile of matches. Each player is allowed to remove 1 match.

> **What are the winning positions?**

2. There is one pile of matches. Each player is allowed to remove 0 matches, but must remove at least 1 match.

> **What are the winning positions?**

3. Can you see a pattern in the last two problems and the example discussed above (in which a player is allowed to remove 1 or 2 matches)?

> **In other words, can you see how to win a game in which an allowed move is to remove at least 1 and at most N matches, where N is some number fixed in advance?**

4. There is one pile of matches. Each player is allowed to remove 1, 3 or 4 matches.

> **What are the winning positions and what is the winning strategy?**

---

[1] Recall that n mod 3 denotes the remainder after dividing n by 3.

5. There is one pile of matches. Each player is allowed to remove 1, 3 or 4 matches, except that it is not allowed to repeat the opponent's last move. (So, if, say, your opponent removes 1 match, your next move must be to remove 3 or 4 matches.)

What are the winning positions and what is the winning strategy?

6. There are two piles of matches. A move is to choose one pile and, from that pile, remove 1, 2 or 3 matches.

What are the winning positions and what is the winning strategy?

7. There are two piles of matches. A move is to choose one pile; from the left pile 1, 2 or 3 matches may be removed, and from the right pile 1 thru 7 matches may be removed.

What are the winning positions and what is the winning strategy?

8. There are two piles of matches. A move is to choose one pile; from the left pile, 1, 3 or 4 matches may be removed, and, from the right pile, 1 or 2 matches may be removed.

What are the winning positions and what is the winning strategy?

4.2 WINNING STRATEGIES

In this section, we formulate what is required of a winning strategy. We begin with the simple matchstick game where a move is to remove one or two matches from a single pile of matches; we show how to search systematically through all the positions of the game, labelling each as either a winning or a losing position. Although a brute-force search, and thus not practical for more complicated games, the algorithm does give a better understanding of what is involved and can be used as a basis for developing more efficient solutions in particular cases.

4.2.1 Assumptions

We make a number of assumptions about the game, in order that the search will work.

- We assume that the number of positions is finite.
- We assume that the game is guaranteed to terminate no matter how the players choose their moves.

The first assumption is necessary because a one-by-one search of the positions can never be complete if the number of positions is infinite. The second assumption is necessary because the algorithm relies on being able to characterise all positions as either losing or winning; we exclude the possibility that there are stalemate positions. Stalemate positions are ones from which the players can continue the game indefinitely, so that neither player can win.

4.2.2 Labelling Positions

The first step is to draw a *directed graph* depicting positions and moves in the game. Figure 4.1 is a graph of the matchstick game described at the beginning of Section 4.1 for the first nine positions.

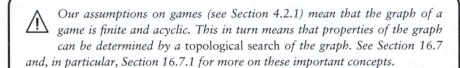

🔵 **Figure 4.1: Matchstick game. Players may take one or two matches at each turn.**

A directed graph has a set of *nodes* and a set of *edges*. Each edge is *from* one node *to* another node. When graphs are drawn, nodes are depicted by circles, and edges are depicted by arrows pointing from the *from* node to the *to* node.

> ⚠️ *Our assumptions on games (see Section 4.2.1) mean that the graph of a game is finite and acyclic. This in turn means that properties of the graph can be determined by a topological search of the graph. See Section 16.7 and, in particular, Section 16.7.1 for more on these important concepts.*

The nodes in Figure 4.1 are labelled by the number of matches remaining in the pile. From the node labelled 0, there are no edges. It is impossible to move from the position in which no matches remain. From the node labelled 1, there is exactly one edge, to the node labelled 0. From the position in which one match remains, there is exactly one move that can be made, namely to remove the remaining match. From all other nodes, there are two edges. From the node labelled n, where n is at least 2, there is an edge to the node labelled n−1 and an edge to the node labelled n−2. That is, from a position in which the number of remaining matches is at least 2, one may remove one or two matches.

Having drawn the graph, we can begin labelling the nodes as either losing positions or winning positions. A player who finds themself in a losing position will inevitably lose, if playing against a perfect opponent. A player who finds themself in a winning position is guaranteed to win, provided the right choice of move is made at each turn.

The labelling rule has two parts, one for losing positions, the other for winning positions:

- A node is labelled *losing* if *every* edge from the node is to a winning position.

- A node is labelled *winning* if *there is* an edge from the node to a losing position.

At first sight, it may seem that it is impossible to begin to apply these rules; after all, the first rule defines losing positions in terms of winning positions, while the second rule does the reverse. It seems like a vicious circle! However, we can begin by labelling as losing positions all the nodes with no outgoing edges. This is because, if there are no edges from a node, the statement "every edge from the node is to a winning position" is true. It is indeed the case that all of the (non-existent) edges are to a winning position.

This is an instance of a general rule of logic. A statement of the form "every x has property p" is called a *for-all quantification*, or a *universal quantification*. Such a statement is said to be *vacuously* true when there are no instances of the "x" in the quantification. In a sense, the statement is "vacuous" (i.e. empty) because it is a statement about nothing.

> ⚠ A "quantification" extends a binary operator (a function on two values) to a collection of values. Summation is an example of a quantification: the binary operator is adding two numbers. In the case of universal quantification, the binary operator is logical "and". See Chapter 14 for full details.

Returning to Figure 4.1, node 0 is labelled "losing" because there are no edges from it. It is indeed a losing position, because the rules of the game specify that a player who cannot make a move loses.

Next, nodes 1 and 2 are labelled "winning", because, from each, there is an edge to 0, which we know to be a losing position. Note that the edges we have identified dictate the move that should be made from these positions if the game is to be won.

Now, node 3 is labelled "losing", because both edges from node 3 are to nodes (1 and 2) that we have already labelled "winning". From a position in which there are 3 matches remaining, every move is to a position starting from which a win is guaranteed. A player that finds themself in this position will eventually lose.

The process we have described repeats itself until all nodes have been labelled. Nodes 4 and 5 are labelled "winning", then node 6 is labelled "losing", then nodes 7 and 8 are labelled "winning", and so on.

Figure 4.2 shows the state of the labelling process at the point that node 7 has been labelled but not node 8. The circles depicting losing positions are drawn with thick lines; the circles depicting winning positions are the ones from which there is an edge drawn with a thick line. These edges depict the winning move from that position.

Clearly, a pattern is emerging from this process: a losing position is one where the number of matches is a multiple of 3, and all others are winning positions. The winning

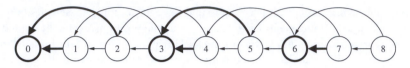

○ **Figure 4.2: Labelling positions. Winning edges are indicated by thick edges.**

strategy is to remove one or two matches so as to leave the opponent in a position where the number of matches is a multiple of 3.

4.2.3 Formulating Requirements

The terminology we use to describe the winning strategy is to "maintain" the property that the number of matches is a multiple of 3. In programming terms, we express this property using Hoare triples. Let n denote the number of matches in the pile. Then, the correctness of the winning strategy is expressed by the following annotated program segment:

$$\{ \ n \text{ is a multiple of 3, and } n \neq 0 \ \}$$

$$\text{if } 1 \leq n \ \rightarrow \ n := n-1 \ \square \ \ 2 \leq n \ \rightarrow \ n := n-2 \text{ fi}$$

; $\{ \ n \text{ is not a multiple of 3} \ \}$

$$n := n - (n \bmod 3)$$

$$\{ \ n \text{ is a multiple of 3} \ \}$$

This program segment has five components, each on a separate line. The first line, the precondition, expresses the assumption that execution begins from a position in which the number of matches is a multiple of 3 and is non-zero.

The second line uses a non-deterministic conditional statement[2] to model an arbitrary move. Removing one match is allowed only if $1 \leq n$; hence, the statement $n := n-1$ is "guarded" by this condition. Similarly, removing two matches – modelled by the assignment $n := n-2$ – is "guarded" by the condition $2 \leq n$. At least one of these guards, and possibly both, is true because of the assumption that $n \neq 0$.

The postcondition of the guarded command is the assertion "n is not a multiple of 3". The triple comprising the first three lines thus asserts that if the number of matches is a multiple of 3, and a valid move is made that reduces the number of matches by one or two, then, on completion of the move, the number of matches is not a multiple of 3.

[2] You may wish to review Section 3.6 on the formulation and use of conditional statements.

The fourth line of the sequence is the implementation of the winning strategy; specifically, remove n mod 3 matches. The fifth line is the final postcondition, which asserts that, after execution of the winning strategy, the number of matches is again a multiple of 3.

In summary, beginning from a state in which n *is* a multiple of 3, and making an arbitrary move, results in a state in which n is *not* a multiple of 3. Subsequently, removing n mod 3 matches results in a state in which n is again a multiple of 3.

In general, a winning strategy is obtained by characterising the losing positions by some property, losing say. The end positions (the positions where the game is over) must satisfy the property losing. The winning positions are then the positions that do not satisfy losing. For each winning position, one has to identify a way of calculating a losing position to which to move; the algorithm that is used is the *winning strategy*. More formally, the losing and winning positions and the winning strategy must satisfy the following specification.

> { losing position, and not an end position }
>
> make an arbitrary (legal) move

; { winning position, i.e. not a losing position }

> apply winning strategy
>
> { losing position }

In summary, a winning strategy is a way of choosing moves that divides the positions into two types, the losing positions and the winning positions, such that the following three properties hold:

- End positions are losing positions.
- From a losing position that is not an end position, every move is to a winning position. That is, every move *falsifies* the property of being a losing position.
- From a winning position, it is always possible to apply the winning strategy, resulting in a losing position. That is, it is always possible to choose a move that *truthifies*[3] the property of being a losing position.

If both players are perfect, the winner is decided by the starting position. If the starting position is a losing position, the second player is guaranteed to win. And if the starting position is a winning position, the first player is guaranteed to win. The perfect player wins from a winning position by truthifying the invariant, thus placing the opponent in

---

[3] The word "falsify" can be found in an English dictionary, but not "truthify". "Falsify" means to make something false; we use "truthify" for the opposite: making something true. It is so common in algorithmic problem solving that it deserves to be in the dictionary. "Truthify" was coined by David Gries.

a losing position. Starting from a losing position, one can only hope that one's opponent is not perfect, and will make a mistake.

We recommend that you now try to solve the matchstick-game problem when the rule is that any number of matches from 1 thru M may be removed at each turn. The number M is a natural number, fixed in advance. We recommend that you try to solve this general problem by first considering the case where M is 0. This case has a very easy solution, although it is a case that is very often neglected. Next, consider the case where M is 1. This case also has an easy solution, but slightly more complicated. Now, combine these two cases with the case where M is 2, which is the case we have just considered. Do you see a pattern in the solutions? If you do not see a pattern immediately, try a little harder. As a last resort, try working out the case where M is 3. (It is better to construct a table rather than draw a diagram. At this stage a diagram is becoming too complicated.) Then return to the cases where M is 0, 1 and 2 (in particular, the extreme cases 0 and 1) in order to check the pattern you have identified. Finally, formulate the correctness of the strategy by a sequence of assertions and statements, as we did above for the case where M is 2.

Exercise 4.1 (31st December Game)   Two players alternately name dates. The winner is the player who names 31st December, and the starting date is 1st January.

Each part of this exercise uses a different rule for the dates that a player is allowed to name. For each, devise a winning strategy, stating which player should win. State also if it depends on whether the year is a leap year or not.

Hint: in principle, you have to determine for each of 365 days (or 366 in the case of a leap year) whether naming the day results in losing against a perfect player. In practice, a pattern soon becomes evident and the days in each month can be grouped together into winning and losing days. Begin by identifying the days in December that one should avoid naming.

(a) (Easy) A player can name the 1st of the next month, or increase the day of the month by an arbitrary amount. (For example, the first player begins by naming 1st February, or a date in January other than the 1st.)

(b) (Harder) A player can increase the day by one, leaving the month unchanged, or name the 1st of the next month.

4.3 SUBTRACTION-SET GAMES

A class of matchstick games is based on a single pile of matches and a (finite) set of numbers; a move is to remove m matches, where m is an element of the given set. A game in this class is called a *subtraction-set game*, and the set of numbers is called the *subtraction set*.

The games we have just discussed are examples of subtraction-set games; if the rule is that 1 thru M matches may be removed at each turn, the subtraction set is {1..M}. More interesting examples are obtained by choosing a subtraction set with less regular structure.

For any given subtraction set, the winning and losing positions can always be computed. We exemplify the process in this section by calculating the winning and losing positions when the allowed moves are:

- remove one match,
- remove three matches,
- remove four matches.

In other words, the subtraction set is {1, 3, 4}.

Positions in the game are given by the number of matches in the pile. We refer to the positions using this number. So, "position 0" means the position in which there are no matches remaining in the pile, "position 1" means the position in which there is just one match in the pile, and so on.

Beginning with position 0, and working through the positions one by one, we identify whether each position is a winning position using the rules that

- a position is a losing position if every move from it is to a winning position, and
- a position is a winning position if there is a move from it to a losing position.

The results are entered in a table. The top half of Table 4.1 shows the entries when the size of the pile is at most 6. The first row is the position, and the second row shows whether or not it is a winning (W) or losing position (L). In the case where the position is a winning position, the third row shows the number of matches that should be removed in order to move from the position to a losing position. For example, 2 is a losing position because the only move from 2 is to 1; positions 3 and 4 are winning positions because from both a move can be made to 0. Note that there may be a choice of winning move. For example, from position 3 there are two winning moves – remove 3 matches to move to position 0, or remove 1 match to move to position 2. It suffices to enter just one move in the bottom row of the table.

Continuing this process, we get the next seven entries in the table: see the bottom half of Table 4.1. Comparing the two halves of the table, we notice that the pattern of winning and losing positions repeats itself. Once the pattern begins repeating in this way, it will continue to do so forever. We may therefore conclude that, for the subtraction set {1, 3, 4}, whether or not the position is a winning position can be determined by computing the remainder, r say, after dividing the number of matches by 7. If r is 0 or 2, the position is a losing position. Otherwise, it is a winning position. The winning strategy is to remove 1 match if r is 1, remove 3 matches if r is 3 or 5, and remove 4 matches if r is 4 or 6.

Position	0	1	2	3	4	5	6
Type	L	W	L	W	W	W	W
Move		1		3	4	3	4

Position	7	8	9	10	11	12	13
Type	L	W	L	W	W	W	W
Move		1		3	4	3	4

○ Table 4.1: **Winning (W) and losing (L) positions for subtraction set $\{1,3,4\}$.**

The repetition in the pattern of winning and losing positions that is evident in this example is a general property of subtraction-set games, with the consequence that, for a given subtraction set, it is always possible to determine for an arbitrary position whether or not it is a winning position (and, for the winning positions, a winning move). The following argument gives the reason why.

Suppose a subtraction set is given. Since the set is assumed to be finite, it must have a largest element. Let this be M. Then, from each position, there are at most M moves. For each position k, let $W(k)$ be true if k is a winning position, and false otherwise. When k is at least M, $W(k)$ is completely determined by the sequence $W(k-1)$, $W(k-2)$, ..., $W(k-M)$. Call this sequence $s(k)$. Now, there are only 2^M different sequences of booleans of length M. As a consequence, the sequence $s(M+1)$, $s(M+2)$, $s(M+3)$, ... must eventually repeat, and it must do so within at most 2^M steps. That is, for some j and k, with $M \leq j < k < M + 2^M$, we must have $s(j) = s(k)$. It follows that $W(j) = W(k)$ and the sequence W repeats from the kth position onwards.

For the example above, this analysis predicts that the winning–losing pattern will repeat from the 20th position onwards. In fact, it begins repeating much earlier. Generally, we can say that the pattern of win–lose positions will repeat at position $2^M + M$, *or before*. To determine whether an arbitrary position is a winning or losing position involves computing the status of each position k, for successive values of k, until a repetition in $s(k)$ is observed. If the repetition occurs at position R, then, for an arbitrary position k, $W(k)$ equals $W(k \bmod R)$.

Exercise 4.2   Suppose there is one pile of matches. In each move, 2, 5 or 6 matches may be removed. (That is, the subtraction set is $\{2,5,6\}$.)

(a) For each n, $0 \leq n < 22$, determine whether a pile of n matches is a winning or losing position.

(b) Identify a pattern in the winning and losing positions. Specify the pattern by giving precise details of a boolean function of n that determines whether a pile of n matches is a winning position or not.

Verify the pattern by constructing a table showing how the function's value changes when a move is made.

Exercise 4.3 This exercise is challenging; its solution involves thinking beyond the material presented in the rest of the chapter.

Figure 4.3 shows a variant of snakes and ladders. In this game, there is just one counter. The two players take it in turn to move the counter at most four spaces forward. The start is square 1 and the finish is square 25; the winner is the first to reach the finish. As in the usual game of snakes and ladders, if the counter lands on the head of a snake, it falls down to the tail of the snake; if the counter lands at the foot of a ladder, it climbs to the top of the ladder.

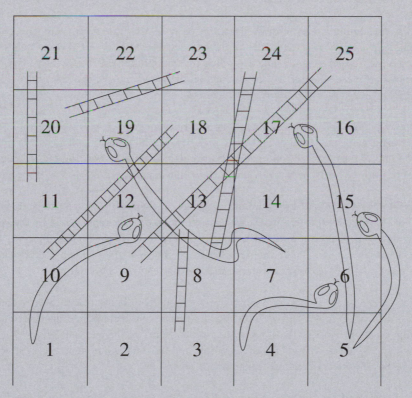

Figure 4.3: Snakes and ladders. Players take it in turn to move the counter at most four spaces forward.

(a) List the positions in this game. (These are not the same as the squares. Think carefully about squares linked by a snake or a ladder.)

(b) Identify the winning and losing positions. Use the rule that a losing position is one from which every move is to a winning position, and a winning position is one from which there is a move to a losing position.

(c) Some of the positions cannot be identified as winning or losing in this way. Explain why.

4.4 SUMS OF GAMES

In this section we look at how to exploit the structure of a game in order to compute a winning strategy more effectively.

The later examples of matchstick games in Section 4.1 have more than one pile of matches. When a move is made, one of the piles must first be chosen; then, matches may be removed from the chosen pile according to some prescribed rule, which may differ from pile to pile. The game is thus a combination of two games; this particular way of combining games is called *summing* the games.

In general, given two games each with its own rules for making a move, the *sum* of the games is the game described as follows. For clarity, we call the two games the *left* and the *right* game. A position in the sum game is the combination of a position in the left game and a position in the right game. A move in the sum game is a move in one of the games.

Figure 4.4 is an example of the sum of two games. Each graph represents a game, where the positions are represented by the nodes, and the moves are represented by the edges. Imagine a coin placed on a node. A move is then to displace the coin along one of the edges to another node. The nodes in the left graph and right graphs are named by capital letters and small letters, respectively, so that we can refer to them later.

In the "sum" of the games, two coins are used, one coin being placed over a node in each of the two graphs. A move is then to choose one of the coins, and displace it along an edge to another node. Thus, a position in the "sum" of the games is given by a pair Xx where "X" names a node in the left graph, and "x" names a node in the right graph; a move has the effect of changing exactly one of "X" or "x".

Both the left and right games in Figure 4.4 are unstructured; consequently, the brute-force search procedure described in Section 4.2.2 is unavoidable when determining their winning and losing positions. However, the left game in Figure 4.4 has 15 different positions, and the right game has 11; thus, the sum of the two games has 15×11 different

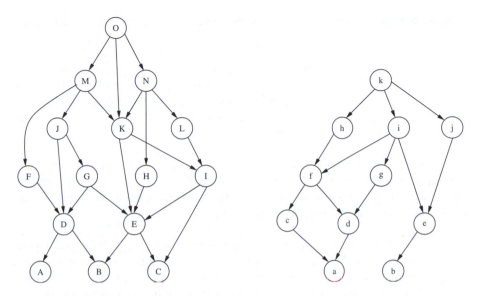

Figure 4.4: A sum game. The left and right games are represented by the two graphs. A position is a pair Xx where "X" is the name of a node in the left graph, and "x" is the name of a node in the right graph. A move changes exactly one of X or x.

positions. For this game, and for sums of games in general, a brute-force search is highly undesirable. In this section, we study how to compute a winning strategy for the sum of two games. We find that the computational effort is the sum (in the usual sense of addition of numbers) of the effort required to compute winning and losing positions for the component games, rather than the product. We find, however, that it is not sufficient to know just the winning strategy for the individual games. Deriving a suitable generalisation forms the core of the analysis.

> ⚠ *The set of positions in a sum game is the* cartesian product *of the sets of positions in the component games. This explains why the number of positions in the sum game is the product of the number of positions in the component games. See Section 12.4.1.*

4.4.1 A Simple Sum Game

We begin with a very simple example of the sum of two games. Suppose there are two piles of matches. An allowed move is to choose any one of the piles and remove at least one match from the chosen pile. Otherwise, there is no restriction on the number of matches that may be removed. As always, the game is lost when a player cannot make a move.

This game is the "sum" of two instances of the same, very, very simple, game: given a (single) pile of matches, a move is to remove at least one match from the pile. In this simple game, the winning positions are, obviously, the positions in which the pile has at least one match, and the winning strategy is to remove all the matches. The position in which there are no matches remaining is the only losing position.

It quickly becomes clear that knowing the winning strategy for the individual games is insufficient to win the sum of the games. If a player removes all the matches from one pile – that is, applies the winning strategy for the individual game – the opponent wins by removing the remaining matches in the other pile.

The symmetry between left and right allows us to easily spot a winning strategy. Suppose we let m and n denote the number of matches in the two piles. In the end position, there is an equal number of matches in both piles, namely 0. That is, in the end position, $m = n = 0$. This suggests that the losing positions are given by $m = n$. This is indeed the case. From a position in which $m = n$ and a move is possible (i.e. either $1 \leq m$ or $1 \leq n$), any move will be to a position where $m \neq n$. Subsequently, choosing the pile with the larger number of matches, and removing the excess matches from this pile, will restore the property that $m = n$.

Formally, the correctness of the winning strategy is expressed by the following sequence of assertions and program statements.

$$\{ \ m = n \ \wedge \ (m \neq 0 \ \vee \ n \neq 0) \ \}$$

$$\textbf{if} \ \ 1 \leq m \ \rightarrow \ \text{reduce } m$$

$$\square \ \ 1 \leq n \ \rightarrow \ \text{reduce } n$$

$$\textbf{fi}$$

$$; \quad \{ \ m \neq n \ \}$$

$$\textbf{if} \ \ m < n \ \rightarrow \ n := n - (n-m)$$

$$\square \ n < m \ \rightarrow \ m := m - (m-n)$$

$$\textbf{fi}$$

$$\{ \ m = n \ \}$$

The non-deterministic choice between reducing m, in the case where $1 \leq m$, and reducing n, in the case where $1 \leq n$, models an arbitrary choice of move in the sum game. The fact that either m changes in value, or n changes in value, but not both, guarantees $m \neq n$ after completion of the move.

The property $m \neq n$ is the precondition for the winning strategy to be applied. Equivalently, $m < n$ or $n < m$. In the case where $m < n$, we infer that $1 \leq n-m \leq n$, so that $n-m$ matches can be removed from the pile with n matches. Since, $n-(n-m)$ simplifies to m, it is clear that after the assignment $n := n-(n-m)$, the property $m = n$ will hold. The case $n < m$ is symmetric.

The following sequence of assertions and program statements summarises the argument just given for the validity of the winning strategy. Note how the two assignments have been annotated with a precondition and a postcondition. The precondition expresses the legitimacy of the move; the postcondition is the losing property that the strategy is required to establish.

$$\{ \ m \neq n \ \}$$

$$\{ \ m < n \ \vee \ n < m \ \}$$

$$\text{if} \ \ m < n \ \rightarrow \ \{ \ 1 \leq n-m \leq n \ \} \ \ n := n-(n-m) \ \{ \ m = n \ \}$$

$$\square \ \ n < m \ \rightarrow \ \{ \ 1 \leq m-n \leq m \ \} \ \ m := m-(m-n) \ \{ \ m = n \ \}$$

$$\text{fi}$$

$$\{ \ m = n \ \}$$

4.4.2 Maintain Symmetry!

The game in Section 4.4.1 is another example of the importance of symmetry; the winning strategy is to ensure that the opponent is always left in a position of symmetry between the two individual components of the sum game. We see shortly that this is how to win all sum games, no matter what the individual components are.

There are many examples of games where symmetry is the key to winning. Here are a couple. The solutions can be found at the end of the chapter.

The Daisy Problem Suppose a daisy has 16 petals arranged symmetrically around its centre (Figure 4.5). There are two players. A move involves removing one petal or two adjacent petals. The winner is the one who removes the last petal. Who should win and what is the winning strategy? Generalise your solution to the case that there are initially n petals and a move consists of removing between 1 and M adjacent petals (where M is fixed in advance of the game).

The Coin Problem Two players are seated at a rectangular table which initially is bare. They each have an unlimited supply of circular coins of varying diameter. The players take it in turns to place a coin on the table, such that it does not overlap any coin already on the table. The winner is the one who puts the last coin on the table. Who should win and what is the winning strategy? (*Harder*) What, if anything, do you assume about the coins in order to justify your answer?

Figure 4.5: A 16-petal daisy.

4.4.3 More Simple Sums

Let us return to our matchstick games. A variation on the sum game in Section 4.4.1 is to restrict the number of matches that can be removed. Suppose the restriction is that at most K matches can be removed from either pile (where K is fixed, in advance).

The effect of the restriction is to disallow some winning moves. If, as before, m and n denote the number of matches in the two piles, it is not allowed to remove m−n matches when $K < m-n$. Consequently, the property $m = n$ no longer characterises the losing positions. For example, if K is fixed at 1, the position in which one pile has two matches while the second pile has no matches is a losing position: in this position a player is forced to move to a position in which one match remains; the opponent can then remove the match to win the game.

A more significant effect of the restriction seems to be that the strategy of establishing symmetry is no longer applicable. Worse is if we break symmetry further by imposing different restrictions on the two piles: suppose, for example, we impose the limit M on the number of matches that may be removed from the left pile, and N on the number of matches that may be removed from the right pile, where $M \neq N$. Alternatively, suppose the left and right games are completely different, for example, if one is a matchstick game and the other is the daisy game. If this is the case, how is it possible to maintain symmetry? Nevertheless, a form of "symmetry" is a key to the winning strategy: symmetry is too important to abandon so easily!

We saw, in Section 4.2, that the way to win the one-pile game, with the restriction that at most M matches can be removed, is to continually establish the property that the remainder after dividing the number of matches by M+1 is 0. Thus, for a pile of m matches, the number m mod (M+1) determines whether the position is a winning position or not. This suggests that, in the two-pile game, "symmetry" between the piles is formulated as the property that

$$m \bmod (M+1) = n \bmod (N+1).$$

(M is the maximum number of matches that can be removed from the left pile, and N is the maximum number that can be removed from the right pile.)

This, indeed, is the correct solution. In the end position, where both piles have 0 matches, the property is satisfied. Also, the property can always be maintained following an arbitrary move by the opponent, as given by the following annotated program segment:

{ m mod (M+1) = n mod (N+1) ∧ (m ≠ 0 ∨ n ≠ 0) }

if 1 ≤ m → reduce m by at most M

☐ 1 ≤ n → reduce n by at most N

fi

;   { m mod (M+1) ≠ n mod (N+1) }

if m mod (M+1) < n mod (N+1) → n := n − (n mod (N+1) − m mod (M+1))

☐ n mod (N+1) < m mod (M+1) → m := m − (m mod (M+1) − n mod (N+1))

fi

{ m mod (M+1) = n mod (N+1) }

(We discuss later the full details of how to check the assertions made in this program segment.)

4.4.4 Evaluating Positions

The idea of defining "symmetric" to be "the respective remainders are equal" can be generalised to an arbitrary sum game.

Consider a game that is the sum of two games. A position in the sum game is a pair (l,r) where l is a position in the left game, and r is a position in the right game. A move affects just one component; so a move is modelled by either a (guarded) assignment l := l′ (for some l′) to the left component or a (guarded) assignment r := r′ (for some r′) to the right component.

The idea is to define two functions L and R, say, on left and right positions, respectively, in such a way that a position (l,r) is a losing position exactly when L(l)=R(r). The question is: what properties should these functions satisfy? In other words, how do we specify the functions L and R?

The analysis given earlier of a winning strategy allows us to distil the specification.

First, since (l,r) is an end position of the sum game exactly when l is an end position of the left game and r is an end position of the right game, it must be the case that L and R have equal values on end positions.

Second, every allowed move from a losing position – a position (l,r) satisfying $L(l) = R(r)$ – that is not an end position, should result in a winning position – a position (l,r) satisfying $L(l) \neq R(r)$. That is,

> $\{\ L(l) = R(r) \land (l \text{ is not an end position} \lor r \text{ is not an end position})\ \}$
>
> if   l is not an end position → change l
>
> ☐ r is not an end position → change r
>
> fi
>
> $\{\ L(l) \neq R(r)\ \}$

Third, applying the winning strategy from a winning position – a position (l,r) satisfying $L(l) \neq R(r)$ – should result in a losing position – a position (l,r) satisfying $L(l) = R(r)$. That is,

> $\{\ L(l) \neq R(r)\ \}$
>
> apply winning strategy
>
> $\{\ L(l) = R(r)\ \}.$

We can satisfy the first and second requirements if we define L and R to be functions with range the set of natural numbers, and require that:

- For end positions l and r of the respective games, $L(l) = 0 = R(r)$.

- For every l' such that there is a move from l to l' in the left game, $L(l) \neq L(l')$. Similarly, for every r' such that there is a move from r to r' in the right game, $R(r) \neq R(r')$.

Note that the choice of the natural numbers as range of the functions, and the choice of 0 as the functions' value at end positions, is quite arbitrary. The advantage of this choice arises from the third requirement. If L(l) and R(r) are different natural numbers, either $L(l) < R(r)$ or $R(r) < L(l)$. This allows us to refine the process of applying the winning strategy, by choosing to move in the right game when $L(l) < R(r)$ and choosing to move in the left game when $R(r) < L(l)$. (See below.)

$$\{ \ L(l) \neq R(r) \ \}$$

if $\ L(l) < R(r) \ \rightarrow \ $ change r

$\Box \ \ R(r) < L(l) \ \rightarrow \ $ change l

fi

$$\{ \ L(l) = R(r) \ \}$$

For this to work, we require that:

- For any number m less than $R(r)$, it is possible to move from r to a position r' such that $R(r') = m$. Similarly, for any number n less than $L(l)$, it must be possible to move from l to a position l' such that $L(l') = n$.

The bulleted requirements are satisfied if we define the functions L and R to be the so-called "mex" function. The precise definition of this function is as follows.

Definition 4.4 (Mex Function) Let p be a position in a game G. The mex value of p, denoted $mex_G(p)$, is defined to be the smallest natural number, n, such that

- for all positions q such that there is a move in G from p to q, $n \neq mex_G(q)$.

The name "mex" is short for "minimal excludant". A brief, informal description of the mex number of a position p is the minimum number that is excluded from the mex numbers of positions q to which a move can be made from p. By choosing the mex number to be *excluded* from the mex numbers of positions to which there is a move, it is guaranteed that in any sum game if the left and right positions have equal mex numbers, any choice of move will falsify the equality. By choosing $mex_G(p)$ to be the *minimum* number different from the mex numbers of positions to which there is a move, it is guaranteed that

- for every natural number m less than $mex_G(p)$, there exist a position q and a move in the game G from p to q satisfying $mex_G(q) = m$.

This is the basis for the choice of move from a position in a sum game where the left and right positions have different mex numbers: choose to move in the component game where the position has the larger number and choose a move to a position that equalises the mex numbers. Note, finally, that if there are no moves from position p (i.e. p is an end position), the number 0 satisfies the definition of $mex_G(p)$.

Exercise 4.5 In Section 4.2.2 we showed how to calculate for each position in a game whether or not it is a winning position. In principle, we can do the same for sum games. If two games with m and n positions, respectively, are summed, the sum game has m×n positions. The game graph of the sum game is essentially a combination of m copies of one game and n copies of the second game. Determining the winning and losing positions in the sum game takes time proportional to the product m×n, whereas calculating the mex numbers for each game takes time proportional to m+n. For large m and n this is a very big saving. (To be more precise, the two methods of determining winning and losing positions take time proportional to the product and sum, respectively, of the number of *edges* in the two game graphs. If the number of choices of move from any one position can be very large, the saving is yet more.)

A question we might ask is whether the calculation of mex numbers is an over-complication: is it possible to combine the winning/losing information on each component of a pair of positions to determine whether the pair is a winning or losing position? Formally, the question is whether or not the winning predicate *distributes* through the operation of summing positions – that is, whether it is possible to define some boolean operator $\oplus$, say, such that for all positions l and r in games G and H, respectively,

$$\mathrm{winning}_{G+H}(l,r) \;=\; \mathrm{winning}_G(l) \oplus \mathrm{winning}_H(r).$$

If this were the case, it would suffice to compute the winning predicate for both games and then combine the results using the operator $\oplus$. The $\oplus$ operator might turn out to be, for example, equality or conjunction.

> ⚠ *The subscripts on* winning *are necessary because the winning predicate must be evaluated with respect to the relevant game. The functions* mex, winning *and* losing *all have two parameters, a game and a position. Their types are more complicated than the function types discussed in Section 12.4.2 because the type of positions depends on the game that is given as the first parameter. They have so-called dependent types.*

Show that this is not the case by giving a counter-example. Hint: the simple sum game discussed in Section 4.4.1 can be used to construct an example. The counter-example can be constructed using a small number of positions.

Show that it is the case that

$$\big[\, \text{losing}_{G+H}(l,r) \;\Leftarrow\; \text{losing}_G(l) \wedge \text{losing}_H(r) \,\big].$$

Do so by giving the winning player's strategy if play is begun from a position (l, r) satisfying $\text{losing}_G(l) \wedge \text{losing}_H(r)$.

4.4.5 Using the Mex Function

We use the game depicted in Figure 4.4 to illustrate the calculation of mex numbers. Figure 4.6 shows the mex numbers of each of the nodes in their respective games.

The graphs do not have any systematic structure; consequently, the only way to compute the mex numbers is by a brute-force search of all positions. This is easily done by hand. The end positions are each given mex number 0. Subsequently, a mex number can be given to a node when all its successors have already been given a mex number. (A successor of a node p is a node q such that there is an edge from p to q.) The number is, by definition, the smallest number that is not included in the mex numbers of its successors. Figure 4.7 shows a typical situation. The node at the top of the figure is given

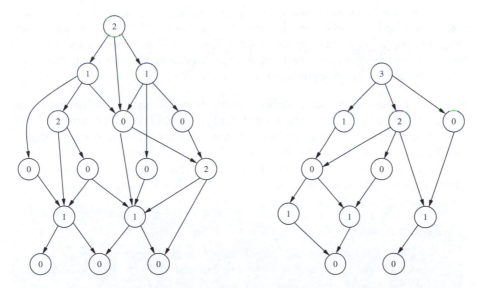

Figure 4.6: Mex numbers. The mex number of a node is the smallest natural number not included among the mex numbers of its successors.

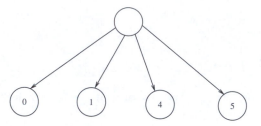

 Figure 4.7: Computing mex numbers. The unlabelled node is given the mex
number 2.

a mex number when all its successors have been given mex numbers. In the situation
shown, the mex number given to it is 2 because none of its successors have been given
this number, but there are successors with the mex numbers 0 and 1.

> ⚠ *The algorithm used to calculate mex numbers is an instance of topological*
> *search. See Section 16.7.1.*

Now, suppose we play this game. Let us suppose the starting position is "Ok". This is
a winning position because the mex number of "O" is different from the mex number
of "k". The latter is larger (3 against 2). So, the winning strategy is to move in the right
graph to the node "i", which has the same mex number as "O". The opponent is then
obliged to move, in either the left or right graph, to a node with mex number different
from 2. The first player then repeats the strategy of ensuring that the mex numbers are
equal, until eventually the opponent can move no further.

Note that, because of the lack of structure of the individual games, we have to search
through all 15 positions of the left game and all 11 positions of the right game, in order to
calculate the mex numbers of each position. In total, therefore, we have to search through
26 different positions. But, this is just the sum (in the usual sense of the word) of 15 and
11, and is much less than their product, 165. This is a substantial saving of computational
effort. Moreover, the saving grows as the size of the component games increases.

Exercise 4.6

(a) Consider the subtraction-set game where there is one pile of matches from
which at most 2, 5 or 6 matches may be removed. Calculate the mex number
for each position until you spot a pattern.

(b) Consider a game which is the sum of two games. In the left game, 1 or 2
matches may be removed at each turn. In the right game, 2, 5 or 6 matches

may be removed. In the sum game, a move is made by choosing to play in the left game, or choosing to play in the right game.

Table 4.2 shows a number of different positions in this game. A position is given by a pair of numbers: the number of matches in the left pile, and the number of matches in the right pile.

Left game	Right game	"losing" or winning move
10	20	?
20	20	?
15	5	?
6	9	?
37	43	?

Table 4.2: Fill in entries marked "?".

For each position, state whether it is a winning or a losing position. For winning positions, give the winning move in the form Xm where "X" is one of "L" (for "left game") or "R" (for "right game"), and m is the number of matches to be removed.

Exercise 4.7 A rectangular board is divided into m horizontal rows and n vertical columns, where m and n are both strictly positive integers, making a total of m×n squares. The number of squares is called the *area* of the board.

A game is played on the board as follows. Each of the two players takes it in turn to cut the board either horizontally or vertically along one of the dividing lines. A cut divides the board into two parts; when a cut has been made a part whose area is at most the area of the other part is discarded. (This means that the part with the smaller area is discarded if the two parts have different areas, and one of the two parts is chosen arbitrarily if the two areas are equal.) For example, if the board has 4×5 squares, a single move reduces it to 2×5, 3×5, 4×3, or 4×4 squares. Also, if the board has 4×4 squares, a single move reduces it to either 2×4 or 3×4 squares. (Boards with 3×4 and 4×3 squares are effectively the same; the orientation of the board is not significant.) The game ends when the board has been reduced to a 1×1 board. At this point, the player whose turn it is to play loses.

This game is a sum game because, at each move, a choice is made between cutting horizontally and cutting vertically. The component games are copies of the same game. This game is as follows. A position in the game is given by a strictly positive integer m. A move in the game is to replace m by a number n such that $n < m \leq 2n$; the game ends when m has been reduced to 1, at which point the player whose turn it is to play loses. For example, if the board has 5 columns, the number of columns can be reduced to 3 or 4 because $3 < 5 \leq 6$ and $4 < 5 \leq 8$. No other moves are possible because, for n less than 3, $2n < 5$, and for n greater than 4, $5 \leq n$.

The game is easy to win if it is possible to make the board square. This question is about calculating the mex numbers of the component games in order to determine a winning move even when the board cannot be made square.

(a) For the component game, calculate which positions are winning and which positions are losing for the first 15 positions. Make a general conjecture about the winning and losing positions in the component game and prove your conjecture.

Base your proof on the following facts. The end position, position 1, is a losing position. A winning position is a position from which there is a move to a losing position. A losing position is a position from which every move is to a winning position.

(b) For the component game, calculate the mex number of each of the first 15 positions.

Give the results of your calculation in the form of a table with two rows. The first row is a number m and the second row is the mex number of position m. Split the table into four parts. Part i gives the mex numbers of positions 2^i thru $2^{i+1} - 1$ (where i begins at 0) as shown below. (The first three entries have been completed as illustration.)

Position:	1
Mex number:	0

Position:	2	3
Mex number:	1	0

Position:	4	5	6	7
Mex number:	?	?	?	?

Position:	8	9	10	11	12	13	14	15
Mex number:	?	?	?	?	?	?	?	?

(You should find that the mex number of each of the losing positions (identified in part (a)) is 0. You should also be able to observe a pattern in the way entries are filled in for part i+1 knowing the entries for part i. The pattern is based on whether the position is an even number or an odd number.)

(c) Table 4.3 shows a position in the board game; the first column shows the number of columns and the second column the number of rows. Using your table of mex numbers, or otherwise, fill in "losing" if the position is a losing position. If the position is not a losing position, fill in a winning move either in the form "Cn" or "Rn", where n is an integer; "C" or "R" indicates whether the move is to reduce the number of columns or the number of rows, and n is the number which it should become.

No. of columns	No. of rows	"losing" or winning move
2	15	?
4	11	?
4	14	?
13	6	?
21	19	?

Table 4.3: Fill in entries marked "?".

4.5 SUMMARY

This chapter has been about determining winning strategies in simple two-person games. The underlying theme of the chapter has been problem *specification*. We have seen how winning and losing positions are specified. A precise, formal specification enabled us to formulate a brute-force search procedure to determine which positions are which.

Brute-force search is only advisable for small, unstructured problems. The analysis of the "sum" of two games exemplifies the way structure is exploited in problem solving. Again, the focus was on problem specification. By formulating a notion of "symmetry" between the left and right games, we were able to determine a specification of the "mex" function on game positions. The use of mex functions substantially reduces the effort needed to determine winning and losing positions in the sum of two games, compared to a brute-force search.

Game theory is a rich, well-explored area of mathematics, which we have only touched upon in this chapter. It is a theory that is becoming increasingly important in computing science. One reason for this is that problems that beset software design, such as the security of a system, are often modelled as a game, with the user of the software as the adversary. Another reason is that games often provide excellent examples of "computational complexity"; it is easy to formulate games having very simple rules but for which no efficient algorithm implementing the winning strategy is known.

Mex numbers were introduced by Sprague and Grundy to solve the "Nim" problem, and mex numbers are sometimes called "Sprague–Grundy" numbers, after their originators. Nim is a well-known matchstick game involving three piles of matches. Formally, it is the sum of three copies of the same trivial game: given a pile of matches, the players take it in turn to remove any number of matches. (The game is trivial because the obvious winning strategy is to remove all the matches.) We have not developed the theory sufficiently in this chapter to show how Nim, and sums of more than two games, are solved using mex numbers. (What is missing is how to compute mex numbers of positions in the sum of two games.)

4.6 BIBLIOGRAPHIC REMARKS

The two-volume book *Winning Ways* [BCG82] by Berlekamp, Conway and Guy is essential reading for anyone interested in the theory of combinatorial games. It contains a great wealth of examples and entertaining discussion of strategies for winning.

I do not know the origins of the daisy problem or the coin problem (Section 4.4.2). Both are solved by the simple tactic of copying the opponent's moves. In the case of the daisy problem, the second player always wins. The first player's first move destroys the symmetry and, subsequently, the second player restores symmetry by removing petals directly opposite those just removed by the first player. In the case of the coin problem, the first player wins. The first player's first move is to place a coin at the exact centre of the table. Subsequently the first player copies the second player's move by placing a coin diagonally opposite the one just placed on the table by the second player. Again, every move made by the second player destroys symmetry and the first player restores the symmetry. The coins may be of any shape (circular, rectangular or even misshapen) provided two conditions are met. Firstly, the coin used for the very first move must be symmetrical about a centre point and should not have a hole in the centre that can be filled by another coin. Secondly, for all other moves, the first player should always be able to choose a coin that is identical to the one just used by the second player.

The 31st December game (Exercise 4.1) is adapted from [DW00]. Exercise 4.7 was suggested to me by Atheer Aheer. (I do not know its origin.)

Chapter

Knights and Knaves

5

The island of knights and knaves is a fictional island that is often used to test students' ability to reason logically. The island has two types of natives, "knights" who always tell the truth, and "knaves" who always lie. Logic puzzles involve deducing facts about the island from statements made by its natives without knowing whether or not the statements are made by a knight or a knave.

The temptation is to solve such problems by case analysis – in a problem involving n natives, consider the 2^n different cases obtained by assuming that the individual natives are knights or knaves. Case analysis is a clumsy way of tackling the problems. In contrast, these and similar logic puzzles are easy exercises in the use of *calculational logic*, which we introduce in this chapter.

The form of this chapter diverges from our usual practice of referring the reader to Part II of the book. This is because the techniques needed are unfamiliar but very necessary. The chapter gives a first introduction to calculational logic – enough to solve the knights-and-knaves puzzles – while Chapter 13 takes the subject further for more general use.

5.1 LOGIC PUZZLES

Here is a typical collection of knights-and-knaves puzzles.

1. It is rumoured that there is gold buried on the island. You ask one of the natives whether there is gold on the island. The native replies: "There is gold on this island is the same as I am a knight."

    The problem is
    (a) Can it be determined whether the native is a knight or a knave?
    (b) Can it be determined whether there is gold on the island?

2. Suppose you come across two of the natives. You ask both of them whether the other one is a knight.

> **Will you get the same answer in each case?**

3. There are three natives A, B and C. Suppose A says "B and C are the same type".

> **What can be inferred about the number of knights?**

4. Suppose C says "A and B are as like as two peas in a pod".

> **What question should you pose to A to determine whether or not C is telling the truth?**

> 5. Devise a question that allows you to determine whether a native is a knight.
>
> 6. What question should you ask A to determine whether B is a knight?
>
> 7. What question should you ask A to determine whether A and B are the same type (i.e. both knights or both knaves)?

8. You would like to determine whether an odd number of A, B and C is a knight. You may ask one yes/no question to any one of them.

> **What is the question you should ask?**

9. A tourist comes to a fork in the road, where one branch leads to a restaurant and one does not. A native of the island is standing at the fork.

> **Formulate a single yes/no question that the tourist can ask such that the answer will be yes if the left fork leads to the restaurant, and otherwise the answer will be no.**

5.2 CALCULATIONAL LOGIC

5.2.1 Propositions

The algebra we learn at school is about calculating with expressions whose values are numbers. We learn, for example, how to manipulate an expression like m^2-n^2 in order to show that its value is the same as the value of $(m+n)\times(m-n)$, independently of the values of m and n. We say that m^2-n^2 and $(m+n)\times(m-n)$ are *equal*, and write

$$m^2-n^2 \ = \ (m+n)\times(m-n).$$

The basis for these calculations is a set of *laws*. Laws are typically primitive, but general, equalities between expressions. They are "primitive" in the sense that they cannot be broken down into simpler laws, and they are "general" in the sense that they hold independently of the values of any variables in the constituent expressions. We call them *axioms*. Two examples of axioms, both involving zero, are

$$n+0 \ = \ n,$$

and

$$n-n \ = \ 0,$$

both of which are true whatever the value of the variable n. We say they are true "for all n". The laws are often given names so that we can remember them more easily. For example, "associativity of addition" is the name given to the equality

$$(m+n)+p \ = \ m+(n+p),$$

which is true for all m, n and p.

(Calculational) logic is about calculating with expressions whose values are so-called "booleans" – that is, either true or false. Examples of such expressions are "it is sunny" (which is either true or false depending on to when and where "it" refers), $n=0$ (which is either true or false depending on the value of n), and $n < n+1$ (which is true for all numbers n). Boolean-valued expressions are called *propositions*. *Atomic* propositions are propositions that cannot be broken down into simpler propositions. The three examples above are all atomic. A non-atomic proposition would be, for example, $m < n < p$, which can be broken down into the so-called *conjunction* of $m < n$ *and* $n < p$.

Logic is not concerned with the truth or otherwise of atomic propositions; that is the concern of the problem domain being discussed. Logic is about rules for manipulating the *logical connectives* – the operators like "and", "or" and "if" that are used to combine atomic propositions.

Calculational logic places emphasis on *equality* of propositions, in contrast to other axiomatisations of logic, which emphasise logical *implication* (if . . . then . . .). Equality is the most basic concept of logic – a fact first recognised by Gottfried Wilhelm Leibniz,[1] who was the first to try to formulate logical reasoning – and equality of propositions is no exception. We see shortly that equality of propositions is particularly special, recognition of which considerably enhances the beauty and power of reasoning with propositions.

5.2.2 Knights and Knaves

Equality of propositions is central to solving puzzles about knights and knaves. Recall that a knight always tells the truth, and a knave always lies. If A is a native of the island,

---

[1] Gottfried Wilhelm Leibniz (1646–1716) was a famous German philosopher and mathematician.

the statement "A is a knight" is either true or false, and so is a proposition. Also, the statements made by the natives are propositions. A statement like "the restaurant is to the left" is either true or false. Suppose A denotes the proposition "A is a knight", and suppose native A makes a statement S. Then, the crucial observation is that the values of these two propositions are the same. That is,

$A = S$.

For example, if A says "the restaurant is to the left", then

$A = L$,

where L denotes the truth value of the statement "the restaurant is to the left". In words, A is a knight and the restaurant is to the left, or A is not a knight and the restaurant is not to the left.

Using this rule, if A says "I am a knight", we deduce

$A = A$.

This does not tell us anything! A moment's thought confirms that this is what one would expect. Both knights and knaves would claim that they are knights.

If native A is asked a yes/no question Q, the response to the question is the truth value of $A = Q$. That is, the response will be "yes" if A is a knight and the answer is really yes, or A is a knave and the answer is really no. Otherwise the response will be "no". For example, asked the question "are you a knight" all natives will answer "yes", as $A = A$. Asked the question "is B a knight?" A will respond "yes" if they are both the same type (i.e. $A = B$), otherwise "no". That is, A's response is "yes" or "no" depending on the truth or falsity of $A = B$.

Because these rules are equalities, the algebraic properties of equality play a central role in the solution of logic puzzles formulated about the island. A simple first example is if A is asked whether B is a knight, and B is asked whether A is a knight. As discussed above, A's response is $A = B$. Reversing the roles of A and B, B's response is $B = A$. But, equality is symmetric; therefore, the two responses will always be the same. Note that this argument does not involve any case analysis on the four different values of A and B.

The calculational properties of equality of booleans are discussed in the next section before we return again to the knights and knaves.

5.2.3 Boolean Equality

Equality – on any domain of values – has a number of characteristic properties. First, it is *reflexive*. That is, $x = x$ whatever the value (or type) of x. Second, it is *symmetric*.

That is, $x=y$ is the same as $y=x$. Third, it is *transitive*. That is, if $x=y$ and $y=z$ then $x=z$. Finally, if $x=y$ and f is any function then $f(x)=f(y)$ (where the parentheses denote function application). This last rule is called *substitution of equals for equals* or *Leibniz's rule*.

Equality is a binary relation. When studying relations, reflexivity, symmetry and transitivity are properties that we look out for. Equality is also a function. It is a function with range the boolean values true and false. When we study functions, the sort of properties we look out for are associativity and symmetry. For example, addition and multiplication are both associative: for all x, y and z,

$$x+(y+z) = (x+y)+z$$

and

$$x \times (y \times z) = (x \times y) \times z.$$

They are also both symmetric: for all x and y,

$$x+y = y+x$$

and

$$x \times y = y \times x.$$

Symmetry of equality, viewed as a function, is just the same as symmetry of equality, viewed as a relation. But, what about associativity of equality? Is equality an associative operator?

The answer is that, in all but one case, the question does not make sense. Associativity of a binary function only makes sense if the domains of its two arguments and the range of its result are all the same. The expression $(p=q)=r$ just does not make sense when p, q and r are numbers, or characters, or sequences, etc. The one exception is equality of boolean values. When p, q and r are all booleans it makes sense to compare the boolean $p=q$ with r for equality. That is, $(p=q) = r$ is a meaningful boolean value. Similarly, so too is $p = (q=r)$. It also makes sense to compare these two values for equality. In other words, it makes sense to ask whether equality of boolean values is associative – and, perhaps surprisingly, *it is*. That is, for all booleans p, q and r,

$$[\text{\textbf{Associativity}}] \quad [((p=q) = r) = (p = (q=r))]. \tag{5.1}$$

The associativity of equality is a very powerful property, for one because it enhances economy of expression. We will see several examples; an elementary example is the following.

The reflexivity of equality is expressed by the rule

$$[(p=p) = \text{true}].$$

The square "everywhere" brackets emphasise that this holds for all p, whatever its type (number, boolean, string, etc.). But, for boolean p, we can apply the associativity of equality to get

$$[p = (p = \text{true})].$$

This rule is most commonly used to simplify expressions by eliminating "true" from an expression of the form p = true. We use it several times below.

5.2.4 Hidden Treasures

We can now return to the island of knights and knaves, and discover the hidden treasures. Let us consider the first problem posed in Section 5.1. What can we deduce if a native says "I am a knight equals there is gold on the island"? Let A stand for "the native is a knight" and G stand for "there is gold on the island". Then the native's statement is A = G, and we deduce that

$$A = (A = G)$$

is true. So,

$$
\begin{aligned}
& \text{true} \\
=\ & \qquad \{ \qquad \text{A's statement} \quad \} \\
& A = (A = G) \\
=\ & \qquad \{ \qquad \text{equality of booleans is associative} \quad \} \\
& (A = A) = G \\
=\ & \qquad \{ \qquad [(A = A) = \text{true}], \\
& \qquad\qquad\qquad \text{substitution of equals for equals} \quad \} \\
& \text{true} = G \\
=\ & \qquad \{ \qquad \text{equality is symmetric} \quad \} \\
& G = \text{true} \\
=\ & \qquad \{ \qquad [G = (G = \text{true})] \quad \} \\
& G.
\end{aligned}
$$

We conclude that there is gold on the island, but it is not possible to determine whether the native is a knight or a knave.

Suppose, now, that the native is at a fork in the road, and you want to determine whether the gold can be found by following the left or right fork. You want to formulate a question such that the reply will be "yes" if the left fork should be followed, and "no" if the right fork should be followed.

As usual, we give the unknown a name. Let Q be the question to be posed. Then, as we saw earlier, the response to the question will be $A = Q$. Let L denote "the gold can be found by following the left fork". The requirement is that L is the same as the response to the question. That is, we require that $L = (A = Q)$. But,

$$L = (A = Q)$$
$$= \qquad \{ \qquad \text{equality is associative} \quad \}$$
$$(L = A) = Q \ .$$

So, the question Q to be posed is $L = A$. That is, ask the question "Is the truth value of 'the gold can be found by following the left fork' equal to the truth value of 'you are a knight'?".

⚠️ *Some readers might object that the question is too "mathematical"; a question that cannot be expressed in everyday language is not a valid solution to the problem. An alternative way of phrasing Q in "natural" language is presented in Section 5.4.3.*

Note that this analysis is valid independently of what L denotes. It might be that you want to determine whether there is a restaurant on the island, or whether there are any knaves on the island, or whatever. In general, if it is required to determine whether some proposition P is true or false, the question to be posed is $P = A$. In the case of more complex propositions P, the question may be simplified.

5.2.5 Equals for Equals

Equality is distinguished from other logical connectives by Leibniz's rule: if two expressions are equal, one expression can be substituted for the other. Here, we consider one simple example of the use of Leibniz's rule:

Suppose there are three natives of the island, A, B and C, and C says "A and B are both the same type". Formulate a question that, when posed to A, determines whether C is telling the truth.

To solve this problem, we let A, B and C denote the propositions A, B and C is a knight, respectively. We also let Q be the unknown question.

The response we want is C. So, by the analysis in Section 5.2.4, $Q=(A=C)$. But C's statement is $A=B$. So we know that $C=(A=B)$. Substituting equals for equals, $Q=(A=(A=B))$. But $A=(A=B)$ simplifies to B. So the question to be posed is "Is B a knight?". Here is this argument again, but set out as a calculation of Q, with hints showing the steps taken at each stage.

$$Q$$
$$=\quad\{\quad\text{rule for formulating questions}\quad\}$$
$$A=C$$
$$=\quad\{\quad\text{from C's statement, } C=(A=B),$$
$$\text{substitution of equals for equals}\quad\}$$
$$A=(A=B)$$
$$=\quad\{\quad\text{associativity of equality}\quad\}$$
$$(A=A)=B$$
$$=\quad\{\quad(A=A)=\text{true}\quad\}$$
$$\text{true}=B$$
$$=\quad\{\quad(\text{true}=B)=B\quad\}$$
$$B.$$

5.3 EQUIVALENCE AND CONTINUED EQUALITIES

Associative functions are usually denoted by infix operators.[2] The benefit in calculations is immense. If a binary operator $\oplus$ is associative (that is, $(x\oplus y)\oplus z=x\oplus(y\oplus z)$ for all x, y and z), we can write $x\oplus y\oplus z$ without fear of ambiguity. The expression becomes more compact because of the omission of parentheses. More importantly, the expression is unbiased; we may choose to simplify $x\oplus y$ or $y\oplus z$ depending on which is the most convenient. If the operator is also symmetric (that is, $x\oplus y=y\oplus x$ for all x and y) the gain is even bigger, because then, if the operator is used to combine several subexpressions, we can choose to simplify $u\oplus w$ for any pair of subexpressions u and w.

---

[2] An *infix operator* is a symbol used to denote a function of two arguments that is written between the two arguments. The symbols "+" and "×" are both infix operators, denoting addition and multiplication, respectively.

Infix notation is also often used for binary relations. We write, for example, $0 \leq m \leq n$. Here, the operators are being used *conjunctionally*: the meaning is $0 \leq m$ *and* $m \leq n$. In this way, the formula is more compact (since m is not written twice). More importantly, we are guided to the inference that $0 \leq n$. The algebraic property that is being hidden here is the transitivity of the at-most relation. If the relation between m and n is $m < n$ rather than $m \leq n$ and we write $0 \leq m < n$, we may infer that $0 < n$. Here, the inference is more complex since there are two relations involved. But, it is an inference that is so fundamental that the notation is designed to facilitate its recognition.

> ⚠ *Refer to Section 12.3.2 for a detailed discussion of infix (and other) notation for binary operators like addition and multiplication. Section 12.5 discusses important algebraic properties like associativity and symmetry. Section 12.7 extends the discussion to binary relations.*

In the case of equality of boolean values, we have a dilemma. Do we understand equality as a relation and read a continued expression of the form

$$x = y = z$$

as asserting the equality of all of x, y and z? Or do we read it "associatively" as

$$(x = y) = z,$$

or, equally, as

$$x = (y = z),$$

in just the same way as we would read $x+y+z$? The two readings are, unfortunately, not the same (for example $true = false = false$ is false according to the first reading but true according to the second and third readings). There are advantages in both readings, and it is a major drawback to have to choose one in favour of the other.

It would be very confusing and, indeed, dangerous to read $x = y = z$ in any other way than $x = y$ and $y = z$; otherwise, the meaning of a sequence of expressions separated by equality symbols would depend on the type of the expressions. Also, the conjunctional reading (for other types) is so universally accepted – for good reasons – that it would be quite unacceptable to try to impose a different convention.

The solution to this dilemma is to use two different symbols to denote equality of boolean values – the symbol "=" when the transitivity of the equality relation is to be emphasised and the symbol "≡" when its associativity is to be exploited. Accordingly, we write both

$p=q$ and $p\equiv q$. When p and q are expressions denoting boolean values, these both mean the same. But a continued expression

$$p\equiv q\equiv r,$$

comprising more than two boolean expressions connected by the "$\equiv$" symbol, is to be evaluated *associatively* – i.e. as $(p\equiv q)\equiv r$ or $p\equiv(q\equiv r)$, whichever is the most convenient – whereas a continued expression

$$p=q=r$$

is to be evaluated *conjunctionally* – that is, as $p=q$ *and* $q=r$. More generally, a continued *equality* of the form

$$p_1=p_2=\ldots=p_n$$

means that all of $p_1, p_2, \ldots, p_n$ are equal, while a continued *equivalence* of the form

$$p_1\equiv p_2\equiv\ldots\equiv p_n$$

has the meaning given by fully parenthesising the expression (in any way whatsoever, since the outcome is not affected) and then evaluating the expression as indicated by the chosen parenthesisation.

Moreover, we recommend that the "$\equiv$" symbol is pronounced as "equivales"; being an unfamiliar word, its use will help to avoid misunderstanding.

Shortly, we introduce a number of laws governing boolean equality. They invariably involve a continued equivalence. A first example is its reflexivity.

$$[\textbf{Reflexivity}]\qquad [\,\text{true}\equiv p\equiv p\,]. \qquad\qquad (5.2)$$

5.3.1 Examples of the Associativity of Equivalence

This section contains a couple of beautiful examples illustrating the effectiveness of the associativity of equivalence.

Even and Odd Numbers   The first example is the following property of the predicate even on numbers. (A number is even exactly when it is a multiple of 2.)

$$[\,\text{m+n is even}\ \equiv\ \text{m is even}\ \equiv\ \text{n is even}\,].$$

It will help if we refer to whether or not a number is even or odd as the *parity* of the number. Then, if we parenthesise the statement as

$$[\,\text{m+n is even}\ \equiv\ (\text{m is even}\ \equiv\ \text{n is even})\,],$$

it states that the number m+n is even exactly when the parities of m and n are the same. Parenthesising it as

$$[\,(\text{m+n is even} \;\equiv\; \text{m is even}) \;\equiv\; \text{n is even}\,],$$

it states that the operation of adding a number n to a number m does not change the parity of m exactly when n is even.

Another way of reading the statement is to use the fact that, in general, the equivalence $p \equiv q \equiv r$ is true exactly when an odd number of p, q and r is true. So the property captures four different cases:

	((m+n is even)	and (m is even)	and	(n is even))
or	((m+n is odd)	and (m is odd)	and	(n is even))
or	((m+n is odd)	and (m is even)	and	(n is odd))
or	((m+n is even)	and (m is odd)	and	(n is odd)).

The beauty of this example lies in the avoidance of case analysis. There are four distinct combinations of the two booleans "m is even" and "n is even". Using the associativity of equivalence, the value of "m+n is even" is expressed in one simple formula, without any repetition of the component expressions, rather than as a list of different cases. Avoidance of case analysis is vital to effective reasoning.

Sign of Non-Zero Numbers   The *sign* of a number says whether or not the number is positive. For non-zero numbers x and y, the product $x \times y$ is positive if the signs of x and y are equal. If the signs of x and y are different, the product $x \times y$ is negative.

Assuming that x and y are non-zero, this rule is expressed as

$$[\,x \times y \text{ is positive} \;\equiv\; x \text{ is positive} \;\equiv\; y \text{ is positive}\,].$$

Just as for the predicate even, this one statement neatly captures a number of different cases, even though no case analysis is involved. Indeed, our justification of the rule is the statement

$$[\,x \times y \text{ is positive} \;\equiv\; (x \text{ is positive} \;\equiv\; y \text{ is positive})\,].$$

The other parenthesisation – which states that the sign of x is unchanged when it is multiplied by y exactly when y is positive – is obtained "for free" from the associativity of boolean equality.

5.3.2 On Natural Language

Many mathematicians and logicians appear not to be aware that equality of booleans is associative. Most courses on logic first introduce implication ("only if") and then briefly mention "follows from" ("if") before introducing boolean equality as "if and only if". This is akin to introducing equality of numbers by first introducing the at-most ($\leq$) and at-least ($\geq$) relations, and then defining an "at most and at least" operator.

The most probable explanation lies in the fact that many logicians view the purpose of logic as formalising "natural" or "intuitive" reasoning, and our "natural" tendency is not to reason in terms of equalities, but in causal terms. ("If it is raining, I will take my umbrella.") The equality symbol was first introduced into mathematics by Robert Recorde in 1557, which, in the history of mathematics, is quite recent; were equality "natural" it would have been introduced much earlier. Natural language has no counterpart to a continued equivalence.

This fact should not be a deterrent to the use of continued equivalence. At one time (admittedly, a very long time ago) there was probably similar resistance to the introduction of continued additions and multiplications. The evidence is still present in the language we use today. For example, the most common way to express time is in words – "quarter to ten" or "ten past eleven". Calculational requirements (e.g. wanting to determine how long is it before the train is due to arrive) have influenced natural language so that, nowadays, people sometimes say, for example, "nine forty-five" or "eleven ten" in everyday speech. But we still do not find it acceptable to say "ten seventy"! Yet this is what we actually use when we want to calculate the time difference between 9.45 and 11.10. In fact, several laws of arithmetic, including associativity of addition, are fundamental to the calculation. Changes in natural language have occurred, and will continue to occur, as a result of progress in mathematics, but will always lag a long way behind. The language of mathematics has developed in order to overcome the limitations of natural language. The goal is not to mimic "natural" reasoning, but to provide a more effective alternative.

5.4 NEGATION

Consider the following knights-and-knaves problem. There are two natives, A and B. Native A says, "B is a knight equals I am not a knight". What can you determine about A and B?

This problem involves a so-called *negation*: the use of "not". Negation is a unary operator (meaning that it is a function with exactly one argument) mapping a boolean to a boolean, and is denoted by the symbol "$\neg$", written as a prefix to its argument. If p is a boolean expression, "$\neg$p" is pronounced "*not* p".

Using the general rule that if A makes a statement S, we know that $A \equiv S$, we get, for this problem,

$$A \equiv B \equiv \neg A.$$

(We switch from "=" to "≡" here in order to exploit associativity.) The goal is to simplify this expression.

In order to tackle this problem, it is necessary to begin by formulating calculational rules for negation. For arbitrary proposition p, the law governing ¬p is:

[Negation]   [¬p ≡ p ≡ false] .   (5.3)

Reading this as

¬p = (p≡false),

it functions as a definition of negation. Reading it the other way,

(¬p≡p) = false,

it provides a way of simplifying propositional expressions. In addition, the symmetry of equivalence means that we can rearrange the terms in a continued equivalence in any order we like. So we also get the property

p = (¬p≡false).

Returning to the knights-and-knaves problem, we are given that

A ≡ B ≡ ¬A.

This simplifies to ¬B as follows:

$$
\begin{aligned}
&\quad A \equiv B \equiv \neg A \\
= &\quad \{ \quad\quad\quad \text{rearranging terms} \quad \} \\
&\quad \neg A \equiv A \equiv B \\
= &\quad \{ \quad\quad\quad \text{law (5.3) with } p := A \quad \} \\
&\quad \text{false} \equiv B \\
= &\quad \{ \quad\quad\quad \text{law (5.3) with } p := B \text{ and rearranging} \quad \} \\
&\quad \neg B.
\end{aligned}
$$

So, B is a knave, but A could be a knight or a knave. Note how (5.3) is used in two different ways.

The law (5.3), in conjunction with the symmetry and associativity of equivalence, provides a way of simplifying continued equivalences in which one or more terms are repeated and/or negated. Suppose, for example, we want to simplify

$$\neg p \equiv p \equiv q \equiv \neg p \equiv r \equiv \neg q.$$

We begin by rearranging all the terms so that repeated occurrences of "p" and "q" are grouped together. Thus we get

$$\neg p \equiv \neg p \equiv p \equiv q \equiv \neg q \equiv r.$$

Now we can use (5.2) and (5.3) to reduce the number of occurrences of "p" and "q" to at most one (possibly negated). In this particular example we obtain

$$\text{true} \equiv p \equiv \text{false} \equiv r.$$

Finally, we use (5.2) and (5.3) again. The result is that the original formula is simplified to

$$\neg p \equiv r.$$

Just as before, this process can be compared with the simplification of an arithmetic expression involving continued addition, where now negative terms may also appear. The expression

$$p + (-p) + q + (-p) + r + q + (-q) + r + p$$

is simplified to

$$q + 2r$$

by counting all the occurrences of p, q and r, an occurrence of −p cancelling out an occurrence of p. Again, the details are different but the process is essentially identical.

The two laws (5.2) and (5.3) are all that is needed to define the way that negation interacts with equivalence; using these two laws, we can derive several other laws. A simple example of how these two laws are combined is a proof that $\neg\text{false} = \text{true}$:

$$\neg\text{false}$$

$$= \qquad \{ \qquad \text{law } \neg p \equiv p \equiv \text{false with } p := \text{false} \quad \}$$

$$\text{false} \equiv \text{false}$$

$$= \qquad \{ \qquad \text{law true} \equiv p \equiv p \text{ with } p := \text{false} \quad \}$$

$$\text{true}.$$

Exercise 5.4   Prove that $\neg\text{true} = \text{false}$.

Exercise 5.5 (Double Negation) Prove the rule of double negation,

$$[\neg\neg p = p].$$

5.4.1 Contraposition

A rule that should now be obvious, but which is surprisingly useful, is the rule we call *contraposition*.[3]

[Contraposition] $[p \equiv q \equiv \neg p \equiv \neg q]$.   (5.6)

The name refers to the use of the rule in the form $(p \equiv q) = (\neg p \equiv \neg q)$.

We used the rule of contraposition implicitly in the river-crossing problems (see Chapter 3). Recall that each problem involves getting a group of people from one side of a river to another, using one boat. If we let n denote the number of crossings, and ℓ denote the boolean "the boat is on the left side of the river", a crossing of the river is modelled by the assignment

$$n, \ell \ := \ n+1, \neg\ell.$$

In words, the number of crossings increases by one, and the boat changes side. The rule of contraposition tells us that

$$even(n) \equiv \ell$$

is invariant under this assignment. This is because

$$(even(n) \equiv \ell)[n, \ell \ := \ n+1, \neg\ell]$$

$$= \quad \{ \quad \text{rule of substitution} \quad \}$$

$$even(n+1) \equiv \neg\ell$$

$$= \quad \{ \quad even(n+1)$$

$$= \quad \{ \quad \text{distributivity} \quad \}$$

$$even(n) \equiv even(1)$$

$$= \quad \{ \quad even(1) \equiv false \quad \}$$

$$even(n) \equiv false$$

---

[3] Other authors use the name "contraposition" for a less general rule combining negation with implication.

$$= \qquad \{ \qquad \text{negation} \quad \}$$

$$\neg(\text{even}(n)) \quad \}$$

$$\neg(\text{even}(n)) \equiv \neg\ell$$

$$= \qquad \{ \qquad \text{contraposition} \quad \}$$

$$\text{even}(n) \equiv \ell.$$

We are given that, initially, the boat is on the left side. Since zero is an even number, we conclude that $\text{even}(n) \equiv \ell$ is invariantly true. In words, the boat is on the left side equivales the number of crossings is even.

Another example is the following. Suppose it is required to move a square armchair sideways by a distance equal to its own width (see figure 5.1). However, the chair is so heavy that it can only be moved by rotating it through $90°$ around one of its four corners. Is it possible to move the chair as desired? If so, how? If not, why not?

Figure 5.1: Moving a heavy armchair.

The answer is that it is impossible. Suppose the armchair is initially positioned along a north–south axis. Suppose, also, that the floor is painted alternately with black and white squares, like a chess board, with each of the squares being the same size as the armchair. (see Figure 5.2). Suppose the armchair is initially on a black square. The requirement is to move the armchair from a north–south position on a black square to a north–south position on a white square.

Now, let boolean col represent the colour of the square that the armchair is on (say, true for black and false for white), and dir represent the direction that the armchair is facing (say, true for north–south and false for east–west). Then, rotating the armchair about any corner is represented by the assignment

$$\text{col}, \text{dir} := \neg\text{col}, \neg\text{dir}$$

The rule of contraposition states that an invariant of this assignment is

$$\text{col} \equiv \text{dir}.$$

So the value of this expression will remain equal to its initial value, no matter how many times the armchair is rotated. But, moving the armchair sideways one square changes the

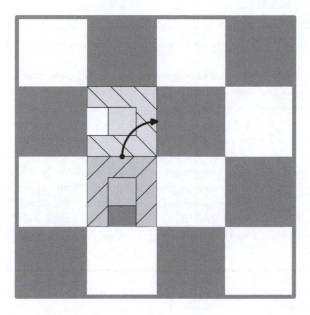

○ **Figure 5.2: Invariant when moving a heavy armchair.**

colour but does not change the direction. That is, it changes the value of col ≡ dir, and is impossible to achieve by continually rotating the armchair as prescribed.

In words, an invariant of rotating the armchair through 90° around a corner point is

> the chair is on a black square ≡ the chair is facing north–south

which is false when the chair is on a white square and facing north–south.

Exercise 5.7 (Knight's Move)   In the game of chess, a knight's move is two places up or down and one place left or right, or two places left or right and one place up or down. A chessboard is an 8×8 grid of squares.

Show that it is impossible to move a knight from the bottom-left corner of a chessboard to the top-right corner in such a way that every square on the board is visited exactly once.

Hint: How many moves have to be made? Model a move in terms of the effect on the number of moves and the colour of the square on which the knight is standing; identify a relation between the two that is invariant under a move.

5.4.2 Handshake Problems

Logical properties of negation are fundamental to solving so-called *handshake problems*.

The simplest example of a handshake problem is this: Suppose that at a party, some people shake hands and some do not. Suppose each person counts the number of times they shake hands. Show that at least two people have the same count.

Crucial to how we solve this problem are the properties of shaking hands. These are that it is a *binary relation*; it is *symmetric*, and it is *anti-reflexive*. It being a "binary relation" on people, means that, for any two people – Jack and Jill, say – Jack shakes hands with Jill is either true or false. (In general, a *relation* is any boolean-valued function. Binary means that it is a function of two arguments.) It being a "symmetric" relation means that, for any two people – Jack and Jill, say – Jack shakes hands with Jill equivales Jill shakes hands with Jack. Finally, it being "anti-reflexive" means that no one shakes hands with themselves.

 Refer to Section 12.7 for a basic introduction to binary relations and their properties.

We are required to show that (at least) two people shake hands the same number of times. Let us explore the consequences of the properties of the shake-hands relation with respect to the number of times that each person shakes hands.

Suppose there are n people. Then, everyone shakes hands with at most n people. However, the anti-reflexivity property is that no one shakes hands with themselves. We conclude that everyone shakes hands with between 0 and n−1 people.

There are n numbers in the range 0 thru n−1. The negation of "two people shake hands the same number of times" is "everyone shakes hands a distinct number of times". In particular, someone shakes hands 0 times and someone shakes hands n−1 times. The symmetry of the shake-hands relation makes this impossible.

Suppose we abbreviate "shake hands" to S, and suppose we use x and y to refer to people. In this way, xSy is read as "person x shakes hands with person y", or just x shakes hands with y. Then the symmetry of "shakes hands" gives us the rule, for all x and y,

$$xSy \equiv ySx.$$

The contrapositive of this rule is that, for all x and y,

$$\neg(xSy) \equiv \neg(ySx).$$

In words, x does not shake hands with y equals y does not shake hands with x. Now, suppose person a shakes hands with no one and person b shakes hands with everyone. Then, in particular, a does not shake hands with b, that is, ¬(aSb) has the value true, and b shakes hands with a, that is, bSa also has the value true. But then, substituting equals for equals, we have that aSb has both the value false (because of the contrapositive of the symmetry of S and the fact that ¬(aSb) has the value true) and true (because bSa has the value true and S is symmetric). This is impossible.

The assumption that everyone shakes hands with a distinct number of people has led to a contradiction, and so we conclude that two people must shake hands the same number of times.

Note carefully how the symmetry and anti-reflexivity of the shakes-hands relation are crucial. Were we to consider a similar problem involving a different relation, the outcome might be different. For example, if we replace "shake hands" by some other form of greeting like "bows or curtsies", which is not symmetric, the property need not hold. (Suppose there are two people, and one bows to the other, but the greeting is not returned.) However, if "shake hands" is replaced by "rub noses", the property does hold. Like "shake hands", "rub noses" is a symmetric and anti-reflexive relation.

> **Exercise 5.8** Here is another handshaking problem. It is a little more difficult to solve, but the essence of the problem remains the same: "shake hands" is a symmetric relation, as is "do not shake hands".
>
> Suppose a number of couples (husband and wife) attend a party. Some people shake hands, others do not. Husband and wife never shake hands. One person, the "host", asks everyone else how many times they have shaken hands, and gets a different answer every time. How many times did the host and the host's partner shake hands?

5.4.3 Inequivalence

In the knights-and-knaves problem mentioned at the beginning of Section 5.4, A might have said "B is different from myself". This statement is formulated as $B \neq A$, or $\neg(B = A)$. This is, in fact, the same as saying "B is a knight equals I am not a knight", as the following calculation shows (note that we switch from "=" to "≡" once again, in order to exploit associativity):

$$\neg(B \equiv A)$$
$$= \qquad \{ \qquad [\; \neg p \equiv p \equiv false \;] \text{ with } p := (B \equiv A) \quad \}$$
$$B \equiv A \equiv false$$

$$= \qquad \{ \qquad [\ \neg p \equiv p \equiv \text{false}\ ] \text{ with } p := A \ \}$$

$$B \equiv \neg A.$$

We have thus proved, for all propositions p and q,

[Inequivalence] $[\ \neg(p \equiv q) \equiv p \equiv \neg q\ ]$.   (5.9)

Note how associativity of equivalence has been used silently in this calculation. Note also how associativity of equivalence in the summary of the calculation gives us two properties for the price of one. The first is the one proved directly,

$$[\ \neg(p \equiv q) = (p \equiv \neg q)\ ],$$

and the second comes free with associativity,

$$[\ (\neg(p \equiv q) \equiv p) = \neg q\ ].$$

The proposition $\neg(p \equiv q)$ is usually written $p \not\equiv q$. The operator is called *inequivalence* (or *exclusive-or*, abbreviated *xor*).

> ⚠ *Calling inequivalence "exclusive-or" can be misleading because* $p \not\equiv q \not\equiv r$ *does not mean that "exclusively" one of* p, q *and* r *is true. On the contrary,* true $\not\equiv$ true $\not\equiv$ true *simplifies to* true. *We occasionally use this name, but only when the operator has two arguments.*

Inequivalence is also associative:

$$(p \not\equiv q) \not\equiv r$$

$$= \qquad \{ \qquad \text{definition of "}\not\equiv\text{", applied twice} \ \}$$

$$\neg(\neg(p \equiv q) \equiv r)$$

$$= \qquad \{ \qquad (5.9), \text{ with } p,q := \neg(p \equiv q), r \ \}$$

$$\neg(p \equiv q) \equiv \neg r$$

$$= \qquad \{ \qquad \text{contraposition (5.6), with } p,q := p \equiv q, r \ \}$$

$$p \equiv q \equiv r$$

$$= \qquad \{ \qquad \text{contraposition (5.6), with } p,q := p, q \equiv r \ \}$$

$$\neg p \equiv \neg(q \equiv r)$$

$$= \qquad \{ \qquad (5.9), \text{with } p,q := p, q \equiv r \quad \}$$

$$\neg(p \equiv \neg(q \equiv r))$$

$$= \qquad \{ \qquad \text{definition of "}\not\equiv\text{", applied twice} \quad \}$$

$$p \not\equiv (q \not\equiv r).$$

As a result, we can write the *continued inequivalence* $p \not\equiv q \not\equiv r$ without fear of ambiguity.[4] Note that, as a byproduct, we have shown that $p \not\equiv q \not\equiv r$ and $p \equiv q \equiv r$ are equal.

⚠ *We can now return to formulating a more "natural" question that enables gold to be found on the island of knights and knaves (see Section 5.2.4). Recall that, if L denotes "the gold can be found by following the left fork in the road" and A denotes "the native is a knight", the question to be asked is: are L and A equal? The rule of contraposition combined with inequivalence allows the question to be formulated in terms of exclusive-or. We have:*

$$L = A$$

$$= \qquad \{ \qquad \textit{contraposition} \quad \}$$

$$\neg L = \neg A$$

$$= \qquad \{ \qquad \textit{inequivalence and double negation} \quad \}$$

$$L \not\equiv \neg A \ .$$

Expressing the inequivalence in the formula $L \not\equiv \neg A$ in terms of exclusive-or, the question becomes: "Of the two statements 'the gold can be found by following the left fork' and 'you (the native) are a knave' is one and only one of them true?". Other formulations are, of course, possible.

As a final worked example, we show that inequivalence associates with equivalence:

$$(p \not\equiv q) \equiv r$$

$$= \qquad \{ \qquad \text{expanding the definition of } p \not\equiv q \quad \}$$

$$\neg(p \equiv q) \equiv r$$

$$= \qquad \{ \qquad \neg(p \equiv q) \equiv p \equiv \neg q \quad \}$$

$$p \equiv \neg q \equiv r$$

---

[4]This is to be read associatively, and should not be confused with $p \not\equiv q \not\equiv r$, which some authors occasionally write. Inequality is not transitive, so such expressions should be avoided.

$$= \qquad \{ \qquad \text{using symmetry of equivalence, the law (5.9)}$$

$$\text{is applied in the form } \neg(p \equiv q) \equiv \neg q \equiv p$$

$$\text{with p,q := q,r} \quad \}$$

$$p \equiv \neg(q \equiv r)$$

$$= \qquad \{ \qquad \text{definition of } q \not\equiv r \quad \}$$

$$p \equiv (q \not\equiv r) \quad .$$

Exercise 5.10 Simplify the following. (Note that in each case it does not matter in which order you evaluate the subexpressions. Also, rearranging the variables and/or constants does not make any difference.)

(a) $\text{false} \not\equiv \text{false} \not\equiv \text{false}$

(b) $\text{true} \not\equiv \text{true} \not\equiv \text{true} \not\equiv \text{true}$

(c) $\text{false} \not\equiv \text{true} \not\equiv \text{false} \not\equiv \text{true}$

(d) $p \equiv p \equiv \neg p \equiv p \equiv \neg p$

(e) $p \not\equiv q \equiv q \equiv p$

(f) $p \not\equiv q \equiv r \equiv p$

(g) $p \equiv p \not\equiv \neg p \not\equiv p \equiv \neg p$

(h) $p \equiv p \not\equiv \neg p \not\equiv p \equiv \neg p \not\equiv \neg p$

Exercise 5.11 (Encryption) The fact that inequivalence is associative, that is,

$$(p \not\equiv (q \not\equiv r)) \equiv ((p \not\equiv q) \not\equiv r),$$

is used to encrypt data. To encrypt a single bit b of data, a key a is chosen and the encrypted form of b that is transmitted is $a \not\equiv b$. The receiver decrypts the received bit, c, using the same operation.[5] That is, the receiver uses the same key a to compute $a \not\equiv c$. Show that, if bit b is encrypted and then decrypted in this way, the result is b independently of the key a.

[5]This operation is usually called "exclusive-or" in texts on data encryption; it is not commonly known that exclusive-or and inequivalence are the same. Inequivalence can be replaced by equivalence in the encryption and decryption process. But very few scientists and engineers are aware of the algebraic properties of equivalence, and this possibility is never exploited!

Exercise 5.12   On the island of knights and knaves, you encounter two natives, A and B. What question should you ask A to determine whether A and B are different types?

5.5 SUMMARY

In this chapter, we have used simple logic puzzles to introduce logical equivalence (the equality of boolean values), the most fundamental logical operator. Equivalence has the remarkable property of being associative, in addition to the standard properties of equality. Exploitation of the associativity of equivalence eliminates the tedious and ineffective case analysis that is often seen in solutions to logic puzzles.

The associativity of equivalence can be difficult to get used to, particularly if one tries to express its properties in natural language. However, this should not be used as an excuse for ignoring it. The painful, centuries-long process of accepting zero as a number, and introducing the symbol 0 to denote it, provides ample evidence that the adherence to "natural" modes of reasoning is a major impediment to effective reasoning. The purpose of a calculus is not to mimic "natural" or "intuitive" reasoning, but to provide a more powerful alternative.

5.6 BIBLIOGRAPHIC REMARKS

The fact that equality of boolean values is associative has been known since at least the 1920s, having been mentioned by Alfred Tarski in his PhD thesis, where its discovery is attributed to J. Lukasiewicz. (See the paper "On the primitive term of logistic" [Tar56]; Tarski and Lukasiewicz are both famous logicians.) Nevertheless, its usefulness was never recognised until brought to the fore by E.W. Dijkstra in his work on program semantics and mathematical method (see [DS90]).

The logic puzzles in Section 5.1 were taken from Raymond Smullyan's book *What Is the Name of This Book?* [Smu78]. This is an entertaining book which leads on from simple logic puzzles to a discussion of the logical paradoxes and Gödel's undecidability theorem. But Smullyan's proofs often involve detailed case analyses and use traditional "if and only if" arguments. The exploitation of the associativity of equivalence in the solution of such puzzles is due to Gerard Wiltink [Wil87]. For a complete account of calculational logic, see [GS93].

Chapter

Induction

6

Induction is a very important problem-solving technique based on repeatedly breaking a problem down into subproblems.

Central to the use of induction is the idea of generalising a given problem to a *class* of problems. Specific problems within the class are called *instances* and each has a certain *size*. The "size" is said to be a *parameter* of the problem. For example, the problem might involve a pile of matchsticks, where the number of matches is a parameter; an instance of the problem is then a particular pile of matches, and its size is the number of matches in the pile.

Having decided on a suitable generalisation, the solution process has two steps. First, we consider problems of size 0. This is called the *basis* of the induction. Almost invariably, such problems are very easy to solve. (They are often dismissed as "trivial".) Second, we show how to solve, for an arbitrary natural number n, a problem of size n+1 given a solution to problems of size n. This is called the *induction step*.

By this process, we can solve problems of size 0. We can also solve problems of size 1; we apply the induction step to construct a solution to problems of size 1 from the known solution to problems of size 0. Then, we can solve problems of size 2; we apply the induction step again to construct a solution to problems of size 2 from the known solution to problems of size 1. And so it goes on. We can solve problems of size 3, then problems of size 4, etc. That is, "by induction" we can solve problems of arbitrary size.

A requirement is that the size is a non-negative, whole number: thus 0, 1, 2, 3, etc. We use the term *natural number* for a non-negative, whole number. A word of warning: mathematicians often exclude the number 0 from the natural numbers. For typical real-life computing problems, however, it is very important that 0 should be included, making a break with tradition imperative. (For example, an internet search may yield 0 matches. A robot that processes search information must be programmed to deal with such a possibility.) Very occasionally, problems of size 0 do not make sense. In such cases the basis of the induction is problems of size 1. More generally, the basis may be problems of size n_0, for some number n_0; induction then provides a solution for all instances of size at least n_0.

Textbook problems are often presented in a way that makes the size parameter obvious, but this need not always be the case. For example, a given problem might involve a chessboard, which has 64 squares. There are several ways in which the problem might be generalised. The problem might be generalised to a class of problems where there are instances for each number n; the given problem is an instance such that n is 64. Such a generalisation takes no account of the structure of a chessboard. A second generalisation might exploit the fact that a chessboard is square: a class of problems is identified where an instance is an n×n board, for some n. The "size" of an instance of the class is then n (and not n^2), and the size of the specific chessboard problem is 8. A third generalisation might depend on the fact that 8 is a power of 2; the class of problems is then restricted to square boards where the length of a side is 2^n. In this case, the chessboard problem would have "size" 3 (because $8 = 2^3$).

6.1 EXAMPLE PROBLEMS

All the following problems can be solved by induction. In the first, the size is the number of lines. In the second and third problems, it is explicitly given by the parameter n. In each case, the basis should be easy. You then have to solve the induction step. We discuss each problem in turn in coming sections.

Figure 6.1: Black and white colouring.

1. **Cutting the Plane**   A number of straight lines are drawn across a sheet of paper, each line extending all the way from from one border to another (see Figure 6.1). In this way, the paper is divided into a number of regions.

   > Show that it is possible to colour each region black or white so that no two adjacent regions have the same colour (i.e. so that the two regions on opposite sides of any line segment have different colours).

2. **Triominoes**   A square piece of paper is divided into a grid of size $2^n \times 2^n$, where n is a natural number.[1] The individual squares are called *grid squares*. One grid square is covered, and the others are left uncovered. A triomino is an L-shape made of three grid squares. Figure 6.2 shows, on the left, an 8×8 grid with one square covered. On the right is a triomino.

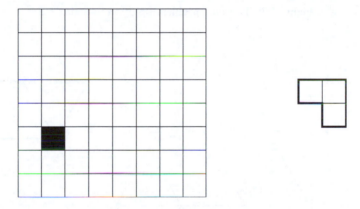

   ◯ **Figure 6.2: Triomino problem.**

   > Show that it is possible to cover the remaining squares with (non-overlapping) triominoes. (Figure 6.3 shows a solution in one case.)

   Note that the case $n = 0$ should be included in your solution.

3. **Trapeziums**   An equilateral triangle, with side of length 3n for some natural number n, is made of smaller equilateral triangles. Figure 6.4 shows the case where n is 2.

   A bucket-shaped trapezium, shown on the right of Figure 6.4, is made from three equilateral triangles.

   > Show that it is possible to cover the remaining triangles with (non-overlapping) trapeziums. See Figure 6.5 for the solution in the case where n is 2.

---

[1] Recall that the natural numbers are the numbers 0, 1, 2, etc.

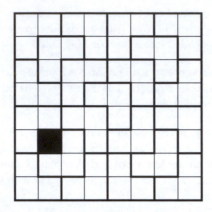

Figure 6.3: Triomino problem: solution to Figure 6.2.

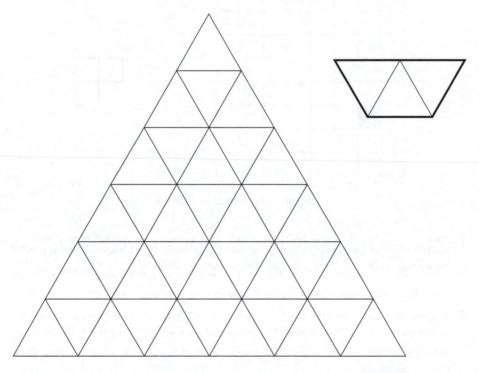

Figure 6.4: A pyramid of equilateral triangles and a trapezium.

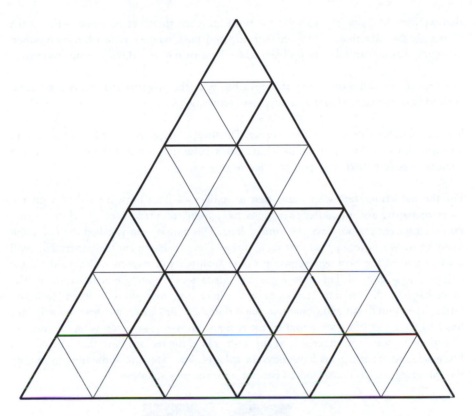

Figure 6.5: Solution to Figure 6.4.

Additional examples, such as fake-coin detection and the Tower of Hanoi problem, are discussed in later chapters.

6.2 CUTTING THE PLANE

Recall the statement of the problem:

> A number of straight lines are drawn across a sheet of paper, each line extending all the way from one border to another (see Figure 6.1). In this way, the paper is divided into a number of regions. Show that it is possible to colour each region black or white so that no two adjacent regions have the same colour (i.e. so that the two regions on opposite sides of any line segment have different colours).

For this problem, the number of lines is an obvious measure of the "size" of the problem. The goal is, thus, to solve the problem "by induction on the number of lines". This means that we have to show how to solve the problem when there are zero lines – this is the "basis" of the induction – and when there are n+1 lines, where n is an arbitrary number, assuming that we can solve the problem when there are n lines – this is the induction step.

For brevity, we call a colouring of the regions with the property that no two adjacent regions have the same colour a *satisfactory colouring*.

The case where there are zero lines is easy. The sheet of paper is divided into one region, and this can be coloured black or white, either colouring meeting the conditions of a solution (because there is no pair of adjacent regions).

For the induction step, we assume that a number of lines have been drawn on the sheet of paper, and the different regions have been coloured black or white so that no two adjacent regions have the same colour. This assumption is called the *induction hypothesis*. We now suppose that an additional line is drawn on the paper. This will divide some of the existing regions into two; such pairs of regions will have the same colour, and so the existing colouring is not satisfactory. Figure 6.6 is an example. The plane has been divided into 12 regions by five lines, and the regions coloured black and white, as required. An additional line, shown dashed for clarity, has been added. This has had the effect of dividing four of the regions into two, thus increasing the number of regions by four. On either side of the dashed line, the regions have the same colour. Elsewhere, adjacent regions have different colours. The task is to show how to modify the colouring so that it does indeed become a satisfactory solution.

Figure 6.6: Cutting the plane. Additional line shown dashed.

The key to a solution is to note that inverting the colours of any satisfactory colouring (i.e. changing a black region to white, and vice versa) also gives a satisfactory colouring. Now, the additional line divides the sheet of paper into two regions. Let us call these regions the *left* and *right* regions. (By this choice of names, we do not imply that the additional line must be from top to bottom of the page. It is just a convenient, easily remembered, way of naming the regions.) Note that the assumed colouring is a satisfactory colouring of the left region and of the right region. In order to guarantee that, either side of the additional line, all regions have opposite colour, choose, say, the left region, and invert all the colours in that region. This gives a satisfactory colouring of the left region (because inverting the colours of a satisfactory colouring gives a satisfactory colouring). It also gives a satisfactory colouring of the right region (because the colouring has not changed, and was satisfactory already). Also, the colouring of adjacent regions at the boundary of the left and right regions is satisfactory, because they have changed from being the same to being different.

Figure 6.7 shows the effect on our example. Grey has been used instead of black in order to make the inversion of the colours more evident.

Figure 6.7: **Cutting the plane. The colours are inverted to one side of the additional line (black is shown as grey to make clear which colours have changed).**

This completes the induction step. In order to apply the construction to an instance of the problem with, say, seven lines, we begin by colouring the whole sheet of paper. Then the lines are added one by one. Each time a line is added, the existing colouring is modified as prescribed in the induction step, until all seven lines have been added.

The algorithm is non-deterministic in several ways. The initial colouring of the sheet of paper (black or white) is unspecified. The ordering of the lines (which to add first, which to add next, etc.) is also unspecified. Finally, which region is chosen as the "left" region, and which the "right" region is unspecified. This means that the final colouring may be achieved in lots of different ways. But that does not matter. The final colouring is guaranteed to be "satisfactory", as required in the problem specification.

Exercise 6.1   Check your understanding by considering variations on the problem.

Why is it required that the lines are straight? How might this assumption be relaxed without invalidating the solution?

The problem assumes the lines are drawn on a piece of paper. Is the solution still valid if the lines are drawn on the surface of a ball, or on the surface of a doughnut?

We remarked that the algorithm for colouring the plane is non-deterministic. How many different colourings does it construct?

6.3 TRIOMINOES

As a second example of an inductive construction, let us consider the triomino problem posed in Section 6.1. Recall the statement of the problem:

A square piece of paper is divided into a grid of size $2^n \times 2^n$, where n is a natural number. The individual squares are called *grid squares*. One grid square is covered, and the others are left uncovered. A triomino is an L-shape made of three grid squares. Show that it is possible to cover the remaining squares with (non-overlapping) triominoes.

The measure of the "size" of instances of the problem in this case is the number n. We solve the problem by induction on n.

The base case is when n equals 0. The grid then has size $2^0 \times 2^0$, that is, 1×1. That is, there is exactly one square. This one square is inevitably the one that is covered, leaving no squares uncovered. It takes 0 triominoes to cover no squares! This, then, is how the base case is solved.

Now consider a grid of size $2^{n+1} \times 2^{n+1}$. Make the *induction hypothesis* that it is possible to cover any grid of size $2^n \times 2^n$ with triominoes if, first, an arbitrary grid square has been covered. We have to show how to exploit this hypothesis in order to cover a grid of size $2^{n+1} \times 2^{n+1}$ of which one square has been covered.

A grid of size $2^{n+1} \times 2^{n+1}$ can be subdivided into four grids each of size $2^n \times 2^n$, simply by drawing horizontal and vertical dividing lines through the middle of each side (see Figure 6.8). Let us call the four grids the *bottom-left*, *bottom-right*, *top-left*, and *top-right* grids. One grid square is already covered. This square will be in one of the four sub-grids. We may assume that it is in the bottom-left grid. (If not, the entire grid can be rotated about the centre so that it does become the case.)

The bottom-left grid is thus a grid of size $2^n \times 2^n$ of which one square has been covered. By the induction hypothesis, the remaining squares in the bottom-left grid can be covered

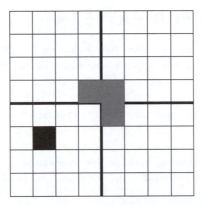

○ **Figure 6.8:** Triomino problem: inductive step. The grid is divided into four sub-grids. The covered square, shown in black, identifies one sub-grid. A triomino, shown in grey, is placed at the junction of the other three grids. The induction hypothesis is then used to cover all four sub-grids with triominoes.

with triominoes. This leaves us with the task of covering the bottom-right, top-left and top-right grids with triominoes.

None of the squares in these three grids is covered, as yet. We can apply the induction hypothesis to them if just one square in each of the three is covered. This is done by placing a triomino at the junction of the three grids, as shown in Figure 6.8.

Now, the inductive hypothesis is applied to cover the remaining squares of the bottom-right, top-left and top-right grids with triominoes. On completion of this process, the entire $2^{n+1} \times 2^{n+1}$ grid has been covered with triominoes.

Exercise 6.2   Test your understanding of the solution to the triomino problem by solving the following problem. The solution is very similar.

An equilateral triangle as illustrated in Figure 6.4 has a side of length 2^n for some n. The topmost triangle (of size 1) is covered. Show that it is possible to cover the remaining triangles with (non-overlapping) buckets like the one shown on the right in Figure 6.2.

Exercise 6.3   Solve the trapezium problem given in Section 6.1. Hint: exploit the assumption that the size of the triangle is divisible by 3. You will need to consider the case $n = 1$ as the basis of the induction.

6.4 LOOKING FOR PATTERNS

In Sections 6.2 and 6.3, we have seen how induction is used to solve problems of a given "size". Technically, the process we described is called "mathematical induction"; "induction", as it is normally understood, is more general.

"Induction", as used in, for example, the experimental sciences, refers to a process of reasoning whereby general laws are inferred from a collection of observations. A famous example of induction is the process that led Charles Darwin to formulate his theory of evolution by natural selection, based on his observations of plant and animal life in remote parts of the world. In simple terms, induction is about *looking for patterns*.

Laws formulated by a process of induction go beyond the knowledge on which they are based, thus introducing inherently new knowledge. In the experimental sciences, however, such laws are only *probably* true; they are tested by the predictions they make, and may have to be discarded if the predictions turn out to be false. In contrast, *deduction* is the process of inferring laws from existing laws, whereby the deductions made are guaranteed to be true provided that the laws on which they are based are true. In a sense, laws deduced from existing laws add nothing to our stock of knowledge since they are, at best, simply reformulations of existing knowledge.

Mathematical induction is a combination of induction and deduction. It is a process of looking for patterns in a set of observations, formulating the patterns as *conjectures*, and then testing whether the conjectures can be *deduced* from existing knowledge. Guess-and-verify is a brief way of summarising mathematical induction. (Guessing is the formulation of a conjecture; verification is the process of deducing whether the guess is correct.)

Several of the matchstick games studied in Chapter 4 provide good examples of mathematical induction. Recall, for example, the game discussed in Section 4.2.2: there is one pile of matches from which it is allowed to remove one or two matches. Exploring this game, we discovered that a pile with 0, 3 or 6 matches is a losing position, and piles with 1, 2, 4, 5, 7 and 8 matches are winning positions. There seems to be a pattern in these numbers: losing positions are the positions in which the number of matches are a multiple of 3, and winning positions are the remaining positions. This is a conjecture about *all* positions made from observations on just nine positions. However, we can verify that the conjecture is true by using mathematical induction to construct a winning strategy.

In order to use induction, we measure the "size" of a pile of matches not by the number of matches but by the number of matches divided by 3, rounded down to the nearest natural number. So, the "size" of a pile of 0, 1 or 2 matches is 0, the "size" of a pile of 3, 4 or 5 matches is 1, and so on. The induction hypothesis is that a pile of $3n$ matches is a losing position, and a pile of $3n+1$ or $3n+2$ matches is a winning position.

The basis for the induction is when n equals 0. A pile of 0 matches is, indeed, a losing position because, by definition, the game is lost when it is no longer possible to move. A pile of 1 or 2 matches is a winning position because the player can remove the matches, leaving the opponent in a losing position.

Now, for the induction step, we assume that a pile of 3n matches is a losing position, and a pile of $3n+1$ or $3n+2$ matches is a winning position. We have to show that a pile of $3(n+1)$ matches is a losing position, and a pile of $3(n+1)+1$ or $3(n+1)+2$ matches is a winning position.

Suppose there are $3(n+1)$ matches. The player, whose turn it is, must remove 1 or 2 matches, leaving either $3(n+1)-1$ or $3(n+1)-2$ behind. That is, the opponent is left with either $3n+2$ or $3n+1$ matches. But, by the induction hypothesis, this leaves the opponent in a winning position. Hence, the position in which there are $3(n+1)$ matches is a losing position.

Now, suppose there are $3(n+1)+1$ or $3(n+1)+2$ matches. By taking 1 match in the first case, and 2 matches in the second case, the player leaves the opponent in a position where there are $3(n+1)$ matches. This we now know to be a losing position. Hence, the positions in which there are $3(n+1)+1$ or $3(n+1)+2$ are both winning positions.

This completes the inductive construction of the winning moves, and thus verifies the conjecture that a position is a losing position exactly when the number of matches is a multiple of 3.

6.5 THE NEED FOR PROOF

When using induction, it is vital that any conjecture is properly verified. It is too easy to extrapolate from a few cases to a more general claim that is *not* true. Many conjectures turn out to be false; only by subjecting them to the rigours of proof can we be sure of their validity. This section is about a non-trivial example of a false conjecture.

Suppose n points are marked on the circumference of a circular cake and then the cake is cut along the chords joining them. The points are chosen in such a way that all intersection points of pairs of chords are distinct. The question is, in how many portions does this cut the cake?

Figure 6.9 shows the case when n is 1, 2, 3 or 4. The number of portions is successively 1, 2, 4 and 8. This suggests that the number of portions, for arbitrary n, is 2^{n-1}. Indeed, this conjecture is supported by the case that $n=5$. (We leave the reader to draw the figure.) In this case, the number of portions is 16, which is 2^{5-1}. However, for $n=6$, the number of portions is 31! (See Figure 6.10.) Note that $n=6$ is the first case in which the points are not allowed to be placed at equal distances around the perimeter.

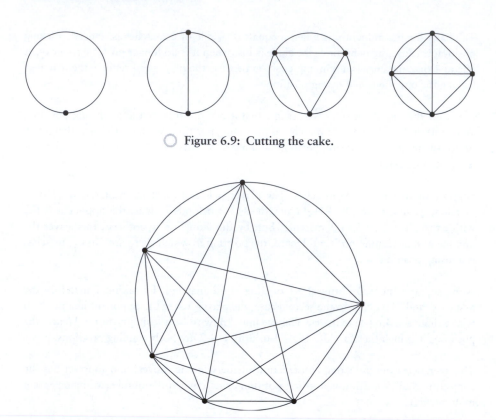

Figure 6.9: Cutting the cake.

Figure 6.10: Cutting the cake: the case $n = 6$. The number of portions is 31, not 2^{6-1}.

Had we begun by considering the case where $n = 0$, suspicions about the conjecture would already have been raised – it does not make sense to say that there are 2^{0-1} portions, even though cutting the cake as stated does make sense! The easy, but inadequate, way out is to dismiss this case, and impose the requirement that n is different from 0. The derivation of the correct formula for the number of portions is too complicated to discuss here, but it does include the case where n equals 0!

6.6 FROM VERIFICATION TO CONSTRUCTION

In mathematical texts, induction is often used to *verify* known formulae. Verification is important but has a major drawback – it seems that a substantial amount of clairvoyance is needed to come up with the formula that is to be verified. And, if one's conjecture is wrong, verification gives little help in determining the correct formula.

Induction is sometimes used in computing science as a verification principle, but it is most important as a fundamental principle in the *construction* of computer programs. This section introduces the use of induction in the *construction* of mathematical formulae.

The problem we consider is how to determine a closed formula for the sum of the kth powers of the first n natural numbers.

A well-known formula gives the sum of the natural numbers from 1 thru n :

$$1 + 2 + \ldots + n = \frac{1}{2}n(n+1).$$

Two other exercises, often given in mathematical texts, are to verify that

$$1^2 + 2^2 + \ldots + n^2 = \frac{1}{6}n(n+1)(2n+1)$$

and

$$1^3 + 2^3 + \ldots + n^3 = \frac{1}{4}n^2(n+1)^2.$$

As well as being good examples of the strength of the principle of mathematical induction, the examples also illustrate the weakness of verification: the technique works if the answer is known, but what happens if the answer is not already known! Suppose, for example, that you are now asked to determine a closed formula for the sum of the 4th powers of the first n numbers,

$$1^4 + 2^4 + \ldots + n^4 = ?.$$

How would you proceed? Verification, using the principle of mathematical induction, does not seem to be applicable unless we already know the right-hand side of the equation. Can you guess what the right side would be in this case? Can you guess what the right side would be if the power, 4, is replaced by, say, 27? Almost certainly not!

Constructing solutions to non-trivial problems involves a creative process. This means that a certain amount of guesswork is necessary, and trial and error cannot be completely eliminated. Reducing the guesswork to a minimum, replacing it by mathematical calculation is the key to success.

Induction can be used to construct closed formulae for such summations. The general idea is to seek a pattern, formulate the pattern in precise mathematical terms and then verify the pattern. The key to success is simplicity. Do not be over-ambitious. Leave the work to mathematical calculation.

A simple pattern in the formulae displayed above is that, for m equal to 1, 2 and 3, the sum of the mth powers of the first n numbers is a polynomial in n of degree m+1. (The sum of the first n numbers is a quadratic function of n, the sum of the first n squares is a cubic function of n, and the sum of the first n cubes is a quartic function of n.) This pattern is also confirmed in the (oft-forgotten) case that m is 0:

$$1^0 + 2^0 + \ldots + n^0 \;=\; n.$$

A strategy for determining a closed formula for, say, the sum of the fourth powers is thus to guess that it is a fifth-degree polynomial in n and then *use induction to calculate the coefficients*. The calculation in this case is quite long, so let us illustrate the process by showing how to construct a closed formula for $1+2+\ldots+n$. (Some readers will already know a simpler way of deriving the formula in this particular case. If this is the case, then bear with us. The method described here is more general.)

We conjecture that the required formula is a second-degree polynomial in n, say $a+bn+cn^2$ and then calculate the coefficients a, b and c. Here is how the calculation goes.

For brevity, let us use S(n) to denote

$$1+2+\ldots+n.$$

We also use P(n) to denote the proposition

$$S(n) \;=\; a+bn+cn^2.$$

Then,

$$\begin{array}{ll}
& P(0) \\[4pt]
= & \qquad \{ \qquad \text{definition of P} \quad \} \\[4pt]
& S(0) \;=\; a+b{\times}0+c{\times}0^2 \\[4pt]
= & \qquad \{ \qquad S(0)=0 \text{ (the sum of an empty set of numbers} \\
& \qquad\qquad\qquad\quad \text{is zero) and arithmetic} \quad \} \\[4pt]
& 0 = a.
\end{array}$$

So the basis of the induction has allowed us to deduce that a, the coefficient of n^0, is 0. Now, we calculate b and c. To do so, we make the induction hypothesis that $0 \le n$ and P(n) is true. Then

$$\begin{array}{ll}
& P(n+1) \\[4pt]
= & \qquad \{ \qquad \text{definition of P, } a = 0 \quad \}
\end{array}$$

$$S(n{+}1) \;=\; b(n{+}1) + c(n{+}1)^2$$

$=$ {   heading for use of the induction hypothesis,

$$S(n{+}1) \;=\; S(n){+}n{+}1 \quad \}$$

$$S(n) + n + 1 \;=\; b(n{+}1) + c(n{+}1)^2$$

$=$ {   assumption: P(n). Also, a = 0.

That is, $S(n) \;=\; bn + cn^2$ }

$$bn + cn^2 + n + 1 \;=\; b(n{+}1) + c(n{+}1)^2$$

$=$ {   arithmetic   }

$$cn^2 + (b{+}1)n + 1 \;=\; cn^2 + (b{+}2c)n + b + c$$

$\Leftarrow$ {   comparing coefficients of powers of n   }

$$c = c \;\wedge\; b{+}1 = b{+}2c \;\wedge\; 1 = b{+}c$$

$=$ {   arithmetic   }

$$\tfrac{1}{2} = c \wedge \tfrac{1}{2} = b.$$

From the conjecture that the sum of the first n numbers is a quadratic in n, we have thus calculated that

$$1 + 2 + \ldots + n \;=\; \frac{1}{2}n + \frac{1}{2}n^2.$$

Extrapolating from this calculation, one can see that it embodies an algorithm to express $1^m + 2^m + \ldots + n^m$ as a polynomial function for any given natural number m. The steps in the algorithm are: postulate that the summation is a polynomial in n with degree m+1. Use the principle of mathematical induction together with the facts that S(0) is 0 and S(n+1) is $S(n)+(n+1)^m$ (where S(n) denotes $1^m + 2^m + \ldots + n^m$) to determine a system of simultaneous equations in the coefficients. Finally, solve the system of equations.

It is worth remarking here that, in the case of the sum $1 + 2 + \ldots + n$, there is an easier way to derive the correct formula. Simply write down the required sum

$$1 \quad + \quad 2 \quad + \quad \ldots \quad + \quad n,$$

and immediately below it

$$n \quad + \quad n{-}1 \quad + \quad \ldots \quad + \quad 1.$$

Then add the two rows together:

$$n{+}1 \quad + \quad n{+}1 \quad + \quad \ldots \quad + \quad n{+}1.$$

From the fact that there are n occurrences of n+1 we conclude that the sum is $\frac{1}{2}n(n+1)$. However, this method cannot be used for determining $1^m + 2^m + \ldots + n^m$ for m greater than 1.

Exercise 6.4   Use the technique just demonstrated to construct closed formulae for

$$1^0 + 2^0 + \ldots + n^0 \quad \text{and} \quad 1^2 + 2^2 + \ldots + n^2.$$

Exercise 6.5   Consider a matchstick game with one pile of matches from which m thru n matches can be removed. By considering a few simple examples (for example, m is 1 and n is arbitrary, or m is 2 and n is 3), formulate a general rule for determining which are the winning positions and which are the losing positions, and what the winning strategy is.

Avoid guessing the complete solution. Try to identify a simple pattern in the way winning and losing positions are grouped. Introduce variables to represent the grouping, and calculate the values of the variables.

6.7 SUMMARY

Induction is one of the most important problem-solving principles. The principle of mathematical induction is that instances of a problem of arbitrary "size" can be solved for all "sizes" if

(a) instances of "size" 0 can be solved,

(b) given a method of solving instances of "size" n, for arbitrary n, it is possible to adapt the method to solve instances of "size" n+1.

Using induction means looking for patterns. The process may involve some creative guesswork, which is then subjected to the rigours of mathematical deduction. The key to success is to reduce the guesswork to a minimum, by striving for simplicity, and using mathematical calculation to fill in complicated details.

6.8 BIBLIOGRAPHIC REMARKS

All the problems in this chapter are very well known. I have not attempted to trace their origin. The trapezium problems were suggested by an anonymous reviewer.

The triomino and trapezium problems are instances of so-called *tiling problems*. Generally the form that such problems take is to determine whether or not it is possible to cover a given area using tiles of a given shape. Some tiling problems have an *ad hoc* solution: the problem cannot be generalised to a class of problems. When a generalisation is possible, and the problem is solvable, we seek an algorithm to perform the tiling. Tiling problems can be very hard to solve and finding the right generalisation can often be critical to success.

Chapter 7

Fake-Coin Detection

This chapter is the first of two considering more demanding applications of induction. The motto of Section 6.6 can be summarised as "Do not guess! Calculate." We put this into practice in this chapter.

Suppose we are given a number of coins, each of the same size and shape. We are told that among them there is at most one "fake" coin, and all the rest are "genuine". All "genuine" coins have the same weight, whereas a "fake" coin has a different weight than a "genuine" coin.

The problem is how to use a pair of scales optimally in order to find the fake coin, if there is one.

Note the element of vagueness in this problem statement; we do not say what we mean by using the scales "optimally". This is deliberate. Often, an essential element of problem solving is to clearly identify the problem itself. Our formulation of the problem and its eventual solution illustrates several other aspects of "real" problem solving. Several stages are needed, including some "backtracking" and revision.

7.1 PROBLEM FORMULATION

When we use a pair of scales to compare two weights – an operation that we call a *comparison* – there are 3 possible outcomes: the scales may tip to the left, they may balance, or they may tip to the right. This means that with n comparisons, there are at most 3^n different outcomes. This gives an upper bound on what can be achieved using a pair of scales.

Now, suppose we are given m coins, of which at most one is fake and the rest are genuine. Then there are $1+2m$ different possibilities that can be observed with a pair of scales: "1" possibility is that all coins are genuine; otherwise, there are "2" ways that one of the "m" coins is fake (by being lighter or heavier than a genuine coin). This means that, with n comparisons, the number of coins among which at most one fake coin can be detected is at most m, where $1+2m=3^n$. More precisely, if the number, m, of coins is greater than $(3^n-1)/2$, it is impossible to guarantee that a fake coin can be found with n comparisons.

 The counting arguments given here are applications of the set theory in Sections 12.4.1 and 12.4.2. Formally, the outcome is a function from comparisons to the three-element set {left, balance, right}, that is, a function of type

> comparison → {left, balance, right}.

The possible observations are a disjoint union of the singleton set {allGenuine} and the cartesian product of {left, right} and the set coin of coins. That is the set of possible observations is

> {allGenuine} + {left, right}×coin.

(The names we have introduced are hopefully self-explanatory.) Sections 12.4.1 and 12.4.2 explain the rules for counting elements of such sets.

We have almost reached the point at which we can state our problem precisely. We conjecture that, given $(3^n-1)/2$ coins of which at most one is fake, it is possible to establish that all are genuine or identify the fake coin (and whether it is lighter or heavier than a genuine coin) using at most n comparisons.

For n equal to 0, the conjecture is clearly true; in this case, there are no coins, all of which are genuine. For n equal to 1, however, we run into a problem. The assumption is that there is one coin (since $(3^1-1)/2=1$). But how can we tell whether this one coin is fake or genuine, if there are no other coins to compare it with? Our conjecture has broken down and needs revision.

We propose to modify the conjecture by assuming that we have at our disposal at least one *additional* coin that is known to be genuine. Thus, we are given $(3^n-1)/2$ coins about which we know nothing except that at most one is fake, and we are also given at least one coin that is known to be genuine. The problem is to construct an algorithm that will identify the fake coin, if it exists, or determine that all coins are genuine, using at most n comparisons.

7.2 PROBLEM SOLUTION

Our formulation of the problem begs the use of induction on the number of comparisons, n, in its solution.

7.2.1 The Basis

With zero comparisons, we can report immediately that all coins in a collection of $(3^0-1)/2$ are genuine. The base case, n equal to 0, is thus solved.

7.2.2 Induction Step

Now we tackle the induction step. Suppose n is at least zero. For brevity, let us use $c(n)$ to denote $(3^n-1)/2$. By induction, we may assume that a fake coin, if it exists, can be found among $c(n)$ coins using at most n comparisons. We have to show how to find a fake coin, if it exists, among $c(n+1)$ coins, using at most n+1 comparisons.

Consider the first comparison. It involves putting some number of coins on the left scale, some on the right scale, and leaving some on the table. To be able to draw any conclusion from the comparison, the number of coins on the two scales must be equal. One possible consequence of the comparison is that the scales balance, from which one infers that none of the coins on the scales is fake. The algorithm would then proceed to try to find a fake coin among the coins left on the table.

Combined with the induction hypothesis, this dictates that $c(n)$ coins must be left on the table. This is because $c(n)$ is the maximum number of coins among which a fake coin can be found with n comparisons.

It also dictates how many coins should be put on the scales – this is the difference between $c(n+1)$ and $c(n)$. Now,

$$c(n+1) \;=\; (3^{n+1}-1)/2 \;=\; 3 \times ((3^n-1)/2)+1 \;=\; 3 \times c(n)+1.$$

So

$$c(n+1)-c(n) \;=\; 2 \times c(n)+1 \;=\; 3^n.$$

This is an odd number; it can be made even by using one of the coins we know to be genuine. (Recall the assumption that we have at least one coin that is known to be genuine, in addition to the $c(n+1)$ coins whose kind we must determine.) We conclude that in the first comparison, $c(n)+1$ coins should be put on each of the two scales.

The next step is to determine what to do after the first comparison is made. There are three possible outcomes, of which we have already discussed one. If the scales balance, the fake coin should be sought among the $c(n)$ coins left on the table. The problem is what to do if the scales tip either to the left or to the right.

At this point, we realise that the induction hypothesis does not help. It is too weak! If the scales tip to one side, we can conclude that all the coins left on the table are genuine, and can be eliminated from consideration. But we are still left with 3^n coins, none of which we know to be genuine. And crucially, 3^n is greater than $c(n)$. We are unable to apply the induction hypothesis to this number of coins.

The comparison does tell us something about the coins on the scales. If the scales tip to one side, we know that all the coins on that side are *possibly heavier* than a genuine coin, and all the coins on the other side are *possibly lighter* than a genuine coin. By "possibly lighter" we mean genuine, or fake and lighter. By "possibly heavier" we mean genuine, or fake and heavier. After the comparison, we can mark all the coins on the scales one way or the other.

7.2.3 The Marked-Coin Problem

In this way, in the case where the scales do not balance, the problem we started with has been reduced to a different problem. The new problem is this. Suppose a number of coins are supplied, each of which is marked either "possibly light" or "possibly heavy". The coins marked "possibly light" have weights at most the weight of a genuine coin and the coins marked "possibly heavy" have weights at least the weight of a genuine coin. Exactly one of the coins is fake, and all the rest are genuine. Construct an algorithm that will determine, with at most n comparisons, the fake coin among 3^n marked coins.

Again, the base case is easy. If n equals 0, there is one coin, which must be the fake coin. That is, 0 (i.e. n) comparisons are needed to determine this fact.

For the induction step, we proceed as for the earlier problem. Suppose we are supplied with 3^{n+1} marked coins. In the first comparison, some coins are put on the left scale, some on the right, and some are left on the table. In order to apply the induction hypothesis in the case where the scales balance, the coins must be divided equally: 3^n coins must be left on the table, and thus 3^n put on the left scale and 3^n on the right scale.

The coins are marked in two different ways. So, we need to determine how to place the coins according to their markings. We calculate the numbers as follows.

Suppose $l1$ possibly light coins are placed on the left scale and $l2$ possibly light coins on the right scale. Similarly, suppose $h1$ possibly heavy coins are placed on the left scale and $h2$ possibly heavy coins on the right scale.

To draw any conclusion from the comparison, we require that the number of coins on the left scale equals the number on the right. That is, $l1+h1$ and $l2+h2$ should be equal. Furthermore, as already determined, they should equal 3^n.

Now, if the comparison causes the scales to tip to the left, we conclude that all coins on the left scale are possibly heavy, and all the coins on the right scale are possibly light. Combining this with the markings, we conclude that the $l1$ possibly light coins on the left scale and the $h2$ possibly heavy coins on the right scale are in fact genuine (since possibly heavy and possibly light equals genuine); this leaves $h1+l2$ coins to be investigated further. Conversely, if the scale tips to the right, the $h1$ possibly heavy coins on the left scale and the $l2$ possibly heavy coins on the right scale are genuine, leaving $l1+h2$ coins to be investigated further.

Again, in order to apply the induction hypothesis, we require that the number of coins not eliminated be equal to 3^n, whatever the outcome of the comparison. This imposes the requirement that $h1+l2 = l1+h2 = 3^n$. Together with $l1+h1 = l2+h2$, we infer that $l1 = l2$ and $h1 = h2$. We must arrange the coins so that each scale contains equal numbers of coins of the same kind.

This requirement can be met. Simply place the coins on the scales two at a time, one on the left and one on the right, until each scale has its full complement of 3^n coins, always choosing two coins with the same marking. The choice can always be made because there are always at least three coins from which to choose; by choosing any three coins, at least two of them will have the same marking.

7.2.4 The Complete Solution

This completes the solution to the marked-coin problem, and thus to the unmarked-coin problem. Figure 7.1 summarises the algorithm diagrammatically in the case where there are $(3^3-1)/2$ coins. The remainder of this section summarises the algorithm in words.

The fake coin is identified from a collection of 3^{n+1} *marked* coins by placing 3^n coins on each scale, in such a way that there is an equal number of possibly light coins on each of the scale. According to the outcome of the comparison, one of the following is executed.

- If the scales balance, all the coins on the scales are genuine. Proceed with the coins left on the table.

- If the scales tip to the left, the coins on the table are genuine. So too are the possibly light coins on the left scale and the possibly heavy coins on the right scale. Proceed with the possibly heavy coins on the left scale and the possibly light coins on the right scale.

- If the scales tip to the right, the coins on the table are genuine. So too are the possibly light coins on the right scale and the possibly heavy coins on the left scale. Proceed with the possibly heavy coins on the right scale and the possibly light coins on the left scale.

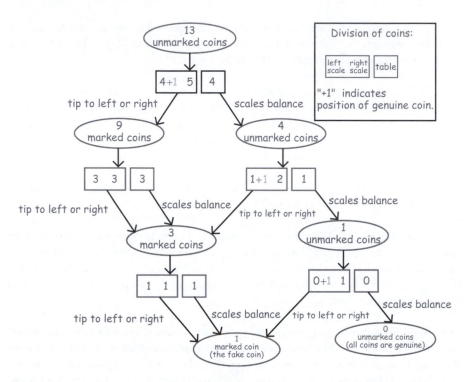

Figure 7.1: Solving the fake-coin problem for $(3^3-1)/2$ coins with 3 comparisons.

The solution to the unmarked-coin problem when the number of coins is $(3^{n+1}-1)/2$ is as follows.

Divide the coins into three groups of sizes $(3^n-1)/2$, $(3^n-1)/2+1$ and $(3^n-1)/2$. Place the first group on the left scale together with the supplied genuine coin. Place the second group on the right scale, and leave the third group on the table. Determine the outcome of the comparison, and proceed as follows:

- If the scales balance, all the coins on the balance are genuine. Apply the solution to the unmarked-coin problem (inductively) to the coins on the table.

- If the scales tip to the left, the coins on the table are genuine. Mark all the coins on the left scale, with the exception of the supplied genuine coin, as "possibly heavy". Mark the coins on the right scale as "possibly light". Apply the solution to the marked-coin problem to the 3^n marked coins.

- If the scales tip to the right, the coins on the table are genuine. Mark all the coins on the left scale, with the exception of the supplied genuine coin, as "possibly light". Mark the coins on the right scale as "possibly heavy". Apply the solution to the marked-coin problem to the 3^n marked coins.

We ask the reader to review the development of this algorithm. Note that at no stage is a *guess* made at an inductive hypothesis, even though the development necessitates several such hypotheses. Quite the opposite: each hypothesis is systematically *calculated* from the available information. This is the epitome of the art of effective reasoning.

Exercise 7.1   The solution to the fake-coin problem assumes that the number of coins is exactly $(3^n-1)/2$ for some n. Parts (a) and (b) of this question are about generalising the solution to an arbitrary number of coins. Part (c) is about eliminating the assumption that a genuine coin is supplied.

> *Solving this exercise requires some reasoning with "inequalities". Refer to Section 15.1 for the calculational rules for doing so.*

(a) Suppose m coins are given of which at most one is fake. Suppose also that one genuine coin is supplied. Construct an algorithm to determine which (if any) is the fake coin and how it differs from a genuine coin (i.e. lighter or heavier) using at most n comparisons, where n is the smallest number such that m is at most $(3^n-1)/2$. Your algorithm will make use of the solution to part (b) of this question.

Use the following induction hypothesis. Given
- one genuine coin,
- a number n,
- m coins, where $0 \leq m \leq (3^n-1)/2$ and at most one of the coins is fake,

it is possible to determine which (if any) is the fake coin using at most n comparisons.

(b) Suppose m coins are given of which exactly one is fake. The coins are all marked either "possibly heavy" or "possibly light". "Possibly heavy" means that the coin is either fake and heavier than a genuine coin or genuine. "Possibly light" means that the coin is either fake and lighter than a genuine coin or genuine. Suppose also that one genuine coin is supplied. Construct an algorithm to determine which is the fake coin and how it differs from the genuine coin (i.e. lighter or heavier) using at most n comparisons, where n is the smallest number such that m is at most 3^n.

Use the following induction hypothesis. Given
- one genuine coin,
- a number n,

- m marked ("possibly heavy" or "possibly light") coins, where $1 \leq m \leq 3^n$ of which exactly one is fake,

it is possible to determine which is the fake coin and how it differs from the genuine coin (i.e. lighter or heavier) using at most n comparisons. Construct your algorithm using induction on n.

(c) If at least three coins are given of which at most one is fake, then one comparison suffices to identify a genuine coin. (One way to do this is to place one coin on each of the scales. If the scales balance, both coins on the balance are genuine; if the scales tip to one side, the unused coins are genuine.) This suggests that it may be possible to eliminate the assumption that a genuine coin has been supplied. Show that this is indeed the case *without the expense of an additional comparison* except in the case where the number of coins equals $(3^n-1)/2$ for some n.

Use the following induction hypothesis. Given
- a number n, where $2 \leq n$,
- m coins, where $3 \leq m < (3^n-1)/2$ of which at most one is fake,

it is possible to determine which (if any) is the fake coin and how it differs from a genuine coin (i.e. lighter or heavier) using at most n comparisons. Construct your algorithm using induction on n. The base case is when n equals 2.

Apply your solution to part (c) to the case where the number of coins is 12. That is, suppose 12 coins are given of which at most one is fake. Show how to determine which, if any, is the fake coin and how it differs from a genuine coin using at most 3 comparisons.

Exercise 7.2 Suppose you are given a number of objects. All the objects have the same weight, with the exception of one, called the *unique* object, which has a different weight. In all other respects, the objects are identical. You are required to determine which is the unique object. For this purpose, you are provided with a pair of scales.

Show, by induction on m, that at most $2 \times m$ comparisons are needed to identify the unique object when the total number of objects is 3^m. (Hint: for the induction step, 3^{m+1} objects can be split into three groups of 3^m objects.)

Can you identify whether the unique object is lighter or heavier than all the other objects?

Exercise 7.3 Given are n objects, where $1 \leq n$, each of different weight. A pair of scales is provided so that it is possible to determine, for any two of the objects, which is the lighter and which is the heavier.

(a) How many comparisons are needed to find the lightest object?

(b) Show, by induction on n, that it is possible to determine which is the lightest and which is the heaviest object using $2n - 3$ comparisons. Assume that $2 \leq n$.

(c) Suppose there are four objects with weights A, B, C and D, and suppose $A < B$ and $C < D$. Show how to find the lightest and heaviest of all four with two additional comparisons. Use this to show how to find the lightest and heaviest of four objects using 4 comparisons (and not 5, as in your solution to part (b)).

(d) Suppose there are 2m objects, where $1 \leq m$. Show, by induction on m, that it is possible to find the lightest and heaviest objects using $3m - 2$ comparisons. (Hint: make use of (c).)

Exercise 7.4 Suppose you have a balance. You are allowed to choose the weights to use with the balance. The objective is to choose the weights in such a way that you maximise the number of weights that you can check. For example, if you have a 1 gram weight and a 2 gram weight, it is possible to weigh items of 1, 2 or 3 grams. However, if you have a 1 gram weight and a 3 gram weight, it is possible to weigh items of 1, 2 or 3 grams and also items of 4 grams. (Items of weight 2 grams are weighed by putting the item on one side of the balance together with the 1 gram weight; the 3 gram weight is placed on the other side of the balance. If the two sides balance, the item does indeed have weight 2 grams.)

For clarity, let us call the weights that are chosen "widgets" and the items to be weighed "fudgets".

(a) Given n widgets all of which are different, how many different ways are there of arranging them on the scales of a balance? (Hint: how many different ways are there of placing each widget?) Assume that the two sides of the balance are indistinguishable. (So, for example, placing a widget of weight 1 on one side and a widget of weight 2 on the opposite side is only counted once.) What conclusion can you make about the maximum range of weights that can be measured?

(b) Show by induction that it is possible to check all weights in the range given in your solution to part (a) by using widgets of weights $3^0, 3^1, 3^2, \ldots, 3^n$, one of each weight. State your induction hypothesis clearly. (Note that it should have as parameter the side s on which the fudget is placed.)

7.3 SUMMARY

The solution to the fake-coin problem combines several elements of algorithmic problem solving. The first step is a non-trivial abstraction in order to identify a suitable induction hypothesis. Subsequently the problem is decomposed, leading to a new problem, the marked-coin problem. The marked-coin problem has a stronger precondition, given by the markings on the coins, which makes it more straightforward to solve, also by induction. The algorithm that is obtained is surprisingly efficient.

7.4 BIBLIOGRAPHIC REMARKS

The solution to the fake-coin problem is a combination of two papers by E.W. Dijkstra [Dij90, Dij97]. The case of finding a fake coin among 12 coins with 3 comparisons (see Exercise 7.1) appears widely. Exercise 7.4 is a disguised version of a number system called *balanced ternary notation*: a base 3 system in which the digits – called *trits* – are −1, 0 and +1. See [Knu69] for more details.

Chapter

The Tower of Hanoi

8

The topic of this chapter is a problem that is discussed in many books on recreational mathematics and often used in computing science and artificial intelligence as an illustration of "recursion" as a problem-solving strategy.

The Tower of Hanoi problem is quite difficult to solve without a systematic problem-solving strategy. Induction gives a systematic way of constructing a first solution. However, this solution is undesirable. A better solution is obtained by observing an invariant of the inductive solution. In this way, this chapter brings together a number of the techniques discussed earlier: principally induction and invariants, but also the properties of logical equivalence.

For this problem, we begin with the solution of the problem. One reason for doing so is to make clear where we are headed; the Tower of Hanoi problem is one that is not solved in one go – several steps are needed before a satisfactory solution is found. Another reason is to illustrate how difficult it can be to understand *why* a correct solution has been found if no information about the solution method is provided.

8.1 SPECIFICATION AND SOLUTION

8.1.1 The End of the World!

The Tower of Hanoi problem comes from a puzzle marketed in 1883 by the French mathematician Édouard Lucas, under the pseudonym M. Claus.

The puzzle is based on a legend according to which there is a temple in Brahma where there are three giant poles fixed in the ground. On the first of these poles, at the time of the world's creation, God placed 64 golden discs, each of different size, in decreasing order of size (see Figure 8.1). The monks were given the task of moving the discs, one per day, from one pole to another according to the rule that no disc may ever be above a smaller disc.

The monks' task would be complete when they succeeded in moving all the discs from the first of the poles to the second and, on the day that they completed their task, the world would come to an end!

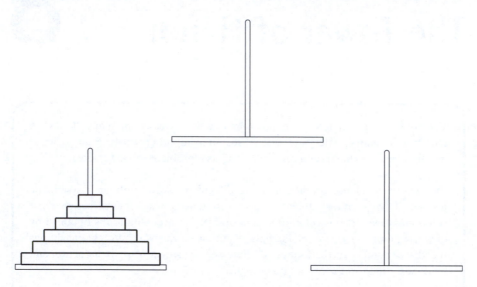

○ **Figure 8.1: Tower of Hanoi problem.**

8.1.2 Iterative Solution

There is a very easy solution to the Tower of Hanoi problem that is easy to remember and easy to execute. To formulate the solution, we assume that the poles are arranged at the three corners of a triangle. Movements of the discs can then be succinctly described as either clockwise or anticlockwise movements. We assume that the problem is to move all the discs from one pole to the next in a clockwise direction. We also assume that days are numbered from 0 onwards. On day 0, the discs are placed in their initial position and the monks begin moving the discs on day 1. With these assumptions, the solution is the following.

On every alternate day, beginning on the first day, the smallest disc is moved. The rule for moving the smallest disc is that it should *cycle* around the poles. The direction of rotation depends on the total number of discs. If the total number of discs is odd, the smallest disc should cycle in a clockwise direction. Otherwise, it should cycle in an anticlockwise direction.

On every other day, a disc other than the smallest disc is moved – subject to the rule that no disc may ever be above a smaller disc. It is easy to see that because of this rule there is exactly one move possible so long as not all the discs are on one pole.

The algorithm terminates when no further moves are possible, that is, on an even-numbered day when all the discs are on one and the same pole.

Try executing this algorithm yourself on, say, a 4-disc puzzle. Take care to cycle the smallest disc on the odd-numbered moves and to obey the rule not to place a disc on top of a disc smaller than itself on the even-numbered moves. If you do, you will find that the algorithm works. Depending on how much patience you have, you can execute the algorithm on larger and larger problems – 5-disc, 6-disc, and so on.

8.1.3 Why?

Presenting the problem *and* its solution, like this, provides no help whatsoever in understanding how the solution is constructed. If anything, it only serves to impress – look at how clever I am! – but in a reprehensible way. Matters would be made even worse if we now proceeded to give a formal mathematical verification of the correctness of the algorithm. This is not how we intend to proceed! Instead, we first present an inductive solution of the problem. Then, by observing a number of invariants, we show how to derive the algorithm above from the inductive solution.

8.2 INDUCTIVE SOLUTION

Constructing a solution by induction on the number of discs is an obvious strategy.

Let us begin with an attempt at a simple-minded inductive solution. Suppose that the task is to move M discs from one specific pole to another specific pole. Let us call these poles A and B, and the third pole C. (Later, we see that naming the poles is inadvisable.)

As often happens, the basis is easy. When the number of discs is 0 no steps are needed to complete the task. For the inductive step, we assume that we can move n discs from A to B, and the problem is to show how to move n+1 discs from A to B.

Here, we soon get stuck! There are only a couple of ways that the induction hypothesis can be used, but these lead nowhere:

1. Move the top n discs from A to B. After doing this, we have exhausted all possibilities of using the induction hypothesis because n discs are now on pole B, and we have no hypothesis about moving discs from this pole.

2. Move the smallest disc from A to C. Then move the remaining n discs from A to B. Once again, we have exhausted all possibilities of using the induction hypothesis, because n discs are now on pole B, and we have no hypothesis about moving discs from this pole.

The mistake we have made is to be too specific about the induction hypothesis. The way out is to generalise by introducing one or more parameters to model the start and finish positions of the discs.

At this point, we make a crucial decision. Rather than name the poles (A, B and C, say), we observe that the problem exhibits a *rotational* symmetry. The rotational symmetry is obvious when the poles are placed at the corners of an equilateral triangle, as we did in Figure 8.1. (This rotational symmetry is obscured by placing the poles in a line, as is often done.) The problem does not change when we rotate the poles and discs about the centre of the triangle.

The importance of this observation is that only *one* additional parameter needs to be introduced, namely, the direction of movement. That is, in order to specify how a particular disc is to be moved, we need only say whether it is to be moved clockwise or anticlockwise from its current position. Also, the generalisation of the Tower of Hanoi problem becomes how to move n discs from one pole to the next in the direction d, where d is either clockwise or anticlockwise. The alternative of naming the poles leads to the introduction of two additional parameters, the start and finish positions of the discs. This is much more complicated since it involves unnecessary additional detail.

Now, we can return to the inductive solution again. We need to take care in formulating the induction hypothesis. It is not sufficient to simply take the problem specification as induction hypothesis. This is because the problem specification assumes that there are exactly M discs that are to be moved. When using induction, it is necessary to move n discs in the presence of M−n other discs. If some of these M−n discs are smaller than the n discs being moved, the requirement that a larger disc may not be placed on top of a smaller disc may be violated. We need a stronger induction hypothesis.

In the case where n is 0, the sequence of moves is the empty sequence. In the case of n+1 discs we assume that we have a method of moving the n smallest discs from one pole to either of its two neighbours. We must show how to move n+1 discs from one pole to its neighbour in direction d, where d is either clockwise or anticlockwise. For convenience, we assume that the discs are numbered from 1 upwards, with the smallest disc being given number 1.

Given the goal of exploiting the induction hypothesis, there is little choice of what to do. We can begin by moving the n smallest discs in the direction d, or in the direction ¬d. Any other initial choice of move would preclude the use of the induction hypothesis. Some further thought (preferably assisted by a physical model of the problem) reveals that the solution is to move the n smallest discs in the direction ¬d. Then disc n+1 can be moved in the direction d. (This action may place disc n+1 on top of another disc. However, the move is valid because the n discs smaller than disc n+1 are not on the pole to which disc n+1 is moved.) Finally, we use the induction hypothesis again to move the n smallest discs in the direction ¬d. This places them above disc n+1, and all n+1 smallest discs have now been moved from their original position to the neighbouring pole in direction d.

The following code summarises this inductive solution to the problem. The code defines $H_n(d)$ to be a sequence of pairs $\langle k, d' \rangle$ where n is the number of discs, k is a disc number and d and d′ are directions. Discs are numbered from 1 onwards, disc 1 being the smallest. Directions are boolean values, true representing a clockwise movement and false an anticlockwise movement. The pair $\langle k, d' \rangle$ means move the disc numbered k from its current position in the direction d′. The semicolon operator concatenates sequences together, "[]" denotes an empty sequence and [x] is a sequence with exactly one element x. Taking the pairs in order from left to right, the complete sequence $H_n(d)$ prescribes how to move the n smallest discs one by one from one pole to its neighbour in the direction d, following the rule of never placing a larger disc on top of a smaller disc:

$$H_0(d) = [] \ ,$$
$$H_{n+1}(d) = H_n(\neg d); \left[\langle n{+}1 \ , \ d \rangle\right] ; H_n(\neg d).$$

Note that the procedure name H recurs on the right-hand side of the equation for $H_{n+1}(d)$. Because of this we have what is called a *recursive* solution to the problem. Recursion is a very powerful problem-solving technique, but unrestricted use of recursion can be unreliable. The form of recursion used here is limited; describing the solution as an "inductive" solution makes clear the limitation on the use of recursion.

This inductive procedure gives us a way to generate the solution to the Tower of Hanoi problem for any given value of n – we simply use the rules as left-to-right rewrite rules until all occurrences of H have been eliminated. For example, here is how we determine $H_2(cw)$. (We use cw and aw, meaning clockwise and anticlockwise, rather than true and false in order to improve readability.)

$$H_2(cw)$$
$$= \qquad \{ \qquad \text{2nd equation, n,d}:=1,\text{cw} \ \}$$
$$H_1(aw); [\langle 2,cw \rangle] ; H_1(aw)$$
$$= \qquad \{ \qquad \text{2nd equation, n,d}:=0,\text{aw} \ \}$$
$$H_0(cw); [\langle 1,aw \rangle] ; H_0(cw); [\langle 2,cw \rangle] ; H_0(cw); [\langle 1,aw \rangle] ; H_0(cw)$$
$$= \qquad \{ \qquad \text{1st equation} \ \}$$
$$[] ; [\langle 1,aw \rangle] ; [] ; [\langle 2,cw \rangle] ; [] ; [\langle 1,aw \rangle] ; []$$
$$= \qquad \{ \qquad \text{concatenation of sequences} \ \}$$
$$[\langle 1,aw \rangle , \langle 2,cw \rangle , \langle 1,aw \rangle].$$

As an exercise you should determine $H_3(aw)$ in the same way. If you do, you will quickly discover that this inductive solution to the problem takes a lot of effort to put into practice. The complete expansion of the equations in the case of $n = 3$ takes 16 steps, in the case of $n = 4$ takes 32 steps, and so on. This is not the easy solution that the monks are using! The solution given in Section 8.1.1 is an *iterative* solution to the problem. That is, it is a solution that involves iteratively (i.e. repeatedly) executing a simple procedure dependent only on the current state. The implementation of the inductive solution, on the other hand, involves maintaining a stack of the sequence of moves yet to be executed. The memory of Brahman monks is unlikely to be large enough to do that!

Exercise 8.1   The number of days the monks need to complete their task is the length of the sequence $H_{64}(cw)$. Let $T_n(d)$ denote the length of the sequence $H_n(d)$. Derive an inductive definition of T from the inductive definition of H. (You should find that $T_n(d)$ is independent of d.) Use this definition to evaluate T_0, T_1 and T_2. Hence, or otherwise, formulate a conjecture expressing T_n as an arithmetic function of n. Prove your conjecture by induction on n.

Exercise 8.2   Use induction to derive a formula for the number of different states in the Tower of Hanoi problem.

Use induction to show how to construct a state-transition diagram that shows all possible states of n discs on the poles, and the allowed moves between states.

Use the construction to show that the above solution optimises the number of times that discs are moved.

Exercise 8.3 (Constant Direction)

(a) Suppose the discs must always be moved in a constant direction, say clockwise. That is, every move of a disc should be clockwise and no anticlockwise moves are allowed.

Use induction to devise an algorithm to move n discs, for arbitrary n, in the direction d. Use the same induction hypothesis as for the standard Tower of Hanoi problem, namely that it is possible to move the n *smallest* discs – under the new constraints – from one pole to its neighbour in the direction d, beginning from any valid starting position. Since the direction of movement is constant, it suffices to determine the sequence of discs that are moved. For example, to move 2 discs clockwise, the solution is the sequence

[1,1,2,1,1].

(Disc 1 – the smallest disc – is moved twice clockwise, then disc 2 is moved clockwise, and finally disc 1 is moved twice clockwise.)

(b) Now suppose that the direction each disc is moved must be constant, but may differ between discs. Formally, suppose dir is a function from discs to booleans such that, for each n, the direction of movement of disc n is given by dir(n); true means that disc n must always be moved clockwise, and false means that disc n must always be moved anticlockwise. Use induction to devise an algorithm to move n discs, for arbitrary n, in the direction d. (Again it suffices to determine the sequence of discs that are moved.)

8.3 THE ITERATIVE SOLUTION

Recall the iterative solution to the problem, presented in Section 8.1.2. It has two main elements: the first is that the smallest disc cycles around the poles (i.e. its direction of movement is invariantly clockwise or invariantly anticlockwise), the second is that the disc to be moved alternates between the smallest disc and some other disc. In this section, we show how these properties are derived from the inductive solution.

Cyclic Movement of the Discs

In this section, we show that the smallest disc always cycles around the poles. In fact, we do more than this. We show that *all* the discs cycle around the poles, and we calculate the direction of movement of each.

The key is that, for all pairs $\langle k, d' \rangle$ in the sequence $H_{n+1}(d)$, the boolean value $even(k) \equiv d'$ is invariant (i.e. always true or always false). This is a simple consequence of the rule of contraposition discussed in Section 5.4.1. When the formula for $H_{n+1}(d)$ is applied, the parameter "n+1" is replaced by "n" and "d" is replaced by "¬d". Since $even(n+1) \equiv \neg(even(n))$, the value of $even(n+1) \equiv d$ remains constant under this assignment.

Whether $even(k) \equiv d'$ is true or false (for all pairs $\langle k, d' \rangle$ in the sequence $H_{n+1}(d)$) will depend on the initial values of n and d. Let us suppose these are N and D. Then, for all moves $\langle k, d \rangle$, we have

$$even(k) \equiv d \equiv even(N) \equiv D.$$

This formula allows us to determine the direction of movement d of disc k. Specifically, if it is required to move an even number of discs in a clockwise direction, all even-numbered discs should cycle in a clockwise direction, and all odd-numbered discs should cycle in an anticlockwise direction. Likewise, if it is required to move an odd number of discs in a clockwise direction, all even-numbered discs should cycle in an anticlockwise direction, and all odd-numbered discs should cycle in a clockwise direction. In particular, the smallest disc (which is odd-numbered) should cycle in a direction opposite to D if N is even, and in the same direction as D if N is odd.

Exercise 8.4   An explorer once discovered the Brahman temple and was able to secretly observe the monks performing their task. At the time of his discovery, the monks had got some way to completing their task, so that the discs were arranged on all three poles. The poles were arranged in a line and not at the corners of the triangle so he was not sure which direction was clockwise and which anticlockwise. However, on the day of his arrival he was able to observe the monks move the smallest disc from the middle pole to the rightmost pole. On the next day, he saw the monks move a disc from the middle pole to the leftmost pole. Did the disc being moved have an even number or an odd number?

Alternate Discs

We now turn to the second major element of the solution, namely that the disc that is moved alternates between the smallest disc and some other disc.

By examining the puzzle itself, it is not difficult to see that this must be the case. After all, two consecutive moves of the smallest disc are wasteful as they can always be combined into one. And two consecutive moves of a disc other than the smallest have no effect on the state of the puzzle. We now want to give a formal proof that the sequence $H_n(d)$ satisfies this property.

Let us call a sequence of numbers *alternating* if it has two properties. The first property is that consecutive elements alternate between one and a value greater than one; the second property is that if the sequence is non-empty then it begins and ends with the value one. We write alt(ks) if the sequence ks has these two properties.

The sequence of discs moved on successive days, which we denote by $disc_n(d)$, is obtained by taking the first component of each of the pairs in $H_n(d)$ and ignoring the second. Let the sequence that is obtained in this way be denoted by $disc_n(d)$. Then, from the definition of H we get:

$$disc_0(d) = [] \ ,$$
$$disc_{n+1}(d) = disc_n(\neg d) \ ; \ [n+1] \ ; \ disc_n(\neg d).$$

Our goal is to prove $alt(disc_n.d)$. The proof is by induction on n. The base case, $n = 0$, is clearly true because an empty sequence has no consecutive elements. For the induction step, the property of alternating sequences on which the proof depends is that, for a sequence ks and number k,

$$alt(ks ; [k] ; ks) \quad \Leftarrow \quad alt(ks) \wedge ((ks = []) \equiv (k = 1)).$$

The proof is then:

$$alt(disc_{n+1}(d))$$

$$= \qquad \{ \qquad \text{definition} \quad \}$$

$$alt(disc_n(\neg d) ; [n+1] ; disc_n(\neg d))$$

$$\Leftarrow \qquad \{ \qquad \text{above property of alternating sequences} \quad \}$$

$$alt(disc_n(\neg d)) \wedge ((disc_n(\neg d) = []) \equiv (n+1 = 1))$$

$$= \qquad \{ \qquad \text{induction hypothesis applied to the first conjunct,}$$

$$\text{straightforward property of } disc_n \text{ for the second} \quad \}$$

$$\text{true.}$$

Exercise 8.5 The explorer left the area and did not return until several years later. On his return, he discovered the monks in a state of great despair. It transpired that one of the monks had made a mistake shortly after the explorer's first visit but it had taken the intervening time before they had discovered the mistake. The state of the discs was still valid but the monks had discovered that they were no longer making progress towards their goal; they had got into a never-ending loop!

Fortunately, the explorer was able to tell the monks how to proceed in order to return all the discs to one and the same pole while still obeying the rules laid down to them on the day of the world's creation. They would then be able to begin their task afresh.

What was the algorithm the explorer gave to the monks? Say why the algorithm is correct. (Hint: The disc being moved will still alternate between the smallest and some other disc. You only have to decide in which direction the smallest disc should be moved. Because of the monks' mistake this will not be constant. Make use of the fact that, beginning in a state in which n discs are all on the same pole, maintaining invariant the relationship

$$even(n) \equiv d \equiv even(k) \equiv d'$$

for the direction d' moved by disc k will move n discs in the direction d.)

Exercise 8.6 [Coloured Discs]   Suppose each disc is coloured red, white or blue. The colouring of discs is random; different discs may be coloured differently.

Devise an algorithm that will sort the discs so that all the red discs are on one pole, all the white discs are on another pole, and all the blue discs are on the third pole. You may assume that, initially, all discs are on one pole.

8.4 SUMMARY

In this chapter we have seen how to use induction to construct a solution to the Tower of Hanoi problem and then how to transform the inductive solution to an iterative solution that is easy for human beings to execute. An essential component of the inductive solution, which is often overlooked, is the proper formulation of an inductive hypothesis. The transformation to an interative solution involves identifying an invariant of the inductive solution: the odd-numbered disks cycle around the poles in one direction whilst the even-numbered poles cycle around in the opposite direction. The invariant is easy to spot if the poles are arranged at the corners of a triangle rather than in a straight line. This illustrates the importance of recognising and exploiting inherent symmetry in order to avoid unnecessary complexity.

The chapter has also illustrated two important design considerations: the inclusion of the 0-disc problem as the basis for the construction (rather than the 1-disc problem) and the avoidance of unnecessary detail by not naming the poles and referring to the direction of movement of the discs (clockwise or anticlockwise) instead.

8.5 BIBLIOGRAPHIC REMARKS

Information on the history of the Tower of Hanoi problem is taken from [Ste97]. Martin Gardner [Gar08] cites a paper by R.E. Allardice and A.Y. Fraser published in 1884 as describing the iterative solution. Gardner also discusses several related problems. A proof of the correctness of the iterative solution was published in [BL80]. The formulation and proof presented here is based on [BF01].

Chapter 9

Principles of Algorithm Design

This chapter collects together the basic principles of algorithm design. The main focus is the design of *iterative* algorithms. These are algorithms that achieve a given task by repeatedly ("iteratively") executing the same actions in a so-called *loop*. We use three problems to illustrate the method. The first is deliberately very simple, the second and third are more challenging.

The principles themselves have already been introduced individually in earlier chapters. In summary, they are:

Sequential (De)composition   Sequential decomposition breaks a problem down into two or more subproblems that are solved in sequence. The key creative step in the use of sequential decomposition is the invention of intermediate properties that link the components.

Case Analysis   Case analysis involves splitting a problem into separate cases which are solved independently. The creative step is to identify an appropriate separation: avoiding unnecessary case analysis is often crucial to success.

Induction   Induction entails identifying a class of problems each of which has a certain "size" and of which the given problem is an instance. The solution to any problem in the class is to repeatedly break it down into strictly smaller subproblems together with a mechanism for combining the solutions to the subproblems into a solution to the whole problem. Problems of the smallest size cannot be broken down; they are solved separately and form the basis of the induction.

Induction is perhaps the hardest algorithm-design principle to apply because it involves simultaneously inventing a class of problems and a measure of the size of a problem. Its use is, however, unavoidable except for the most trivial of problems. In Chapter 6 we saw several examples of the direct use of induction. In these examples, the generalisation to a class of problems and the "size" of an instance were relatively straightforward to identify. We saw induction used again in Chapters 7 and 8 where we also introduced the notion of an *iterative* algorithm.

Induction is the basis of the construction of iterative algorithms, although in a different guise. We discuss the general principles of constructing iterative algorithms in Section 9.1. This section may be difficult to follow on a first reading. We recommend reading through it briefly and then returning to it after studying each of the examples in the later sections. Section 9.2 is about designing a (deliberately) simple algorithm to illustrate the principles. Section 9.4 is about a more challenging problem, the solution to which involves combining sequential decomposition, case analysis and the use of induction. The chapter is concluded with a couple of non-trivial algorithm-design exercises for you to try.

9.1 ITERATION, INVARIANTS AND MAKING PROGRESS

An iterative algorithm entails repeated execution of some action (or combination of actions). If S is the action, we write

 do S od

for the action of repeatedly executing S. Such a do–od action is called a *loop* and S is called the *loop body*.

A loop is potentially never-ending. Some algorithms are indeed never-ending – computer systems are typically never-ending loops that repeatedly respond to their users' actions – but our concern is with algorithms that are required to "terminate" (i.e. stop) after completion of some task.

Typically, S is a collection of *guarded* actions, where the guards are boolean expressions. That is, S takes the form

 $b_1 \rightarrow S_1 \ \square \ b_2 \rightarrow S_2 \ \square \ \ldots$

Execution of S then means choosing an index i such that the expression b_i evaluates to true and then executing S_i. Repeated execution of S means terminating if no such i can be chosen and, otherwise, executing S once and then executing S repeatedly again. For example, the loop

 $do \ 100 < n \ \rightarrow \ n := n - 10$

 $\square \ n \leq 100 \land n \neq 91 \ \rightarrow \ n := n + 11$

 od

repeatedly decreases n by 10 while $100 < n$ and increases n by 11 while $n \leq 100$ and $n \neq 91$. The loop terminates when neither of the guards is true, that is when $n = 91$. For example, if n is initially 100, the sequence of values assigned to n is 90, 101 and 91. (This is, in fact, an example of a loop for which it is relatively difficult to prove that it will eventually terminate in all circumstances.)

If a loop is one of a sequence of actions, the next action in the sequence is begun immediately the loop has terminated.

The most common form of a loop is do $b \rightarrow S$ od. (In many programming languages, a notation like **while** b **do** S is used instead; such statements are called *while* statements.) It is executed by testing whether or not b has the value true. If it does, S is executed and then execution of the do–od statement begins again from the new state. If not, execution of the do–od statement is terminated without any change of state. The negation of b, $\neg b$, is called the *termination condition*.

Induction is the basis of the design of (terminating) loops, but the terminology that is used is different. Recall that algorithmic problems are specified by the combination of a precondition and a postcondition; starting in a state that satisfies the precondition, the task is to specify actions that guarantee transforming the state to one that satisfies the postcondition. A loop is designed to achieve such a task by generalising from both the precondition and the postcondition an *invariant* – that is, the precondition and the postcondition are instances of the invariant. Like the precondition and the postcondition, the invariant is a predicate on the current state which may, at different times during execution of the algorithm, have the value true or false. The body of the loop is constructed so that it *maintains* the invariant in the sense that, assuming the invariant has the value true before execution of the loop body, it will also have the value true after execution of the loop body.[1] Simultaneously, the loop body is constructed so that it *makes progress* towards the postcondition and *terminates* immediately the postcondition is truthified. Progress is measured by identifying a function of the state with range the natural numbers; progress is made if the value of the function is strictly reduced by each execution of the loop body.

In summary, the design of a loop involves the invention of an *invariant* and a *measure of progress*. The invariant is chosen so that the precondition satisfies the invariant, as does the postcondition. The loop body is designed to make progress from any state satisfying the given precondition to one satisfying the given postcondition by always reducing the measure of progress while maintaining the invariant. Since the invariant is initially true

---

[1] Strictly, a loop invariant is not an invariant but what is sometimes called a *mono-invariant*. A mono-invariant is a value in an ordered set that always changes monotonically, that is, either remains constant or increases at each step. A loop invariant is a boolean function of the state that either remains constant or increases with respect to the implication ordering on booleans. This means that, if the value of the loop invariant is false before execution of the loop body, its value may change to true.

(the precondition satisfies the invariant), it will remain true after 0, 1, 2, etc. executions of the loop body. The measure of progress is chosen so that it cannot decrease indefinitely, so eventually – by the principle of mathematical induction – the loop will terminate in a state where the postcondition is true. Let us illustrate the method with concrete examples.

9.2 A SIMPLE SORTING PROBLEM

In this section we solve a simple sorting problem. Here is the statement of the problem.

> A robot has the task of sorting a number of coloured pebbles, contained in a row of buckets. The buckets are arranged in front of the robot, and each contains exactly one pebble, coloured either red or blue. The robot is equipped with two arms, on the end of each of which is an eye. Using its eyes, the robot can determine the colour of the pebble in each bucket; it can also swap the pebbles in any pair of buckets. The problem is to issue a sequence of instructions to the robot, causing it to rearrange the pebbles so that all the red pebbles come first in the row, followed by all the blue pebbles.

Let us suppose the buckets are indexed by numbers i such that $0 \leq i < N$. The number of pebbles is thus N. We assume that boolean-valued functions red and blue on the indices determine the colour of the pebble in a bucket. That is, red.i equivales the pebble in bucket i is red, and similarly for blue.i. The fact that pebbles are either red or blue is expressed by

$$\langle \forall i \ :: \ \text{red.i} \not\equiv \text{blue.i} \rangle .$$

We do not assume that there is at least one value of each colour. (That is, there may be no red pebbles or there may be no blue pebbles.) We assume that swapping the pebbles in buckets i and j is effected by executing swap(i,j).

 The range of the bound variable i has been omitted in this universal quantification. This is sometimes done for brevity where the range is clear from the context. See Section 14.4.1 for further explanation.

It is clear that a solution to the problem will involve an iterative process. Initially all the colours are mixed and on termination all the colours should be sorted. We therefore seek an invariant property that has both the initial and final states as special cases.

A reasonably straightforward idea is to strive for an invariant that partitions the array of values into three segments, two of the segments containing values all of the same colour (red or blue) and the third containing a mixture of colours. Because of the symmetry between the colours red and blue, the mixed segment should separate the red and blue segments. This is depicted in Figure 9.1.

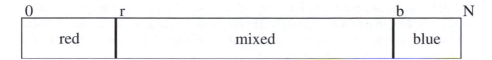

0		r		b	N
red		mixed		blue	

Figure 9.1: The invariant property.

Note that, as required, the precondition is an instance of the invariant shown in Figure 9.1: the precondition is that the entire row of pebbles is mixed and the red and blue segments are empty. The postcondition is also an instance: the postcondition is that the mixed segment is empty. In this way, the invariant generalises from the precondition and postcondition. An obvious measure of progress is the size of the mixed segment. Our goal is to write a loop that maintains the invariant while making progress by always reducing the size of the mixed segment.

Figure 9.1 introduces the variables r and b to represent the extent of the red and blue segments. Expressed formally, the invariant is

$$0 \leq r \leq b \leq N \ \wedge \ \langle \forall i : 0 \leq i < r : red.i \rangle \ \wedge \ \langle \forall i : b \leq i < N : blue.i \rangle .$$

In the initial state, the red and blue segments are empty. We express this by beginning the algorithm with the assignment

$$r,b := 0,N.$$

This assignment is said to *truthify* the invariant. The inequality

$$0 \leq r \leq b \leq N$$

is truthified because the size of the row, N, is at least 0 and the two universal quantifications are truthified because $0 \leq i < 0$ and $N \leq i < N$ are everywhere false.

The size of the mixed segment is $b-r$; this is our measure of progress. The mixed segment becomes empty by truthifying $b-r = 0$, that is, by truthifying $r = b$; so $r = b$ will be our termination condition.

> ⚠ *Refer to Section 14.3 for the meaning of "∀". Note in particular the "empty range" rule (14.16). If the range of a universal quantification is false, the quantification is said to be* vacuously true. *Truthifying universal quantifications in an invariant by making them vacuously* true *is very common.*

In order to make progress towards the termination condition, we must increase r and/or decrease b. We can do this by examining the colour of the elements at the boundaries of the "mixed" segment. If the pebble with index r is red, the red segment can be extended by incrementing r. That is, execution of

$$\text{red.r} \ \rightarrow \ r := r+1$$

is guaranteed to reduce b−r and maintain the invariant. Similarly, if the pebble with index b is blue, the blue segment can be extended by decrementing b. That is, execution of

$$\text{blue.}(b-1) \ \rightarrow \ b := b-1$$

is guaranteed to reduce b−r and maintain the invariant. Finally, since red.r $\neq$ blue.r and red.(b−1) $\neq$ blue.(b−1), if the pebble with index r is not red and the pebble with index b−1 is not blue, they must be blue and red, respectively; so they can be swapped, and r can be incremented and b can be decremented. That is, execution of

$$\text{blue.r} \ \wedge \ \text{red.}(b-1) \ \rightarrow \ \text{swap}(r,b-1) \ ; \ r,b := r+1,b-1$$

is guaranteed to reduce b−r and maintain the invariant. The complete solution is shown in Figure 9.2.

$\{ \ 0 \leq N \ \}$

r,b := 0,N ;

$\{$ **Invariant:**

$\quad 0 \leq r \leq b \leq N \ \wedge \ \langle \forall i : 0 \leq i < r : \text{red.i} \rangle \ \wedge \ \langle \forall i : b \leq i < N : \text{blue.i} \rangle$

$\quad$ **Measure of progress:** b−r $\}$

do r < b → $\quad$ if red.r → r := r+1

$\qquad\qquad\quad$ □ blue.r $\wedge$ red.(b−1) → swap(r,b−1) ; r,b := r+1,b−1

$\qquad\qquad\quad$ □ blue.(b−1) → b := b−1

$\qquad\qquad$ fi

od

$\{ \ r = b \ \wedge \ 0 \leq r \leq N \ \wedge \ \langle \forall i : 0 \leq i < r : \text{red.i} \rangle \ \wedge \ \langle \forall i : r \leq i < N : \text{blue.i} \rangle \ \}$

○ **Figure 9.2: A simple sorting algorithm.**

Take care to study this algorithm carefully. It exemplifies how to document loops. The boolean expressions in curly brackets are called *assertions*; they document properties of the state during the execution of the algorithm. The first and last lines document the precondition and postcondition; the precondition is assumed, the postcondition is the goal. The invariant states precisely the function of the variables r and b, and the measure of progress indicates why the loop is guaranteed to terminate. Note that the postcondition is the conjunction of the invariant and the termination condition. Make sure that you understand why the invariant is maintained by the loop body, and why b−r functions as a measure of progress. (We have omitted some essential details in our informal justification of the algorithm. Can you explain, for example, why $r \leq b$ is maintained by the loop body, and why that is important?)

9.3 BINARY SEARCH

The so-called *intermediate-value theorem* in mathematics states that if a continuous function is negative at one end of a (non-empty) interval and positive at the other end, it must equal 0 at some "intermediate" point in the interval. The theorem is illustrated in Figure 9.3. The left figure shows the graph of a continuous function in a certain interval; the function's value is 0 where it crosses the horizontal line. At the left end of the interval the function's value is negative and at the right end it is positive. In this case there happens to be three points, indicated in the figure by short vertical lines, at which the function's value is 0; the theorem states that there must be at least one such point.

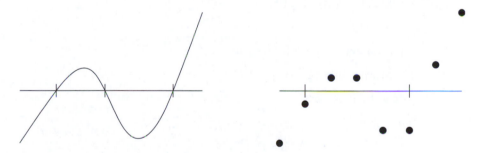

Figure 9.3: The intermediate-value theorem and its discrete counterpart.

The right part of Figure 9.3 illustrates the discrete analogue of the intermediate-value theorem. Suppose a function f is defined on some non-empty interval of the natural numbers and suppose at the left end of the interval the function's value is at most 0 and at the right end the function's value is at least 0. Then there must be a point i in the interval such that $f(i) \leq 0 \leq f(i+1)$. (In our example, there are two possible values for i indicated by short vertical lines.) In this section, we show how to search for such a point in a very efficient way. The method is called *binary search*.

We assume that the interval is given by two (natural) numbers M and N. The precondition is that the interval is non-empty, i.e. M<N, and the function f has opposite sign at the

two ends of the interval, i.e. $f(M) \leq 0 \leq f(N)$. The goal is to determine a number i such that $f(i) \leq 0 \leq f(i+1)$.

Comparing the precondition

$$M < N \wedge f(M) \leq 0 \leq f(N)$$

with the postcondition

$$f(i) \leq 0 \leq f(i+1),$$

it is obvious that both are instances of

$$i < j \wedge f(i) \leq 0 \leq f(j) \tag{9.1}$$

where i and j are variables. This suggests that our algorithm should introduce two variables i and j which are initialised to M and N, respectively; the algorithm will then be a loop that *maintains* (9.1) whilst *making progress* to the condition that $i+1 = j$. An obvious measure of progress is the size of the interval $j-i$.

Formally, this is the structure of the algorithm so far:

$$\{ \ M < N \ \wedge \ f(M) \leq 0 \leq f(N) \ \}$$

$$i,j := M,N$$

$$\{ \ \textbf{Invariant:} \ \ i < j \ \wedge \ f(i) \leq 0 \leq f(j)$$

$$\quad \textbf{Measure of progress:} \ \ j-i \ \};$$

$$\text{do } i+1 \neq j \ \rightarrow \ \text{body}$$

$$\text{od}$$

$$\{ \ i+1 = j \ \wedge \ f(i) \leq 0 \leq f(i+1) \ \}$$

The initial assignment truthifies the invariant. Assuming that the loop body maintains the invariant, when the loop terminates we have:

$$i+1 = j \ \wedge \ i < j \ \wedge \ f(i) \leq 0 \leq f(j)$$

which simplifies to

$$i+1 = j \ \wedge \ f(i) \leq 0 \leq f(i+1).$$

The value of i thus satisfies the goal.

Now we have to construct the loop body. We make progress by reducing the size of the interval, which is given by $j-i$. Reducing $j-i$ is achieved either by reducing j or by increasing i. Clearly, in order to simultaneously maintain the invariant, it is necessary to examine the value of f(k) for at least one number k in the interval. Suppose we choose an arbitrary k such that i<k<j and inspect f(k). Then either $f(k) \leq 0$ or $0 \leq f(k)$ (or both, but that is not important). In the former case, the value of i can be increased to k and, in the latter case, the value of j can be decreased to k. In this way, we arrive at a loop body of the form:

$$\{ \ i+1 \neq j \ \wedge \ i<j \ \wedge \ f(i) \leq 0 \leq f(j) \ \}$$

choose k such that i<k<j

$$\{ \ i<k<j \ \wedge \ f(i) \leq 0 \leq f(j) \ \};$$

$$\text{if} \ \ f(k) \leq 0 \ \rightarrow \ i := k$$

$$\square \ 0 \leq f(k) \ \rightarrow \ j := k$$

fi

$$\{ \ i<j \ \wedge \ f(i) \leq 0 \leq f(j) \ \}$$

Note that $i+1 \neq j \wedge i<j$ simplifies to $i+1 < j$ or equally $i < j-1$ so that it is always possible to choose k: two possible choices are $i+1$ and $j-1$. The final step is to decide how to choose k.

Always choosing $i+1$ for the value of k gives a so-called *linear search* whereby the value of j is constant and i is incremented by 1 at each iteration. (For those familiar with a conventional programming language, such a search would be implemented by a so-called for loop.) Symmetrically, always choosing $j-1$ for the value of k also gives a linear search whereby the value of i is constant and j is decremented by 1 at each iteration. In both cases, the size of the interval is reduced by exactly one at each iteration --- which isn't very efficient. *Binary search* is somewhat better. By choosing a value k roughly half-way between i and j, it is possible to reduce the size of the interval by roughly a half at each iteration. This choice is implemented by the assignment:

$$k := (i+j) \div 2.$$

Substituting these design decisions in the algorithm above, we get the complete algorithm:

$$\{ \ M<N \ \wedge \ f(M) \leq 0 \leq f(N) \ \}$$

$$i,j := M,N$$

$$\{ \ \textbf{Invariant:} \ \ i<j \ \wedge \ f(i) \leq 0 \leq f(j)$$

$$\quad \textbf{Measure of progress:} \ \ j-i \ \};$$

$$\text{do} \ i+1 \neq j \ \rightarrow \quad \{ \ i+1 \neq j \ \wedge \ i<j \ \wedge \ f(i) \leq 0 \leq f(j) \ \}$$

$$k := (i+j) \div 2$$

$$\{ \ i<k<j \ \wedge \ f(i) \leq 0 \leq f(j) \ \};$$

$$\text{if} \ \ f(k) \leq 0 \ \rightarrow \ i := k$$

$$\square \ \ 0 \leq f(k) \ \rightarrow \ j := k$$

$$\text{fi}$$

$$\{ \ i<j \ \wedge \ f(i) \leq 0 \leq f(j) \ \}$$

od

$$\{ \ i+1=j \ \wedge \ f(i) \leq 0 \leq f(i+1) \ \}$$

The correctness of the algorithm relies on the property that

$$[\ i+1 \neq j \ \wedge \ i<j \ \ \Rightarrow \ \ i < (i+j) \div 2 < j \ ].$$

This property can be proven using the properties of integer division discussed in section 15.4.1. The measure of progress, the size of the interval, only gives an upper bound on the number of iterations of the loop body. In this algorithm, because $j-i$ is halved at each iteration, the number of iterations is approximately $\log_2(N-M)$. So, for example, if $N-M$ is 1024 (i.e. 2^{10}), the number of iterations is 10. This is independent of the function f. The number of iterations required by a linear search is at least 1 and at most 1023, depending on the function f. So linear search is much worse in the worst case (although it is not always worse).

9.4 SAM LOYD'S CHICKEN-CHASING PROBLEM

For our next example of algorithm design, we construct an algorithm to solve a puzzle invented by Sam Loyd. Here is Loyd's (slightly modified) description of the problem:[2]

> On a New Jersey farm, where some city folks were wont to summer, chicken-chasing became an everyday sport, and there were two chickens which could always be found in the garden ready to challenge any one to catch them. It reminded one of a game of tag, and suggests a curious puzzle which I am satisfied will worry some of our experts.
>
> The object is to prove in just how many moves the good farmer and his wife can catch the two chickens.
>
> The field is divided into sixty-four square patches, marked off by the corn hills. Let us suppose that they are playing a game, moving between the corn rows from one square to another, directly up and down or right and left.
>
> Play turn about. First let the man and woman each move one square, then let each of the chickens make a move. The play continues in turns until you find out in how many moves

[2]See http://www.cut-the-knot.org/SimpleGames/RFWH.shtml.

it is possible to drive the chickens into such positions that both of them are cornered and captured. A capture occurs when the farmer or his wife can pounce on a square occupied by a chicken.

The game can be played on any checkerboard by using two checkers of one color to represent the farmer and his wife, and two checkers of another color to represent the hen and rooster.

The game is easy to solve; the only trick in the problem is that, in the initial state depicted in Loyd's accompanying illustration (see Figure 9.4), the farmer cannot catch the rooster and his wife cannot catch the hen. This is obvious to anyone trained to look out for invariants. The farmer is given the first move and his distance from the rooster (measured by smallest number of moves needed to reach the rooster) is initially even. When the farmer moves the distance becomes odd. The rooster's next move then makes the distance even again. And so it goes on. The farmer can thus never make the distance zero, which is an even number. The same argument applies to his wife and the hen. However, the farmer is initially at an odd distance from the hen and his wife is an odd distance from the rooster, so the problem has to be solved by the farmer chasing the hen and his wife chasing the rooster. This argument is even more obvious when the game is played on a chessboard. Squares on a chessboard that have the same colour are an even distance apart (where distance is measured as the smallest number of horizontal

○ **Figure 9.4: The chicken-chasing problem.**

and/or vertical moves needed to move from one square to the other) and squares that have different colours are an odd distance apart. Any single horizontal or vertical move is between squares of different colour.

As we said, the game is easy to solve. Try it and see. (It is possible to play the game on the Internet. See the bibliographic remarks in Section 9.7.) The real challenge is to articulate the solution to the problem sufficiently precisely that it can be executed by a dumb machine. This is what this section is about.

In some respects, Loyd's formulation of the problem is unclear. He does not say whether or not the farmer and his wife can occupy the same square on the board and he does not say what happens if the hen or rooster moves to a square occupied by the farmer or his wife. Partly to avoid the distractions of such details, we consider a simplified form of the game.

The problem we consider assumes a rectangular checkerboard of arbitrary, but finite, dimension. There are just two players, the *hunter* and the *prey*. The hunter occupies one square of the board and the prey occupies another square. The hunter and prey take it in turns to move; a single move is one square vertically or horizontally (up or down or to the right or left) within the bounds of the board (see Figure 9.5). The hunter *catches* the prey if the hunter moves to the square occupied by the prey. The problem is to formulate an algorithm that guarantees that the hunter catches the prey with the smallest number of moves.

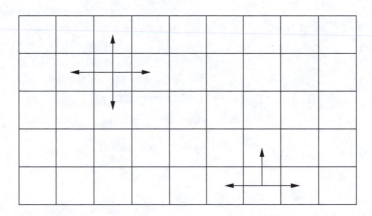

○ **Figure 9.5: Allowed moves in the catching game.**

Our solution is to first formulate an algorithm that guarantees the capture of the prey. Then we will argue that the algorithm achieves its task in the smallest possible number of moves.

The distance between the prey and the hunter clearly plays a fundamental role in the algorithm, so we begin by formulating the notion precisely.

Given any two squares on the board we can identify the *horizontal* distance, h, and the *vertical* distance, v, between them, as shown in Figure 9.6. (To be completely precise, if each square is assigned cartesian coordinates, the horizontal distance between square (i, j) and square (k, l) is $|i-k|$ and the vertical distance between them is $|j-l|$.) The (total) *distance*, d, between the two squares is h+v. (This is sometimes called the *Manhattan distance* after the layout of streets in Manhattan, New York.)

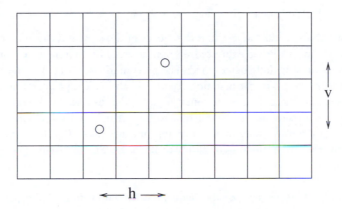

Figure 9.6: Horizontal and vertical distances.

If the prey and hunter are initially distance d apart and one of them makes a single move, d is either incremented or decremented by one. If they each take a turn to move, the effect is to execute the sequence of assignments

$$d := d \pm 1 \; ; \; d := d \pm 1.$$

This is equivalent to executing

$$d := d-2 \; \square \; d := d+0 \; \square \; d := d+2.$$

(Recall that "$\square$" denotes a non-deterministic choice – see Section 2.3.1.) An obvious invariant is the boolean quantity even(d). (If d is even, i.e. even(d) has the value true, it will remain even and if d is odd, i.e. even(d) has the value false, it will remain odd.) Since the goal is to reduce the distance to 0, which is even, it is necessary to assume that the prey and hunter are an odd distance apart when the hunter makes its first move. This assumption becomes a precondition of our algorithm.

Loyd's statement of the problem suggests the obvious strategy: the goal is to *corner* the prey. But what is meant precisely by "corner"? We let the mathematics be our guide.

Let h and v denote, respectively, the (absolute) horizontal and vertical distances between the hunter and the prey. Let us suppose the hunter is allowed the first move. Then the problem is to formulate an algorithm S satisfying

> { odd(h+v) }
>
> S
>
> { h＝0＝v }.

The form of S must reflect the fact that the moves of the prey and the hunter alternate, with the prey's moves being expressed as non-deterministic choices. In contrast, the hunter's moves must be fully determined. The precondition odd(h+v) is essential in the case where the hunter makes the first move, as argued above. The postcondition expresses formally the requirement that, on termination of S, the distance between the prey and hunter is zero. Furthermore, it is important to note that h and v are natural numbers and not arbitrary integers (since they record absolute distances). For the moment, we say nothing about the size of the board, although this is clearly an essential component of any solution.

The postcondition suggests a possible sequential decomposition of the problem: first the hunter "corners" the prey by truthifying h＝v and then, assuming h＝v, the hunter catches the prey.

> { odd(h+v) }
>
> get the prey into a corner
>
> { h＝v };
>
> catch the prey
>
> { h＝0＝v }.

Diagrammatically one can understand why truthifying h＝v is expressed in words as "cornering" the prey. In such a state, the hunter and prey are connected by a diagonal line which identifies a unique corner of the board: each diagonal identifies two corners and, of these, the one closest to the prey is chosen. For example, in the state shown in Figure 9.7, the hunter's task is to drive the prey into the bottom-left corner of the board.

9.4.1 Cornering the Prey

We begin with the task of truthifying h＝v. Initially, h＝v is false (because h+v is odd). That is, h < v ∨ v < h. Now note that what we call "horizontal" and what we call "vertical" is somewhat arbitrary since rotating the board through 90° interchanges the

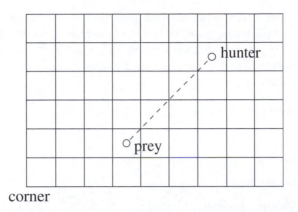

corner

○ **Figure 9.7: The prey is cornered.**

two. So, by rotating the board if necessary, we may assume that h < v. Then all the hunter has to do is to repeatedly move vertically, in the direction towards the prey thus decreasing v, until h = v is true, irrespective of the prey's moves.

Is this really correct? Are we not forgetting that the prey moves too? Let us put it to the test. Below we give a skeleton of the algorithm showing just the hunter's moves. The precondition is odd(h+v) ∧ h < v and the postcondition is h = v. The hunter's moves are modelled by the assignments v := v−1. The hunter makes its first move and then the prey and hunter alternate in making a move. The loop is terminated if h and v are equal (this is the function of the guard h ≠ v).

$$\{ \ odd(h+v) \land h < v \ \}$$

$$v := v-1 \ ;$$

$$do \ h \neq v \rightarrow \quad prey's \ move \ ;$$

$$v := v-1$$

$$od$$

$$\{ \ h = v \ \}$$

Now we add to this skeleton an if–fi statement that reflects a superset of the options open to the prey. (We explain later why it is a superset.) In addition, we document the loop with an all-important *invariant* property and *measure of progress*. These are the key to the correctness of this stage of the algorithm. Several assertions have also been added in the body of the loop; the one labelled PreP is the precondition for the prey's move. The variable vp has also been introduced; this is the vertical distance of the prey from the "bottom" of the board. Very importantly, we define the *bottom* of the board so that the prey is below the hunter on the board, that is, the bottom is the side of the board such that the vertical distance of the prey from the bottom is smaller than the vertical distance of the hunter from the bottom. (If necessary, the board can always be rotated through $180°$ so that what we normally understand by "'bottom" and "below" fits with the definition.) The reason why this is important becomes clear when we discuss the termination of the loop.

$\{ \ odd(h+v) \wedge h < v \ \}$

/* hunter's move */

$v := v-1$

$\{$ **Invariant:** $even(h+v) \wedge h \leq v$

   Measure of progress: $v+vp \ \}$;

$do \ h \neq v \rightarrow$ /* prey's move */

   $\{ \ PreP: \ even(h+v) \wedge h+1 < v \ \}$

   $if \ \ h \neq 0 \rightarrow h := h-1$

   $\Box \ \ true \rightarrow h := h+1$

   $\Box \ \ vp \neq 0 \rightarrow v, vp := v+1, vp-1$

   $\Box \ \ true \rightarrow v, vp := v-1, vp+1$

   fi

   $\{ \ odd(h+v) \wedge h < v \ \}$;

   /* hunter's move */

   $v := v-1$

   $\{ \ even(h+v) \wedge h \leq v \ \}$

od

$\{ \ h = v \ \}$

The precondition of the hunter's first move is

$odd(h+v) \wedge h < v.$

We see shortly that this is a precondition of all of the hunter's moves in this cornering phase of the algorithm. From such a state, the hunter's move truthifies the property

$even(h+v) \wedge h \leq v.$

This is the invariant of the loop.

Now, either h=v or h<v. In the former case, the loop terminates and the desired postcondition has been truthified. In the latter case, the conjunction of h<v and the invariant becomes the precondition, PreP, of the prey's move. But

$$\left[\; \text{even}(h+v) \wedge h \leq v \wedge h < v \; \equiv \; \text{even}(h+v) \wedge h+1 < v \; \right]$$

so the prey chooses a move with precondition

$$\text{even}(h+v) \wedge h+1 < v.$$

 Check this claim by doing the calculation in complete detail. Refer to Chapter 15 for properties of inequalities. You will also need to exploit the properties of the predicate even *discussed in Section 5.3.1.*

This assertion is labelled PreP above. Now we show that with precondition PreP, a move by the prey truthifies the condition

$$\text{odd}(h+v) \wedge h < v \tag{9.2}$$

which, we recall, was the precondition of the hunter's first move.

The prey can choose between four options: increase/decrease the horizontal/vertical distance from it to the hunter. These are the four branches of the if–if statement. The guard "h≠0" has been added to the option of decreasing the horizontal distance; if h is 0, a horizontal move by the prey will increase its horizontal distance from the hunter. The guard on the action of increasing v and decreasing vp is necessary for our argument; it constrains the movements of the prey in a vertical direction. The guards on horizontal movements could be strengthened in a similar way; we have not done so because constraints on the prey's horizontal movements are not relevant at this stage. Indeed, the hunter's algorithm has to take account of all possible moves the prey is allowed to make; if the algorithm takes account of a superset of such possibilities, the correctness is still assured.

Because the hunter has no control over the prey's choice of move, we have to show that (9.2) is truthified irrespective of the choice. It is obvious that all four choices falsify even(h+v) and truthify odd(h+v) (because exactly one of h and v is incremented or decremented by 1). Also, all four choices truthify h < v. In the two cases where the prey's move increases h or decreases v, we need to exploit the fact that h+1 < v before the move. The other two cases are simpler. The guard on increasing the vertical distance is not needed at this stage in the argument.

We have shown that, if the loop begins in a state that satisfies the invariant, re-execution of the loop will also begin in a state that satisfies the invariant. The question that remains is whether or not the loop is guaranteed to terminate. Do we indeed make progress to the state where h and v are equal?

It is at this point that the variable vp is needed. Recall that vp is the distance of the prey from the bottom of the board. Recall also that the definition of "bottom" is such that the prey is closer to the bottom than the hunter. This means that v+vp is the distance of the hunter from the bottom of the board.

The crucial fact is that, when the prey increases v, the value of vp decreases by the same amount; conversely, when the prey decreases v, the value of vp increases by the same amount. Thus v+vp is an invariant of the prey's move. However, since the hunter's move decreases v, the net effect of a move by the hunter followed by the prey is to decrease v+vp by 1; but its value is always at least zero. So the repetition of such a pair of moves can only occur a finite number of times (in fact, at most the initial vertical distance of the hunter from the bottom of the board). The loop is guaranteed to terminate in a state where h and v are equal and the prey is cornered.

9.4.2 Catching the Prey

Unlike the cornering process, catching the prey requires the hunter to adapt its moves according to the moves made by the prey.

The precondition for this stage is $h=v$. Recall that this condition identifies a unique corner of the board, which we call "the" corner. If hp is the horizontal distance of the prey from the corner, the horizontal distance of the hunter from the corner is h+hp. Similarly, if vp is the vertical distance of the prey from the corner, the vertical distance of the hunter from the corner is v+vp.

Starting in a state that satisfies $h=v$, any move made by the prey will falsify the property; the hunter's response is to truthify the property while making progress to the termination condition $h=0$.

It is easy to truthify $h=v$ following a move by the prey. Figure 9.8 shows two ways this can be done when the prey moves in a way that increases h; the hunter may respond by moving horizontally or vertically. Although the vertical move may not be possible because of the boundary of the board, the horizontal move is always possible. Moreover, the horizontal move makes progress in the sense that the hunter moves closer to the corner.

The full details of how the hunter should respond to a move by the prey are shown below. The tests $hp \neq 0$ and $vp \neq 0$ prevent the prey from moving off the board in the direction away from the hunter. The distance of the hunter from the corner is h+hp+v+vp. This is the bound on the number of times the loop body is executed.

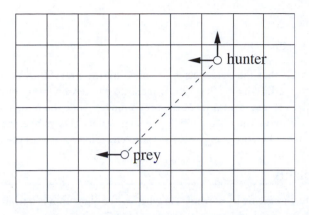

○ **Figure 9.8: Maintaining the catching invariant.**

{ **Invariant:**   h = v

  Measure of progress: h+hp+v+vp }

do 0 < h →   if   hp ≠ 0 →   /* prey's move */

                              hp,h := hp−1,h+1 ;

                              /* hunter's move */

                              h := h−1

      □ true →   /* prey's move */

                    hp,h := hp+1,h−1 ;

                    /* hunter's move */

                    v := v−1

      □ vp ≠ 0 →   /* prey's move */

                    vp,v := vp−1,v+1 ;

                    /* hunter's move */

                    v := v−1

      □ true →   /* prey's move */

                    vp,v := vp+1,v−1 ;

                    /* hunter's move */

                    h := h−1

      fi

od

$\{\ h=0=v\ \}$

It is easy to check that the net effect of a move by the prey followed by a move by the hunter is to truthify $h=v$. Progress is made to the termination condition because both $h+hp$ and $v+vp$ are invariants of the prey's moves while the hunter's move always decreases either h or v. The distance $h+hp+v+vp$ is thus always decreased but cannot be decreased forever because it is always at least zero. This completes the algorithm.

9.4.3 Optimality

We conclude the discussion by considering whether the algorithm is optimal. For brevity, the argument is informal, although it can be made formal. Once again, the notion of an invariant plays an important role.

We have established that the hunter can always catch the prey (assuming the two are initially at an odd distance apart) by presenting an algorithm whereby the hunter chooses its moves. To establish the optimality of the hunter's algorithm, we have to switch the focus to the prey. Although the prey cannot avoid capture, it can try to evade the hunter for as long as possible. We must investigate the prey's algorithm to do this.

The hunter's algorithm has two phases. In the cornering phase, the hunter continually moves in one direction, vertically downwards. In the catching phase, the hunter moves steadily towards "the" corner, either horizontally or vertically. The total distance moved by the hunter is thus at most its initial distance from the corner to which the prey is driven.

The corner to which the prey is driven is not chosen by the hunter; it is determined by the prey's moves in the cornering phase. A choice of two possible corners *is* made, however, prior to the cornering phase. (It is this choice that allows us to assume that $h<v$ initially.) Let us call these two corners A and B, and the remaining two corners C and D. Initially, the prey is closer than the hunter to A and to B; conversely, the hunter is closer than the prey to C and to D.

The hunter cannot catch the prey in corners C or D because, after each of the hunter's moves, the prey can always truthify the property that the hunter is closer than the prey to C and to D. The hunter must therefore catch the prey in corner A or B.

Now suppose corner A is strictly closer to the hunter than corner B. (If the two corners are at equal distance from the hunter, it does not matter which of the two the prey is caught in.) Now the prey can always force the hunter to move a distance at least equal to the hunter's initial distance from corner B. One way the prey can do this is to continually choose the option of reducing its horizontal distance, h, from the hunter during the cornering phase; when forced to increase h – when h=0 – the prey moves towards corner B. This guarantees making progress to the postcondition h=v=1 while maintaining the property that the prey is closer to corner B than the hunter. In the catching phase, the prey continually chooses between increasing h and increasing v while it still can. (It cannot do so indefinitely because of the boundaries of the checkerboard.) The invariant in this phase is that either 0<h or 0<v or the prey is at corner B. When the prey is at corner B, it will be caught after its next move.

In this way it is proven that the hunter moves a distance that is at least its initial distance from corner B. Since we have already shown that the hunter moves a distance that is at most its initial distance from corner B, we have established that the hunter's algorithm is optimal.

> **Exercise 9.3**   Formulate an algorithm for the prey that ensures that it will avoid capture for as long as possible against any algorithm used by the hunter. That is, the prey's algorithm should make no assumption about the hunter's algorithm except that the hunter will capture the prey if the two are adjacent.

9.5 PROJECTS

The following are exercises in algorithm design similar to the chicken-chasing problem. They are non-trivial, which is why we have titled the section "Projects". Do not expect to solve them in a short time: algorithm design demands careful work in order to get it right. The solution to the first exercise is provided at the end of the book, the second is not.

> **Exercise 9.4**   Given is a bag containing three kinds of objects. The total number of objects is reduced by repeatedly removing two objects of different kinds, and replacing them by one object of the third kind.
>
> Identify exact conditions in which it is possible to remove all the objects except one. That is, identify when it is not possible and, when it is possible, design an algorithm to achieve the task. You should assume that initially there are objects of different kinds.
>
> Note that this problem is about invariants and not about making progress: termination is guaranteed because the number of objects is reduced at each iteration.

Exercise 9.5 (Chameleons of Camelot)   On the island of Camelot there are three different types of chameleons: grey, brown and crimson. Whenever two chameleons of different colours meet, they both change colour to the third colour.

For which numbers of grey, brown and crimson chameleons is it possible to arrange a succession of meetings that results in all the chameleons displaying the same colour? For example, if the number of the three different types of chameleons is 4, 7 and 19 (irrespective of the colour), we can arrange a succession of meetings that results in all the chameleons displaying the same colour. An example is

$$(4,7,19) \rightarrow (6,6,18) \rightarrow (0,0,30).$$

On the other hand, if the number of chameleons is 1, 2, and 3, it is impossible to make them all display the same colour. In the case where it is possible, give the algorithm to be used.

Hint: Begin by introducing variables g, b, and c to record the number of green, brown, and crimson chameleons, respectively, and then model repeated meetings by a simple loop. Identifying an invariant of the loop should enable you to determine a general condition on g, b, and c when it is not possible to make all chameleons display the same colour. Conversely, when the negation of the condition is true, you must design an algorithm to schedule a sequence of meetings that guarantees that all chameleons eventually do display the same colour. As in the chicken-chasing problem, one solution is to decompose the algorithm into two phases, the first of which results in a state from which it is relatively easy to arrange an appropriate sequence of meetings.

9.6 SUMMARY

Three basic principles of algorithm design are sequential decomposition, case analysis and induction. Induction is the hardest principle to apply but it is essential because, for all but the most trivial problems, some form of repetitive process – so-called iteration – is needed in their solution.

Invariants are crucial to constructing iterative algorithms; they are the algorithmic equivalent of the mathematical notion of an induction hypothesis. This is why they were introduced as early as Chapter 2. In Chapter 2 the focus was on identifying invariants of repetitive processes. Often problems *cannot* be solved because the mechanisms available for their solution maintain some invariant that *cannot* be satisfied by both the precondition and the postcondition. Conversely, the key to solving many problems is the identification of an invariant that has both the given precondition and postcondition as instances and *can* be maintained by a repetitive process that makes progress from the precondition to the postcondition. Success in algorithmic problem solving can only be achieved by sustained practice in the skill of recognising and exploiting invariants.

The combination of an invariant and a measure of progress is the algorithmic counterpart of the mathematical notion of induction. The induction hypothesis is the invariant; it is parameterised by a natural number, which is the measure of progress. So, if you are prepared to put on your algorithmic spectacles, you can gain much benefit from studying proofs by induction in mathematics.

Exercise 9.6 Consider the tumbler problem discussed in Section 2.3. Suppose the tumblers are placed in a line and the rule is that when two tumblers are turned, they must be *adjacent*. (So it is not possible to choose two arbitrary upside-down tumblers and turn them upside up.) Determine an algorithm to turn all the tumblers upside up, placing the emphasis in your solution on the invariant and the measure of progress. You should assume, of course, that the number of upside-down tumblers is even.

Exercise 9.7 (*Difficult*) Recall the nervous-couples problem discussed in Section 3.3. Show that it is impossible to transport four or more couples across the river with a two-person boat.

Show that it is impossible to transport six or more couples across the river with a three-person boat.

Both problems can be handled together. The crucial properties are as follows:

- At most half of the bodyguards can cross together.
- The boat can only hold one couple.

The following steps may help you to formulate the solution.

Let M denote the capacity of the boat, and N denote the number of couples. Assume that N is at least 2 and M is at least 2 and at most the minimum of 3 and N/2. (These properties are common to the cases of a two-person boat and four couples, and a three-person boat and six couples.)

Let lB denote the number of bodyguards on the left bank. The number of bodyguards on the right bank, denoted rB, is then N−lB. Similarly, let lP denote the number of presidents on the left bank. The number of presidents on the right bank, denoted rP, is then N−lP.

Formulate a property of lB and lP that characterises the valid states. Call this property the *system invariant*.

Express the movement of bodyguards and presidents across the river in the form of a loop with two phases: crossing from left to right and from right to left. (Assume that crossings begin from the left bank.) Show how to strengthen the system invariant when the boat is at the left bank and at the right bank in such a way that precludes the possibility that lB is 0.

9.7 BIBLIOGRAPHIC REMARKS

Section 9.2 is a simplification of a sorting problem (involving three colours) called the Dutch national flag problem, introduced by E.W. Dijkstra. Dijkstra's original description of the Dutch national flag problem can be found in his classic text, *A Discipline of Programming* [Dij76]. There, you will also find many other examples of derivations of non-trivial algorithms. The Dutch national flag problem is a subroutine in a general-purpose sorting algorithm called Quicksort and a program called Find for finding the k smallest elements in an array, both of which were designed by C.A.R. Hoare. These algorithms are discussed in many texts on algorithm design.

Binary search is often used as an introductory example of algorithm design, but most texts – including one written by myself – assume a much stronger precondition. (It is common to assume that the function f is monotonic.) The fact that the precondition can be significantly weakened, as here, is not well known; it is due to David Gries [Gri81].

The chicken-chasing problem was invented by Sam Loyd (*Cyclopedia of Puzzles*, Lamb Publishing, New York, 1914). It is one of many mathematical puzzles listed at http://www.cut-the-knot.org; the website has an applet so that you can play the game. The algorithm presented here is based on a derivation by Diethard Michaelis.

The Chameleons of Camelot problem (Exercise 9.5) is a generalisation of a problem found in [Hon97, page 140]. The problem was formulated and solved by João F. Ferreira [Fer10].

Exercise 9.4 was posed to me by Dmitri Chubarov. I have been told that it was posed in a slightly different form in the Russian national Mathematics Olympiad in 1975 and appears in a book by Vasiliev entitled *Zadachi Vsesoyuzynykh Matematicheskikh Olympiad*, published in Moscow in 1988. The author of the problem is apparently not stated.

Chapter

The Bridge Problem

10

In this chapter, we present a solution to a more general version of the problem in Section 3.5. The generalisation is to consider an arbitrary number of people; the task is to get all the people across a bridge in the optimal time. Specifically, the problem we discuss is the following:

N people wish to cross a bridge. It is dark, and it is necessary to use a torch when crossing the bridge, but they only have one torch between them. The bridge is narrow and at most 2 people can be on it at any one time. The people are numbered from 1 thru N. Person i takes time t.i to cross the bridge; when two cross together they must proceed at the speed of the slowest.

Construct an algorithm that will get all N people across in the shortest time.

For simplicity, we assume that $t.i < t.j$ whenever $i < j$. (This means that we assume the people are ordered according to crossing time and that their crossing times are distinct. Assuming that the crossing times are distinct makes the arguments simpler, but is not essential. If the given times are such that $t.i = t.j$ for some i and j, where $i < j$, we can always consider pairs $(t.i, i)$, where i ranges over people, ordered lexicographically. Renaming the crossing "times" to be such pairs, we obtain a total ordering on times with the desired property.)

10.1 LOWER AND UPPER BOUNDS

The derivation that follows is quite long and surprisingly difficult, particularly in comparison to the final algorithm, which is quite simple. It is important to appreciate where precisely the difficulties lie. This has to do with the difference between establishing an "upper bound" and a "lower bound" on the crossing times.

A lexicograpic ordering on a pair of numbers is defined by

$$[\ (m, n) < (p, q)\ \equiv\ m < p \ \lor\ (m = p \land n < q)\ ].$$

See Section 12.7.6 for more on ordering relations.

Because this is a problem about minimising total times, its solution exploits the algebraic properties of minimum and addition. See Section 15.2 for full details of these properties.

In the original problem given in Chapter 1, there are four people with crossing times of 1, 2, 5 and 10 minutes. Crucially, the question asked was to show that all four can cross the bridge *within* 17 minutes. In other words, the question asks for a so-called *upper bound* on the time taken. In general, an upper bound is established by exhibiting a sequence of crossings that takes the required time.

A much harder problem is to show that 17 minutes is a *lower bound* on the time taken. Showing that it is a lower bound means showing that the time can never be bettered.

We can use the same instance of the bridge problem to further illustrate the difference between lower and upper bounds. Most of us, when confronted with the bridge problem, will first explore the solution in which the fastest person accompanies the others across the bridge. Such a solution takes a total time of 2+1+5+1+10 (i.e. 19 minutes). By exhibiting the crossing sequence, we have established that 19 minutes is an upper bound on the crossing time; we have *not* established that it is a lower bound. (Indeed, it is not.) Similarly, exhibiting the crossing sequence that gets all four people across in 17 minutes does not prove that this time cannot be bettered. Doing so is much harder than just constructing the sequence.

In this chapter, the goal is to construct an algorithm for scheduling N people to cross the bridge. The algorithm we derive is quite simple but, on its own, it only establishes an upper bound on the optimal crossing time. The greatest effort goes into showing that the algorithm simultaneously establishes a lower bound on the crossing time. The combination of equal lower and upper bounds is called an *exact* bound; this is what is meant by an optimal solution.

In Section 10.6, we present two algorithms for constructing an optimal sequence. The more efficient algorithm assumes a knowledge of algorithm development that goes beyond the material in this book.

10.2 OUTLINE STRATEGY

Once again, the main issue we have to overcome is the avoidance of unnecessary detail. The problem asks for a *sequence* of crossings, but there is an enormous amount of freedom in the order in which crossings are scheduled. It may be, for example, that the optimal solution is to let one person accompany all the others one by one across the bridge, each time returning with the torch for the next person. If our solution method requires that we detail in what order the people cross, then it is extremely ineffective. The number of different orderings is $(N-1)!$, which is a very large number even for quite small values of N.

 m! *is the number of different permutations of* m *objects. So-called "combinatorics", introduced in Section 16.8, is the theory of how to count the elements in sets like this.*

The way to avoid unnecessary detail is to focus on what we call the "forward trips". Recall that, when crossing the bridge, the torch must always be carried. This means that crossings alternate between "forward" and "return" trips, where a *forward trip* is a crossing in the desired direction, and a *return trip* is a crossing in the opposite direction. Informally, the forward trips do the work while the return trips service the forward trips. The idea is that, if we can compute the optimal collection of forward trips, the return trips needed to sequence them correctly can be easily deduced.

In order to turn this idea into an effective solution, we need to proceed more formally. First, by the "collection" of forward trips, we mean a "bag" of sets of people. The mathematical notion of a "bag" (or "multiset" as it is sometimes called) is similar to a set but, whereas a set is defined solely by whether or not a value is an element of the set, a bag is defined by the number of times each value occurs in the set. For example, a bag of coloured marbles would be specified by saying how many red marbles are in the bag, how many blue marbles, and so on. We will write, for example, $\{1*a, 2*b, 0*c\}$ to denote a bag of as, bs and cs in which a occurs once, b occurs twice and c occurs no times. For brevity, we also write $\{1*a, 2*b\}$ to denote the same bag.

It is important to stress that a bag is different from a sequence. Even though when we write down an expression denoting a bag we are forced to list the elements in a certain order (alphabetical order in $\{1*a, 2*b, 0*c\}$, for example), the order has no significance. The expressions $\{1*a, 2*b, 0*c\}$ and $\{2*b, 1*a, 0*c\}$ both denote the same bag.

A *trip* is given by the set of people involved in the trip. So, for example, $\{1, 3\}$ is a trip in which persons 1 and 3 cross. If we are obliged to distinguish between forward and return trips, we prefix the trip with either "+" (for forward) or "−" (for return). So +{1,3} denotes a forward trip made by persons 1 and 3 and −{2} denotes a return trip made by person 2.

As we said above, our focus will be on computing the *bag* of forward trips in an optimal sequence of trips. We begin by establishing a number of properties of sequences of trips that allow us to do this.

We call a sequence of trips that gets everyone across in accordance with the rules a *valid sequence*. We will say that one valid sequence *subsumes* another valid sequence if the time taken by the first is at most the time taken for the second. Note that the subsumes relation is reflexive (every valid sequence subsumes itself) and transitive (if valid sequence a subsumes valid sequence b and valid sequence b subsumes valid sequence c then valid sequence a subsumes valid sequence c). The problem is to find a valid sequence that subsumes all valid sequences.

> ⚠ *Reflexivity and transitivity are important properties of a relation discussed in Section 12.7. Note that the subsumes relation is not anti-symmetric and so is not an ordering relation on sequences. (It is what is called a* pre-order.*)*
> *An optimal sequence will typically not be unique: there will typically be many sequences that take the same optimal time.*

Formally, a *valid sequence* is a set of numbered trips with the following two properties:

- The trips are sets; each set has one or two elements, and the number given to a trip is its position in the sequence (where numbering begins from 1).

- Odd-numbered trips in the sequence are called forward trips; even-numbered trips are called return trips. The length of the sequence is odd.

- The trips made by each individual person alternate between forward and return trips, beginning and ending with forward trips. (A trip T is made by person i if i∈T.)

Immediate consequences of this definition which play a crucial role in finding an optimal sequence are as follows:

- The number of forward trips is one more than the number of return trips.

- The number of forward trips made by each individual person is one more than the number of return trips made by that person.

A *regular forward trip* means a forward trip *made by two people*, and a *regular return trip* means a return trip *made by exactly one person*. A *regular sequence* is a valid sequence that consists entirely of regular forward and return trips.

The first step (Lemma 10.1) is to show that every valid sequence is subsumed by one in which all trips are regular. The significance of this is threefold.

- In a regular sequence, the number of forward trips is N−1 and the number of return trips is N−2. (Recall that N is the number of people.)

- The time taken by a regular sequence can be evaluated knowing only which forward trips are made; not even the order in which they are made needs to be known. (Knowing the bag of forward trips, it is easy to determine how many times each person makes a return trip. This is because each person makes one fewer return trips than forward trips. In this way, the time taken for the return trips can be calculated.)

- Most importantly, knowing just the bag of forward trips in a regular sequence is sufficient to reconstruct a valid regular sequence. Since all such sequences take the same total time, we can thus replace the problem of finding an optimal sequence of forward and return trips by the problem of finding an optimal bag of forward trips.

Finding an optimal bag of forward trips is then achieved by focusing on which people do not make a return trip. We prove the obvious property that, in an optimal solution, the two slowest people do not return. We can then use induction to determine the complete solution.

10.3 REGULAR SEQUENCES

Recall that a "regular" sequence is a sequence in which each forward trip involves two people and each return trip involves one person. We can always restrict attention to regular sequences because of the following lemma.

Lemma 10.1 Every valid sequence containing irregular trips is subsumed by a strictly faster valid sequence without irregular trips.

Proof Suppose a given valid sequence contains irregular trips. We consider two cases: the first irregular trip is backward and the first irregular trip is forward.

If the first irregular trip is backward, choose an arbitrary person, p say, making the trip. Identify the forward trip made by p prior to the backward trip, and remove p from both trips. More formally, suppose the sequence has the form

$$u +\{p,q\} \ v \ -\{p,r\} \ w$$

where q and r are people, u, v and w are subsequences and p occurs nowhere in v. (Note that the forward trip made by p involves two people because it is assumed that the first irregular trip is backward.) Replace the sequence by

$$u +\{q\} \ v \ -\{r\} \ w.$$

This results in a valid sequence, the time for which is no greater than the original sequence. (To check that the sequence remains valid, we have to check that the trips made by each individual continue to alternate between forward and return. This is true for individuals other than p because the points at which they cross remain unchanged, and it is true for p because the trips made by p have changed by the removal of consecutive forward and return trips. The time taken is no greater since, for any x and y, $t.p \uparrow x + t.p \uparrow y \geq x+y$.) The number of irregular crossings is not reduced, since a new irregular forward trip has been introduced, but the total number of person-trips *is* reduced.

Now suppose the first irregular trip is forward. There are two cases to consider: the irregular trip is the very first in the sequence, and it is not the very first.

If the first trip in the sequence is not regular, it means that one person crosses and then immediately returns. (We assume that N is at least 2.) These two crossings can be removed. Clearly, since times are positive, the total time taken is reduced. Also, the number of person-trips is reduced.

If the first irregular crossing is a forward trip but not the very first, let us suppose it is person p who crosses, and suppose q is the person who returns immediately before this forward trip. (There is only one such person because of the assumption that p's forward trip is the first irregular trip.) That is, suppose the sequence has the form

$$u -\{q\} +\{p\} \ v.$$

Consider the latest crossing that precedes q's return trip and involves p or q. There are two cases: it is a forward trip or it is a return trip.

If it is a forward trip, it must involve q and not p. Swap p with q in this trip and remove q's return trip and p's irregular crossing. That is, transform

$$u +\{q,r\} \ w \ -\{q\} +\{p\} \ v$$

(where w does not involve p or q) to

$$u +\{p,r\} \ w \ v.$$

The result is a valid sequence. Moreover, the total crossing time is reduced (since, for any x, $t.q \uparrow x + t.q + t.p > t.p \uparrow x$), and the number of person-trips is also reduced.

If it is a return trip, it is made by one person only. (This is because we assume that p's forward trip is the first irregular trip in the sequence.) That person must be p. Swap p with q in this return trip, and remove q's return trip and p's irregular crossing. That is, transform

$$u \; -\{p\} \; w \; -\{q\} \; +\{p\} \; v$$

(where w does not involve p or q) to

$$u \; -\{q\} \; w \; v.$$

The result is a valid sequence. Moreover, the total crossing time is reduced (since $t.p + t.q + t.p > t.q$), and the number of person-trips is also reduced.

We have now described how to transform a valid sequence that has at least one irregular crossing; the transformation has the effect of strictly decreasing the total time taken. Repeating this process while there are still irregular crossings is therefore guaranteed to terminate with a valid sequence that is regular, subsumes the given valid sequence and has a smaller person-trip count.

10.4 SEQUENCING FORWARD TRIPS

Lemma 10.1 has three significant corollaries. First, it means that the number of forward trips in an optimal sequence is $N-1$ and the number of return trips is $N-2$. This is because every subsequence comprising a forward trip followed by a return trip increases the number of people that have crossed by one, and the last trip increases the number by two. Thus, after the first $2 \times (N-2)$ trips, $N-2$ people have crossed and 2 have not, and after $2 \times (N-2) + 1$ trips everyone has crossed.

Second, it means that the total time taken to complete any regular sequence can be evaluated if only the bag of forward trips in the sequence is known; not even the order in which the trips are made is needed. This is because the bag of forward trips enables us to determine how many times each individual makes a forward trip. Hence, the number of times each individual returns can be computed, from which the total time for the return trips can be computed.

For example, suppose the forward trips in a regular sequence are as follows:

$$3*\{1,2\} \; , \; 1*\{1,6\} \; , \; 1*\{3,5\} \; , \; 1*\{3,4\} \; , \; 1*\{7,8\}.$$

(The trips are separated by commas; recall that $3*\{1,2\}$ means that persons 1 and 2 make 3 forward trips together, $1*\{1,6\}$ means that persons 1 and 6 make one forward trip together, etc. Note that no indication is given of the order in which the forward trips occur in the sequence.) Then, counting the number of occurrences of each person in the bag, person 1 makes 4 forward trips, and hence 3 return trips; similarly, person 2 makes 3 forward trips and hence 2 return trips, while person 3 makes 2 forward trips and hence 1 return trip. The remaining people (4, 5, 6, 7 and 8) all make 1 forward trip and, hence, no return trips. The total time taken is thus:

$$3 \times (t.1{\uparrow}t.2) + 1 \times (t.1{\uparrow}t.6) + 1 \times (t.3{\uparrow}t.5) + 1 \times (t.3{\uparrow}t.4) + 1 \times (t.7{\uparrow}t.8)$$

$$+ \quad 3 \times t.1 + 2 \times t.2 + 1 \times t.3.$$

(The top line gives the time taken by the forward trips, and the bottom line gives the time taken by the return trips.) Note that the total number of forward trips is 7 (one less than the number of people), and the total number of return trips is 6.

The third important corollary of Lemma 10.1 is that, given just the bag of forward trips corresponding to a regular sequence, it is possible to construct a regular sequence to get everyone across with the same collection of forward trips. This is a non-obvious property of the forward trips and to prove that it is indeed the case we need to make some crucial observations.

Suppose F is a bag of forward trips corresponding to some regular sequence. That is, F is a collection of sets, each with exactly two elements and each having a certain multiplicity. The elements of the sets in F are people, which we identify with numbers in the range 1 thru N, and each number in the range must occur at least once. The number of times a person occurs is the number of forward trips made by that person.

We will call a person a *settler* if they make only one forward trip; we call a person a *nomad* if they make more than one forward trip. Division of people into these two types causes the trips in F to be divided into three types depending on the number of settlers in the trip. If both people in a trip are settlers we say the trip is *hard*; if one of the people is a settler and the other a nomad, we say the trip is *firm*; finally, if both people are nomads we say the trip is *soft*.

Suppose we use #nomad, #hard, #firm and #soft to denote the number of nomads, the number of hard trips, the number of firm trips and the number of soft trips, respectively, in the collection F. Then, the number of trips in F is

$$\#hard + \#firm + \#soft.$$

The number of return trips equals the total number of forward trips made by individual nomads less the number of nomads, since each nomad makes one more forward trip than return trip. Since each soft trip contributes 2 to the number of forward trips made by nomads, and each firm trip contributes 1, the number of return trips is thus

$$2 \times \#soft + \#firm - \#nomad.$$

But the number of forward trips is one more than the number of return trips. That is,

$$\#\text{hard} + \#\text{firm} + \#\text{soft} = 2 \times \#\text{soft} + \#\text{firm} - \#\text{nomad} + 1.$$

Equivalently,

$$\#\text{hard} + \#\text{nomad} = \#\text{soft} + 1.$$

We summarise these properties in the following definition.

Definition 10.2 (Regular Bag) Suppose N is at least 2. A bag of subsets of $\{i \mid 1 \leq i \leq N\}$ is called a *regular* N-*bag* if it has the following properties:

- Each element of F has size 2. (Informally, each trip in F involves two people.)

- $\langle \forall i : 1 \leq i \leq N : \langle \exists T : T \in F : i \in T \rangle \rangle$. (Informally, every person is an element of at least one trip in F.)

- If #hard.F, #soft.F and #nomad.F denote, respectively, the number of trips in F that involve two settlers, the number of trips in F that involve no settlers, and the number of nomads in F, then

$$\#\text{hard.F} + \#\text{nomad.F} = \#\text{soft.F} + 1. \tag{10.3}$$

Formally, what we have proved is the following.

 "∀" and "∃" denote the so-called universal *and* existential *quantifiers. Later we use "Σ" for summation. We use a uniform notation for all quantifiers which is explained in Chapter 14.*

Lemma 10.4 Given a valid regular sequence of trips to get N people across, where N is at least 2, the bag of forward trips F that is obtained from the sequence by forgetting the numbering of the trips is a regular N-bag. Moreover, the time taken by the sequence of trips can be evaluated from F. Let $\#_F T$ denote the multiplicity of T in F. Then, the time taken is

$$\langle \Sigma T : T \in F : \langle \Uparrow i : i \in T : t.i \rangle \times \#_F T \rangle + \langle \Sigma i :: t.i \times r_F i \rangle \tag{10.5}$$

where

$$r_F i = \langle \Sigma T : T \in F \wedge i \in T : \#_F T \rangle - 1. \tag{10.6}$$

($r_F i$ is the number of times that person i returns.)

Combining the definitions of the trip types with (10.3), we make a number of deductions. If #nomad.F is zero, there are no nomads and hence, by definition, no soft or firm trips. So, by (10.3), #hard.F is 1. That is,

$$\#nomad.F = 0 \ \Rightarrow \ \#hard.F = 1 \ \wedge \ \#firm.F = 0 = \#soft.F. \tag{10.7}$$

If there is only one nomad, there are no trips involving two nomads. That is #soft.F is zero. It follows from (10.3) that #hard.F also equals zero. The converse is immediate from (10.3). That is,

$$\#nomad.F = 1 \ \equiv \ \#hard.F = 0 = \#soft.F. \tag{10.8}$$

If N (the number of people) is greater than 2, not all can cross at once, and so #nomad.F is at least 1. It follows from (10.3) that #soft.F is at least 1:

$$N > 2 \ \wedge \ \#hard.F \geq 1 \ \Rightarrow \ \#soft.F \geq 1. \tag{10.9}$$

Now we can show how to construct a regular sequence from F.

Lemma 10.10 Given N (at least 2) and a regular N-bag, a valid regular sequence of trips can be constructed from F to get N people across. The time taken by the sequence is given by (10.5).

Proof The proof is by induction on the size of the bag F. We need to consider three cases.

The easiest case is when F consists of exactly one trip (with multiplicity one). The sequence is then just this one trip.

The second case is also easy. It is the case where #nomad.F = 1. In this case, every trip in F is firm. That is, each trip has the form {n,s} where n is the nomad and s is a settler. The sequence is simply obtained by listing all the elements of F in an arbitrary order and inserting a return trip by the nomad n in between each pair of forward trips of which the first is the trip {n,s} for some s.

The third case is that #hard.F is non-zero and F has more than one trip. In this case, by (10.9), #soft.F is at least 1. It follows, by definition of soft, that #nomad.F is at least 2. Choose any soft trip in F. Suppose it is {n,m}, where n and m are both nomads. Construct the sequence which begins with the trip {n,m} and is followed by the return of n, then an arbitrary hard trip and then the return of m. Reduce the multiplicity of the chosen hard trip and the chosen soft trip in F by 1. (That is, remove one occurrence of each from F.) We get a new bag F′ in which the number of trips made by each of n and m has been reduced by 1 and the number of people has been reduced by 2. By induction, there is a regular sequence corresponding to F′ which gets the remaining people across.

Optimisation Problem   Lemmas 10.4 and 10.10 have a significant impact on how to solve the general case of the bridge problem. Instead of seeking a sequence of crossings of optimal duration, we seek a regular bag as defined in Definition 10.2 that optimises the time given by (10.5). It is this problem that we now solve.

In solving this problem, it is useful to introduce some terminology when discussing the time taken as given by (10.5). There are two summands in this formula: the value of the first summand we call F's *total forward time*, and the value of the second summand F's *total return time*. Given a bag F and a trip T in F, we call $\langle \Uparrow i : i \in T : t.i \rangle \times \#_F T$ the *forward time of* T *in* F. (Sometimes "in F" is omitted if this is clear from the context.) For each person i, we call the value of $t.i \times r_F i$ the *return time of person* i.

10.5 CHOOSING SETTLERS AND NOMADS

This section is about how to choose settlers and nomads. We establish that the settlers are the slowest people and the nomads are the fastest. More specifically, we establish that in an optimal solution there are at most 2 nomads. Person 1 is always a nomad if N is greater than 2; additionally, person 2 may also be a nomad.

Lemma 10.11   Every regular bag is subsumed by a regular bag for which all settlers are slower than all nomads.

Proof Suppose the regular N-bag F is given. Call a pair of people (p, q) an *inversion* if, within F, p is a settler, q is a nomad and p is faster than q.

Choose any inversion (p, q). Suppose q and p are interchanged everywhere in F. We get a regular N-bag. Moreover, the return time is clearly reduced by at least $t.q - t.p$.

The forward times for the trips not involving p or q are, of course, unchanged. The forward time for the trips originally involving q are not increased (because $t.p < t.q$). The forward time for the *one* trip originally involving p is increased by an amount that is at most $t.q - t.p$. This is verified by considering two cases. The first case is when the trip involving p is {p,q}. In this case, swapping p and q has no effect on the trip, and the increase in time taken is 0. In the second case, the trip involving p is {p,r} where $r \neq q$. In this case, it suffices to observe that

$$t.p \uparrow t.r + (t.q - t.p)$$

$$=\qquad \{ \qquad \text{distributivity of addition over max, arithmetic}\quad \}$$

$$t.q \uparrow (t.r + (t.q - t.p))$$

$$\geq \qquad \{ \qquad t.p \leq t.q, \text{ monotonicity of max}\quad \}$$

$$t.q \uparrow t.r.$$

Finally, the times for all other forward trips are unchanged.

The net effect is that the total time taken does not increase. That is, the transformed bag subsumes the original bag. Also, the number of inversions is decreased by at least one. Thus, by repeating the process of identifying and eliminating inversions, a bag F is obtained that subsumes the given bag.

Corollary 10.12 Every regular N-bag is subsumed by a regular N-bag F with the following properties:

- In any firm trip in F, the nomad is person 1.

- Every soft trip in F is {1,2}. (Note that the multiplicity of this trip in the bag can be an arbitrary number, including 0.)

- The multiplicity of {1,2} in F is j, for some j where $1 \leq j \leq N \div 2$, and the hard trips are {k: $0 \leq k < j-1$: {N $- 2 \times k$, N $- 2 \times k - 1$}}. (Note that this is the empty set when j equals 1.)

 The set of hard trips is a set of sets. Standard mathematical notation for the set

$$\{\{N - 2 \times k , N - 2 \times k - 1\} \mid 0 \leq k < j-1\}$$

does not make clear that the variable k is bound and variables j and N are free. See Section 14.2.2 for further discussion.

Proof Suppose F is a regular N-bag that optimises the total travel time. From Lemma 10.11, we may assume that the settlers are slower than the nomads.

Suppose there is a firm trip in F in which the nomad is person i where i is not 1. Replace i in one occurrence of the trip by person 1. This has no effect on the forward time, since i is slower than the other person in the trip. However, the total return time is reduced (by t.i − t.1). We claim that this results in a regular N-bag, which contradicts F being optimal. (See Lemma 10.4 for the properties required of a regular bag.)

Of course, the size of each set in F is unchanged. The number of trips made by i decreases by one, but remains positive because i is a nomad in F. The number of trips made by all other persons either remains unchanged or, in the case of person 1, increases. So it remains to check property (10.3). If person i is still a nomad after the replacement, property (10.3) is maintained because the type (hard, firm or soft) of each trip remains unchanged. However, person i may become a settler. That is, the number of nomads may be decreased by the replacement. If so, person i is an element of two trips in F. The second trip is either a firm trip in F and becomes a hard trip, or it is a soft trip in F and becomes firm. In both cases, it is easy to check that (10.3) is maintained.

Now suppose there is a soft trip in F different from {1,2}. A similar argument to the one above shows that replacing the trip by {1,2} results in a regular bag with a strictly smaller total travel time, contradicting F being optimal.

We may now conclude from (10.3) that either there are no soft trips or the multiplicity of {1,2} in F is j, for some j which is at least 2, and there are j−1 hard trips. When there are no soft trips, all the trips are firm or hard. But, as we have shown, person 1 is the only nomad in firm trips and there are no nomads in hard trips; it follows that person 1 is the only nomad in F and, from (10.3), that there are no hard trips. Thus persons 1 and 2 are the elements of one (firm) trip in F.

It remains to show that, when j is at least 2, the hard trips form the set

$$\{k: 0 \leq k < j-1: \{N-2 \times k, N-2 \times k-1\}\}.$$

(The multiplicity of each hard trip is 1, so we can ignore the distinction between bags and sets.)

Assume that the number of soft trips is j, where j is at least two. Then the settlers are persons 3 thru N, and $2 \times (j-1)$ of them are elements of hard trips, the remaining $N - 2 \times (j-2)$ being elements of firm trips. Any regular bag clearly remains regular under any permutation of the settlers. So we have to show that choosing the settlers so that the hard trips are filled in order of slowness gives the optimal arrangement. This is done by induction on the number of settlers in the hard trips.

Corollary 10.13 Suppose F is an optimal solution satisfying the properties listed in Corollary 10.12. Then, if j is the multiplicity of {1,2} in F, the total time taken by F is

$$HF.j + FF.j + j \times t.2 + (N-j-1) \times t.1 + (j-1) \times t.2, \tag{10.14}$$

where

$$HF.j = \langle \Sigma i : 0 \leq i < j-1 : t.(N-2i) \rangle$$

and

$$FF.j = \langle \Sigma i : 3 \leq i \leq N-2 \times (j-1) : t.i \rangle.$$

(The first three terms give the forward times, and the last two terms give the return times.)

Proof There are two cases to consider. If there are no soft trips, the value of j is 1. In this case, the total time taken is

$$\langle \Sigma i : 2 \leq i \leq N : t.i \rangle + (N-2) \times t.1.$$

But

$$HF.1 + FF.1 + 1 \times t.2 + (N{-}1{-}1) \times t.1 + (1{-}1) \times t.2$$

$$= \qquad \{ \qquad \text{definition of HF and FF, arithmetic} \quad \}$$

$$0 + \langle \Sigma i : 3 \leq i \leq N : t.i \rangle + t.2 + (N{-}2) \times t.1$$

$$= \qquad \{ \qquad \text{arithmetic} \quad \}$$

$$\langle \Sigma i : 2 \leq i \leq N : t.i \rangle + (N{-}2) \times t.1.$$

If there are soft trips, the value of j is equal to the number of soft trips and is at least 2. In this case, HF.j is the forward time for the hard trips in F and FF.j is the forward time for the firm trips in F. Also, $j \times t.2$ is the forward time for the j soft trips. Finally, person 1's return time is $(N{-}j{-}1) \times t.1$ and person 2's return time is $(j{-}1) \times t.2$. (Person 2 is an element of j forward trips, and person 1 is an element of $j + (N{-}2 \times (j{-}1){-}3{+}1)$ forward trips. Note that the sum of $j{-}1$ and $N{-}j{-}1$ is $N{-}2$, which is what we expect the number of return trips to be.)

10.6 THE ALGORITHM

For all j, where j is at least 2, define OT.j to be the optimal time taken by a regular N-bag where the multiplicity of {1,2} in the bag is j. That is, OT.j is given by (10.14). Now, we observe that

$$HF.(j{+}1) - HF.j = t.(N{-}2j{+}2)$$

and

$$FF.(j{+}1) - FF.j = -(t.(N{-}2j{+}2) + t.(N{-}2j{+}1)).$$

As a consequence,

$$OT.(j{+}1) - OT.j = -t.(N{-}2j{+}1) + 2 \times t.2 - t.1.$$

Note that

$$OT.(j{+}1) - OT.j \leq OT.(k{+}1) - OT.k$$

$$= \qquad \{ \qquad \text{above} \quad \}$$

$$-t.(N{-}2j{+}1) + 2 \times t.2 - t.1 \leq -t.(N{-}2k{+}1) + 2 \times t.2 - t.1$$

$$= \qquad \{ \qquad \text{arithmetic} \quad \}$$

$$t.(N{-}2k{+}1) \leq t.(N{-}2j{+}1)$$

$$= \qquad \{ \qquad \text{t increases monotonically} \quad \}$$

$$j \leq k.$$

That is, OT.(j+1) − OT.j *increases* as j *increases*. A consequence is that the minimum value of OT.j can be determined by a search for the point at which the difference function changes from being negative to being positive.

The simplest way to do this and simultaneously construct a regular sequence to get all N people across is to use a linear search, beginning with j assigned to 1. At each iteration the test $2 \times t.2 \leq t.1 + t.(N-2j+1)$ is performed. If it evaluates to true, the soft trip {1,2} is scheduled; this is followed by the return of person 1, then the hard trip {N−2j+2 , N−2j+1} and then the return of person 2. If the test evaluates to false, the remaining N−2j+2 people are scheduled to cross in N−2j+1 firm trips. In each trip one person crosses accompanied by person 1; in between two such trips person 1 returns. This algorithm is documented below. For brevity, the details of the trip schedules have been omitted. Note that the loop is guaranteed to terminate because j is increased by 1 at each iteration so that eventually N−2j+1 equals 1 or 2. In either case, the test for termination will succeed (because t.1 < t.2). The invariant documents the optimal time needed to get all N people across when the multiplicity of {1,2} in the bag of forward trips is j.

$\{ \ 2 \leq N \wedge t.1 < t.2 \ \}$

$j,T := 1,0 \ ;$

$\{$ **Invariant:**

$\qquad 1 \leq j \leq N \div 2$

$\qquad \wedge \ \ OT.j \ = \ T + \langle \Sigma i : 2 \leq i \leq N-2j+2 : t.i \rangle + (N-2j-2) \times t.1$

Measure of progress: N−2j $\}$

$do \ 2 \times t.2 \leq t.1 + t.(N-2j+1) \ \rightarrow \qquad$ schedule settlers {N−2j+2 , N−2j+1} ;

$\qquad\qquad\qquad\qquad\qquad\qquad\qquad T \ := \ T + 2 \times t.2 + t.1 + t.(N-2j+2) \ ;$

$\qquad\qquad\qquad\qquad\qquad\qquad\qquad j := j+1$

od

$\{ \qquad 2 \times t.2 \ > \ t.1 + t.(N-2j+1)$

$\quad \wedge \ \ OT.j \ = \ \langle \Downarrow k : 1 \leq k \leq N \div 2 : OT.k \rangle$

$\quad \wedge \ \ OT.j \ = \ T + \langle \Sigma i : 2 \leq i \leq N-2j+2 : t.i \rangle + (N-2j-2) \times t.1 \ \};$

schedule firm trips for persons {i | 2 ≤ i ≤ N−2j+2} .

 Linear search is a very elementary algorithmic technique. Those familiar with a programming language will recognise a linear search as a so-called for *loop. Binary search is typically more efficient than linear search, but*

is not always applicable. Binary search is used as an example of algorithm design in Section 9.3. The algorithm presented there can be adapted to solve Exercise 10.15.

Exercise 10.15   When the number N is large, the number of tests can be reduced by using binary search to determine the optimal value of j. Show how this is done.

⚠ *In Chapter 3, we argued that brute-force search should be avoided whenever possible. Brute-force search is applicable to river-crossing problems where the issue is whether there is a way of crossing according to the given constraints. In the bridge problem, finding at least one way of getting the people across the bridge is clearly not an issue; the problem is getting the people across in the fastest time.*

The state-transition graph for the bridge problem is acyclic. A method akin to brute-force search for solving optimisation problems on an acyclic graph is so-called "dynamic programming". Like brute-force search, it involves constructing a state-transition diagram and then using topological search to explore the different paths through the diagram to determine the best path. See Section 16.7 for more information on acylic graphs and topological search.

Dynamic programming is useful for some problems where the state-transition diagram has little or no structural properties but, just as for brute-force search, it should not be used blindly. The execution time of dynamic programming depends on the number of states in the state-transition diagram. This is typically substantially smaller than the total number of different paths – making dynamic programming substantially more efficient than a brute-force search of all paths – but, even so, the number of states can grow exponentially, making dynamic programming impractical except for small instances.

Exercise 10.16 is about quantifying the number of states and the number of different ways (including suboptimal ways) of solving the bridge problem. The conclusion is that dynamic programming is unacceptably inefficient except for relatively small numbers of people.

Exercise 10.16 In this exercise, consider only solutions to the problem in which, repeatedly, two people cross and one returns. Thus, every solution has $N-1$ forward trips and $N-2$ return trips.

(a) Calculate the number of states in the state-transition diagram for the bridge problem.

(b) Calculate the number of different ways of getting everyone across the bridge.

Tabulate your answers for N equal to 2, 3, 4, 5 and 6.

10.7 SUMMARY

In this chapter, we have presented an algorithm to solve the bridge problem for an arbitrary number of people and arbitrary individual crossing times. The greatest challenge in an optimisation problem of this nature is to establish without doubt that the algorithm constructs a solution that cannot be improved. A major step in solving the problem was to eliminate the need to consider *sequences* of crossings and to focus on the bag of forward trips. Via a number of lemmas, we established a number of properties of an optimum bag of forward trips that enabled us to construct the required algorithm.

Many of the properties we proved are not surprising. An optimal sequence is "regular" – that is, each forward trip is made by two people and each return trip is made by one; the "settlers" (the people who never make a return trip) are the slowest, and the "nomads" (the people who do make return trips) are the fastest. Less obvious is that there are at most two nomads and the number of "hard" trips (trips made by two settlers) is one less than the number of trips that the two fastest people make together. The proof of the fact that there are at most two nomads is made particularly easy by the focus on the bag of forward trips; if we had to reason about the sequence of trips, this property could have been very difficult to establish.

Even though these properties may seem unsurprising and the final algorithm (in retrospect) perhaps even "obvious", it is important to appreciate that proof is required: the interest in the bridge problem is that the most "obvious" solution (letting the fastest person accompany everyone else across the bridge) is not always the best solution. Always beware of claims that something is "obvious".

10.8 BIBLIOGRAPHIC REMARKS

In American English, the bridge problem is called the "flashlight problem"; it is also sometimes called the "torch problem". The solution presented here is based on a solution to the yet more general problem in which the capacity of the bridge is a parameter [Bac08]. In terms of this more general problem, this chapter is about the capacity-2 problem; the solution is essentially the same as a solution given by Rote [Rot02]. Rote gives a comprehensive bibliography, including pointing out one publication where the algorithm is incorrect.

When the capacity of the bridge is also a parameter, the problem is much harder to solve. Many "obvious" properties of an optimal solution turn out to be false. For example, it is no longer the case that an optimal solution uses a minimum number of crossings. (If $N = 5$, the capacity of the bridge is 3 and the travel times are 1, 1, 4, 4 and 4, the shortest time is 8, which is achieved using 5 crossings. The shortest time using 3 crossings is 9.)

Chapter 11

Knight's Circuit

The problem tackled in this chapter is a particularly hard one. Yet, by suitably decomposing the problem combined with effective reasoning skills, the problem becomes solvable.

> **The problem is to find a Knight's *circuit* of a chessboard. That is, find a sequence of moves that will take a Knight in a circuit around all the squares of a chessboard, visiting each square exactly once, and ending at the square at which the circuit began.**

The problem is an instance of a search problem; in principle, it can be solved by a systematic, exhaustive examination of all the paths a Knight can follow around a chessboard – a *brute-force* search. However, there are 64 squares on a chessboard; that means 64 moves have to be chosen, one for each square. From each of the corner squares, there is a choice of just 2 moves, but from each of the 16 central squares, there is a choice of 8 moves (see Figure 11.1); from the remaining squares either 4 or 6 moves are possible. This gives a massive amount of choice in the paths that can be followed. Lots of choice is usually not a problem but, when combined with the very restrictive requirement that the path forms a circuit that visits every square exactly once, it does become a problem. The Knight's circuit problem is hard because of this critical combination of an *explosion* with an *implosion* of choice.

But, all is not lost. The squares on a chessboard are arranged in a very simple pattern, and the Knight's moves, although many, are specified by one simple rule (two squares horizontally or vertically, and one square in the opposite direction). There is a great deal of structure, which we must endeavour to exploit.

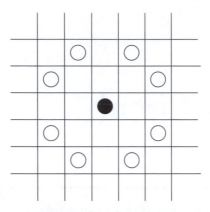

Figure 11.1: Knight's moves.

11.1 STRAIGHT-MOVE CIRCUITS

Finding a Knight's circuit is too difficult to tackle head on. Some experience of tackling simpler circuit problems is demanded.

Let's turn the problem on its head. Suppose you want to make a circuit of a chessboard and you are allowed to choose a set of moves that you are allowed to make. What sort of moves would you choose?

The obvious first answer is to allow moves from any square to any other square. In that case, it's always possible to construct a circuit of any board, whatever its size – starting from any square, choose a move to a square that has not yet been visited until all the squares are exhausted; then return to the starting square. But that is just too easy. Let's consider choosing from a restricted set of moves.

The simplest move is one square horizontally or vertically. (These are the moves that a King can make, but excluding diagonal moves.) We call these moves *straight* moves. Is it possible to make a circuit of a chessboard just with straight moves?

The answer is yes, although it isn't immediately obvious. You may be able to find a straight-move circuit by trial and error, but let us try to find one more systematically. As is often the case, it is easier to solve a more general problem; rather than restrict the problem to an 8×8 board, let us consider an arbitrary rectangular board. Assuming each move is by one square only, to the left or right, or up or down, is it possible to complete a straight-move circuit of the entire board? That is, is it possible to visit every square exactly once, beginning and ending at the same square, making "straight" moves at each step?

In order to gain some familiarity with the problem, please tackle the following exercise. Its solution is relatively straightforward.

Exercise 11.1

(a) What is the relation between the number of moves needed to complete a circuit of the board and the number of squares? Use your answer to show that it is impossible to complete a circuit of the board if both sides have odd length. (Hint: crucial is that each move is from one square to a different coloured square. Otherwise, the answer does not depend on the sort of moves that are allowed.)

(b) For what values of m is it possible to complete a straight-move circuit of a board of size 2m×1? (A 2m×1 board has one column of squares; the number of squares is 2m.)

(c) Show that it is possible to complete a straight-move circuit of a 2×n board for all (positive) values of n. (A 2×n board has two rows, each row having n squares.)

The conclusion of exercise 11.1 is that a straight-move circuit is only possible if the board has size 2m×n, for positive numbers m and n. That is, one side has length 2m and the other has length n. (Both m and n must be non-zero because the problem assumes the existence of at least one starting square.) Also, a straight-move circuit can always be completed when the board has size 2×n, for positive n. This suggests that we now try to construct a straight-move circuit of a 2m×n board, for m at least one and n greater than one, by induction on m, the 2×n case providing the basis for the inductive construction.

To complete the inductive construction, we need to consider a board of size $2m \times n$, where m is greater than 1. Such a construction is hopeful because, when m is greater than 1, a $2m \times n$ board can be split into two boards of sizes $2p \times n$ and $2q \times n$, say, where both p and q are smaller than m and p+q equals m. We may take as the inductive hypothesis that a straight-move circuit of both boards can be constructed. We just need to combine the two constructions.

In our description of the solution below, we use the convention that the first component of the size of a board gives the number of rows and the second the number of columns.

The key to the combination is the corner squares. There are two straight moves from each of the corner squares, and any straight-move circuit must use both. In particular, it must use the horizontal moves. Now, imagine that a $2m \times n$ board is divided into a $2p \times n$ board and a $2q \times n$ board, with the former above the latter. The bottom-left corner of the $2p \times n$ board is immediately above the top-left corner of the $2q \times n$ board. Construct straight-move circuits of these two boards. Figure 11.2 shows the result diagrammatically. The two solid horizontal lines at the middle-left of the diagram depict moves that we know must form part of the two circuits. The dashed lines depict the rest of the circuits. (Of course, the shape of the dashed lines gives no indication of the shape of the circuit that is constructed.)

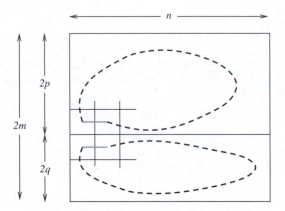

Figure 11.2: **Combining straight-move circuits. First, split the board into two smaller boards and construct straight-move circuits of each.**

Now, to combine the circuits to form one circuit of the entire board, replace the horizontal moves from the bottom-left and top-left corners by vertical moves, as shown by the vertical solid lines in Figure 11.3. This completes the construction.

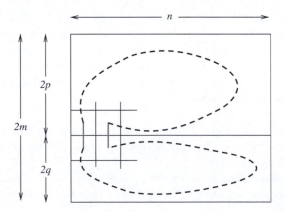

Figure 11.3: **Second, combine the two circuits as shown.**

Figure 11.4 shows the circuit that is constructed in this way for a 6 × 8 board. Effectively, the basis of the inductive algorithm constructs straight-move circuits of three 2 × 8 boards. The induction step then combines them by replacing horizontal moves by the vertical moves shown in Figure 11.4.

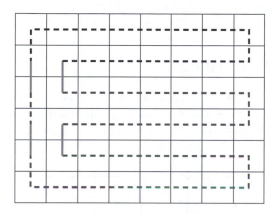

○ **Figure 11.4: A straight-move circuit for a 6 × 8 board.**

Exercise 11.2 As mentioned above, when a board has an odd number of squares, no circuit is possible.

Consider a 3×3 board. It is easy to construct a straight-move circuit of all its squares but the middle square. (See Figure 11.5.) It is also possible to construct a straight-move circuit of all its squares but one of the corner squares. However, a

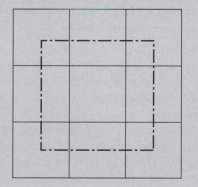 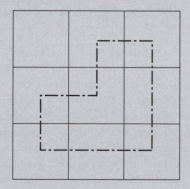

Figure 11.5: Straight-move circuits of a 3 × 3 board, omitting one of the squares.

straight-move circuit of all but one of the other four squares – the squares adjacent to a corner square, for example, the middle-left square – cannot be constructed.

Explore when it is possible, and when it is not possible, to construct a straight-move circuit of all the squares but one in a board of odd size.

11.2 SUPERSQUARES

Let us now return to the Knight's-circuit problem. The key to a solution is to exploit what we know about straight moves. The way this is done is to imagine that the 8×8 chessboard is divided into a 4×4 board by grouping together 2×2 squares into "supersquares", as shown in Figure 11.6.

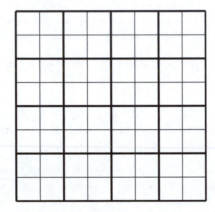

Figure 11.6: Chessboard divided into a 4×4 board of supersquares.

If this is done, the Knight's moves can be classified into two types: *Straight moves* are moves that are "straight" with respect to the supersquares; that is, a Knight's move is *straight* if it takes it from one supersquare to another supersquare either vertically above or below, or horizontally to the left or to the right. *Diagonal moves* are moves that are not straight with respect to the supersquares; a move is *diagonal* if it takes the Knight from one supersquare to another along one of the diagonals through the starting supersquare. In Figure 11.7, the boundaries of the supersquares are indicated by thickened lines; the starting position of the Knight is shown in black, the straight moves are to the white positions, and the diagonal moves are to the grey positions.

Focusing on the straight moves, we now make a crucial observation. Figure 11.8 shows the straight moves from one supersquare – the bottom-left supersquare – vertically upwards

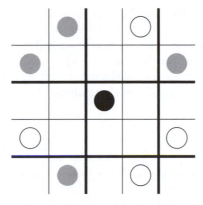

Figure 11.7: Straight (white) and diagonal (grey) knight's moves from some starting position (black). Boundaries of the supersquares are indicated by thickened lines.

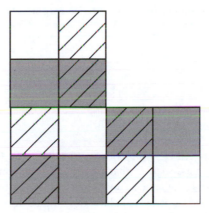

Figure 11.8: Straight moves from the bottom-left supersquare.

and horizontally rightwards. The "colours" (the combination of stripes and shading) indicate the moves that can be made. For example, from the bottom-left white square a straight move can be made to the top-left white square or to the bottom-right white square. However, it is not possible to move from a square to another square of a different "colour".

Observe the pattern. Vertical moves flip the "colours" around a vertical axis, whilst horizontal moves flip them around a horizontal axis. (The vertical moves interchange striped and not-striped squares; the horizontal moves interchange shaded and not-shaded squares.)

Let us denote by v the operation of flipping the columns of a 2×2 square (v is short for "vertical"). Similarly, let us denote by h (short for "horizontal") the operation of flipping the rows of the square. Now, let an infix semicolon denote doing one operation after another. So, for example, $v ; h$ denotes the operation of first flipping the columns and then flipping the rows of the square. Flipping the columns and then flipping the rows is the same as flipping the rows and then the columns. That is,

$$v ; h \ = \ h ; v.$$

Both are equivalent to rotating the 2×2 square through $180°$ about its centre. So, let us use c (short for "centre") as its name. That is, by definition of c,

$$v ; h \ = \ c \ = \ h ; v. \tag{11.3}$$

We have now identified three operations on a 2×2 square. There is a fourth operation, which is the do-nothing operation. Elsewhere, we have used skip to name such an operation. Here, for greater brevity we use n (short for "no change"). Flipping twice vertically, or twice horizontally, or rotating twice through $180°$ about the centre, all amount to doing nothing. That is;

$$v ; v \ = \ h ; h \ = \ c ; c \ = \ n. \tag{11.4}$$

Also, doing nothing before or after any operation is the same as doing the operation.

$$n ; x \ = \ x ; n \ = \ x. \tag{11.5}$$

The three equations (11.3), (11.4) and (11.5), together with the fact that doing one operation after another is associative (that is, doing one operation x followed by two operations y and z in turn is the same as doing first x followed by y and then concluding with z – in symbols, $x ; (y ; z) = (x ; y) ; z$ allow the simplification of any sequence of the operations to one operation. For example,

$$\begin{aligned}
& v ; c ; h \\
= \quad & \{ \quad v ; h \ = \ c \ \} \\
& v ; v ; h ; h \\
= \quad & \{ \quad v ; v \ = \ h ; h \ = \ n \ \} \\
& n ; n \\
= \quad & \{ \quad n ; x \ = \ x, \text{ with } x := n \ \} \\
& n.
\end{aligned}$$

In words, flipping vertically, then rotating through 180° about the centre, and then flipping horizontally is the same as doing nothing. (Note how associativity is used implicitly between the first and second steps. The use of an infix operator for "followed by" facilitates this all-important calculational technique.)

Exercise 11.6 Construct a two-dimensional table that shows the effect of executing two operations x and y in turn. The table should have four rows and four columns, each labelled by one of n, v, h and c. (Use the physical process of flipping squares to construct the entries.)

Use the table to verify that, for x and y in the set {n,v,h,c},

$$x\,;y \ = \ y\,;x. \tag{11.7}$$

Check also that, for x and y in the set {n,v,h,c},

$$x\,;(y\,;z) \ = \ (x\,;y)\,;z. \tag{11.8}$$

(In principle, you need to consider 4^3, i.e. 64, different combinations. Think of ways to reduce the amount of work.)

Exercise 11.9 Two other operations that can be done on a 2×2 square are to rotate it about the centre through 90°, in one case clockwise and in the other anticlockwise. Let r denote the clockwise rotation and let a denote the anticlockwise rotation. Construct a table that shows the effect of performing any two of the operations n, r, a or c in sequence.

11.3 PARTITIONING THE BOARD

The identification of the four operations on supersquares is a significant step towards solving the Knight's-circuit problem. Suppose one of the supersquares is labelled "n". Then the remaining fifteen supersquares can be uniquely labelled as n, v, h or c squares, depending on their position relative to the starting square. Figure 11.9 shows how this is done. Suppose we agree that the bottom-left square is an "n" square. Then immediately above it is a "v" square, to the right of it is an "h" square, and diagonally adjacent to it is a "c" square. Supersquares further away are labelled using the rules for composing the operations.

As a consequence, all 64 squares of the chessboard are split into four disjoint sets. In Figure 11.9, the different sets are easily identified by the colour of the square[1]. Two squares have the same colour equivales they can be reached from each other by straight Knight's moves. (That is, two squares of the same colour *can* be reached from each other by straight Knight's moves, and two squares of different colour *cannot* be reached from each other by straight Knight's moves.)

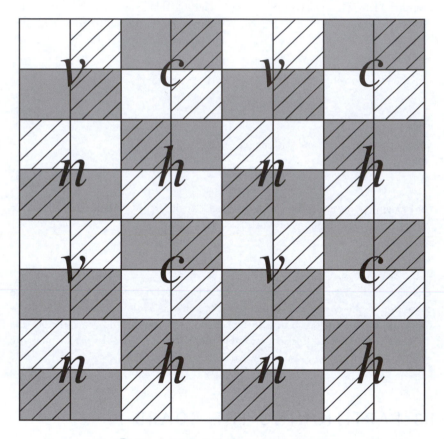

○ **Figure 11.9: Labelling supersquares.**

Recall the discussion of straight-move circuits in section 11.1. There we established the simple fact that it is possible to construct a straight-move circuit of a board of which one side has even length and the other side has length at least two. In particular, we can construct a straight-move circuit of a 4×4 board.

---

[1] Because we are unable to use true colours, like red and blue, we use "colour" to refer to the different combinations of shaded/not-shaded and striped/not-striped.

Now, a "straight" Knight's move is "straight" with respect to the supersquares of a chessboard. That means we can construct straight-move circuits of each of the four sets of squares on the chessboard. In Figure 11.9, this means constructing a circuit of all the white squares, a circuit of all the striped squares, a circuit of all the shaded squares, and a circuit of all the shaded-and-striped squares. Figure 11.10 shows how we distinguish the four different circuits. Specifically, moves connecting white squares are shown as 0-dot, dashed lines, moves connecting striped squares are shown as 1-dot, dashed lines, moves connecting shaded squares are shown as 2-dot, dashed lines, and moves connecting shaded-and-striped squares are shown as 3-dot, dashed lines.

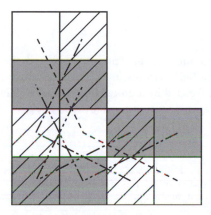

Figure 11.10: Moves from the bottom-left supersquare. The number of dots (0, 1, 2 or 3) corresponds to the "colour" of connected squares (white, striped, shaded and striped-and-shaded).

We now have four *disjoint* circuits that together visit all the squares of the chessboard. The final step is to combine the circuits into one. The way to do this is to exploit the "diagonal" Knight's moves. (Refer back to Figure 11.7 for the meaning of "diagonal" in this context.)

A simple way of combining the four circuits is to combine them in pairs, and then combine the two pairs. For example, we can combine the circuits of the white and striped squares into a "non-shaded" circuit of half the board; similarly, we can combine the circuits of the shaded and shaded-and-striped squares into a "non-white" circuit. Finally, by combining the non-shaded and non-white circuits, a complete circuit of the board is obtained.

Figure 11.11 shows schematically how non-shaded and non-white circuits are formed; in each case, two straight moves (depicted by dotted lines) in the respective circuits are replaced by diagonal moves (depicted by solid lines). Figure 11.12 shows one way of

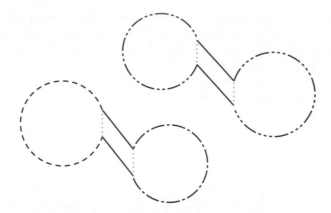

○ **Figure 11.11:** Schema for forming "non-shaded" and "non-white" circuits. The straight-move circuits are depicted as circles, a single move in each being depicted by a dotted line. These straight moves are replaced by the diagonal moves, shown as solid lines.

choosing the straight and diagonal moves in order to combine striped and white circuits, and shaded and shaded-and-striped circuits – in each case, two "parallel" straight moves are replaced by two "parallel" diagonal moves. Exploiting symmetry, it is easy to find similar "parallel moves" with which to combine striped and shaded-and-striped circuits, or shaded and white circuits. On the other hand, there are no diagonal moves from striped to shaded, or from shaded-and-striped to white squares; consequently, it is impossible to construct a "non-striped" or a "non-plain" circuit.

Striped and white straight-move circuits have been combined in Figure 11.13 to form a "non-shaded" circuit. The method of combination is indicated by the dotted and solid lines: the straight moves (dotted lines) are replaced by diagonal moves (solid lines). To complete a circuit of the whole board, with this "non-shaded" circuit as basis, a "non-white" circuit has to be constructed, and this circuit combined with the "non-shaded" circuit. This is left as an exercise.

A slight difficulty of this method is that it constrains the straight-move circuits that can be made. For example, considering the suggested method for combining striped and white circuits in Figure 11.12, no constraint is placed on the white circuit (because there is only one way a straight-move circuit of the white squares can enter and leave the bottom-left corner of the board). However, the straight-move circuit of the striped squares is constrained by the requirement that it make use of the move shown as a dotted line. The difficulty is resolved by first choosing the combining moves and then constructing the straight-move circuits appropriately.

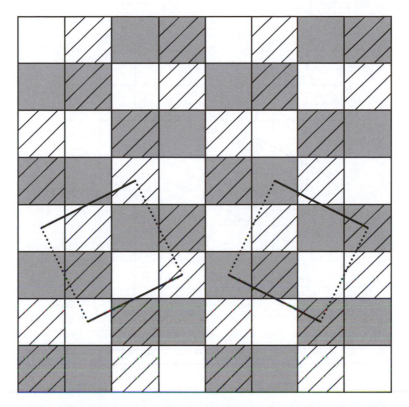

Figure 11.12: Forming circuits of the "non-shaded" and "non-white" squares. The straight moves shown as dotted lines are replaced by the diagonal moves shown as solid lines.

In order to construct a Knight's circuit of smaller size boards, the different pairs of combining moves need to be positioned as close as possible together. This is possible in the case of an 8×6 board, but not for smaller boards.

Exercise 11.10 Construct a Knight's circuit of an 8×8 board using the scheme discussed above. Do the same for an 8×6 board. Indicate clearly how the individual circuits have been combined to form the entire circuit.

Exercise 11.11 Figure 11.14 illustrates another way that the circuits can be combined. The four straight-move circuits are depicted as circles, one segment of which has been flattened and replaced by a dotted line. The dotted lines represent

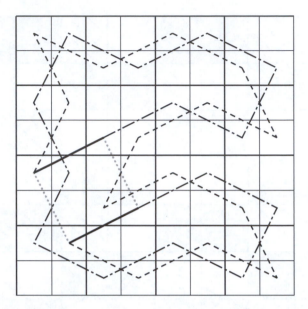

○ Figure 11.13: A circuit of the "non-shaded" squares. Parallel straight moves, shown as thicker dotted lines, are replaced by parallel diagonal moves, shown as thicker solid lines, thus combining the two circuits.

straight moves between consecutive points. If these are replaced by diagonal moves (represented in the diagram by solid black lines), the result is a circuit of the complete board.

To carry out this plan, the four diagonal moves in Figure 11.14 have to be identified. The key to doing this with a minimum of effort is to seek parallel striped and shaded moves, and parallel white and shaded-and-striped moves, whilst exploiting symmetry. (In contrast, the above solution involved seeking parallel striped and white moves.) Choosing to start from, say, the pair of shaded moves in the bottom-left corner, severely restricts the choice of diagonal moves; in combination with symmetry, this makes the appropriate moves easy to find.

Construct a knight's circuit of an 8 × 8 and a 6 × 8 board using the above scheme. Explain how to extend your construction to any board of size 4m × 2n for any m and n such that m ≥ 2 and n ≥ 3.

(The construction of the circuit is easier for an 8 × 8 board than for a 6 × 8 board because, in the latter case, more care has to be taken in the construction of the straight-move circuits. If you encounter difficulties, try turning the board through 90° whilst maintaining the orientation of the combining moves.)

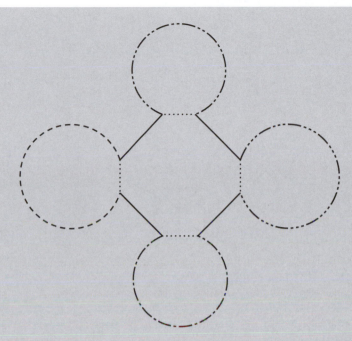

Figure 11.14: Schema for Combining Straight-Move Circuits. Four straight moves (indicated by dotted lines) are replaced by four diagonal moves (indicated by solid black lines).

Exercise 11.12 Division of a board of size $(4m+2) \times (4n+2)$ into supersquares yields a $(2m+1) \times (2n+1)$ "super" board. Because this superboard has an odd number of (super) squares, no straight-move circuit is possible, and the strategy used in exercise 11.10 is not applicable. However, it is possible to construct Knight's circuits for boards of size $(4m+2) \times (4n+2)$, whenever both m and n are at least 1, by exploiting exercise 11.2.

The strategy is to construct four straight-move circuits of the board omitting one of the supersquares. (Recall exercise 11.2 for how this is done.) Then, for each circuit, one move is replaced by two moves – a straight move and a diagonal move – both with end points in the omitted supersquare. This scheme is illustrated in Figure 11.15.

Complete the details of this strategy for a 6×6 board. Make full advantage of the symmetry of a 6×6 board. In order to construct the twelve combining moves depicted in Figure 11.15, it suffices to construct just three; the remaining nine can be found by rotating the moves through a right angle.

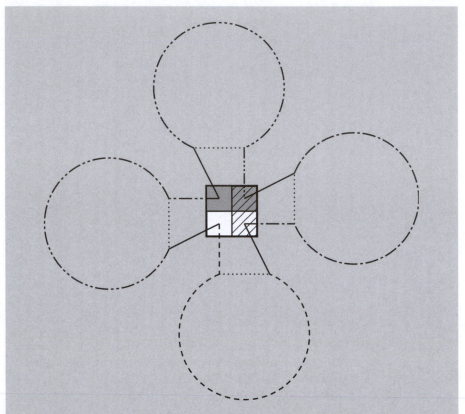

Figure 11.15: Strategy for Constructing a Knight's Circuit of $(4m+2)$ $\times (4n+2)$ boards. One supersquare is chosen, and four straight-move circuits are constructed around the remaining squares. These are then connected as shown.

Explain how to use your solution for the 6×6 board to construct Knight's circuits of any board of size $(4m+2) \times (4n+2)$, whenever, both m and n are at least 1.

11.4 SUMMARY

In the absence of a systematic strategy, the Knight's circuit problem is a truly difficult problem to solve, which means it is a very good example of disciplined problem-solving skills. The method we have used to solve the problem is essentially problem decomposition – reducing the Knight's circuit problem to constructing straight-move circuits, and combining these together.

The key criterion for a good *method* is whether or not it can be extended to other related problems. This is indeed the case for the method we have used to solve the Knight's circuit problem. The method has been applied to construct a circuit of an 8×8 chessboard, but the method can clearly be applied to much larger chessboards.

The key ingredients are

- the classification of moves as "straight" or "diagonal",
- straight-move circuits of supersquares, and
- using diagonal moves to combine straight-move circuits.

Once the method has been fully understood, it is easy to remember these ingredients and reproduce a Knight's circuit on demand. Contrast this with remembering the circuit itself, which is obviously highly impractical, if not impossible.

A drawback of the method is that it can only be applied to boards that can be divided into supersquares. As we have seen, it is not possible to construct a Knight's circuit of a board with an odd number of squares. That leaves open the cases where the board has size $(2m) \times (2n + 1)$, for some m and n. (That is, one side has even length and the other has odd length.) There are lots of websites where information on this case can be obtained; a couple are mentioned in section 11.5.

The Knight's-circuit problem exemplifies a number of mathematical concepts discussed in part II. The n, v, h and c operations together form an example of a "group": see definition 12.22 in section 12.5.6. The relation on squares of being connected by straight moves is an example of an "equivalence relation", and the fact that this relation partitions the squares into four disjoint sets is an example of a general theorem about equivalence relations: see section 12.7.8.

The Knight's-circuit problem is an instance of a general class of problems called "Hamiltonian-Circuit Problems". In general, the input to a Hamiltonian-circuit problem is a graph (a network of nodes with edges connecting the nodes: see chapter 16) and the requirement is to find a path through the graph that visits each node exactly once, before returning to the starting node. Hamiltonian-circuit problems are, in turn, instances of a class of problems called "NP-complete" problems. NP-complete problems are problems characterised by ease of verification but difficulty of construction. That is, given a putative solution, it is easy to check whether or not it is correct (for example, given any sequencing of the squares on a chessboard, it is easy to check whether or not it is a Knight's circuit); however, for the class of NP-complete problems, no efficient methods are known at this time for constructing solutions. "Complexity theory" is the name given to the area of computing science devoted to trying to quantify how difficult algorithmic problems really are.

11.5 BIBLIOGRAPHIC REMARKS

Solutions and historical information on the Knight's circuit problem can easily be found on the internet. According to one of these [MacQuarrie, St. Andrews Univ.] the first Knight's tour is believed to have been found by al-Adli ar-Rumni in the ninth century, long before chess was invented.

I learnt about the use of supersquares in solving the Knight's circuit problem from Edsger W. Dijkstra [Dij92]. Dijkstra's solution is for a standard-sized chessboard and uses the method of combining straight-move circuits described in exercise 11.11. The pairwise combination of straight-move circuits was suggested by Diethard Michaelis. Both solutions involve searching for "parallel moves". Michaelis's solution is slightly preferable because just two pairs of "parallel moves" have to be found at each stage. Dijkstra's solution involves searching for four pairs (twice as many) at the same time, making it a little bit harder to do. The solution to exercise 11.12 was constructed by the author, with useful feedback from Michaelis.

Since first writing this chapter (in 2003), I have learnt that the use of supersquares was devised by Peter Mark Roget (better known for his Thesaurus) in 1840. According to George Jelliss [google "Knight's Tours"], H.J.R.Murray introduced the terminology "straights" and "slants" for the two types of move in a book entitled *History of Chess* and published in 1913. Jellis's website gives an encyclopaedic account of Knight's tours and Knight's circuits.

Part II
Mathematical Techniques

Chapter 12

The Language of Mathematics

Mathematics is the art of effective reasoning. Progress in mathematics is encoded and communicated via its own language, a universal language that is understood and accepted throughout the world. Indeed, in appropriate contexts, communication via the language of mathematics is typically easier than communication via a natural language. This is because mathematical language is clear and concise.

Mathematical language is more than just the formulae that are instantly recognised as part of mathematics. The language is sometimes called mathematical "vernacular"[1] because it is a form of natural language with its own style, idioms and conventions. It is impossible to teach mathematical vernacular, but we can summarise some of its vocabulary. This chapter is about elements of the vocabulary that occur in almost all mathematical texts, namely sets, predicates, functions and relations. Later chapters expand on these topics in further detail.

Mathematical notation is an integral part of the language of mathematics, so notational issues are a recurring theme in the chapter. Well-designed mathematical notation is of tremendous value in problem solving. By far the best example is the positional notation we use to denote numbers (for example, 12, 101, 1.31; note the use of "0" and the decimal point). Thanks to this notation, we are all able to perform numerical calculations that are unimaginable with Roman numerals. (Try multiplying MCIV by IV without translating to positional notation.)

Mathematical notation has evolved over centuries of use. Sometimes this has led to good notational conventions, but sometimes to poor conventions that are difficult to change. If you have experienced difficulty understanding mathematics, it may simply be that your difficulty is with a confusing notation.

[1]"Vernacular" means commonly spoken language.

In this text, we occasionally break with mathematical tradition and employ a non-standard notation. Of course, such a step should never be taken lightly. Whenever we do, the reason is to improve understanding by improving uniformity.

12.1 VARIABLES, EXPRESSIONS AND LAWS

Mathematical expressions form an instantly recognisable part of mathematical language. Expressions like $2+3$ and 4×5 are familiar to us all. These are examples of *arithmetic* expressions: their value is a number. Expressions often involve so-called *constants*: symbols that have a particular, unchanging value. The Greek symbol π, for example, is used in formulae for the perimeter and area of a circle. We say that it *denotes* a number (which happens to be approximately 3.1). "Denotes" means "is a notation for" or "stands for".

Expressions are often confused with the values that they denote. Most of the time this causes no problems, but occasionally (as now) it is important to make a clear distinction. The analogy is with names of people: a name and the person it names are different things. For example, "Winston Churchill" is the name of a famous man; the name and the person are different. The name "Winston Churchill" has two parts, called the "forename" and "surname", consisting respectively of seven and eight letters, while the person, Winston Churchill, has a date of birth, a mother and father, etc. However, when we refer to Winston Churchill, it is usually clear whether we mean the person or the name.

Expressions often involve *variables*. These are symbols that denote values that change ("vary") depending on the context. In Einstein's famous equation

$$E = mc^2,$$

c is a constant denoting the speed of light and E and m are both variables. The formula relates energy and mass; to evaluate energy using the formula we need to know the value of the mass m of the body in question. Similarly, the formulae $2\pi r$ and πr^2 give the length of the perimeter and the area of a circle with radius r, respectively: π denotes a constant and r denotes a variable.

A class of expressions that is particularly important is the class of *boolean expressions*. These are the expressions that evaluate to one of the two *boolean values*, true or false. For example, $1^2 = 1$, $0 < 1$ and $1+2 = 2+1$ are all examples of expressions that evaluate to true while $2^2 = 1$, $1 < 0$ and $1+1 = 1$ are examples of expressions that evaluate to false. The value of expressions like $m=0$ and $i<j$, which depend on variables, can of course be either true or false; we cannot tell until we know the values of the variables.

(The name "boolean" is in recognition of George Boole (1815–1864) whose book *The Laws of Thought* introduced a calculus of reasoning, now called "boolean algebra". Boolean algebra has evolved considerably since the publication of Boole's book; we discuss it in Chapter 13. Boole's book is available on the Internet through Project Gutenberg.)

Mathematics is traditionally about giving a catalogue of true statements. So traditional mathematics includes statements like "let m=0" and "suppose i<j" and the reader is meant to understand the boolean expressions as always evaluating to true. In computing, however, such expressions are used differently. For example, the expression "m=0" may be a test in a program; an action is chosen depending on the value of the expression, true or false, at the time that it is evaluated. In this text, our use of boolean expressions conforms to the computing scientist's usage. This has important but sometimes subtle consequences.

One important consequence is how we deal with mathematical laws. An elementary example of a mathematical law is that adding 0 has no effect. Traditionally, the law would be expressed by the equation $x+0=x$. Here x is a variable denoting a number and $x+0=x$ is a boolean expression; the law of arithmetic is that the expression evaluates to true *whatever the value of* x. There is thus an important difference between an expression like $0=x$ and the expression $x+0=x$, even though both are boolean expressions. The value of the former expression *does* depend on the value of x, while the value of the latter expression *does not* depend on the value of x. To emphasise the difference, we use square brackets to indicate that the value of a boolean expression is always true (i.e. the expression is a law), as in

$$[\,x+0=x\,].$$

The square brackets are pronounced "everywhere". "Everywhere" is short for "for all values of the variables". In the expression $x+0=x$, the variable x is *free*; in the expression $[\,x+0=x\,]$ the variable x is *bound*. We discuss this terminology in more detail in Chapter 14.

Expressions have *instances* obtained by *instantiating* the variables in the expression. Instances of the expression $x+0$ are $0+0$ and $1+0$; these are instances where the variable x has been instantiated with numbers. Other instances are $2x+0$ and y^2+0; here expressions are used to instantiate the variable x. Note that x is an expression as well as a variable, so $0, 1, 2x$ and y^2 are all instances of the expression x.

If an expression includes more than one occurrence of a variable, it is important to instantiate every occurrence in the same way. For example, x^2+x has instances 0^2+0 and 1^2+1, but x^2+0 is not an instance of the expression.

Since laws are boolean expressions that are everywhere true, every instance of the expression also gives a law. The law $[x+0=x]$ has instances $0+0=0$, $1+0=1$,

$[x \times y + 0 = x \times y]$ and so on. Note that the everywhere brackets are not needed for statements like $1+0=1$ because the expression does not include any variables.

12.2 SETS

The *set* is one of the most fundamental mathematical notions. It is best introduced by example: {Monday, Tuesday, Wednesday, Thursday, Friday} is the set of weekdays and {red, green, blue} is a set of primary colours.

In general, a set is defined by its *elements*. The set of weekdays has five elements: Monday, Tuesday, Wednesday, Thursday and Friday. The set of primary colours has three elements: red, green and blue.

These two examples both have a *finite* number of elements, and are sufficiently small that we are able to list all the elements. In the case of a (small) finite set, the set can be defined by *enumerating* (i.e. listing) its elements. The notation that is used is to enclose the list of elements in curly brackets. For example, {0,1} is a set with just two elements, while {a,b,c,d} is a set with four elements. The order in which the elements are listed is not significant. For example, the expressions {0,1} and {1,0} both denote the same set, the set with two elements 0 and 1.

The set {true,false}, whose elements are the two booleans, is particularly important. We use the abbreviation Bool for {true,false}.

12.2.1 The Membership Relation

The symbol "∈" is the standard notation for the so-called *membership relation*. The symbol is pronounced "is an element of" or "is a member of" or, most simply, just "in". An expression of the form $x \in S$ denotes a boolean value which is true if x is an element of the set S and false otherwise. For example, $0 \in \{0,1\}$ is true while $b \in \{a,c,d\}$ is false.

12.2.2 The Empty Set

An extreme example of a set with a finite number of elements is the *empty set*. The empty set has zero elements. It is usually denoted by the symbol "∅" but sometimes by {} (in line with the notation for other enumerated sets). It is an important example of a set, particularly in computing applications: the empty set is what is returned by an internet search engine when nothing matches with the given query. Formally, the empty set is such that $x \in \emptyset$ is false for all x.

12.2.3 Types/Universes

There is no restriction on the elements of a set. They can be colours, days, months, people, numbers, etc. They can also be sets. So, for example, {{0,1}} is a set with one element – the one element is the set {0,1}, which is a set with two elements. Another example of a set with one element is {∅}; the single element of the set is the empty set, ∅. The two sets {∅} and ∅ should not be confused; they are different because they have different elements.

The word *type* is often used in a way that is almost synonymous with set. "Colour", "day" and "number" are examples of "types". Most often, the elements of a set all have the same type, but that is not a requirement. For example, {Monday,1} is a perfectly well-defined set; but it is not a set that is likely to occur in any meaningful application. In all the other examples of sets we have given so far, all the elements have had the same type. Mathematics texts often use the word *universe* instead of "type"; the elements of a set are drawn from a "universe" of values.

Basic types are the integers (numbers like 0, 10, −5), the natural numbers (integers at least zero; note that zero is included), the real numbers (which includes the integers but also includes numbers like $\sqrt{2}$ and π), the booleans (true and false) and characters (letters of some alphabet).

12.2.4 Union and Intersection

Two ways of combining sets are *union* and *intersection*. The union of two sets is the set formed by combining all the elements that are in (at least) one of the two sets. For example, the union of the sets {0,1} and {1,4} is {0,1,4}. We write

$$\{0,1\} \cup \{1,4\} \ = \ \{0,1,4\}.$$

The symbol "∪" denotes set union. Note that in this example two sets each with two elements combine to form a set with three elements (and not four).

The intersection of two sets is the set formed from the elements that are in both of the sets. The intersection of the sets {0,1} and {1,4} is {1}. We write

$$\{0,1\} \cap \{1,4\} \ = \ \{1\}.$$

The symbol "∩" denotes set intersection.

Laws involving set union and set intersection are discussed in Chapter 13.

12.2.5 Set Comprehension

Defining a set by enumerating the elements becomes impractical very quickly, even for relatively small sets. The set of months in the year can, of course, be defined by enumeration but it is tedious to do so. The set of all days in a year can also be enumerated, but that would be very tedious indeed!

A very common way to define a set is called *set comprehension*. Set comprehension entails assuming that some set – the universe or type – is given, and then defining the set to be those elements of the universe that have a certain property.

For example, we may consider the set of all natural numbers that are at most one trillion and are divisible by 2 or 5. This is a finite set and so – in principle – it can be enumerated. However, enumerating its elements would take a long time, especially by a human being! In this example, the universe is the set of all natural numbers and the property is "at most one trillion and divisible by 2 or 5". Another example is the set of all students at the University of Poppleton who are between the ages of 60 and 70. (This example may well be the empty set – the university may not exist and, if it does, there may be no students between the ages of 60 and 70.) The universe in this case is the set of students at the University of Poppleton, and the property is "between the ages of 60 and 70".

The traditional mathematical notation for set comprehension is exemplified by

$$\{n \mid 10 \leq n \leq 1000\}.$$

This expression denotes the set of n such that n is in the range from 10 to 1000 (inclusive). The opening curly bracket is read as "the set of" and the "|" symbol is read as "such that".

In this example – which is not atypical – it is not clear what the universe is. It could be the natural numbers or the real numbers. The variable n is a so-called *dummy* or *bound variable*. Texts often use a naming convention on variables because it avoids clutter. A common convention is that m and n stand for natural numbers, while x and y stand for real numbers. We often use this convention.

The expression

$$10 \leq n \leq 1000$$

is called a *predicate* on n. For some values of n, the expression is true (for example, 10, 11 and 12) and for some values it is false (for example, 0, 1 and 2). The expression $\{n \mid 10 \leq n \leq 1000\}$ denotes the set of all (natural numbers) n for which the predicate $10 \leq n \leq 1000$ evaluates to true.

The difference between free and bound variables is important. Expressions have values which depend on the values of their free variables, but it is meaningless to say that the value of an expression depends on the values of its bound variables. Because the expression $\{n \mid 10 \leq n \leq 1000\}$ has no free variables, it denotes a constant. Compare this with

$$\{n \mid 0 \leq n < k\}$$

which is an expression with one free variable, k. This is an expression denoting a set whose value depends on the value of the variable k. (By convention, k denotes a natural number.) One instance is $\{n \mid 0 \leq n < 1\}$, which evaluates to $\{0\}$ since 0 is the only instance of natural number n for which $0 \leq n < 1$ evaluates to true. Another instance is $\{n \mid 0 \leq n < 2\}$, which evaluates to $\{0,1\}$. In general, $\{n \mid 0 \leq n < k\}$ denotes the set containing the first k natural numbers. The extreme case is $\{n \mid 0 \leq n < 0\}$: the expression $0 \leq n < 0$ always has the value false irrespective of the value of n and so the set, $\{n \mid 0 \leq n < 0\}$, is the empty set, $\varnothing$. See Chapter 14 for further discussion of free and bound variables.

12.2.6 Bags

Recall that a set is defined by its elements. That is, two sets are equal if they have the same elements. A *bag* is like a set but with each element is associated a number, which can be thought of as the number of times the element occurs in the bag. Bags are sometimes called *multisets* in order to suggest a set in which each element occurs a given multiple of times. Bags, rather than sets, are sometimes useful.

Some authors introduce special-purpose brackets replacing the curly brackets for sets, to denote a bag. We use the well-known curly brackets but write each element in the form $m*x$ where m is a number and x is the element. For example, $\{2*red, 1*green\}$ denotes a bag of colours: two red and one green.

12.3 FUNCTIONS

A *function* assigns outputs to inputs. More precisely, a function assigns to each element of a set of so-called *input* values a single *output* value. Familiar examples of functions are mother, father, and date of birth. In these examples, the "input" is a person and the "output" is some characteristic of that person; in all cases, the output is uniquely defined by the input – we all have just one mother, one father and one date of birth. Other familiar examples of functions are age and weight; because our age and weight change over time, the "input" is a combination of a person and a time. (For example, the age of Winston Churchill on VE Day was 61.)

Nationality is an example of a characteristic of a person that is not a function because some people have more than one nationality. Spouse is also not a function because some people do not have a spouse and, in polygamous societies, some have more than one. Nationality and spouse are examples of relations, a topic we return to shortly.

An example of a function in mathematics is even, which assigns the value true to the numbers 0, 2, 4, 6, etc. and the value false to the numbers 1, 3, 5, 7, etc. In this case, the set of inputs is the set of natural numbers and the set of outputs is the set of booleans.

The word "map" is often used to describe the action of a function, as in "the function even maps the even numbers to true and the odd numbers to false".

In mathematics, there are lots of well-known functions that map real numbers to real numbers. Negation is the function that maps, for example, 0.1 to -0.1 and -2 to 2. The square function maps, for example, 1 to 1, 2 to 4, 10 to 100, and 0.1 to 0.01. Note that the square function maps both 1 and -1 to 1; a function maps each input value to a single output value, but several input values may be mapped to the same output value. Other well-known functions are the sine, cosine and tangent functions, which map angles to reals, and area and volume. Area maps a two-dimensional object to a real number; volume does the same to a three-dimensional object.

12.3.1 Function Application

Functions are everywhere; they come in all shapes and sizes and there is a myriad of notations used to denote them and their application. The following are all commonly used notations for the application of well-known arithmetic functions to an argument x; the form that the notation takes is different in each case:

$$\sin x \;,\; x^2 \;,\; -x \;,\; \sqrt{x} \;,\; e^x \;,\; \lfloor x \rfloor.$$

The examples illustrate the fact that functions may be written as prefixes to their argument (as in $\sin x$ and $-x$), as postfixes (as in x^2, in which case it is common to write the function name as a superscript) or as parentheses (as in $\lfloor x \rfloor$).

Additional notations that are used, typically for a temporary purpose, are exemplified by $\hat{x}$ and $\check{x}$. Sometimes it is not at all clear whether or not a function is being defined. The use of an overbar (as in $\overline{x}$), underlining (as in $\underline{x}$) and primes (as in x') are examples. When, say, x' is used it could simply be an identifier having the same status as x or y, or it could be that a function is being introduced denoted by a prime and written as a postfix to its argument (for example, f' is a standard notation for the derivative of f). An overbar is sometimes used as a replacement for parentheses (as in $\sqrt{x}$) in order to indicate the scope of the function rather than being the name of a function, and sometimes to denote complementation. In the first case it does not denote a function, in the second case it does.

A case where a function is defined but the function is seldom made explicit is when subscripts are used. If a text introduces two variables x_0, x_1, say, then x is a function with *domain* the two-element set $\{0, 1\}$. Application of the function to an argument is denoted by subscripting. Similarly, if a sequence is denoted by x_0, x_1, ..., then x is a function with domain the natural numbers.

When introducing functions, standard mathematical vernacular can be mistifying. One often reads statements like "the function $f(x) = 2x$". This is mathematical shorthand for several things at once. It is important to understand that the function is not $f(x) = 2x$ and nor is it $f(x)$. These are expressions with one free variable, x. The function that is being introduced in this example is the function that multiplies a number by 2; the statement gives it the name "f". Another name for the function is the "doubling function". Simultaneously, the statement states that application of the function to an argument will be written by enclosing the argument in parentheses and preceding it by the name "f", as indicated by the pronunciation of $f(x)$ as "eff of eks". The symbol x in the statement is a dummy. Its choice has a hidden significance. To a large extent it is insignificant since one could equally write "the function $f(y) = 2y$". The hidden significance is that it indicates that the function maps real numbers to real numbers since standard mathematical convention dictates that x denotes a real number. By way of comparison, the statement "the function $f(n) = 2n$" would implicitly define a function on natural numbers since mathematical convention dictates that n denotes a natural number. Finally, the boolean expression $f(x) = 2x$ is a so-called *definitional equality*: because its purpose is to define the name "f", it evaluates to true whatever the value of x.

Mathematical vernacular was copied in early programming languages. For example, FORTRAN, a programming language first developed in the 1950s, had the convention that variables beginning with the letters I thru N denoted integer values. But, in the course of time, it was realised that mathematical traditions are untenable in software development. For instance, much mathematical notation (such as juxtaposition, fx, for function application) relies on the names of variables and functions being a single symbol, but in computer programs it is inevitable that multi-character names like "person" and "age" are used. Modern programming languages require the names of variables and functions to be declared, making their types explicit, and different notations are used for function application. Some languages use a space for function application, as in `age person`; this is really just juxtaposition but the space is necessary for parsing purposes. Other languages use an infix dot, as in `person.age`. In this text, we try to heed the lessons of the computer age. But the reader will also have to get used to traditional mathematical shorthands in order to benefit from the vast wealth of mathematical literature. We have therefore adopted a compromise, in particular with regard to notation for functions and their application. In those parts of the text where there are long-standing mathematical conventions we adopt those conventions, but elsewhere we use non-conventional notation.

The examples above are all of functions with just one argument. They are called *unary* functions and the symbols used to denote them (such as the square-root symbol or the symbol "$-$" for negation) are called *unary operators*. When functions with two or more arguments are added to the list, the diversity becomes even greater. The most common notation for binary functions (functions with two arguments) is *infix* notation, as in $a+b$, where the operator is written in between the two operands. Sometimes, however, the function is not denoted (or denoted "by juxtaposition" in the jargon of mathematics) as is the case for multiplication in $2y$; alternatively, it may be denoted by subscripting or superscripting as in x^y, or using a two-dimensional notation as in $\dfrac{x}{y}$. Another example is $\log_b x$. The two arguments are the base b of the logarithm and the argument x. (This example illustrates a general phenomenon whereby arguments that are relevant but the author wants you to ignore are hidden away as subscripts. They function a bit like the small print in legal documents.) In more advanced areas of mathematics, notations like A_i^j are used.

12.3.2 Binary Operators

A *binary* function is a function that has two arguments. A *binary operator* is, strictly speaking, the symbol used to denote a binary function. For example, the symbols "+" and "×" are binary operators, denoting respectively addition and multiplication. Often, however, no distinction is made between the symbol and the function it denotes. Usually, it is clear from the context which is meant. In this text, we use "binary operator" to mean a function of two arguments, and we use "operator symbol" when we want to refer to the symbol itself. As mentioned earlier, binary operators are often written in *infix* form (as in $2+3$ and 2×3), but sometimes they are written as prefixes to their arguments (as in $\log_2 10$ and $\gcd(10,12)$). (The use of a prefix notation for greatest common divisors[2] is an example of a bad choice of notation, as we see later.) They are rarely written in postfix form.

The symbols "$\oplus$" and "$\otimes$" will be used as variables standing for binary operators (in just the same way as we use m and n as variables standing for numbers). We write $\oplus$ and $\otimes$ in infix form, but you should remember that they may also stand for binary operators that are not normally written in infix form.

The symbols f and g will be used as variables to stand for unary functions. Their application to an argument will be denoted in this chapter in the traditional way, as exemplified by "$f(x)$".

12.3.3 Operator Precedence

In any expression involving more than one function application, there is a danger of ambiguity in the order in which the functions are evaluated. Take, for example, the expression $8\div4\div2$. The expression contains two instances of the division operator "$\div$" so there is a question about the order in which the operators are evaluated. Do we first evaluate $8\div4$ (giving 2) and then evaluate $2\div2$ (giving the final answer 1), or should $4\div2$ be evaluated first (giving 2) and then $8\div2$ (giving the final answer 4)? The two different evaluation orders are made clear by introducing parentheses: $(8\div4)\div2$ versus $8\div(4\div2)$. Another example is 8^{4^2}. This is, in fact, the same example except that division

---

[2]Another name for "greatest common divisor" is "highest common factor"; where this name is used, $\gcd(10,12)$ is written $\mathrm{hcf}(10,12)$.

has been replaced by exponentiation. A third example is -2^3. Here the two functions are negation and exponentiation; the question is whether negation is evaluated before exponentiation, as in $(-2)^3$, or the other way around, as in $-(2^3)$. Of course, in this example it makes no difference – the answer is -8 in both cases – but it does make a difference in the expression -2^2.

Mathematical expressions are often ambiguous in this way. As we discuss below, the ambiguity can be deliberate and is exploited in mathematical calculations. This is the case when the ambiguity has no effect on the value of the expression. Where an ambiguity does have an effect on the value, the ambiguity is resolved by specifying an evaluation order and/or an order of *precedence* on the functions involved. The rules are often referred to as mathematical *conventions*. Unfortunately, because mathematical notation has evolved over centuries, traditional conventions are often not stated, causing difficulty for students. (Mathematicians often blame students for the resulting mistakes but should actually blame themselves!)

An example of a "well-known" convention is that subtraction is evaluated from left to right. For example, the expression $1-2-3$ evaluates to -4 (i.e. $(1-2)-3$) and not 2 (which is the value of $1-(2-3)$). In contrast, exponentiation is conventionally evaluated from right to left: the value of 10^{2^3} is $100\,000\,000$ (i.e. 10^8) and not $1\,000\,000$ (i.e. 100^3). An example of where the order is irrelevant, and the resulting ambiguity exploited, is addition: $1+2+3$ has the value 6 irrespective of whether addition is evaluated from left to right or from right to left. (See Section 12.5.4 for further discussion.)

Operator precedence is often necessary when different operators are involved. The best-known example of operator precedence is multiplication versus addition – the standard rule is that multiplication has precedence over addition. Thus when evaluating, say, $1+2\times3$ the value of 2×3 is first computed and then 1 is added to the result. If a different order of evaluation is demanded, this is indicated by the use of parentheses, as in $(1+2)\times3$.

Elementary textbooks often do not mention precedence rules. One reason is that arithmetic notation has evolved in a way that avoids the need to explicitly state the rules. Multiplication is commonly denoted by juxtaposition which has the effect that in an expression like $1+2x$ the human eye naturally groups the symbols 2 and x together. This is also aided by the spaces around the "+" symbol. Similarly, in an expression like 2×3^2 the human eye naturally sees "3^2" as a group, thus suggesting the rule that exponentiation has precedence over multiplication. Adding more space, as in 2×3^2, also helps.

Another reason why operator precedence is not mentioned is that, sometimes, expressions are only meaningful if evaluated in a certain order. This is true of expressions like $m\leq n\times p$ that involve a combination of arithmetic operators (like addition and multiplication) and relations (here the at-most relation denoted by "$\leq$"). It just does not make sense to read this expression as "$(m\leq n)\times p$" because it does not make sense to multiply a boolean and a number. A convention on precedences is unnecessary.

Identifying the structure of an expression is called *parsing* the expression. The parsing problem emerged as an important issue when programming languages were being developed in the 1960s. At that time, the problem was how to instruct a dumb machine to parse expressions of arbitrary complexity. But that experience made us aware that parsing is a problem for human beings too! The more complicated expressions become, the more difficult they become to parse, which is the first step towards understanding their meaning. Unfortunately, many mathematicians rely on the reader's understanding of the meaning of an expression in order to understand its structure. This is a practice we eschew because clarity of expression is vital to problem solving. As a consequence, we strive to ensure that our expressions are easy to parse – wherever possible in the blink of an eye by the use of spacing and choice of operators. But precedence rules are unavoidable. The rules we use divide operators into a number of categories as shown in the table below. Within each category, further precedence rules apply, which are made clear when the operators are first introduced.

Precedence	Operator
highest	unary (prefix or postfix)
	function application (infix dot)
	binary arithmetic ($+$, $\times$ etc.)
	arithmetic relation ($=$, $\leq$ etc.)
lowest	logical connectives ($\equiv$, $\vee$ etc.)

12.4 TYPES AND TYPE CHECKING

As mentioned in Section 12.2.3, the word "type" is often used synonymously with "set". One difference is in the way that "types" are used to avoid mistakes, particularly in computer programs. The process is called "type checking".

For many schoolchildren, the first encounter with type checking is in physics where "types" are called "dimensions". The quantities that are measured (velocity, energy, power, etc.) all have a dimension; for example, the dimension of velocity is distance divided by time and the dimension of acceleration is distance divided by time squared. Whenever an equation is formulated in physics it is useful to check that both sides of the equation have the same dimension. It is relatively easy to do, and is useful in avoiding silly mistakes like equating a velocity with an acceleration.

Computer programs are unbelievably massive in comparison to the formulae used in physics and mathematics, and type checking plays a very significant role in the avoidance of error.

Type checking involves identifying certain *base types* and mechanisms for constructing more complex types from existing types. Examples of base types include the different types of numbers – natural numbers, integers and reals – and the booleans. These types are denoted by $\mathbb{N}$ (the natural numbers), $\mathbb{Z}$ (the integers), $\mathbb{R}$ (the reals) and Bool (the booleans). The simplest mechanisms for constructing more complex types are *cartesian product*, *disjoint sum* and *function spaces*. These three are discussed below. More complicated mechanisms include sets, matrices, polynomials and induction.

12.4.1 Cartesian Product and Disjoint Sum

If A and B are both sets, then their *cartesian product*, $A \times B$, is the set of pairs (a, b), where $a \in A$ and $b \in B$. For example, taking A to be {red,green,blue} and B to be {true,false} then $A \times B$ is

$$\{(\text{red}, \text{true}), (\text{red}, \text{false}), (\text{green}, \text{true}), (\text{green}, \text{false}), (\text{blue}, \text{true}), (\text{blue}, \text{false})\}.$$

The *disjoint sum*, $A+B$, of A and B is a set formed by choosing an element of A or an element of B and tagging the element to indicate from which of the two it was chosen. Various notations are used for the elements of $A+B$. Let us use l (for left) and r (for right) for the tags. Then the disjoint sum of {red,green,blue} and {true,false} is

$$\{\text{l.red}, \text{l.green}, \text{l.blue}, \text{r.true}, \text{r.false}\}.$$

Disjoint sum is sometimes called disjoint *union* because it has similarities to forming the union of two sets; indeed, in the example we have just given the disjoint sum of {red,green,blue} and {true,false} has exactly the same number of elements as the union of {red,green,blue} and {true,false}. Disjoint sum and set union differ when the two sets being combined have elements in common. In particular, for any set A, the set $A+A$ has twice as many elements as the set $A \cup A$. For example, {true,false}+{true,false} is

$$\{\text{l.true}, \text{l.false}, \text{r.true}, \text{r.false}\}.$$

The elements l.true and r.true are distinguished by their tags, as are l.false and r.false.

The use of the arithmetic operators $\times$ and $+$ for cartesian product and disjoint sum is an example of *overloading* of notation. A symbol is "overloaded" if the symbol is used for different types of argument. (Readers familiar with modern programming languages will be aware of the problems of overloading. The symbol "/" is often overloaded so that 1/2 has a different meaning than 1.0/2.0, the former evaluating to 0 and the latter to 0.5. Type "coercions" are sometimes necessary in programs in order to enforce the desired meaning.) An explanation for the overloading is that it makes operations on sets look familiar even though they may be unfamiliar. This is deliberate and is based on correspondences between the two types of operator.

One correspondence is the number of elements in a set. If A and B are both finite sets with p and q elements, respectively, then A×B has p×q elements and A+B has p+q elements. Writing |C| for the number of elements in the (finite) set C, we have the laws

$$[\ |A{\times}B| \ = \ |A| \times |B| \ ]$$

and

$$[\ |A{+}B| \ = \ |A| + |B| \ ].$$

(Recall the discussion of the square "everywhere" brackets in Section 12.1.) In both these equations, on the left "×" and "+" denote operations on sets, whereas on the right they denote operations on numbers. Recalling that Ø denotes the empty set, we have

$$|\emptyset| \ = \ 0.$$

As a consequence, for any finite set A,

$$|A{+}\emptyset| \ = \ |A| + |\emptyset| \ = \ |A| + 0 \ = \ |A|.$$

Similarly,

$$[\ |A{\times}\emptyset| \ = \ |\emptyset| \ = \ 0 \ ].$$

Formally, the sets A+Ø and A are never the same, although they have the same number of elements – the difference is that all the elements of A+Ø have a tag. So we cannot write [A+Ø=A]. When two (finite) sets have the same number of elements they are said to be *isomorphic*. The symbol "≅" is used to denote isomorphism, so we have the law

$$[\ A{+}\emptyset \ \cong \ A \ ].$$

Similarly,

$$[\ A{\times}\emptyset \ \cong \ \emptyset \ ].$$

In the above paragraph, we limited the discussion to finite sets. However, the properties hold also for infinite sets. This involves some advanced mathematics which is beyond the scope of this text. The notion of "number" has to be extended to the so-called "transfinite" numbers and the number of elements of a set is called the *cardinality* of the set. That the properties hold for all sets, and not just finite sets, is a justification for overloading the notation.

12.4.2 Function Types

A function maps input values to output values. The type of a function therefore has two components, the type of the input and the type of the output. The type of the input values is called the *domain* and the type of the output values is called the *range*. We write

$$A \rightarrow B$$

for the type of a function with domain A and range B. Examples are $\mathbb{Z} \rightarrow \mathsf{Bool}$, the type of the function even which determines whether a given integer is even or odd, $\mathbb{R} \rightarrow \mathbb{R}$, the type of negation, doubling, squaring etc., and $\mathbb{R} \rightarrow \mathbb{Z}$, the type of the so-called floor and ceiling functions.

The domain and range of a function are integral to its definition. For example, the process of adding 1 to a number has different properties depending on the type of the number. (See Section 15.1.) It is important, therefore, to distinguish between the function +1 of type $\mathbb{N} \rightarrow \mathbb{N}$ and the function +1 of type $\mathbb{R} \rightarrow \mathbb{R}$. The type of a function is particularly important when overloaded notation is used (for example, the use of + and × for operations on numbers and operations on sets).

The domain type of a binary operator is a cartesian product of two types. Addition and multiplication of real numbers both have type $\mathbb{R} \times \mathbb{R} \rightarrow \mathbb{R}$. Functions can also have functions as arguments; such functions are called *higher-order* functions. Function application is the first example we all encounter. As stated in Section 12.3.2, we use an infix dot to denote function application; every use of function application has type $(A \rightarrow B) \times A \rightarrow B$ for some types A and B. That is, the first argument of function application is a function of type $A \rightarrow B$, for some A and B, and the second argument is a value of type A; the result of applying the function to the value then has type B. (Function application is an example of what computing scientists call a *polymorphic* function. There is not just one function application – there is a distinct instance for each pair of types A and B, but the distinction is not important. The simplest example of a polymorphic function is the so-called *identity function*. This is the function that maps every value to itself. There is an identity function for every type A.)

Function types are sometimes denoted by using superscripts. Instead of writing $A \rightarrow B$ the notation B^A is used. This is done for the same reason that + and × are used for disjoint sum and cartesian product. It is the case that, for all sets A and B,

$$|B^A| \;=\; |B|^{|A|}.$$

To see this for finite sets A and B, consider how one might define a function f of type $A \rightarrow B$. For each element a of A there are $|B|$ choices for the value of $f(a)$. So, if A has one element there are $|B|$ choices for f, if A has two elements, there are $|B| \times |B|$ choices for f, if A has three elements there are $|B| \times |B| \times |B|$ choices for f, etc. That is, the number of different choices for f is $|B|^{|A|}$.

A consequence is that function spaces enjoy properties like exponentiation in normal arithmetic. For example,

$$\left[\;\; |A^{B+C}| \;=\; |A^B \times A^C| \;\;\right].$$

Equivalently,

$$\left[\;\; A^{B+C} \;\cong\; A^B \times A^C \;\;\right].$$

The sets A^{B+C} and $A^B \times A^C$ are never the same (one is a set of functions, the other is a set of pairs) but they have the same cardinality. This is an important elementary property in combinatorics. See Section 16.8 for further discussion.

If arrow notation is used to denote function spaces, this rule (and others) looks less familiar and so may be less easy to remember:

$$[\;\; (B+C) \to A \;\;\cong\;\; (B \to A) \times (C \to A) \;\;].$$

The exponent notation is not used as frequently as the arrow notation but it is commonly used for the so-called *power set* of a set. A set A is a *subset* of a set B if every element of A is an element of the set B. The *power set* of set A is the set of all subsets of A. The subset relation is denoted by the symbol "$\subseteq$". For example, {Monday,Tuesday} is a subset of the set of weekdays, and the set of weekdays is a subset of the set of days. The empty set is a subset of every set and every set is a subset of itself so we have the two laws:

$$[\;\emptyset \subseteq A\;] \quad \text{and} \quad [\;A \subseteq A\;].$$

The power set of the empty set has exactly one element (the empty set) and the power set of any non-empty set has at least two elements. One way of specifying a subset of a set A is to specify a function with range Bool and domain A; applied to an element of A, the function has value true if the element is in the subset and false otherwise. (This function is called the *characteristic* function of the subset.) The number of subsets of A is thus $|\text{Bool}^A|$, which equals $|\text{Bool}|^{|A|}$ (i.e. $2^{|A|}$). This suggests the notation 2^A for the set of subsets of A – this is the explanation for the curious name "power set". (Some authors use the notation $\wp(A)$, where the "$\wp$" abbreviates "power", but then the motivation completely disappears.)

12.5 ALGEBRAIC PROPERTIES

The use of a mathematical notation aids problem solving because mathematical expressions are typically more concise than statements in natural language. Clarity is gained from economy of expression. But mathematical notation is not just an abbreviated form of natural language – the real benefit of mathematical expressions is in calculations.

All of the objects of mathematical discourse that we have introduced so far (numbers, sets, functions, etc.) have properties that are captured in mathematical laws. Such mathematical laws form the basis of mathematical calculations.

Arithmetic is the sort of calculations done with specific numbers, sometimes by hand and sometimes with the help of a calculator. An example of an arithmetic calculation is calculating income tax for an individual given their income and outgoings and the tax laws that are in force. *Algebra* is about calculations on arbitrary mathematical expressions and often involving objects and functions other than numbers and the standard arithmetic operators. Boolean algebra, for example, is about calculating with boolean expressions formed from the two boolean values true and false, variables (denoting boolean values) and the *boolean operators*, operators such as "conjunction" and "disjunction". Relation algebra is about calculating with relations and operators such as "transitive closure". We introduce these operators in later sections.

When studying new operators, mathematicians investigate whether or not certain kinds of algebraic law hold. Although much more general than arithmetic, the properties that one looks out for are very much informed by the laws of arithmetic. This section introduces the terminology that is used.

In the section, we use the symbols "$\oplus$" and "$\otimes$" as variables denoting binary operators. We assume that each operator has type $A \times A \to A$ for some type A, called the *carrier* of the operator. Instances include addition, multiplication, minimum and maximum – for each of these the carrier is assumed to be R (the set of real numbers). Other instances include set union, and intersection – for which the carrier is a power set 2^A, for some A. We also use greatest common divisor (abbreviated gcd) and least common multiple (abbreviated lcm) as examples. For these, the carrier is N (the set of natural numbers).

12.5.1 Symmetry

A binary operator $\oplus$ is said to be *symmetric* (or *commutative*) if

$$[\ x \oplus y = y \oplus x\ ] .$$

(Recall that the square brackets are read as "everywhere" or, in this case, for all values of x and y in the carrier of the operator $\oplus$.)

Examples   Addition and multiplication are symmetric binary operators:

$$[\text{Symmetry}]\quad [\ x+y = y+x\ ], \tag{12.1}$$

$$[\text{Symmetry}]\quad [\ x \times y = y \times x\ ]. \tag{12.2}$$

The minimum and maximum operators on numbers are also symmetric. For the minimum of two numbers x and y, we write $x \downarrow y$; for their maximum, we write $x \uparrow y$. (We explain why we use an infix notation rather than the more common $\min(x, y)$ and $\max(x, y)$ shortly.)

Non-examples   Division and exponentiation are not symmetric binary operators:

$$\frac{1}{2} \neq \frac{2}{1}$$

and

$$2^3 \neq 3^2.$$

(To show that a property does not hold everywhere, we only need to give one counterexample.)

12.5.2 Zero and Unit

Suppose that $\otimes$ is symmetric. Then the value z is said to be the *zero* of $\otimes$ if, for all x,

$$x \otimes z = z.$$

The value e is said to be the *unit* of $\otimes$ if, for all x,

$$x \otimes e = x.$$

The number 0 is the zero of multiplication, and the number 1 is the unit of multiplication. That is,

$$[\text{Zero}] \quad [\, x \times 0 = 0 \,], \tag{12.3}$$

$$[\text{Unit}] \quad [\, x \times 1 = x \,]. \tag{12.4}$$

Note that 0 is the *unit* of addition since

$$[\text{Unit}] \quad [\, x + 0 = x \,]. \tag{12.5}$$

Least common multiple (lcm) and greatest common divisor (gcd) are both symmetric operators. The number 0 is the zero of lcm,

$$[\text{Zero}] \quad [\, m \text{ lcm } 0 = 0 \,], \tag{12.6}$$

and the number 1 is the unit of lcm,

$$[\text{Unit}] \quad [\, m \text{ lcm } 1 = m \,]. \tag{12.7}$$

Note that 0 is the only common multiple of m and 0 so it is inevitably the least.

For greatest common divisors, the terms "zero" and "unit" can, at first, be confusing. The zero of gcd is 1,

$$[\textbf{Zero}] \quad [\ m \text{ gcd } 1 \ = \ 1\ ], \quad\quad\quad (12.8)$$

and the unit of gcd is 0,

$$[\textbf{Unit}] \quad [\ m \text{ gcd } 0 \ = \ m\ ]. \quad\quad\quad (12.9)$$

(An instance of the unit rule is that 0 gcd 0 is 0. This may seem strange: how can 0 be a divisor of itself? The problem is that we have not yet given a precise definition of "greatest common divisor". This we do in Section 12.7.)

There is no unit of minimum in $\textbf{R}$. It is possible to augment $\textbf{R}$ with a new number, called *infinity* and denoted by ∞. It then becomes necessary to extend the definition of addition, multiplication etc. to include this number. By definition, ∞ is the unit of minimum,

$$[\textbf{Unit}] \quad [\ x{\downarrow}\infty \ = \ x\ ], \quad\quad\quad (12.10)$$

and the zero of maximum,

$$[\textbf{Zero}] \quad [\ x{\uparrow}\infty \ = \ \infty\ ]. \quad\quad\quad (12.11)$$

(The everywhere brackets now mean "for all x in $\textbf{R}\cup\{\infty\}$".) Note that the introduction of infinity introduces complications when, as is usually the case, other operators such as addition and subtraction are involved.

If the operator $\otimes$ is not symmetric it is necessary to distinguish between a left zero and a right zero and between a left unit and a right unit. These definitions are easily given where necessary.

12.5.3 Idempotence

A binary operator $\oplus$ is said to be *idempotent* if

$$[\ x{\oplus}x \ = \ x\ ].$$

Examples Minimum, maximum, greatest common divisor and least common multiple are all examples of idempotent operators. For example,

$$[\textbf{Idempotence}] \quad [\ x{\downarrow}x \ = \ x\ ] \quad\quad\quad (12.12)$$

and

$$[\textbf{Idempotence}] \quad [\ m \text{ gcd } m \ = \ m\ ]. \quad\quad\quad (12.13)$$

Set union and set intersection are also idempotent.

Non-examples   Addition and multiplication are non-examples of idempotence since, for example, $1+1 \neq 1$ and $2 \times 2 \neq 2$.

Typically (although not necessarily), idempotent operators are linked to "ordering relations": minimum is linked to the at-least relation and greatest common divisor is linked to the divides relation. See Section 12.7.6 and the exercises at the end of the chapter.

12.5.4 Associativity

A binary operator $\oplus$ is said to be *associative* if

$$[\ x \oplus (y \oplus z)\ =\ (x \oplus y) \oplus z\ ].$$

Examples   Addition and multiplication are associative binary operators:

$$\text{[Associativity]} \quad [\ x+(y+z) = (x+y)+z\ ], \qquad\qquad (12.14)$$

$$\text{[Associativity]} \quad [\ x \times (y \times z) = (x \times y) \times z\ ]. \qquad\qquad (12.15)$$

Non-examples   Division and exponentiation are not associative:

$$1/(2/3) \neq (1/2)/3$$

and

$$2\char`^(3\char`^4) \neq (2\char`^3)\char`^4.$$

(In the second statement, we have used the symbol "$\char`^$" for exponentiation, rather than the conventional superscript notation, because it makes the comparison with division clearer.)

When an operator is associative and it is denoted using an infix operator symbol we can omit parentheses, without fear of confusion, in a so-called *continued* expression. For example, the *continued addition*

$$1+2+3+4+5$$

is equal to $(((1+2)+3)+4)+5$, $((1+2)+3)+(4+5)$, $(1+2)+(3+(4+5))$ and so on. Parentheses indicate in what order the expression is to be evaluated but, because addition is associative, the order does not matter. This is a very, very important aspect of infix notation.

When an operator is symmetric as well as associative, we are free to rearrange terms in a continued expression as well as omit parentheses. For example,

$$2 \times 4 \times 5 \times 25$$

is easiest to evaluate when written as

$$(2 \times 5) \times (4 \times 25).$$

(This, of course, you would normally do in your head.)

We mentioned earlier that the usual prefix notation for greatest common divisors is a poor choice of notation. The reason is that "gcd" is associative and symmetric. That is, using prefix notation,

[**Symmetry**] $\left[gcd(x, y) = gcd(y, x) \right]$ (12.16)

and

[**Associativity**] $\left[gcd(x, gcd(y, z)) = gcd(gcd(x, y), z) \right].$ (12.17)

Try evaluating

$$gcd(5, gcd(10, gcd(24, 54))).$$

Now use an infix notation so that the problem becomes to evaluate

5 gcd 10 gcd 24 gcd 54.

The infix notation makes it much easier to spot that 5 gcd 24 equals 1, and so the value of the expression is 1. The prefix notation requires you to work out three different gcd values, beginning with 24 gcd 54, which is not so easy to do in your head.

Minimum and maximum are also commonly denoted by prefix operators but, because they are both associative and symmetric, it makes much more sense to write them as infix operators. Throughout this book, the symbol "↓" is used for minimum, and "↑" is used for maximum. For example,

u↓v↓w↓x

denotes the minimum of four values u, v, w and x.

12.5.5 Distributivity/Factorisation

A function f is said to *distribute* over the operator $\oplus$ if there is an operator $\otimes$ such that

$$\left[f(x \oplus y) = f(x) \otimes f(y) \right].$$

Examples   Multiplication distributes through addition:

[**Distributivity**] $[x \times (y+z) = x \times y + x \times z].$ (12.18)

Exponentiation also distributes through addition:

[**Distributivity**] $\left[\ b^{y+z} = b^y \times b^z\ \right].$ (12.19)

Note how addition changes to multiplication in the process of "distributing" the exponentiation over the terms in the addition. The function f in this example is "b to the power". That is, it is the function that maps a value x to b^x.

Because logarithms are the inverse of exponentiation, there is an inverse distributivity law:

[**Distributivity**] $\left[\ \log_b(x \times y) = \log_b x + \log_b y\ \right].$ (12.20)

Multiplication changes to addition in the process of "distributing" the logarithm over the terms in the multiplication.

(In each of these examples, we actually have a *family* of distributivity properties. For example, property (12.18) states that multiplication by x distributes through addition, *for each value of* x. So, multiplication by 2 (doubling) distributes through addition; so does multiplication by 3 and by 4, etc.)

Non-example   Addition does not distribute through multiplication:

$$1+(2\times3) \neq ((1+2)\times(1+3)).$$

Continued Expressions   When a function distributes through an associative binary operator, the use of an infix notation is again very helpful. For example, $2\times$ can be distributed through the addition in

$$2\times(5+10+15+20)$$

to give

$$2\times5 + 2\times10 + 2\times15 + 2\times20.$$

The converse of distribution is called *factorisation*. The use of an infix notation is helpful in factorisation as well. For example, the log function can be factorised from

$$\log_b 5 + \log_b 10 + \log_b 15 + \log_b 20$$

giving

$$\log_b(5\times10\times15\times20).$$

12.5.6 Algebras

The algebraic properties we have discussed are so important that mathematicians have studied them in great depth. The word "algebra" is used in, for example, "elementary algebra", "boolean algebra" and "relation algebra" to mean the rules governing a collection of operators defined on a set (or collection of sets). ("Elementary algebra" is the collection of rules governing the arithmetic operators such as addition and multiplication on the real numbers.) Certain algebras are basic to many applications. In this section, we give the definitions of a "monoid", a "group" and a "semiring". Monoids and groups are quite universal. Semirings are basic to many path-finding problems. Elsewhere you will find definitions of "rings", "fields" and "vector spaces".

Definition 12.21 (Monoid) A *monoid* is a triple $(A,1,\times)$ where A is a set, 1 is an element of A and $\times$ is a binary operator on A. It is required that $\times$ is associative and 1 is the (left and right) unit of $\times$.

A monoid is said to be *symmetric* (or *commutative*) if $\times$ is symmetric.

The triple $(\mathbb{N},1,\times)$ (the set of natural numbers, the number 1 and multiplication of numbers) is the archetypical example of a symmetric monoid. The triple $(\mathbb{N},0,+)$ is also a symmetric monoid.

Definition 12.22 (Group) A *group* is a 4-tuple $(A,1,\times,^{-1})$ such that $(A,1,\times)$ is a monoid and $^{-1}$ is a unary operator on A such that

$$\left[x\times(x^{-1}) = 1 = (x^{-1})\times x \right].$$

A group is said to be *abelian* (or *symmetric*, or *commutative*) if the operator $\times$ is symmetric. (Other synonyms for abelian are *symmetric* and *commutative*.)

The 4-tuple $(\mathbb{Z},0,+,-)$, where "$-$" denotes the unary negation operator and not binary subtraction, is an example of an abelian group. (The triple $(\mathbb{Z},0,+)$ is a symmetric monoid and $[m+(-m) = 0]$.)

Monoids and groups frequently arise when considering a set of transformations on an object (e.g. rotating and/or translating a physical three-dimensional object). The transformations form a group when each is "invertible" (i.e. the transformation can be reversed), otherwise they form a monoid. The unit is the do-nothing transformation. Section 11.2 gives an example of flipping the rows and columns of a 2×2 square.

Definition 12.23 (Semiring) A *semiring* is a 5-tuple $(A,1,0,\times,+)$ such that:

- $(A,1,\times)$ is a monoid;
- $(A,0,+)$ is a symmetric monoid;

- 0 is the zero of $\times$;
- $\times$ distributes over +, that is,

$$[\ x\times(y+z)\ =\ (y\times x)+(z\times x)\ ]$$

and

$$[\ (y+z)\times x\ =\ (x\times y)+(x\times z)\ ]\ .$$

The operator $\times$ is said to be the *product* operator of the semiring and the operator + is said to be its *addition* operator. A semiring is *idempotent* if the operator + is idempotent.

Semirings are fundamental to the use of "quantifiers" (see Chapter 14) which are an integral part of many problems and, specifically, in path-finding problems. See Chapter 16 for a number of applications. A *ring* is a semiring $(A,1,0,\times,+)$ with an additional unary operator "$-$" (called the *additive inverse* operator) such that $(A,0,+,-)$ is an abelian group.

12.6 BOOLEAN OPERATORS

Because set comprehension is such a ubiquitous method of defining sets, functions on booleans are very important. For example, corresponding to the union of sets, there is a binary operation from booleans to booleans called *disjunction* and, corresponding to intersection, there is a binary operation (also from booleans to booleans) called *conjunction*. Boolean-valued operators are relations; when the arguments are also booleans, the operators are called *logical connectives* because they relate ("connect") the basic primitives of logic, the boolean values true and false. *Equality* is the most fundamental logical connective; *implication* is another. We introduce these boolean operators in this section. Chapter 13 goes into much more detail about their properties; see also Chapter 5.

Since the domain and range of boolean operators are (small) finite sets we can give them a precise mathematical meaning by simply enumerating all possible combinations of input and output value. This is done in a *truth table*.

There are two booleans and hence 2^2 functions that map a single boolean value into a boolean value. These four truth tables are as follows:

p	true	p	¬p	false
true	true	true	false	false
false	true	false	true	false

The first column of this table enumerates the different values that the variable p can take. Each of the columns after the vertical line lists the values returned by one of the four functions when applied to the input value p. In order from left to right, these are the *constant-true* function, the *identity* function, *negation*, and the *constant-false* function. The constant-true function always returns the value true and the constant-false function always returns the value false. The identity function returns the input value. Finally, negation returns false given input true and returns true given input false.

Because these are the only functions of type Bool→Bool any boolean expression in one boolean variable p can always be simplified to either true, p, ¬p, or false.

There are $2^{2 \times 2}$ (i.e. 16) binary functions from booleans to booleans. Eight correspond to the most frequently used ones: six binary operators and the constant true and false functions. These eight are shown in the following table:

p	q	true	$p = q$ $p \equiv q$	$p \neq q$ $p \not\equiv q$	$p \vee q$	$p \wedge q$	$p \Leftarrow q$	$p \Rightarrow q$	false
true	true	true	true	false	true	true	true	true	false
true	false	true	false	true	true	false	true	false	false
false	true	true	false	true	true	false	false	true	false
false	false	true	true	false	false	false	true	true	false

To the left of the vertical line, all four different combinations of input values p and q are listed. To the right of the vertical line, the values returned by the eight binary operators are listed. Above each column is the notation that is used for the operator. From left to right, the operators are the constant-true function, (boolean) equality, (boolean) inequality, disjunction, conjunction, if, only if, and the constant-false function.

The truth table for equality needs no explanation: the value of p=q is true when p and q have the same value, and false otherwise. (For example, the value of true=true is true while the value of false=true is false.) Inequality (≠) is the opposite. Equality and inequality of booleans are also denoted by the symbols "≡" and "≢", respectively. See Section 5.3 for further explanation.

Disjunction is also called "(logical) or" and conjunction is called "(logical) and". The "or" of two booleans has the value true when at least one has the value true; the "and" of two booleans has the value true when both have the value true. The symbols "∨" and "∧" (pronounced "or" and "and") are used to denote these operators. To enhance clarity, disjunction is sometimes called "inclusive-or" to distinguish it from "exclusive-or"; the "exclusive-or" of two booleans has the value true when exactly one of them has the value true. "Exclusive-or" is the same as "different from", as can be checked by examining the truth table for inequality.

The symbol "$\Leftarrow$" is pronounced "if" or "follows from". The value of false$\Leftarrow$true is false; all other values of p$\Leftarrow$q are true. The symbol "$\Rightarrow$" is pronounced "only if" or "implies". The value of true$\Rightarrow$false is false; all other values of p$\Rightarrow$q are true.

12.7 BINARY RELATIONS

A *binary relation* is a function of two arguments that is boolean-valued. An example of a binary relation is the equality relation. Two objects of the same type (two numbers, two apples, two students, etc.) are either equal or not equal. Another example of a relation is the divides relation. Given two numbers, either the first divides the second or it does not.

Infix notation is often used for binary relations. This reflects the usual practice in natural language – we say "Anne is married to Bill" (the relation "is married to" is written between the two arguments), and "Anne is the sister of Clare". (Note that "Anne is married to Bill" is either true or false.)

Relations are often depicted graphically. The values in the relation are the nodes in a graph and directed edges connect related values. As a simple example, consider the two letters "A" and "B" in the sequence "ABBA". The letter "B" follows both the letter "A" and the letter "B"; the letter "A" follows only the letter "B". We can depict the "follows" relation in a graph with two nodes, labelled "A" and "B", and three edges. This is shown in Figure 12.1(a). Figure 12.1(b) shows the follows relation on the letters "C" and "D" in the sequence "CCDD". Note the arrows – the arrow from D to C indicates that D follows C. It is not the case that C follows D.

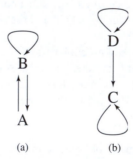

(a)   (b)

○ **Figure 12.1: The follows relation on the letters in the sequences (a) ABBA and (b) CCDD.**

A genealogy tree depicts the "is a parent of" relation on members of a family. (A genealogy tree also depicts the ancestor relation – see the discussion of Hasse diagrams below.) Arrows are often not drawn on a genealogy tree because the dates shown make them unnecessary.

Important properties of binary relations are *reflexivity*, *symmetry* and *transitivity*. We discuss these in turn and explain how the use of an infix notation helps to exploit the properties.

Examples of relations that are used below include the at-most relation on numbers, denoted by "$\leq$", and the different-from relation on numbers, denoted by "$\neq$". A third example is the divides relation on integers, which we denote by the symbol "\". (So m\n is read as "m divides n".) We say n *is a multiple of* m whenever there is some integer k such that m×k equals n and we say that m *divides* n whenever n is a multiple of m. For example, 3 divides 6 because 3×2 equals 6. It is important to note that every integer divides 0 because m×0 equals 0 for all m. That is,

[m\0].

In particular, 0\0. In words, zero divides itself. If this seems odd, the problem is the use of the English word "divides" which may be understood differently. Here we have defined the divides relation to be the *converse* of the "is a multiple of" relation. This defines precisely the meaning of the word "divides" and it is important to stick to the definition. Do not confuse m\n with $\frac{m}{n}$ or m÷n; the former is a boolean while the latter two are numbers.

The variables R, S and T will be used to stand for binary relations.

12.7.1 Reflexivity

A relation R is *reflexive* if

[x R x].

Examples Equality is a reflexive relation:

[**Reflexivity**]   [x = x].   (12.24)

The at-most relation on numbers is reflexive:

[**Reflexivity**]   [x ≤ x].   (12.25)

(Warning: learn to pronounce "$\leq$" as "at most". Saying "less than or equal to" is an awful mouthful! It also has the disadvantage that it suggests a case analysis on "less than" and "equal to" when reasoning about the operator; case analyses should be avoided wherever possible. Similarly, pronounce "$\geq$" as "at least" rather than "greater than or equal to".)

The divides relation is reflexive:

[**Reflexivity**]   [m\m].   (12.26)

(Note the convention: m denotes an integer.)

An example of an everyday reflexive relation is "has the same birthday as" (everyone has the same birthday as themselves). Note that this is just equality ("the same") in disguise; generally, if f is an arbitrary function, we get a reflexive relation by defining x and y to be related whenever f(x) equals f(y). In this example, the function is "birthday". Indeed, the same trick is used to construct relations with properties other than reflexivity, in particular so-called "equivalence relations". See Section 12.7.8 for details.

Non-examples   The less-than relation on numbers is not reflexive:

$0 < 0 \equiv$ false.

(This is sometimes written "$0 \not< 0$". By a common mathematical convention, "$\not<$" denotes the complement of the less-than relation; it so happens that $\not<$ is reflexive, i.e. [$x \not< x$].) The different-from relation is not reflexive. (No value is different from itself.) The "is a sibling of" relation on family members is also not reflexive. No one is a sibling of themselves.

12.7.2 Symmetry

A relation R is *symmetric* if

[$x R y = y R x$].

Recall that a relation is a boolean-valued function. So $x R y$ is either true or false, depending on the values of x and y. Similarly, the value of $y R x$ is either true or false, depending on the values of x and y. A relation is symmetric if the value of $x R y$ is equal to the value of $y R x$ whatever the values of x and y.

Examples   Equality is a symmetric relation:

[**Symmetry**]   [$(x = y) = (y = x)$].   (12.27)

The different-from relation is symmetric:

[**Symmetry**]   [$(x \neq y) = (y \neq x)$].   (12.28)

An example of an everyday symmetric relation is "is married to".

These examples may seem confusing at first. Natural language is focused on true statements, and it is unnatural to allow false statements. George Boole, who originated the "boolean values", had the great insight that a statement can have the value true or false. This means that we can compare them for equality. For given values of x and y, the expression $x = y$ evaluates to either true or false (for example, $0 = 0$ has the value true, and $0 = 1$ has the value false). The symmetry of equality states that the value of $x = y$ is always the same as the value of $y = x$.

(To appreciate the confusion of natural language better, note that the symmetry of equality means that $x = 0$ is the same as $0 = x$. However, many people are very reluctant to write "$0 = x$" because it seems to be a statement about 0, in contrast to the statement "$x = 0$", which seems to be a statement about x. You will need to unlearn this "natural" or "intuitive" way of thinking; train yourself to accept George Boole's insight that they are identical.)

Non-examples The at-most relation on numbers is not symmetric:

$$(0 \leq 1) \neq (1 \leq 0).$$

The value of $0 \leq 1$ is true, and the value of $1 \leq 0$ is false, and true and false are not equal. The divides relation is not symmetric:

$$1 \backslash 2 \neq 2 \backslash 1.$$

12.7.3 Converse

The *converse* of relation R is the relation $R^{\cup}$ defined by

$$[\text{Converse}] \quad \left[x\,R^{\cup}\,y \ = \ y\,R\,x \right]. \tag{12.29}$$

For example, the converse of "at most" ($\leq$) is "at least" ($\geq$) and the converse of the divides relation is the "is a multiple of" relation. Note that a relation R is symmetric exactly when R and $R^{\cup}$ are equal. We do not use the notation $R^{\cup}$, but we often refer to the converse of a (non-symmetric) relation.

12.7.4 Transitivity

A relation R is said to be *transitive* if, for all x, y and z, whenever $x\,R\,y$ is true and $y\,R\,z$ is true, it is also the case that $x\,R\,z$ is true.

Examples Equality is a transitive relation:

$$[\text{Transitivity}] \quad [\ x = y \wedge y = z \ \Rightarrow \ x = z\ ]. \tag{12.30}$$

(Recall that the symbol "$\wedge$" means "and" and the symbol "$\Rightarrow$" means "implies" or "only if".)

The at-most relation on numbers is transitive:

[**Transitivity**] $[\ x \leq y \wedge y \leq z \ \Rightarrow\ x \leq z\ ]$.   (12.31)

The divides relation is transitive:

[**Transitivity**] $[\ m \backslash n \wedge n \backslash p \ \Rightarrow\ m \backslash p\ ]$.   (12.32)

(Read this as: for all m, n and p, if m divides n and n divides p then m divides p.)

Non-examples   The different-from relation is not transitive. We have $0 \neq 1$ and $1 \neq 0$ but this does not imply that $0 \neq 0$. Formally, $0 \neq 1 \wedge 1 \neq 0 \Rightarrow 0 \neq 0$ has the value false.

The "child of" relation is clearly not transitive. Perhaps surprisingly, the sibling relation is also *not* transitive. Because it is symmetric, if it were transitive it would also be reflexive, which we know is not the case. For example, suppose Ann is a sibling of Bob. Then Bob is a sibling of Ann. Now suppose the sibling relation is transitive. Then it follows that Ann is a sibling of Ann. But no one is a sibling of themself. So the sibling relation cannot be transitive.

Note how unreliable the use of natural language can be. "Siblings of siblings are siblings" sounds perfectly plausible, but it is false.

Continued Expressions   When a relation is transitive, it is often used in *continued expressions*. We might write, for example, $m \leq n \leq p$. Here, the expression must be read *conjunctionally*: the meaning is $m \leq n$ *and* $n \leq p$. In this way, the formula is more compact (since n is not written twice). Moreover, we are guided to the inference that $m \leq p$. The transitivity of the at-most relation is implicit in the notation.

Similarly, we might write $m = n = p$. This too should be read conjunctionally. And, because equality is transitive, we infer directly that $m = p$. This is what is happening in a calculation like the one below. (In the calculation A, B and C are sets. Refer back to Section 12.4 for discussion of the laws that are used in the calculation.)

$$|A^{B+C}|$$

$=$ $\{$ law: $[\ |A^B| \ = \ |A|^{|B|}\ ]$ with $B := B+C\ \}$

$$|A|^{|B+C|}$$

$=$ $\{$ law: $[\ |A+B| \ = \ |A| + |B|\ ]$ with $A,B := B,C\ \}$

$$|A|^{|B|+|C|}$$

$=$ $\{$ exponentiation distributes over addition $\}$

$$|A|^{|B|} \times |A|^{|C|}$$

$$= \qquad \{ \qquad \text{law: } [\ |A^B|\ =\ |A|^{|B|}\ ] \text{ used twice,}$$

$$\text{the second time with } B := C \ \ \}$$

$$|A^B| \times |A^C|$$

$$= \qquad \{ \qquad \text{law: } [\ |A \times B|\ =\ |A| \times |B|\ ] \text{ with } A,B := A^B, A^C \ \ \}$$

$$|A^B \times A^C|.$$

The calculation asserts that each expression is equal to the following expression. But, just as importantly, it asserts that the first and the last expressions are equal. That is, the conclusion of the calculation is the law

$$[\ |A^{B+C}|\ =\ |A^B \times A^C|\ ].$$

(The everywhere brackets are introduced in the conclusion because at no point does the calculation depend on the values of A, B or C.) The advantage of the conjunctional meaning of a continued equality is that long expressions do not have to be written twice (which would make it harder to read and give greater scope for error) and the transitivity of equality comes for free.

Sometimes different relations are combined in continued expressions. For example, we might write $0 \leq m < n$. This is read conjunctionally as $0 \leq m$ and $m < n$, from which we infer that $0 < n$. Here, the inference is more complex since there are two relations involved. But it is an inference that is so fundamental that the notation is designed to facilitate its recognition.

12.7.5 Anti–symmetry

An *anti-symmetric* relation is a relation R such that, for all x and y, whenever $x\,R\,y$ is true and $y\,R\,x$ is true, it is the case that x and y are equal.

Examples The at-most relation on numbers is anti-symmetric:

$$\textbf{[Anti-symmetry]} \quad [\ x \leq y \wedge y \leq x\ \Rightarrow\ x = y\ ]. \tag{12.33}$$

The divides relation *on natural numbers* is anti-symmetric:

$$\textbf{[Anti-symmetry]} \quad [\ m \backslash n \wedge n \backslash m\ \Rightarrow\ m = n\ ]. \tag{12.34}$$

Non-examples The different-from relation is not anti-symmetric: $0 \neq 1$ and $1 \neq 0$, but it is not the case that $0 = 1$.

The divides relation *on integers* is not anti-symmetric: 1 divides -1 and -1 divides 1, but 1 and -1 are not equal. This example shows that it is sometimes important to know the type of a relation; the type of a relation defines the set of values on which the relation is defined. The divides relation on natural numbers is not the same as the divides relation on integers; the two relations have different properties.

12.7.6 Orderings

A relation that is reflexive, transitive and anti-symmetric is called an *ordering* relation.

Examples   The equality relation is an ordering relation.

The at-most relation is an ordering relation. It is an example of a so-called *total* ordering. That is, for all numbers x and y, either $x \leq y$ or $y \leq x$.

The divides relation is an ordering relation. It is a *partial* ordering. This is because it is not the case that, for all natural numbers m and n, either m\n or n\m. For example, it is neither the case that 2 divides 3 nor 3 divides 2.

We can now give a precise definition of the "greatest common divisor" of two numbers m and n. It is the greatest – *in the partial ordering defined by the divides relation* – number p such that p\m and p\n. Thus "greatest" does *not* mean with respect to the at-most relation on numbers. This explains why 0 gcd 0 equals 0. In the partial ordering defined by the divides relation, 0 is the greatest number because every number divides 0. There is, however, no "largest" divisor of 0, where "largest" means with respect to the at-most ordering on numbers. It would be very unfortunate indeed if 0 gcd 0 were not defined because then gcd would not be associative. (For example, (1 gcd 0) gcd 0 would equal 1 but 1 gcd (0 gcd 0) would be undefined.) See Section 15.3 for more details.

Hasse Diagrams   Ordering relations are often depicted in a diagram, called a *Hasse diagram*. The values in the ordering are depicted by nodes in the diagram. Two values that are "ordered" are connected by an upward path, of edge-length zero or more, in the diagram. Figure 12.2 depicts a partial ordering of a set with six elements (named by the numbers from 0 thru 5).

The Hasse diagram does not actually depict the relation itself. Rather it depicts a relation whose so-called *reflexive transitive closure* is the relation of interest. For example, the Hasse diagram for the at-most relation on natural numbers (Figure 12.3(a)) actually depicts the predecessor relation (the relation that holds between a number m and m+1, but is true nowhere else). "At most" is the "reflexive transitive closure" of the predecessor relation. Similarly, Figure 12.3(b) is the Hasse diagram for the divides relation on the first six natural numbers but, even though 1 divides all numbers and 0 is divisible by all numbers, there is not an edge from the node labelled 1 to every node nor is there an edge to the node labelled 0 from every node. "Reflexive closure" means allowing paths of length zero – there is a path of length zero from each node to itself – and transitive closure means allowing paths of length two or more.

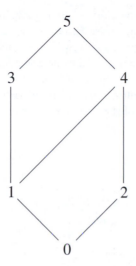

Figure 12.2: Hasse diagram of a partial ordering.

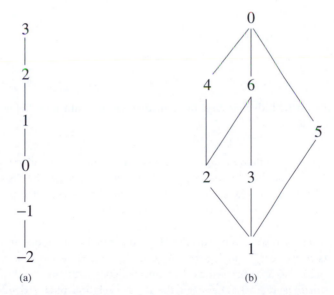

Figure 12.3: (Partial) Hasse diagrams of (a) the at-most relation and (b) the divides relation.

Figure 12.4 shows (a) the reflexive closure, (b) the transitive closure and (c) the reflexive transitive closure of the relation shown earlier in Figure 12.2. The reflexive closure is simply formed by adding loops from each node to itself (thus making the relation reflexive). The transitive closure is formed by adding additional edges from one node to another where there is a path (upwards) of length two or more connecting the nodes (thus making the relation transitive). The convention that the relation holds between two numbers only if the level of the first is at most the level of the second applies to these figures.

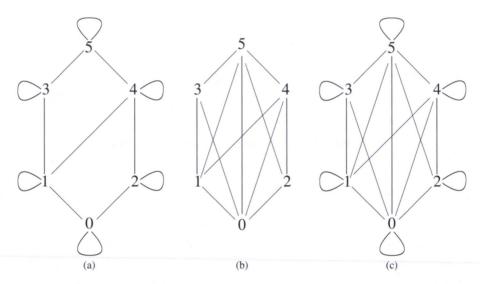

(a)   (b)   (c)

Figure 12.4: (a) Reflexive closure, (b) transitive closure and (c) reflexive transitive closure.

A genealogy tree is a familiar example of "transitive closure". Such a tree depicts the "is a parent of" relation, but, by following paths in the tree, we get the "is an ancestor of" relation. The ancestor relation is transitive, while the parent relation is not; the ancestor relation is the "transitive closure" of the parent relation.

Because there are no arrowheads on edges, a Hasse diagram is ambiguous about whether a relation or its converse is being depicted. A genealogy tree depicts the "is a parent of" relation but could also be construed as depicting the converse "is a child of" relation. We have described Figure 12.3 as depicting the at-most relation and the divides relation, but they can also be construed as depicting the at-least relation and the "is a multiple of" relation. Adding arrowheads always pointing up or always pointing down would remove the ambiguity, but the ambiguity is harmless because the converse of the reflexive transitive closure of a relation equals the reflexive transitive closure of the converse of the relation.

In conclusion, a Hasse diagram is an economical way of presenting a (small finite) ordering relation; it is easy for us to see paths through the graph and, in this way, the relation is made much clearer. It is an example of how economy of expression can be extremely helpful. When relations are too large to depict in a diagram, techniques for computing the transitive closure become very important; efficient algorithms for doing so are fundamental in computing science. See Section 16.2 for further discussion.

12.7.7 Equality

We have seen that equality is reflexive, symmetric and transitive. Equality is the most fundamental relation in mathematics, but it was a very long time before this was properly recognised. Indeed, the equality symbol was only introduced in 1557, which is very recent by mathematical standards, by Robert Recorde.[3] Before then, when two expressions were equal they were written next to each other, leaving the reader to surmise their equality.

The importance of equality was properly recognised by Leibniz, who set himself the goal of reducing all mathematics to calculation (an extract from his writings is shown in Figure 12.5). Leibniz is acknowledged for formulating the first rule of logic – the rule of *substitution of equals for equals*. It is a rule that is used all the time in mathematical calculation, but lots of books fail to mention it. Here is a (very!) simple example of the use of Leibniz's rule:

$$(2-1) \times 3$$
$$= \qquad \{ \qquad \text{arithmetic} \quad \}$$
$$1 \times 3.$$

The step uses the fact that $2-1$ equals 1 in order to substitute the former by the latter.

Formulated precisely, Leibniz's rule states that if f is a function and x and y are equal, then $f(x)$ and $f(y)$ are equal. In the above example, the function f is "multiply by 3" ($\times 3$).

Normally, when Leibniz's rule is used, it is not necessary to be explicit about the function; "substitution of equals for equals" simply means that a subexpression of an expression can be replaced by an equal expression. In the example the subexpression "$2-1$" is replaced by "1". Of course, it could also have been replaced by "$3-2$" or any other expression that equals 1.

Recorde's symbol for equality is used universally to denote the fact that two values are the same. It is used, for example, for equality of numbers (integers, reals, complex

---

[3] Robert Recorde (c. 1510–1558) was a Welsh physician and mathematician; he is credited with introducing algebra to England with the publication of his book *The Whetstone of Whitte*, in which the equality symbol was first introduced. Other symbols for equality, such as $\propto$, had been used earlier but Recorde deliberately chose a symbol composed of two "equale" parallel lines.

Definition 1.   *Same* or *coincident* terms are those which can be substituted for each other everywhere without affecting truth. For example, 'triangle' and 'trilateral', for in all the propositions demonstrated by Euclid about a triangle, *trilateral* can be substituted, and the converse, without affecting their truth.

A∞B signifies that A and B are the same; thus we may say of the straight lines XY and YX: YX∞XY, or the shortest distance of motion from X to Y and from Y to X coincides (Figure 15).

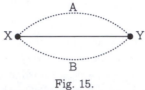

Fig. 15.

Definition 2. Diverse terms are those which are not the same or in which substitution sometimes doesn't work. Such are the circle and the triangle , also the square (that is, the perfect square, as geometricians always understand it) and the equilateral quadrangle, for the latter can be said of the rhombus, which cannot however be called a square.

A non ∞ B signifies that A and B are diverse, as are XY and RS (Figure 16).

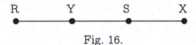

Fig. 16.

○ **Figure 12.5: Extract from Leibniz's writings. [Lei69]**

numbers etc.), for equality of sets, for equality of functions, and so on. It is the most frequently encountered example of overloading of notation. On many occasions the overloading is beneficial, but sometimes it is not.

12.7.8 Equivalence Relations

A common strategy in problem solving is to group together several objects that, for the purpose of solving the problem, are considered to be identical or "equivalent". The underlying mathematical notion is an "equivalence relation". An *equivalence relation* is a (binary) relation that is reflexive, symmetric and transitive. Equality is the simplest example of an equivalence relation.

Typically, an equivalence relation on a set A is defined by combining a function with domain A with the equality on the range of the function. For example, suppose we consider the function even of type $\mathbb{Z} \to \text{Bool}$. We define the relation "has the same parity as" on $\mathbb{Z}$ by, for all integers m and n,

$$m \text{ has the same parity as } n \quad \equiv \quad \text{even}(m) = \text{even}(n).$$

This relation groups all the even integers together and all the odd integers together. It is easily checked that the relation is reflexive: for all integers m,

m has the same parity as m

(because equality is reflexive). It is also symmetric: for all integers m and n,

m has the same parity as n $\equiv$ n has the same parity as m

(because equality is symmetric). Finally, it is transitive: for all integers m, n and p,

m has the same parity as n $\wedge$ n has the same parity as p

$\Rightarrow$ m has the same parity as p

(because equality is transitive). That the relation is an equivalence relation is a direct consequence of the fact that equality is an equivalence relation and (implicitly) Leibniz's rule of substitution of equals for equals.

In general, if A and B are sets and f is a function with domain A and range B, we can define a relation "has the same f value as" by determining, for all x and y in the domain A, the truth value of

f(x) = f(y).

(Note that "=" denotes equality in the range B.) We might, for example, regard two objects as equivalent if they have the same colour (red, blue, green etc.) or two people equivalent if they are the same age. Lots of other examples can be given. In this way, the function f is used to *partition* the set A into groups of "equivalent" elements.

An equivalence relation is, in fact, always defined in this way, at least in principle. Another way of defining an equivalence relation is to consider the reflexive, symmetric and transitive closure of a given relation. Each group of "equivalent" elements is called an *equivalence class*; treating each equivalence class as an object creates what is called a *quotient space*. This is an important mathematical construction, comparable in importance to disjoint sum and cartesian product.

12.8 CALCULATIONS

In this book, we use a style of presenting mathematical calculations that emphasises the documentation of the calculation. The style is quite self-explanatory and has already been used in Section 12.7.4. Here we spend a few words on explaining the style.

Let us base our explanation on a concrete example. Consider the following problem. A student buys a drink for themself and a friend. The friend's drink costs 3 times as much as the student's drink. The student pays with a 5-pound note and gets 1 pound in change. What is the cost of the drinks?

To solve the problem, we introduce two variables s and f for the cost of the student's drink and the cost of the friend's drink. We are given that $f = 3 \times s$ and $s + f + 1 = 5$. Now we can calculate:

$$f = 3 \times s \ \land \ s + f + 1 = 5$$

$=$ {   substitution of equals for equals   }

$$f = 3 \times s \ \land \ s + 3 \times s + 1 = 5$$

$=$ {   arithmetic   }

$$f = 3 \times s \ \land \ s = 1$$

$=$ {   substitution of equals for equals   }

$$f = 3 \times 1 \ \land \ s = 1$$

$=$ {   arithmetic   }

$$f = 3 \ \land \ s = 1.$$

This calculation is deliberately simple so that we can focus on its structure rather than on the details of the specific problem.

The first thing to observe about the calculation is that its conclusion is an equality "everywhere" between the boolean expressions

$$f = 3 \times s \ \land \ s + f + 1 = 5$$

and

$$f = 3 \ \land \ s = 1.$$

By "everywhere" we mean that the two expressions always have the same (boolean) value whatever the values of the variables f and s. For example, if f and s are both 0, the two expressions are both false; if f is 3 and s is 1, the two expressions are both true.

The calculation does not assert that $f = 3$ has the value true (or that $s = 1$ has the value true). It asserts no more and no less than that what is given has the same boolean value as the expression $f = 3 \land s = 1$. This is an important aspect of boolean algebra. The logical connectives, like equality and conjunction, glue together primitive boolean expressions but they do not assert the truth or falsity of these expressions. In this example, the student and the friend may be arguing over the cost of the drinks; the calculation helps to simplify the argument but does no more.

The second thing to observe is that each line of the calculation is connected by boolean equality in just the same way as the calculation in Section 12.7.4 used set equality. The symbol "⇔" is sometimes used to denote boolean equality and, unfortunately, some readers may have been taught to read the symbol as "if and only if". Even worse, some readers may have been taught to connect the statements by implication (⇒). The use of "if and only if" in this context is an over-complication. It is like calling equality of numbers "at most and at least" or equality of sets "is a subset of and is a superset of". The use of implication is wrong in the same way that a calculation that concludes that 2×3 is at most 6 is wrong. The only argument for using a different symbol here for boolean equality is the overloading of the equality symbol in the same calculation: the equality symbol in "$f = 3$" is equality of numbers. However, the layout of the calculation eliminates any possible confusion.

The third thing to note about the calculation is that every step is accompanied by a *hint*. The challenges of programming have taught us that documentation is very important. Documentation of calculations is important as a check in the process of performing the calculation and as a reminder for later. The hints we use vary in detail. Sometimes they are very explicit and sometimes not. The hint "arithmetic", for example, does not provide much information – we assume that the reader has no difficulty with arithmetic calculations – but it does indicate that the logical connectives in the formula (in this case ∧) can be ignored and the reader's attention should focus on the arithmetic operators. This can be very useful in more complicated calculations.

The hint "substitution of equals for equals" occurs twice in the above calculation. This refers to Leibniz's first rule of logic which we introduced in Section 12.7.7. In fact, although the rule is only explicitly mentioned in two of the steps it is used in all four. In the second step the boolean $s + 3 \times s + 1 = 5$ is simplifed to $s = 1$ and this simplification is applied in the context of the function that maps p to $f = 3 \times s \land p$. Similarly, in the final step 3×1 is substituted by its equal 3 in the context of the function that maps n to $f = n \land s = 1$. Leibniz's rule is fundamental to almost all calculations but often not mentioned explicitly. Its importance is another reason for our stressing boolean equality in preference to "if and only if".

12.8.1 Steps in a Calculation

Our calculations have a number of *steps* (usually more than one). A two-step calculation might have the following shape.

$$
\begin{array}{ll}
 & R \\
= & \{ \quad p \quad \} \\
 & S \\
= & \{ \quad q \quad \} \\
 & T.
\end{array}
$$

In this calculation, R, S and T are expressions, and p and q are hints why $[R=S]$ and $[S=T]$, respectively. The *conclusion* of the calculation is that $[R=T]$. (Recall that the square brackets means "everywhere".)

The hints we use are often references to algebraic laws, either explicitly stated or just named. Here is an example of a step where the law is given explicitly:

$$(n+1)^2 - n^2$$
$$= \qquad \{ \qquad [\, x^2 - y^2 \ = \ (x-y)\times(x+y) \,],$$
$$\text{with } x, y \ := \ n+1 \, , \, n \ \}$$
$$((n+1) - n) \times ((n+1) + n)$$

In this case, the step is an instance of a law of arithmetic. The law is enclosed in everywhere brackets to indicate that it is true for all (numbers) x and y and the details of the instance are indicated by the simultaneous assignment. We name the most commonly used laws (e.g. "associativity") rather than state them explicitly. The very simplest rules (e.g. unit laws such as $[x+0=x]$) are often applied silently.

Calculations quickly become very long if all steps are made explicit. To avoid this, we sometimes combine several steps into one. We might, for example, write

$$(n+1)^2 - n^2$$
$$= \qquad \{ \qquad \text{arithmetic} \ \}$$
$$2 \times n + 1.$$

We only do so where the omitted calculation steps are expected to be familiar. This means that when we first introduce a topic we give each step in detail; as familiarity with the topic grows we permit ourselves to take larger steps. Mistakes most often occur in larger steps so our advice is be very cautious about combining many steps into one. A particular case is when applying a definition. Take care to state explicitly the substitutions that are being made for any parameters in the definition, and postpone any simplifications to subsequent steps.

12.8.2 Relations between Steps

A calculation with a number of steps, in which each step relates one expression to the next by equality, establishes that all the expressions are equal (everywhere). However, it is usually the equality between the first and last expressions that is important to us. Formally, we silently exploit the fact that equality is a transitive relation. That is, if $R=S$ and $S=T$, it is also the case that $R=T$.

The less-than relation, denoted by "$<$", is also transitive. Here is a calculation that constructs a rough estimate of the difference between 256 and 367.

$$367 - 256$$

$$< \qquad \{ \qquad 367 < 400 \quad \}$$

$$400 - 256$$

$$< \qquad \{ \qquad 200 < 256 \quad \}$$

$$400 - 200$$

$$= \qquad \{ \qquad \text{arithmetic} \quad \}$$

$$200.$$

The conclusion of this calculation is that $367 - 256 < 200$. It illustrates the so-called *conjunctional* use of the less-than operator. In general, $R < S < T$ means $R < S$ *and* $S < T$. Transitivity of less-than means that a consequence of $R < S < T$ is that $R < T$.

Different relations may be combined in the same proof, but then there should be a logical justification for doing so. For instance, one step of a proof may assert, say, $R < S$, whereas the next asserts $S \leq T$. The inference is then that $R < T$. All such steps can be combined with equality steps, as in the last line above. However, it would be nonsense to combine $<$ with $>$ or $\geq$ in one calculation since then no inference can be made of the relation between the first and last expressions.

The type of the expressions is arbitrary. They may denote real values, integer values, sets, relations etc. In each case, the familiar equality symbol, "$=$", is used to denote equality of values. In particular, if R, S and T denote boolean values we still use the equality symbol to denote equality. For example, a step in a proof might be

$$E \leq F$$

$$= \qquad \{ \qquad \text{E and F denote integer values.}$$

$$\text{Property of integer arithmetic} \quad \}$$

$$E < F + 1$$

Here we are using the fact that the boolean expression $E \leq F$ will always have the same value as the expression $E < F+1$ whenever E and F denote integer values. In other words, the value of $E \leq F$ (which is either true or false) *is equal to* the value of $E < F+1$. In in-line expressions, we often use the symbol "$\equiv$" to denote equality of boolean values. One reason for this is to avoid ambiguity. For example, we write

$$E \leq F \equiv E < F+1$$

in order to avoid confusion with

$$E \leq F = E < F+1$$

which means E $\leq$ F *and* F = E *and* E < F+1. (So equality here means equality of integer values rather than equality of boolean values.) There is another reason for having two notations for equality of boolean values, which is that boolean equality is both transitive and associative. This second reason, which is much more important than the first, is motivated in Section 5.3 and reviewed in Chapter 13.

It is important to realise that a boolean expression will typically evaluate to true or false depending on the values of its free variables. There are two ways in which we assert that a boolean expression always has the value true: the expression in a calculational step and when square brackets surround the expression. If the expression has no free variables the square brackets are omitted (as in 1−1 = 0).

Generally, in calculational steps, the connecting relations have lower precedence than the operators in the expressions they connect, this convention superseding any other precedence conventions. You should have no problem with this convention since it is clearly what is suggested by the layout.

12.8.3 "If" and "Only If"

Steps relating boolean values will sometimes be related by "if" or "only if". The if relation is denoted by "$\Leftarrow$" and the only-if relation by "$\Rightarrow$".

Here is an example of a calculation involving an if step. (Read the second step as $10\times20 \leq 11\times23$ *if* both $10\times20 \leq 11\times20$ and $11\times20 \leq 11\times23$.) It establishes that $200 \leq 11\times23$ is true.

$$
\begin{array}{ll}
& 200 \leq 11\times23 \\
= & \{ \quad 200 = 10\times20 \quad \} \\
& 10\times20 \leq 11\times23 \\
\Leftarrow & \{ \quad \text{``}\leq\text{'' is a transitive relation} \quad \} \\
& 10\times20 \leq 11\times20 \leq 11\times23 \\
= & \{ \quad \text{multiplication is invertible with respect to ``}\leq\text{''} \\
& \qquad \text{(applied twice), and } 10 \leq 11 \text{ and } 20 \leq 23 \quad \} \\
& \text{true.}
\end{array}
$$

An if step is a *strengthening* step. In this example, the inequality $10\times20 \leq 11\times23$ is replaced by the stronger statement $10\times20 \leq 11\times20 \leq 11\times23$. Because they are strengthening steps, if steps in calculations are much less welcome than equality steps;

it may be the case that the strengthening is too coarse. In the following example, the pattern of the above calculation is used, but the strengthening leads to a property that cannot be established. As a consequence, the calculation stalls.

$$243 \leq 11 \times 23$$

$$= \qquad \{ \qquad 243 = 9 \times 27 \quad \}$$

$$9 \times 27 \leq 11 \times 23$$

$$\Leftarrow \qquad \{ \qquad \text{``}\leq\text{'' is a transitive relation} \quad \}$$

$$9 \times 27 \leq 11 \times 27 \leq 11 \times 23.$$

Note that the calculation is correct even though $11 \times 27 \leq 11 \times 23$ is false. The proposition "$243 \leq 11 \times 23$ if false" is a valid, although meaningless, conclusion.

Only-if steps are the converse of if steps; an only-if step is a *weakening* step. An important use of only-if steps is in determining circumstances in which a boolean expression is false. An example is the following:

$$23 \times 11 = 243$$

$$\Rightarrow \qquad \{ \qquad \text{Leibniz (substitution of equals for equals)} \quad \}$$

$$(23 \times 11) \bmod 3 = 243 \bmod 3$$

$$= \qquad \{ \qquad (23 \times 11) \bmod 3 = 1$$

$$243 \bmod 3 = 0$$

$$\text{(details of calculation omitted)} \quad \}$$

$$1 = 0$$

$$= \qquad \{ \qquad \text{arithmetic} \quad \}$$

$$\text{false.}$$

The first step should be read as "$23 \times 11 = 243$ *only if* $(23 \times 11) \bmod 3 = 243 \bmod 3$". The step is unmistakably a direct application of Leibniz's rule that when a function is applied to equal values it gives equal results. In this case, the function that is being applied is the "mod 3" function, which computes the remainder after dividing a given number by 3. The omitted details in the second step involve the use of properties of remainder computation which make it easy to evaluate $(23 \times 11) \bmod 3$ (without evaluating 23×11) and $243 \bmod 3$ (see Section 15.4). The conclusion is that $23 \times 11 = 243$ only if false, that is, $23 \times 11 \neq 243$.

12.9 EXERCISES

1. Say which of the following are everywhere true. In the case where the expression is not everywhere true, give an instance where the expression is false. Assume that x ranges over the real numbers.
   (a) $0 \leq x^2$
   (b) $x < 2x$
   (c) $x^2 - x - 12 = (x-3) \times (x+4)$
   (d) $x^2 + x - 20 = (x-4) \times (x+5)$
   (e) $(-x)^3 = -(x^3)$

2. Enumerate the elements of the following sets.
   (a) $\{0,1,4\} \cup \{4,1,3\}$
   (b) $\{0,1,4\} \cap \{4,1,3\}$
   (c) $(\{2,4,6\} \cup \emptyset \cup \{9\}) \cap \{9,4\}$
   (d) $\{m \mid m \in \{0,1,4\} \cup \{4,1,3\} \land even(m)\}$
   (e) $\emptyset \cap \{2,4\}$
   (f) $\{0,1,4\} + \{4,1,3\}$
   (g) $\{0,1\} \times \{0,1\}$
   (h) $\{0,1,2\} + (\{1\} \times \{3,5\})$
   (i) $2^{\{0\}}$

3. Determine the number of elements in each of the following sets. Try to do so without enumerating all the elements.
   (a) $\{m \mid 0 \leq m < 1000\}$
   (b) $\{m \mid 0 \leq m < 1000\} + \{m \mid 2000 \leq m < 2500\}$
   (c) $\{0,1\} \times \{m \mid 0 \leq m < 1000\}$
   (d) $2^{\emptyset}$
   (e) $2^{\{m \mid 0 \leq m < 3\}}$
   (f) $\{\emptyset, \{a,b\}\}$
   (g) $\{a,b\} \to \{red,green,blue\}$
   (h) $\{red,green,blue\} \to \{a,b\}$

4. Show that a left or right zero of a binary operator is unique. Show that a unit of a symmetric binary operator is unique.

5. Consider the functions double and square defined by:

   $$double(x) = 2 \times x$$

   $$square(x) = x^2.$$

   Say which of the following is true and which is false.
   (a) double distributes through addition
   (b) double distributes through multiplication
   (c) double distributes through exponentiation

    (d) double **distributes through minimum**

    (e) square **distributes through addition**

    (f) square **distributes through multiplication**

    (g) square **distributes through exponentiation**

    (h) square **distributes through minimum**

6. What is the smallest example of a monoid? (The size of a monoid $(A,1,\times)$ is the size of the set A.) What is the smallest example of a semiring?

7. Show that, in a group $(A,1,\times,^{-1})$, $1^{-1}=1$.

8. The follows relation on the letters in the sequence ABBA is symmetric. This is a consequence of the fact that ABBA is a palindrome (a word that reads the same forwards as backwards). Construct a sequence of As and Bs such that the follows relation on the letters in the sequence is symmetric but the sequence is not a palindrome.

9. Is the follows relation on the letters in the sequence ABBA reflexive? Is it transitive?

10. The *empty word* is a sequence of letters of length zero. (Do not confuse the empty word with the empty set.) Is the follows relation on the letters in the empty word symmetric? Is it transitive?

11. Construct a sequence of As and Bs such that the follows relation on the letters in the sequence is

    (a) reflexive and transitive but not symmetric

    (b) transitive but not reflexive or symmetric

    (c) an equivalence relation

    In each case, try to construct a sequence that is as short as possible.

    It is not possible to construct a sequence of As and Bs such that the follows relation is reflexive and symmetric but not transitive. Why is this?

12. Draw the Hasse diagram of the set of subsets of {a,b}.

13. Draw the Hasse diagram of the set of subsets of {a,b,c}.

14. Draw the reflexive transitive closure of both diagrams in Figure 12.3.

15. Draw the Hasse diagram of the numbers from 0 thru 16 under the division ordering.

Chapter
Boolean Algebra
13

This chapter is about the algebra of booleans, which is the basis of logical reasoning. As discussed in Chapter 5, our focus is on equational reasoning. Because equational reasoning is unusual – most introductions to logic focus on implicational reasoning – there is some overlap between Sections 13.1 and 13.2 in this chapter and sections of Chapter 5. This chapter can be read independently, but occasionally we refer the reader to sections of Chapter 5 for further clarification.

13.1 BOOLEAN EQUALITY

Equality – on any domain of values – has a number of characteristic properties. It is *reflexive*, *symmetric* and *transitive*. Most importantly, equal things are indistinguishable in Leibniz's sense of being able to substitute one for the other in any context: the so-called rule of *substitution of equals for equals* or *Leibniz's rule*.

These rules apply, of course, to equality of booleans. So, with variable p ranging over the booleans, we have the law

$$\textbf{[Reflexivity]} \quad [p = p]. \tag{13.1}$$

We can verify this law by constructing a truth table. There are two entries in the table, one for each of the two possibilities for the value of p:

p	p = p
true	true
false	true

The truth table for $p = p$ is true irrespective of the value of p. That is, $p = p$ is "everywhere" true.

Similarly, we have the law

[**Symmetry**] $[(p = q) = (q = p)]$.   (13.2)

We can also verify this law by constructing a truth table. This time, there are four entries in the table, one for each of the 2×2 different combinations of the values of p and q.

p	q	$p = q$	$=$	$q = p$
true	true	true	true	true
false	true	false	true	false
true	false	false	true	false
false	false	true	true	true

Note how the first two columns in the truth table enumerate the four different combinations of the values of p and q. Because the evaluation of the expression $(p=q)=(q=p)$ is more complicated, the values of each subexpression have been detailed to the right of the vertical line. The first and third column show the truth value of $p=q$ and $q=p$, respectively. Note that these are sometimes true and sometimes false but, in each row, their values are always equal. The value of $(p=q)=(q=p)$ given in the middle column is thus always true. In words, the expression $(p=q)=(q=p)$ is "everywhere" true.

Reflexivity and symmetry of boolean equality are unsurprising. Much more interesting is that boolean equality is associative:

[**Associativity**] $[((p=q) = r) = (p = (q=r))]$.   (13.3)

We recommend the reader to check the validity of this law by constructing a truth table. The table will have eight rows, corresponding to the $2 \times 2 \times 2$ different combinations of the values of p, q and r. In order to avoid mistakes, list the truth values of each subexpression under the principal operator of the expression. Once this has been done, try to identify a general rule, based on how many of p, q and r are true, that predicts when the two expressions $((p=q) = r)$ and $(p = (q=r))$ are true.

As discussed in Section 5.3, we use both the symbol "$=$" and the symbol "$\equiv$" for boolean equality. The use of "$=$" emphasises the transitivity of equality. A continued *equality* of the form

$p_1 = p_2 = \ldots = p_n$

means that all of $p_1, p_2, \ldots, p_n$ are equal. A typical use of "$=$" for boolean equality is in the steps of a calculation on boolean expressions; if all steps in a calculation are equality steps, we conclude that the first and the last expressions are equal. The use of "≡" emphasises the associativity of boolean equality. A continued *equivalence* of the form

$$p_1 \equiv p_2 \equiv \ldots \equiv p_n$$

has the meaning given by fully parenthesising the expression (in any way whatsover, since the outcome is not affected) and then evaluating the expression as indicated by the chosen parenthesisation.

When a boolean equality has just two boolean subexpressions, we choose to write $p \equiv q$ whenever p and/or q involves other relations, in particular equality or inequality in some other domain. For example, a simple law of arithmetic is the cancellation law:

$$[\ x = y \ \equiv \ x + z = y + z \ ]$$

The two occurrences of the "=" symbol denote equality of real numbers. Note that "≡" has lower precedence than "=".

The rule (5.2) was our first example of how the associativity of boolean equality is exploited. For convenience, here is the rule again:

$$[\text{Definition}] \quad [\, \text{true} \equiv p \equiv p \,]. \tag{13.4}$$

The rule is a definition of true if we read it as $\text{true} = (p = p)$; in this form, it states that any instance of the expression "$p = p$" can be replaced by "true" (or vice versa, any instance of "true" can be replaced by any instance of the expression "$p = p$"). But it can also be read as $(\text{true} = p) = p$; in this form, it states that true is the unit of boolean equality.

13.2 NEGATION

Negation is discussed in detail in Section 5.4, so this section is very brief.

Negation is a unary operator (meaning that it is a function with exactly one argument) mapping a boolean to a boolean, and is denoted by the symbol "¬", written as a prefix to its argument. If p is a boolean expression, "¬p" is pronounced "not p". The law governing ¬p is:

$$[\text{Negation}] \quad [\, \neg p \equiv p \equiv \text{false} \,]. \tag{13.5}$$

The law introduces both a new unary operator "¬" and a new constant "false".

See Sections 5.4.1 and 5.4.3 for the rule of contraposition and properties of boolean inequality.

13.3 DISJUNCTION

The *disjunction* p ∨ q is the (inclusive) "or" of p and q. Stating that p ∨ q is true means that one or more of p and q is true.

Disjunction has three obvious properties, namely *idempotence*, *symmetry* and *associativity*. *Idempotence* of disjunction is the rule

[Idempotence]   [p ∨ p ≡ p].   (13.6)

Note that, for convenience, we assume that the operator "∨" takes precedence over the operator "≡". Fully parenthesised, (13.6) reads (p ∨ p) ≡ p and *not* p ∨ (p ≡ p).

The *symmetry* and *associativity* of disjunction are expressed as follows:

[Symmetry]   [p ∨ q ≡ q ∨ p];   (13.7)

[Associativity]   [p ∨ (q ∨ r) ≡ (p ∨ q) ∨ r].   (13.8)

The associativity of disjunction allows us to omit parentheses in continued disjunctions, as in, for example,

p ∨ q ∨ p ∨ r ∨ q ∨ q.

The symmetry and associativity of disjunction mean that the terms in such a continued disjunction can be rearranged at will, and the idempotence of disjunction means that multiple occurrences of the same term can be reduced to one. So the above expression would be simplified as follows:

        p ∨ q ∨ p ∨ r ∨ q ∨ q

=   {   rearranging terms – allowed because

              disjunction is symmetric and associative }

        p ∨ p ∨ r ∨ q ∨ q ∨ q

=   {   idempotence of disjunction (applied three times) }

        p ∨ r ∨ q.

The fourth law governing disjunction is not so obvious. Disjunction *distributes through equivalence*:.

[Distributivity]   [p ∨ (q ≡ r) ≡ p ∨ q ≡ p ∨ r].   (13.9)

The fifth and final law is called the rule of the *excluded middle*; it states that, for each proposition p, either p or its negation is true. These are the only two possibilities and a third "middle" possibility is excluded.

[Excluded Middle] $\quad [\,p \vee \neg p\,].$ $\hfill$ (13.10)

Using this basis, we can derive many other laws. Here is how to show that false is a unit of disjunction:

$$p \vee \text{false}$$

$$= \qquad \{ \qquad \text{definition of false (5.3)} \quad \}$$

$$p \vee (\neg p \equiv p)$$

$$= \qquad \{ \qquad \text{disjunction distributes over equivalence (13.9)} \quad \}$$

$$p \vee \neg p \equiv p \vee p$$

$$= \qquad \{ \qquad \text{excluded middle (13.10) and}$$

$$\text{idempotence of disjunction} \quad \}$$

$$\text{true} \equiv p$$

$$= \qquad \{ \qquad \text{unit of equivalence (5.2)} \quad \}$$

$$p.$$

Similarly, it is easy to show that true is the zero of disjunction. In summary, we have the following theorem.

Theorem 13.11 The booleans form a semiring $(\text{Bool}, \text{false}, \text{true}, \vee, \equiv)$ with unit false, zero true, product operator $\vee$ and addition operator $\equiv$.

13.4 CONJUNCTION

In this section, we define conjunction (logical "and") in terms of disjunction and equivalence. We show how to use the definition to derive the basic properties of conjunction.

The definition of conjunction uses the so-called *golden rule*:

[Golden Rule] $\quad [\,p \wedge q \equiv p \equiv q \equiv p \vee q\,].$ $\hfill$ (13.12)

The convention is that the conjunction operator ("$\wedge$", read "and") has the same precedence as disjunction ("$\vee$") which is higher than the precedence of equivalence.

Giving conjunction and disjunction the same precedence means that an expression like $p \wedge q \vee r$ is ambiguous. It is not clear whether it means $(p \wedge q) \vee r$ or $p \wedge (q \vee r)$. You should, therefore, always parenthesise, so that the meaning is clear. (Giving conjunction precedence over disjunction, as is often done, is bad practice, because it obscures symmetries in their algebraic properties.)

The golden rule can be seen as a definition of conjunction in terms of equivalence and disjunction if we read it as

$$[(p \wedge q) \;=\; (p \;\equiv\; q \;\equiv\; p \vee q)].$$

But it can also be read in other ways. For example, the golden rule asserts the equality

$$[(p \wedge q \;\equiv\; p) \;=\; (q \;\equiv\; p \vee q)].$$

This reading will be used later when we define logical implication. It can also be read as a definition of disjunction in terms of conjunction:

$$[(p \wedge q \;\equiv\; p \;\equiv\; q) \;=\; (p \vee q)].$$

This reading is sometimes useful when, in a calculation, it is expedient to replace disjunctions by conjunctions.

The golden rule is so named because it can be used in so many different ways. Its beauty comes from exploiting the associativity and symmetry of equivalence. Here is how it is used to prove that conjunction is symmetric:

$$
\begin{array}{cl}
& p \wedge q \\
= & \qquad \{ \qquad \text{golden rule} \quad \} \\
& p \equiv q \equiv p \vee q \\
= & \qquad \{ \qquad \text{equivalence and disjunction are symmetric} \quad \} \\
& q \equiv p \equiv q \vee p \\
= & \qquad \{ \qquad \text{golden rule, } p,q := q,p \quad \} \\
& q \wedge p.
\end{array}
$$

So-called *absorption* of conjunctions by disjunctions is derived as follows:

$$
\begin{array}{cl}
& p \vee (p \wedge q) \\
= & \qquad \{ \qquad \text{golden rule} \quad \} \\
& p \vee (p \equiv q \equiv p \vee q)
\end{array}
$$

$=$ {   disjunction distributes over equivalence   }

$p \lor p \equiv p \lor q \equiv p \lor (p \lor q)$

$=$ {   idempotence and associativity of disjunction   }

$p \equiv p \lor q \equiv p \lor q$

$=$ {   reflexivity of equivalence (5.2)   }

p.

Thus,

[**Absorption**] $p \lor (p \land q) \equiv p.$ (13.13)

In a similar way, we can prove that conjunction is associative. An outline of the calculation is shown below. (The first and third steps are not given in full.)

$p \land (q \land r)$

$=$ {   expand the definition of $\land$

and use distributivity of $\lor$ over $\equiv$ }

$p \equiv q \equiv r \equiv q \lor r \equiv p \lor q \equiv p \lor r \equiv p \lor q \lor r$

$=$ {   equivalence is symmetric, disjunction is symmetric   }

$r \equiv p \equiv q \equiv p \lor q \equiv r \lor p \equiv r \lor q \equiv r \lor p \lor q$

$=$ {   reverse of first step with $p,q,r := r,p,q$ }

$r \land (p \land q)$

$=$ {   conjunction is symmetric   }

$(p \land q) \land r.$

From now on, we often omit parentheses in continued conjunctions, silently exploiting the associativity property.

Below we list a number of additional properties of disjunction and conjunction. These can all be proved using the rules given above. Alternatively, they can be verified by constructing a truth table. (Note that in the case of the final law, this involves constructing a table with 32 entries!)

[**Distributivity**] $[\, p \lor (q \land r) \equiv (p \lor q) \land (p \lor r) \,].$

[**Distributivity**] $[\, p \land (q \lor r) \equiv (p \land q) \lor (p \land r) \,].$

[**Modus Ponens**] $[\, p \land (p \equiv q) \equiv p \land q \,].$

[**De Morgan**] $[\, \lnot (p \land q) \equiv \lnot p \lor \lnot q \,].$

[De Morgan] $[\ \neg(p \lor q) \equiv \neg p \land \neg q \ ]$.

[Contradiction] $[\ p \land \neg p \equiv \text{false} \ ]$.

[Distributivity] $[\ p \land (q \equiv r \equiv s) \equiv p \land q \equiv p \land r \equiv p \land s \ ]$.

A convenient way to summarise the interaction between disjunction and conjunction is to observe that both operators act like product and addition in a semiring:

Theorem 13.14 The booleans form a semiring $(\text{Bool}, \text{false}, \text{true}, \lor, \land)$ with unit false, zero true, product operator $\lor$ and addition operator $\land$.

The booleans form a semiring $(\text{Bool}, \text{true}, \text{false}, \land, \lor)$ with unit true, zero false, product operator $\land$ and addition operator $\lor$.

This is the basis for what is called a "duality" between the operators. Essentially, many properties can be "dualised" by interchanging true and false, and $\land$ and $\lor$. We do not go into details, but this is the reason for choosing not to give either operator precedence over the other.

13.5 IMPLICATION

Many constructions and proofs involve a logical implication rather than a logical equivalence. Put simply, implications are "if" statements rather than "is" statements. An example is: John and Sue are cousins *if* their fathers are brothers. This is an if statement because the condition given for John and Sue to be cousins is not exhaustive. Another condition is, for example, that their mothers are sisters.

Confusingly, in normal conversation the English word "if" is often used when an equivalence is meant. For instance we might say, Ann and Bob are siblings *if* they have the same father or the same mother. What is meant here, however, is that the definition of *sibling* is having the same father or mother. That is, Ann and Bob are siblings *is* they have the same father or the same mother. In mathematical texts, the distinction between "if" and "is" is often made by writing "iff" when the equality is intended. Often "iff" is pronounced "if and only if" but sometimes it is pronounced "if", as in normal conversation.

The notation we use for the statement "p if q" is $p \Leftarrow q$. The notation we use for "p only if q" is $p \Rightarrow q$. The expression $p \Leftarrow q$ is often verbalised as "p follows from q" and $p \Rightarrow q$ is verbalised as "p implies q".

The statements $p \Leftarrow q$ and $q \Rightarrow p$ mean the same thing. It is useful to use both notations. Sometimes an argument can be easier to construct in one direction than in the other.

13.5.1 Definitions and Basic Properties

Implications are defined equationally. One definition of p⇐q is as follows:

$$[\textbf{Definition of If}] \quad [\; p\Leftarrow q \;\equiv\; p \;\equiv\; p\vee q\;]. \tag{13.15}$$

Note that the precedence of "⇐" is higher than the precedence of "≡" as suggested by the spacing. Henceforth, we give "⇐" and "⇒" lower precedence that "∨" and "∧".

This defines "⇐" in terms of equivalence and disjunction. Alternatively, in terms of equivalence and conjunction,

$$[\textbf{Definition of If}] \quad [\; p\Leftarrow q \;\equiv\; q \;\equiv\; p\wedge q\;]. \tag{13.16}$$

The two definitions are the same because, by the golden rule, $p\equiv p\vee q$ and $q\equiv p\wedge q$ are the same.

Turning the arrows around, we get two definitions of p⇒q:

$$[\textbf{Definition of Only If}] \quad [\; p\Rightarrow q \;\equiv\; q \;\equiv\; p\vee q\;]; \tag{13.17}$$

$$[\textbf{Definition of Only If}] \quad [\; p\Rightarrow q \;\equiv\; p \;\equiv\; p\wedge q\;]. \tag{13.18}$$

Immediate consequences of these definitions are obtained by suitable instantiations of the variables p and q. For example, (13.15) gives us

$$[\textbf{Strengthening}] \quad [\; p\vee q \;\Leftarrow\; q\;]. \tag{13.19}$$

The specific details of the calculation are as follows:

$$
\begin{aligned}
& p\vee q \;\Leftarrow\; q \\
=\;\; & \{ \quad (13.15),\; p,q := p\vee q, q \quad \} \\
& p\vee q \;\equiv\; (p\vee q)\vee q \\
=\;\; & \{ \quad \text{associativity and idempotence of disjunction} \quad \} \\
& p\vee q \;\equiv\; p\vee q \\
=\;\; & \{ \quad \text{reflexivity of} \equiv \quad \} \\
& \text{true.}
\end{aligned}
$$

The rule is called "strengthening" because boolean expressions are often viewed as requirements on the free variables; the rule is used to replace a proof requirement $p\vee q$ by the stronger requirement q. For example, $m\le n$ is the same as $m<n \vee m=n$. The requirement $m=n$ is "stronger" than the requirement $m\le n$.

A second immediate consequence of the definitions is another strengthening rule:

[**Strengthening**] $[\, p \,\Leftarrow\, p \wedge q \,]$.   (13.20)

This is obtained by instantiating q to $p \wedge q$ in (13.15). Other immediate consequences are the following:

[**Absurdity**] $[\, p \Leftarrow \text{false} \,]$;

[**Reflexivity**] $[\, p \Leftarrow p \,]$;

[**De Morgan**]: $[\, p \Leftarrow q \,\equiv\, p \vee \neg q \,]$;

[**Contraposition**] $[\, p \Leftarrow q \,\equiv\, \neg p \Rightarrow \neg q \,]$;

[**Contradiction**] $[\, \neg p \,\equiv\, p \Rightarrow \text{false} \,]$;

[**Distributivity**] $[\, (p \equiv q) \Leftarrow r \,\equiv\, p \wedge r \,\equiv\, q \wedge r \,]$;

[**Distributivity**] $[\, (p \equiv q) \Leftarrow r \,\equiv\, p \Leftarrow r \,\equiv\, q \Leftarrow r \,]$;

[**Shunting**] $[\, p \,\Leftarrow\, q \wedge r \,\equiv\, (p \Leftarrow q) \Leftarrow r \,]$.

The names of these rules are commonly used. For example, a proof that p follows from q (for some properties p and q) is sometimes turned into a proof of the so-called *contrapositive*: a proof that ¬p implies ¬q. "Proof by contradiction" indicates the combined use of the two rules of contradiction we have given, the one above and the one in Section 13.4: to prove that some property p does not hold one shows that p implies false, where the false statement is a "contradiction" of the form $q \wedge \neg q$ for some q.

13.5.2 Replacement Rules

The advantage of using equations over other methods for defining the logical connectives is the opportunity to substitute equals for equals. The definition of $p \Leftarrow q$ provides good examples of this.

An important rule of logic is called *modus ponens*. It is the rule that

$$[\, (p \Leftarrow q) \wedge q \,\equiv\, p \wedge q \,] .$$

Here is one way of proving it. The important step is the middle step, the first step paving the way for this step.

$$(p \Leftarrow q) \wedge q$$

=   {   true is the unit of equivalence   }

$(p \Leftarrow q) \wedge (q \equiv \text{true})$

$=$ 　　　　 {　　　 substitution of equals for equals:

　　　　　　　　　 specifically the value true is substituted for q

　　　　　　　　　 in the term $p \Leftarrow q$　 }

$(p \Leftarrow \text{true}) \wedge (q \equiv \text{true})$

$=$ 　　　　 {　　　 [$p \Leftarrow \text{true} \equiv p$], true is the unit of equivalence　 }

$p \wedge q$.

The middle step uses the intuition that, if we know that q is true, we can substitute true for q in any expression in which it appears. The rule is called a *meta-rule* because it cannot be expressed in the form of an algebraic law, and we need additional language outwith the language of the propositional calculus to explain how the rule is used. A way of expressing the rule is as follows:

[Substitution]　　 $\big[(e = f) \wedge E[x := e] \equiv (e = f) \wedge E[x := f] \big]$.　　　　 (13.21)

The rule expresses the idea that if e and f are equal then e may be replaced by f (and vice versa) in any logical expression E.

Note that the rule does not depend on the type of e and f – they could be numbers, strings, booleans, or whatever. Equivalence of propositions is just equality of boolean values, so the rule applies to equivalences $e \equiv f$ just as well. The types of e, f and x do, however, have to be the same.

The introduction of the variable x in the rule allows the possibility that not every occurrence of e and f is interchanged. For example,

$$(a^2 = b) \wedge (a^2 + 1 = 2a^2 + 3) \equiv (a^2 = b) \wedge (a^2 + 1 = 2b + 3)$$

is an instance of the rule. It is so because

$$(a^2 + 1 = 2x + 3)[x := a^2] \equiv a^2 + 1 = 2a^2 + 3$$

$$(a^2 + 1 = 2x + 3)[x := b] \equiv a^2 + 1 = 2b + 3.$$

Thus, although the subexpression a^2 is repeated, the replacement rule allows a substitution of a value equal to a^2 in selected occurrences of the expression.

Substitution of equals for equals is, in fact, an instance of the rule, first formulated by Leibniz, that application of a function to equal values gives equal results: an expression E parameterised by a variable x is a function of x, and $E[x := e]$ and $E[x := f]$ simply denote the result of applying the function to e and to f, respectively. Sometimes, for brevity and to give credit to Leibniz, we use "Leibniz" as the hint when we mean "substitution of equals for equals".

A more direct formulation of Leibniz's rule is the following. Suppose E is an arbitrary expression. Then, assuming e, f and x all have the same type,

$$\textbf{[Leibniz]} \quad \big[\, (e\!=\!f) \;\equiv\; (e\!=\!f) \wedge (E[x := e] = E[x := f]) \, \big]. \tag{13.22}$$

(Rule (13.22) is a consequence of rule (13.21) because $e\!=\!f$ is equivalent to $(e\!=\!f) \wedge (E\!=\!E)$, to which (13.21) can be applied.)

We use both rules (13.21) and (13.22). Which of the two is being used can be recognised by whether a step does not or does change the number of conjuncts, respectively.

Returning to the properties of logical implication, here is how substitution (of equals for equals) is used to prove that implication is transitive.

$$
\begin{array}{ll}
& (p \Leftarrow q) \wedge (q \Leftarrow r) \\[4pt]
= & \quad \{ \qquad \text{definition} \quad \} \\[4pt]
& (p \;\equiv\; p \vee q) \wedge (q \;\equiv\; q \vee r) \\[4pt]
= & \quad \{ \qquad \text{substitution of equals for equals (13.22),} \\
& \qquad \qquad \text{applied to 2nd term with } E = (p \vee x) \quad \} \\[4pt]
& (p \;\equiv\; p \vee q) \wedge (q \;\equiv\; q \vee r) \wedge (p \vee q \;\equiv\; p \vee q \vee r) \\[4pt]
= & \quad \{ \qquad \text{substitution of equals for equals (13.21):} \\
& \qquad \qquad \text{the two rightmost occurrences of } p \vee q \\
& \qquad \qquad \text{are replaced by } p \quad \} \\[4pt]
& (p \;\equiv\; p \vee q) \wedge (q \;\equiv\; q \vee r) \wedge (p \;\equiv\; p \vee r) \\[4pt]
= & \quad \{ \qquad \text{definition} \quad \} \\[4pt]
& (p \Leftarrow q) \wedge (q \Leftarrow r) \wedge (p \Leftarrow r) \\[4pt]
\Rightarrow & \quad \{ \qquad \text{weakening} \quad \} \\[4pt]
& p \Leftarrow r.
\end{array}
$$

The following rules can all be proved using substitution of equals for equals:

[Mutual Implication (Iff)] $[\, p \equiv q \;\equiv\; (p \Leftarrow q) \wedge (p \Rightarrow q) \,]$;

[Distributivity] $[\ p \Leftarrow q \vee r \ \equiv \ (p \Leftarrow q) \wedge (p \Leftarrow r)\ ]$;

[Distributivity] $[\ p \wedge q \Leftarrow r \ \equiv \ (p \Leftarrow r) \wedge (q \Leftarrow r)\ ]$.

The rule of mutual implication expresses the anti-symmetry of the follows-from relation on booleans. It is comparable to the anti-symmetry of the at-most relation on numbers:

$$[\ x = y \ \equiv \ x \leq y \ \wedge \ x \geq y\ ].$$

For some problems involving the calculation of a number x, say, one is forced to calculate a so-called *upper bound* y, say, on the number. That is, we establish $x \leq y$. Then, in a second step, we establish that y is also a *lower bound* on x, that is, that $x \geq y$. (This often occurs in optimisation problems where the problem is to determine the minimum number x having a certain property: the first step is to exhibit a number y having the desired property and then show that y cannot be reduced without violating the desired property.) In the same way, sometimes one is forced to simplify a given boolean expression p to boolean expression q by first establishing that p follows from q and, separately, that p implies q. This is a commonly used proof technique but which can often be avoided using equational reasoning.

13.6 SET CALCULUS

Sets were introduced in Chapter 12. Set comprehension was introduced in Section 12.2.5 as a common way to define sets. The use of set comprehension entails using boolean expressions to identify a set's elements. As a result, there is a precise connection between boolean algebra and set algebra. In this section, we introduce set algebra via this connection.

We begin with the definition of set equality. Two sets S and T are equal exactly when they have the same elements:

     [Set Equality] $[\ S = T \ \equiv \ \langle \forall x :: x \in S \equiv x \in T \rangle\ ]$.   (13.23)

The rule (13.23) turns reasoning about the equality of two sets into reasoning about the boolean expressions $x \in S$ and $x \in T$ for some arbitrary x. On the right side of the equivalence is a so-called *universal quantification*. The symbol "$\forall$" is read as "for all" and the entire expression is read as "for all x, x is in S equivales x is in T". We discuss universal quantification in detail in Chapter 14; for the moment, the only rule we need is that if we prove some property P that is predicated on x but the proof does not make any assumption about x then we can conclude $\langle \forall x :: P \rangle$.

Here is an example. The union T of two sets S and T is defined formally by the rule

[Set Union] $[\ x \in S \cup T\ \equiv\ x \in S \vee x \in T\ ]$. (13.24)

Using this definition, we show that $S \cup T$ and $T \cup S$ are equal sets:

$$x \in S \cup T$$

$=$ {   definition of set union: (13.24)   }

$$x \in S \vee x \in T$$

$=$ {   disjunction is symmetric   }

$$x \in T \vee x \in S$$

$=$ {   definition of set union: (13.24)   }

$$x \in T \cup S.$$

We have thus proved that

$$\langle \forall x :: x \in S \cup T \equiv x \in T \cup S \rangle .$$

It follows from (13.23) that $[\ S \cup T = T \cup S\ ]$.

Note that the core of this calculation is that disjunction is symmetric. Set union *inherits* the properties of disjunction because the rule (13.24) provides a simple way of rewriting a union of two sets as a disjunction of two booleans, and vice versa. Thus set union is also idempotent and associative. Its unit is the empty set because

[Empty Set] $[\ x \in \emptyset\ \equiv\ \text{false}\ ]$. (13.25)

and false is the unit of disjunction.

Similarly, set intersection T is defined in terms of the conjunction of boolean expressions:

[Set Intersection] $[\ x \in S \cap T\ \equiv\ x \in S \wedge x \in T\ ]$. (13.26)

Consequently, set intersection inherits the properties of conjunction: it is idempotent, symmetric and associative. Also, union distributes through intersection and intersection distributes through union:

[Distributivity] $[\ R \cup (S \cap T)\ =\ (R \cup S) \cap (R \cup T)\ ]$,

[Distributivity] $[\ R \cap (S \cup T)\ =\ (R \cap S) \cup (R \cap T)\ ]$.

The proofs of all these properties are simple: apply the definition of equality of sets to turn the property into an equality of booleans, then apply the relevant property of the boolean operators and, finally, apply the definition of equality of sets once more.

Formally, this duality between set algebra and boolean algebra is captured by two simple rules of set comprehension. Suppose S is a set-valued expression and P is a boolean-valued expression (typically parameterised by variable x). Then

[Set Comprehension] $[e \in \{x \mid P\} \ \equiv \ P[x := e]]$,

[Set Comprehension] $[S = \{x \mid x \in S\}]$.

13.7 EXERCISES

1. Construct truth tables for the following boolean expressions.
   (a) $(p \Leftarrow q) \vee (p \Rightarrow q)$
   (b) $(p \Leftarrow q) \wedge (p \Rightarrow q)$
   (c) $\neg p \vee q$
   (d) $\neg p \wedge q$
   (e) $p \vee q \equiv q$
   (f) $p \wedge q \equiv q$
   (g) $p \vee q \not\equiv q$

   Each of the these expressions defines one of the 16 binary boolean operators. If the operator is shown in the table in Section 12.6, say which it is.

2. Prove the following properties of negation.

   [Negation] $\neg false = true$

   [Double Negation] $[\neg\neg p = p]$

   [Associativity] $[((p \not\equiv q) \equiv r) \equiv (p \equiv (q \not\equiv r))]$

   Use the rules (5.2) and (13.5), stating clearly the instantiations of the variables.

3. Prove:

   $$[p \vee q \equiv p \wedge \neg q \not\equiv q]$$

   using the rules given in this chapter. (Read as

   $$[(p \vee q) = (p \wedge \neg q \not\equiv q)],$$

   the rule expresses an inclusive-or as an exclusive-or. This is useful for counting problems.)

4. Prove each of the rules stated in Section 13.4. Prove them in the order given. You may use previously stated rules but not rules that follow.

5. It is easy to check whether or not a number in decimal notation is even or not: just determine whether the last digit is even. For example, 2437 is odd because 7 is odd. Formulate and prove the rule of arithmetic that is the basis for this method. (Hint: $2437 = 243 \times 10 + 7$. You will need to use the distributivity law formulated in Section 5.3.1. You should also formulate a general rule for determining whether a product of two numbers is even.)

6. Show that the booleans form a semiring[1] ($\mathsf{Bool}, \mathsf{true}, \mathsf{false}, \wedge, \not\equiv$) with unit true, zero false, product operator $\wedge$ and addition operator $\not\equiv$.

   This is a well-known property which leads some authors to write conjunction as an infix dot "•" (to make it look like multiplication) and inequivalence as "$\oplus$" (making it look like addition). Compare this with Theorem 13.11, which is much less well known. In fact, the theorems are duals obtained by interchanging the roles of true and false. The combination of inequivalence and conjunction is often used in the encryption of data. In such applications, equivalence and disjunction could be used instead.

7. Prove the following properties using substitution of equals for equals:

   [Mutual Implication (Iff)] $[\ p \equiv q \equiv (p \Leftarrow q) \wedge (p \Rightarrow q)\ ]$

   [Distributivity]: $[\ p \Leftarrow q \vee r \equiv (p \Leftarrow q) \wedge (p \Leftarrow r)\ ]$

   [Distributivity]: $[\ p \wedge q \Leftarrow r \equiv (p \Leftarrow r) \wedge (q \Leftarrow r)\ ]$

8. Enumerate the elements of the following sets.
   (a) $\{m \mid 0 \le m < 6\}$
   (b) $\{m \mid 3 \le m < 8\}$
   (c) $\{m \mid 0 \le m < 6 \wedge 3 \le m < 8\}$
   (d) $\{m \mid 0 \le m < 6 \vee 3 \le m < 8\}$
   (e) $\{m \mid 0 \le m < 6 \not\equiv 3 \le m < 8\}$

9. When translated to a statement about sets, the golden rule must be formulated as two separate statements, namely:

$$[\ S = T \equiv S \cup T = S \cap T\ ],$$
$$[\ S \cup T = S \equiv T = S \cap T\ ].$$

[1]The most common formulation of this property is that the booleans form something called a *field*, called GF(2): the "Galois field" of order 2. Several additional properties are required for a structure to be a field but, in the case of the booleans, the additional properties are trivial and add nothing to our understanding of their algebraic properties. The significance of identifying the booleans as a field is that they form the simplest possible example of a (Galois) field and the concept of a field is important to the understanding more complex mathematical structures.

The second of these gives two equivalent ways of defining the subset relation on sets:

$$[\ S \supseteq T\ \equiv\ S \cup T = S\ ],$$

$$[\ T \subseteq S\ \equiv\ T = S \cap T\ ].$$

Compare this with the definitions of "if" and "only if" in Section 13.5.1. The subset relation is thus the counterpart in set calculus of implication in boolean algebra.

Formulate and prove each of the rules in Section 13.5.1 in the set calculus. For example, the strengthening rule (13.19) is the rule

$$[\ S \cup T \supseteq S\ ]$$

and the rule of mutual implication (the anti-symmetry of the follows-from relation) is the rule of anti-symmetry of the subset relation

$$[\ S = T\ \equiv\ S \subseteq T \wedge S \supseteq T\ ].$$

You may assume the validity of all the rules in Section 13.5.1.

Chapter

Quantifiers

14

In this chapter, we introduce a uniform notation for quantifiers. We also give rules for manipulating quantifiers and illustrate their use with several examples.

Two quantifers that are particularly important are *universal* quantification and *existential* quantification. Additional rules governing such quantifications are also presented.

14.1 DOTDOTDOT AND SIGMAS

Most readers will have encountered the *dotdotdot* notation already. It is a notation that is rarely introduced properly; mostly, it is just used without explanation as in, for example, "$1 + 2 + \ldots + 20 = 210$" and "let $x_0, x_1, \ldots, x_n$ be".

The dotdotdot notation is used when some operation is to be applied to a bag of values in cases where the bag is too large to be enumerated, or the size of the bag is given by some variable. In the case of "$1 + 2 + \ldots + 20 = 210$", the operation is addition and there are twenty values to be enumerated; in the case of "let $x_0, x_1, \ldots, x_n$ be", the operation is sequencing (indicated by commas) and the number of values is given by the variable n.

The dotdotdot notation is convenient in the very simplest cases. But it puts a major burden on the reader, requiring them to interpolate from a few example values to the general term in a bag of values.

The so-called *Sigma* notation is a well-established notation for continued summations. An example is the sum of the squares of all numbers from 0 up to and including the number n which, in Sigma notation, is written

$$\sum_{k=0}^{n} k^2.$$

Similarly, the *Pi* notation is used to denote a continued product. For example, the factorial of number n is defined to be the product of all numbers from 1 up to and including the number n. In dotdotdot notation this would be written

$$n! = 1 \times 2 \times \ldots \times n.$$

The equivalent in Pi notation is

$$n! = \prod_{k=1}^{n} k.$$

The two-dimensional nature of the Sigma and Pi notations makes them very readable because it is easy to identify the constituent components of the notation. There is a *quantifier* – $\sum$ or $\prod$ in the two examples – which identifies the operation to be carried out (addition in the case of $\sum$ and multiplication in the case of $\prod$). There is also a so-called *bound variable* (k in both examples above) which has a certain *range* (0 thru n in the first example and 1 thru n in the second example). Finally, there is a *term* defining a function of the bound variable which is to be evaluated at each point in the range (k^2 in the first example and k in the second example). The bound variable is always to the left of the equals sign in the expression below the quantifier, and it ranges over a consecutive sequence of numbers, where the lower bound is given to the right of the equals sign and the upper bound is placed above the quantifier. The function of the bound variable is written immediately to the right of the quantifier. The general form of the Sigma and Pi notations is thus

$$\bigoplus_{bv=lb}^{ub} E$$

where $\bigoplus$ is the quantifier, bv is an identifier denoting the bound variable, lb and ub are expressions denoting the lower and upper bounds of the range of the quantification, respectively, and E is an expression denoting the function of the bound variable that is to be evaluated at each point in the range of the bound variable.

Because of their readability, the Sigma and Pi notations are widely used. A major drawback, however, is that they are limited to quantifications over a consecutive sequence of numbers. Problems arise if the notation is to be used for quantifications over non-consecutive numbers. In the next section, we introduce a uniform notation for quantified expressions that avoids this problem.

14.2 INTRODUCING QUANTIFIER NOTATION

Summation and multiplication are just two examples of the quantifiers we want to consider. In general, it is meaningful to "quantify" over a non-empty range with respect to any binary operator that is associative and symmetric. Addition, multiplication, equivalence, inequivalence, set union, set intersection, minimum, maximum, conjunction, disjunction, greatest common divisor and least common multiple are all examples of associative and symmetric operators. In each case, it is meaningful (and useful) to consider the operator applied to a (non-zero) number of values rather than just a pair of values. Moreover, quantifying over an empty range is meaningful provided the operator in question has a unit.

We use a uniform notation to denote quantifications over a number of values. In this way, we can also present a uniform set of laws for manipulating quantifiers, resulting in a substantial reduction in the number of laws one has to remember.

We begin by explaining the particular case of summation, comparing our notation with the Sigma notation discussed above. Then, we consider quantifications with respect to conjunction and disjunction ("for all" quantifications and "there exist" quantifications, respectively) before considering the general case.

14.2.1 Summation

Our notation for summation has the form

$$\langle \Sigma\, bv\ :\ range\ :\ term \rangle .$$

There are five components to the notation, which we explain in turn.

The first component is the *quantifier*, in this case Σ. By a long-standing convention among mathematicians, Σ denotes summation of some arbitrary number of values. The second component is the *dummy* bv. The dummy is said to be *bound* to the quantifier; it is also called the *bound variable*. We use identifiers like i, j and k, or x, y and z as dummies. Later, we allow the possibility of a list of dummies rather than just a single one. The third component is the *range* of the dummy. The range is a boolean-valued expression that determines a set of values of the dummy, specifically, the set of all values of the bound variable for which the range evaluates to true. (Quantifications are not always well defined if the range defines an *infinite* range set; we postpone discussion of this problem until later.) The fourth component is the *term*. In the case of summation, the term is an integer- or real-valued expression. The final component of the notation is the angle brackets; these serve to delimit the *scope* of the bound variable.

The value of a summation of the form $\langle \Sigma\, bv\ :\ range\ :\ term \rangle$ is determined as follows: evaluate the term for each value of the dummy described by the range, and, then, sum all these values together. For example, the value of

$$\langle \Sigma k\ :\ 1 \le k \le 3\ :\ k^3 \rangle$$

is

$$1^3+2^3+3^3.$$

Here, the range $1 \leq k \leq 3$ determines the set $\{k \mid 1 \leq k \leq 3\}$. That is, the dummy k ranges over the three values 1, 2 and 3. The term k^3 is evaluated at these three values and then the values are summed together.

The range can be any boolean expression, and the term any integer or real-valued expression as in, for example,

$$\left\langle \Sigma k \; : \; \text{even}(k) \wedge 0 \leq k < N \; : \; k^3+k^2+N+1 \right\rangle.$$

Sometimes, there may be no value of the dummy in the range, for example, if the dummy is k, the range is $0 \leq k < N$, and N happens to be zero. In this case, the summation is defined to be zero. In words, a sum of no values is zero.

The dummy has a certain type, the knowledge of which is crucial in certain circumstances. A long-standing mathematical convention is that variables i, j and k denote *integer* values; this convention suffices for most problems in this book. Where necessary, the type of the dummy can be indicated by adding it immediately after the first occurrence of the dummy, as in

$$\left\langle \Sigma \, k \in \mathbb{Z} \; : \; \text{even}(k) \wedge 0 \leq k < N \; : \; k^3+k^2+N+1 \right\rangle.$$

Additionally, we sometimes indicate the type of the dummies in the accompanying text rather than in the quantification itself.

Rather than have just one dummy, it is convenient to allow a number of variables to be bound to the same quantifier. An example is

$$\left\langle \Sigma \, i,j \; : \; 0 \leq i < j \leq N \; : \; i+j \right\rangle.$$

This denotes the sum of all values $i+j$ such that i and j satisfy the property $0 \leq i < j \leq N$. Taking N to be 2, the possible values of i and j are: $i=0$ and $j=1$, $i=0$ and $j=2$, $i=1$ and $j=2$, so that

$$\left\langle \Sigma \, i,j \; : \; 0 \leq i < j \leq 2 \; : \; i+j \right\rangle \quad = \quad (0+1)+(0+2)+(1+2).$$

Note that the variables in a list of dummies must all be distinct. It does not make sense to repeat dummies. For example, $\langle \Sigma \, i,i \; : \; 0 \leq i < 2 \; : \; 0 \rangle$ is not meaningful.

14.2.2 Free and Bound Variables

In the next section, we formulate general properties of summation. Several of these rules have so-called *side conditions* that prevent improper use of the rule. The side conditions are, primarily, *syntactic* and not semantic. This means they are conditions on the way expressions are written (their syntax) rather than conditions on the values of the expressions (their semantics). So the conditions may apply to one expression but not to another expression of equal value. For example, the condition "the symbol '0' occurs in the expression" is a syntactic condition on expressions, which is true of "0" but not true of "$1-1$", even though 0 and $1-1$ are equal.

A consequence of the syntactic nature of the side conditions is that they are cumbersome to state even though they are, in fact, quite straightforward. In order to understand them, we need to have a clear understanding of the notions of "free" and "bound" variables in an expression. (These notions provide the semantic justification for the syntactic side conditions.)

Note that, although all the examples given in this section are of summations, the discussion applies equally well to all quantifiers.

Recall that a dummy in a summation is said to be *bound*. For example, all occurrences of "k" in $\langle \Sigma k : 1 \leq k \leq 3 : k \rangle$ are bound to the Σ quantifier. Variables that have occurrences in an expression that are *not* bound to a quantifier are called *free* variables. For example, n is free in 2^n, and m and n are free in $\langle \Sigma k : 0 \leq k < m : k^n \rangle$.

Free and bound variables have different roles. The value of an expression depends on the value of its free variables. For example, the value of 2^n depends on the value of the free variable n, and the value of $\langle \Sigma k : 0 \leq k < m : k^n \rangle$ depends on the values of the free variables m and n. However, it is meaningless to say that the value of an expression depends on the value of any bound variables occurring in the expression. Also, the names given to bound variables can be changed, whereas those given to free variables cannot. So, $\langle \Sigma k : 1 \leq k \leq 3 : k^n \rangle$ and $\langle \Sigma j : 1 \leq j \leq 3 : j^n \rangle$ both have the same meaning – the change of dummy name from "k" to "j" is irrelevant. But, 2^m and 2^n are quite different – the free variables m and n cannot be interchanged at will.

Dummies bound to quantifiers act like local variables in a program. The first occurrence is comparable to a declaration of the variable, the scope of the declaration being delimited by the angle brackets. This means that dummy names may be reused, that is, different quantifications may use the same bound variables, as in, for example,

$$\langle \Sigma k : 0 \leq k < n : k \rangle \times \langle \Sigma k : 1 \leq k \leq n : k^2 \rangle.$$

In this expression, there are two distinct dummies, both having the same name "k". The first is bound to the leftmost Σ and the second to the rightmost Σ. The angle brackets avoid confusion between the two because they clearly delimit the scope of the bindings (the subexpressions in which the dummies have meaning).

Reuse of dummy names is quite common. After all, the name of a dummy is irrelevant, so why bother to think of different names? Reuse of dummy names is not a problem, except where the scope of the bindings overlaps. The only time that scopes overlap is when they are "nested".

Nesting of quantifications is when one quantification is a subexpression in another quantification – as in, for example,

$$\left\langle \Sigma j \, : \, 0 \leq j < n \, : \, \left\langle \Sigma k \, : \, 0 \leq k < n \, : \, j \times k^2 \right\rangle \right\rangle.$$

A variable that is bound at one level in an expression is free within subexpressions. In the above example, all occurrences of "j" are bound, but in the expression

$$\left\langle \Sigma k : 0 \leq k < n : j \times k^2 \right\rangle$$

"j" is free. (This is just like nested declarations in a block-structured programming language. Variables are local to the block in which they are declared but global in any nested blocks.)

Variables may be both free and bound in the same expression. An example is

$$\left\langle \Sigma k : 0 \leq k < n : k^2 \right\rangle + k.$$

In this expression, the rightmost occurrence of "k" is free, whereas all other occurrences are bound to the Σ quantifier. The rightmost occurrence of "k" is distinct from all other occurrences, as is evident from the fact that the other occurrences can be renamed to, say, "j". An equivalent (and perhaps more readable) expression is

$$\left\langle \Sigma j : 0 \leq j < n : j^2 \right\rangle + k.$$

The names of dummies may also be reused in nested quantifications. The summation

$$\langle \Sigma i : i = 0 \vee i = 1 : \langle \Sigma i : i = 2 \vee i = 3 : i \rangle \; - \; 4 \times i \rangle$$

is perfectly meaningful. It evaluates to $((2+3) - 4 \times 0) + ((2+3) - 4 \times 1)$. Renaming the innermost dummy to j, we get the equivalent expression

$$\langle \Sigma i : i = 0 \vee i = 1 : \langle \Sigma j : j = 2 \vee j = 3 : j \rangle \; - \; 4 \times i \rangle.$$

The rule is that in nested quantifications, the innermost bindings take precedence. (The analogy with variable declarations in block-structured languages is again useful.)

A variable can be *captured* by a quantifier when dummies are renamed. Earlier, we gave

$$\langle \Sigma k : 1 \leq k \leq 3 : k^n \rangle \;=\; \langle \Sigma j : 1 \leq j \leq 3 : j^n \rangle$$

as a valid use of renaming. But it would be wrong to rename "k" to "n". Clearly,

$$\langle \Sigma k : 1 \leq k \leq 3 : k^n \rangle \;\neq\; \langle \Sigma n : 1 \leq n \leq 3 : n^n \rangle.$$

In the left-hand summation, n is free; in the right-hand summation, all occurrences of "n" are bound to the quantifier. The left side depends on the value of n, while the right side does not (it equals $1^1 + 2^2 + 3^3$). So, a proviso on dummy renaming is that the new name is not free anywhere in the scope of the quantifier.

Care must be taken when manipulating quantifications to ensure that free variables are not "captured" by a quantifier and, conversely, bound variables are not "released" from their binding. As a general rule, you should always be aware of which variable occurrences in an expression are free and which are bound. Application of algebraic laws is invalid if free variables become bound or if bound variables become free. Care is also needed to ensure that a dummy name does not occur twice in a list of dummies. (This can occur, for example, when unnesting quantifications.) And care is needed in the process of substitution – substituting an expression for a variable should only replace *free* occurrences of the variable. Understanding the distinction between free and bound occurrences of variables will enable you to easily avoid any pitfalls.

14.2.3 Properties of Summation

The main advantage of a formal quantifier notation over the informal dotdotdot notation is that it is easier to formulate and use calculational rules. In this subsection, we formulate rules for summation. Later, we will see that these rules are all instances of more general rules.

We formulate the rules in terms of each of the components of a quantification. Thus, there are rules governing the use of dummies, rules exploiting the structure of the range, and rules exploiting the structure of the term. Additionally, there are two so-called *trading* rules that allow information to be moved to and from the range of the quantification.

Side Condition   A general side condition on all the rules is that their application should not result in the capture of free variables or release of bound variables, and should not result in a variable occurring more than once in a list of dummies.

Dummy Rules   There are three rules governing the use of dummies. The first rule expresses the fact that a "dummy" is just a place-holder, the particular name chosen for the dummy is not relevant provided it does not clash with the names of other variables in the quantified expression. (The rule has already been discussed in Section 14.2.2 but is repeated here for convenience.) Renaming is often used when performing other algebraic manipulations in order to avoid capture of free variables or release of bound variables.

Let $R[j := k]$ and $T[j := k]$ denote, respectively, the expressions obtained by replacing every *free* occurrence of "j" in R and T by "k". Then

$$\textbf{[Dummy Renaming]} \quad [\; \langle \Sigma j : R : T \rangle \; = \; \langle \Sigma k : R[j := k] : T[j := k] \rangle \;]. \tag{14.1}$$

As discussed earlier, the general side condition on application of rules demands that R and T be expressions not containing any free occurrence of "k".

The second rule states, essentially, that the use of more than one dummy is a convenient abbreviation for a collection of quantifications. We use "*js*" in the statement of the rule to denote any list of variables.

$$\textbf{[Nesting]} \quad [\; \langle \Sigma j,js : R \wedge S : T \rangle \; = \; \langle \Sigma j : R : \langle \Sigma js : S : T \rangle \rangle \;]. \tag{14.2}$$

There are two side conditions on this rule. The first side condition is that expression R may not include free occurrences of any variable in the list js. The reason for this is that the scope of the variables in the list js on the right side of the equality is delimited by the innermost angle brackets and, thus, does not extend to the range R of the bound variable j. If R does not satisfy the side condition, those variables would be released in the process of replacing the left side by the right side.

This is an example of avoiding the circumstance that a bound variable becomes free. Were the rule to be used from left to right when a variable in the list js does occur free in R, that variable would be bound by the quantifier in the left side of the equality but free in the right side. The right side would, thus, be an expression that depends on the value of this variable, whereas the left side does not.

The second side condition is that the list js may not include the variable j. This is because "j,js" in the left side of the equality would then include two occurrences of "j", and it would not be possible to distinguish between related and unrelated occurrences of "j" in the range and term. For example, a naive attempt to apply the nesting rule to

$$\langle \Sigma i : i=0 \vee i=1 : \langle \Sigma i : i=2 \vee i=3 : i - 2 \times i \rangle \rangle$$

gives

$$\langle \Sigma i,i : (i=0 \vee i=1) \wedge (i=2 \vee i=3) : i - 2 \times i \rangle.$$

This is meaningless because it is impossible to determine which occurrences of i are related, and which not.

It is always possible to avoid such complications by suitably renaming bound variables before using the nesting rule. Using the renaming rule, the above summation equals

$$\langle \Sigma\, i : i = 0 \vee i = 1 : \langle \Sigma\, j : j = 2 \vee j = 3 : j - 2 \times j \rangle \rangle$$

which, by the nesting rule, equals

$$\langle \Sigma\ i,j\ :\ (i = 0 \vee i = 1) \wedge (j = 2 \vee j = 3)\ :\ j - 2 \times j \rangle.$$

It is worth remarking that the rule is used both from left to right (from which the name "nesting" is derived) and from right to left (in which case quantifications become *un*nested). So, the rule is both a *nesting* and an *unnesting* rule. The first side condition relates to the use of the rule in a left-to-right direction, and the second side condition to its use in a right-to-left direction.

The third rule is very powerful because, in combination with the nesting rule, it allows us to rearrange the order in which the values in a summation are added together. Formally, however, the rule is very simple. It simply states that the order in which the dummies are listed in a summation is irrelevant.

[Rearranging] $\left[\ \langle \Sigma\, j,k : R : T \rangle\ =\ \langle \Sigma\, k,j : R : T \rangle\ \right].$ (14.3)

Here is an example of how the nesting and rearranging rules are combined. The parenthesisation corresponds to the nesting of the summations.

$$(1 \times 1 + 1 \times 2 + 1 \times 3) + (2 \times 2 + 2 \times 3) + 3 \times 3$$

$=$ {   definition of Σ }

$$\langle \Sigma\, i : 1 \leq i \leq 3 : \langle \Sigma\, j : i \leq j \leq 3 : i \times j \rangle \rangle$$

$=$ {   (un)nesting: $1 \leq i \leq 3 \wedge i \leq j \leq 3 \equiv 1 \leq i \leq j \leq 3$ }

$$\langle \Sigma\ i,j : 1 \leq i \leq j \leq 3 : i \times j \rangle$$

$=$ {   rearranging   }

$$\langle \Sigma\ j,i : 1 \leq i \leq j \leq 3 : i \times j \rangle$$

$=$ {   nesting: $1 \leq i \leq j \leq 3 \equiv 1 \leq j \leq 3 \wedge 1 \leq i \leq j$ }

$$\langle \Sigma\, j : 1 \leq j \leq 3 : \langle \Sigma\, i : 1 \leq i \leq j : i \times j \rangle \rangle$$

$=$ {   definition of Σ }

$$1 \times 1 + (1 \times 2 + 2 \times 2) + (1 \times 3 + 2 \times 3 + 3 \times 3).$$

Note that repeated use of nesting and rearranging allows the rearrangement of the order of the values to be summed. The rules depend crucially on the associativity and symmetry of addition.

Range Part   We now come to the laws governing manipulation of the range part. There are four rules. The first two rules govern the case where the range defines the empty set, and the case where the range defines a set with exactly one element:

[Empty Range] $[\ \langle \Sigma k : \text{false} : T \rangle\ =\ 0\ ]$; (14.4)

[One-Point] $[\ \langle \Sigma k : k = e : T \rangle\ =\ T[k := e]\ ]$. (14.5)

The general side condition on use of rules prohibits the use of the one-point rule when e is an expression containing free occurrences of "k", the reason being that this would result in their release when using the rule from left to right and in their capture when using the rule from right to left.

The third rule allows a summation to be split into separate summations:

[Splitting]
$$[\ \langle \Sigma k : P : T \rangle + \langle \Sigma k : Q : T \rangle\ =\ \langle \Sigma k : P \lor Q : T \rangle + \langle \Sigma k : P \land Q : T \rangle\ ].$$
(14.6)

The splitting rule gets its name because it is most often used when P and Q "split" the range into two disjoint sets, that is, when $P \land Q$ is everywhere false. In this case, $\langle \Sigma k : P \land Q : T \rangle$ is zero, by the empty-range rule, and may be eliminated from the right side of the rule. Here is the most common example, where we "split" predicate P into $P \land Q$ and $P \land \neg Q$.

$$\langle \Sigma k : P \land Q : T \rangle + \langle \Sigma k : P \land \neg Q : T \rangle$$

$=$ $\{$ splitting (14.6) with $P, Q := P \land Q, P \land \neg Q\ \}$

$$\langle \Sigma k : (P \land Q) \lor (P \land \neg Q) : T \rangle + \langle \Sigma k : P \land Q \land P \land \neg Q : T \rangle$$

$=$ $\{$ predicate calculus $\}$

$$\langle \Sigma k : P : T \rangle + \langle \Sigma k : \text{false} : T \rangle$$

$=$ $\{$ empty range (14.4), arithmetic $\}$

$$\langle \Sigma k : P : T \rangle.$$

We have thus derived the rule

$$[\ \langle \Sigma k : P : T \rangle\ =\ \langle \Sigma k : P \land Q : T \rangle + \langle \Sigma k : P \land \neg Q : T \rangle\ ].$$
(14.7)

This rule can now be combined with the one-point rule to split off one term in a summation, as in, for example,

$$\langle \Sigma\, i : 0 \leq i \leq N : 2^i \rangle$$

$= \qquad \{ \qquad$ splitting on $i = 0 \vee i \neq 0$

$\qquad\qquad$ (i.e. (14.7) with Q instantiated to $i = 0$) $\}$

$$\langle \Sigma\, i : 0 \leq i \leq N \wedge i = 0 : 2^i \rangle \;+\; \langle \Sigma\, i : 0 \leq i \leq N \wedge i \neq 0 : 2^i \rangle$$

$= \qquad \{ \qquad$ simplification of ranges (assuming $0 \leq N$) $\}$

$$\langle \Sigma\, i : i = 0 : 2^i \rangle \;+\; \langle \Sigma\, i : 1 \leq i \leq N : 2^i \rangle$$

$= \qquad \{ \qquad$ one-point rule $\}$

$$2^0 + \langle \Sigma\, i : 1 \leq i \leq N : 2^i \rangle$$

$= \qquad \{ \qquad$ arithmetic $\}$

$$1 + \langle \Sigma\, i : 1 \leq i \leq N : 2^i \rangle.$$

(It is more common to state the splitting rule in the form (14.7). However, the beautiful symmetry of (14.6) makes it more attractive and easier to remember.)

The final rule is a consequence of the rearrangement rule given earlier. It also allows the terms in a summation to be rearranged. Suppose function f maps values of type J to values of type K, and suppose g is a function that maps values of type K to values of type J. Suppose, further, that f and g are *inverses*. That is, suppose that, for all $j \in J$ and $k \in K$,

$$f(j) = k \;\equiv\; j = g(k).$$

Then,

$\textbf{[Translation]} \quad [\, \langle \Sigma\, k \in K : R : T \rangle \;=\; \langle \Sigma\, j \in J : R[k := f(j)] : T[k := f(j)] \rangle \,].$

$$(14.8)$$

If a function has an inverse, it is called a *bijection*. The most common use of the translation rule is when the source, J, and target, K, of the function f are the same. A bijection that maps a set to itself simply permutes the elements of the set. So, in this case, (14.8) says that it is permissible to arbitrarily permute the values being added.

The rule is, in fact, a combination of the one-point rule (14.5), the nesting rule (14.2) and the rearrangement rule (14.3); see the exercises at the end of the chapter. We call it the *translation* rule because, in general, it translates a summation over elements of one type into a summation of elements of another type. It is useful to list it separately, because it is a quite powerful combination of these earlier rules and finds frequent use.

When we use the translation rule, the function f is indicated in the accompanying hint by giving the substitution "$k := f(j)$".

Trading Rules The range part of a summation is very convenient to use but, in a formal sense, it is redundant because the information can always be shifted either to the type of the dummy or to the term part. Shifting the information to the type of the dummy is expressed by the rule

$$[\textbf{Trading}] \quad \big[\, \langle \Sigma\, k{\in}K : P \wedge Q : T \rangle \;=\; \langle \Sigma\, k \in \{k{\in}K \,|\, P\} : Q : T \rangle \,\big]. \tag{14.9}$$

Here the type K of the dummy k is replaced by the subset $\{k{\in}K \,|\, P\}$. For example, we might consider the natural numbers $\mathbf{N}$ to be a subset of the integers $\mathbb{Z}$, specifically $\{k{\in}\mathbb{Z} \,|\, 0 \leq k\}$.

Rule (14.9) is most often used implicitly; in order to avoid specific mention of the range (e.g. if it is not explicitly used in a calculation), the information about the types of the dummies is given in the text and then omitted in the formal quantifications. In this case, the form

$$\langle \Sigma\, k :: T \rangle$$

of the notation is used. Formally, $\langle \Sigma\, k :: T \rangle$ is a shorthand for $\langle \Sigma\, k{\in}K : \mathsf{true} : T \rangle$ where K is the declared type of k.

Shifting the information in the range to the term part is achieved by exploiting the fact that zero is the unit of addition. For values k not in the given range, we add zero to the sum:

$$[\textbf{Trading}] \quad \big[\, \langle \Sigma k : P \wedge Q : T \rangle \;=\; \langle \Sigma k : Q : \mathsf{if}\ P{\to}T \ \square \ \neg P {\to} 0\ \mathsf{fi} \rangle \,\big]. \tag{14.10}$$

Some texts use a trick peculiar to summation to simplify this rule. The trick is to note that $0{\times}x = 0$ and $1{\times}x = 1$; the boolean value false is mapped to 0 and the boolean value true is mapped to 1. Denoting this mapping by square brackets, the rule reads

$$\langle \Sigma k : P \wedge Q : T \rangle \;=\; \langle \Sigma k : Q : [P] {\times} T \rangle.$$

Term Part There are two rules governing the term part. The first allows us to combine two summations over the same range (or, conversely, split up an addition within a summation into two summations):

$$[\textbf{Rearranging}] \quad \big[\, \langle \Sigma k : R : T_0 + T_1 \rangle \;=\; \langle \Sigma k : R : T_0 \rangle + \langle \Sigma k : R : T_1 \rangle \,\big]. \tag{14.11}$$

Like the translation rule, this rule is also a combination of the nesting (14.2) and rearranging rules (14.3) given earlier – because

$$T_0 + T_1 = \langle \Sigma j : j = 0 \lor j = 1 : T_j \rangle.$$

It is worth listing separately because it is used very frequently.

The final rule allows us to "factor out" multiplication by a constant from a summation (conversely, it allows us to "distribute" multiplication by a constant into a summation):

$$[\text{\textbf{Distributivity}}] \quad [\ \langle \Sigma k : R : c \times T \rangle \ = \ c \times \langle \Sigma k : R : T \rangle \ ]. \tag{14.12}$$

The general side condition on the application of rules prohibits the use of distributivity when "k" occurs free in the expression c. (Otherwise, any such occurrences would be released/captured by application of the rule.)

14.2.4 Warning

We conclude this discussion of summation with a warning. Care must be taken when quantifying over an infinite range. In this case, the value of the expression is defined as a *limit* of a sequence of finite quantifications, and, in some cases, the limit may not exist. For example, $\langle \Sigma i : 0 \leq i : (-1)^i \rangle$ is not defined because the sequence of finite quantifications $\langle \Sigma i : 0 \leq i < N : (-1)^i \rangle$, for N increasing from 0 onwards, alternates between 0 and 1. So it has no limit. The rules we have given are not always valid when the range of the summation is infinite. The so-called *convergence* of infinite summations is a well-studied part of mathematics but beyond the scope of this text.

14.3 UNIVERSAL AND EXISTENTIAL QUANTIFICATION

Summation is just one example of the quantifiers we want to consider. Readers already familiar with the $\prod$ notation for continued multiplications will probably have no difficulty rewriting each of the properties of summation into a form that is applicable to multiplication. In general, it is meaningful to "quantify" with respect to any binary operator that is associative and symmetric. As mentioned earlier, addition, multiplication, equivalence, inequivalence, minimum, maximum, conjunction, disjunction, greatest common divisor, and least common multiple are all examples of associative and symmetric operators, and, in each case, it is meaningful (and useful) to consider the operator applied to a number of values rather than just a pair of values.

Two quantifications that are particularly important in program specification are so-called *universal quantification* and *existential quantification*. Universal quantification extends conjunction to a set of booleans of arbitrary size. Just as for summation, there is a widely accepted symbol denoting universal quantification, namely the "∀" ("for all") symbol. The notation $\langle \forall k : R : T \rangle$ means the logical "and" ("∧") of all values of the boolean expression T determined by assigning to dummy k all values in the range R. In words, it reads

for all   k   in the range   R   it is the case that   T

$\langle \forall$ k   :   R   :   T$\rangle$

For example,

$$\langle \forall k : 0 \leq k < N : 0 \leq f(k) \rangle$$

states that the value of the function f is positive for all inputs in the range 0 thru N−1. In dotdotdot notation this is

$$0 \leq f(0) \ \wedge \ 0 \leq f(1) \ \wedge \ \ldots \ \wedge \ 0 \leq f(N-1).$$

When disjunction is extended to an arbitrary set of boolean values, the long-standing mathematical convention is to use the "∃" ("there exists") symbol. The notation $\langle \exists k : R : T \rangle$ means the logical "or" ("∨") of all values of the boolean expression T determined by assigning to dummy k all values in the range R. In words, it reads

there exists k   in the range R   such that   T

$\langle \exists$ k   :   R   :   T$\rangle$

For example,

$$\langle \exists k : 0 \leq k < N : 0 \leq f(k) \rangle$$

states that there is some number in the range 0 thru N−1 at which the value of the function f is positive. In dotdotdot notation this is

$$0 \leq f(0) \ \vee \ 0 \leq f(1) \ \vee \ \ldots \ \vee \ 0 \leq f(N-1).$$

14.3.1 Universal Quantification

Just as for summation, we can enumerate a list of rules that govern the algebraic properties of universal and existential quantification. The rules have much the same shape. In this section, we list the rules for universal quantification. Only the splitting rule differs in a non-trivial way from the rules for summation.

The side conditions on application of the rules will not be repeated for individual rules. As a reminder, here, once more, is the statement of the condition.

Side Condition The application of a rule is invalid if it results in the capture of free variables or release of bound variables, or it results in a variable occurring more than once in a list of dummies.

The rules governing the dummies are identical to the rules for summation except for the change of quantifier. The side conditions concerning capture of free variables and/or release of bound variables remain as before.

$$[\text{Dummy Renaming}] \quad [\,\langle \forall j : R : T\rangle \;=\; \langle \forall k : R[j := k] : T[j := k]\rangle\,]. \tag{14.13}$$

$$[\text{Nesting}] \quad [\,\langle \forall j, js : R \wedge S : T\rangle \;=\; \langle \forall j : R : \langle \forall js : S : T\rangle\rangle\,]. \tag{14.14}$$

$$[\text{Rearranging}] \quad [\,\langle \forall j, k : R : T\rangle \;=\; \langle \forall k, j : R : T\rangle\,]. \tag{14.15}$$

The rules governing the range are obtained by replacing the quantifier "Σ" by "$\forall$", replacing "$+$" by "$\wedge$" and replacing 0 (the unit of addition) by true (the unit of conjunction). The proviso on the one-point rule (e contains no occurrences of "k") still applies.

$$[\text{Empty Range}] \quad [\,\langle \forall k : \text{false} : T\rangle \;=\; \text{true}\,]. \tag{14.16}$$

$$[\text{One-Point}] \quad [\,\langle \forall k : k = e : T\rangle \;=\; T[k := e]\,]. \tag{14.17}$$

$$[\text{Splitting}] \quad [\,\langle \forall k : P : T\rangle \wedge \langle \forall k : Q : T\rangle \;=\; \langle \forall k : P \vee Q : T\rangle\,]. \tag{14.18}$$

The empty-range rule (for universal quantification) was apparently a subject of fierce debate among logicians and philosophers when it was first formulated. Algebraically, there can be no dispute: it is a logical consequence of the splitting rule, since P (or Q) can be false.

The splitting rule for universal quantification is simpler than that for summation. The difference is that conjunction is idempotent whereas addition is not. When splitting the range in a universal quantification it *does not* matter whether some elements of the range are repeated in the two conjuncts. When splitting the range in a summation it *does* matter whether elements of the range are repeated.

This additional flexibility allows the range in the splitting rule to be generalised from a disjunction $P \vee Q$ of two predicates on the dummy to an arbitrary disjunction of predicates on the dummy. That is, we replace an "or" by an existential quantification.

$$\textbf{[Splitting]} \quad [\, \langle \forall j : R : \langle \forall k : S : T \rangle \rangle \;=\; \langle \forall k : \langle \exists j : R : S \rangle : T \rangle \,]. \tag{14.19}$$

(The side condition on this rule, when used from right to left, demands that "k" is not free in R.)

Trading terms in the range is the same as summation, with the appropriate replacements for the operators and constants. In particular, 0 (the unit of summation) is replaced by true (the unit of conjunction). But, since if $P \rightarrow T \square \neg P \rightarrow$ true fi is the same as $P \Rightarrow T$, trading with the term part can be simplified:

$$\textbf{[Trading]} \quad [\, \langle \forall k \in K : P \wedge Q : T \rangle \;=\; \langle \forall k \in \{k \in K \mid P\} : Q : T \rangle \,]; \tag{14.20}$$

$$\textbf{[Trading]} \quad [\, \langle \forall k : P \wedge Q : T \rangle \;=\; \langle \forall k : Q : P \Rightarrow T \rangle \,]. \tag{14.21}$$

The final rules govern the term part. The distributivity law is just one example of a distributivity property governing universal quantification. We see shortly that there are several more distributivity laws.

$$\textbf{[Rearranging]} \quad [\, \langle \forall k : R : T_0 \wedge T_1 \rangle \;=\; \langle \forall k : R : T_0 \rangle \wedge \langle \forall k : R : T_1 \rangle \,]. \tag{14.22}$$

$$\textbf{[Distributivity]} \quad [\, \langle \forall k : R : p \vee T \rangle \;=\; p \vee \langle \forall k : R : T \rangle \,]. \tag{14.23}$$

14.3.2 Existential Quantification

These are the rules for existential quantification. Not surprisingly, they are entirely dual to the rules for universal quantification. (In the rule (14.32), if $P \rightarrow T \square \neg P \rightarrow$ false fi has been simplified to $P \wedge T$.) Once again, the side condition that free variables may not be captured, and bound variables may not be released, applies to all rules.

$$\textbf{[Dummy Renaming]} \quad [\, \langle \exists j : R : T \rangle \;=\; \langle \exists k : R[j := k] : T[j := k] \rangle \,]. \tag{14.24}$$

$$\textbf{[Nesting]} \quad [\, \langle \exists j, js : R \wedge S : T \rangle \;=\; \langle \exists j : R : \langle \exists js : S : T \rangle \rangle \,]. \tag{14.25}$$

$$\textbf{[Rearranging]} \quad [\, \langle \exists j, k : R : T \rangle \;=\; \langle \exists k, j : R : T \rangle \,]. \tag{14.26}$$

$$\textbf{[Empty Range]} \quad [\, \langle \exists k : \text{false} : T \rangle \;=\; \text{false} \,]. \tag{14.27}$$

[One-Point] $[\ \langle\exists k : k = e : T\rangle\ =\ T[k := e]\ ].$ (14.28)

[Splitting] $[\ \langle\exists k : P : T\rangle \vee \langle\exists k : Q : T\rangle\ =\ \langle\exists k : P \vee Q : T\rangle\ ].$ (14.29)

[Splitting] $[\ \langle\exists j : R : \langle\exists k : S : T\rangle\rangle\ =\ \langle\exists k : \langle\exists j : R : S\rangle : T\rangle\ ].$ (14.30)

[Trading] $[\ \langle\exists k \in K : P \wedge Q : T\rangle\ =\ \langle\exists k \in \{k \in K \mid P\} : Q : T\rangle\ ].$ (14.31)

[Trading] $[\ \langle\exists k : P \wedge Q : T\rangle\ =\ \langle\exists k : Q : P \wedge T\rangle\ ].$ (14.32)

[Rearranging] $[\ \langle\exists k : R : T_0 \vee T_1\rangle\ =\ \langle\exists k : R : T_0\rangle \vee \langle\exists k : R : T_1\rangle\ ].$ (14.33)

[Distributivity] $[\ \langle\exists k : R : p \wedge T\rangle\ =\ p \wedge \langle\exists k : R : T\rangle\ ].$ (14.34)

14.4 QUANTIFIER RULES

We have now seen four different quantifiers: summation, product, universal quantification and existential quantification. We have also seen that the rules governing the manipulation of these quantifiers have much in common. In this section, we generalise the rules to an arbitrary quantifier. The technical name for the process is *abstraction*; we "abstract" *from* particular operators *to* an arbitrary associative and symmetric operator, which we denote by "⊕".

The rules are grouped, as before, into rules for manipulating the dummy, rules for the range part and the term part, and trading rules. The process of abstraction has the added benefit of enabling us to relate different quantifiers, based on distributivity properties of the operators involved. A separate section discussing distributivity has, therefore, also been added.

Warning: In general, the rules given in this section apply only when the range of the quantification is finite. They can all be proved by induction on the size of the range. Fortunately, in the case of universal and existential quantification, this restriction can be safely ignored. In all other cases, it is not safe to ignore the restriction. We have previously mentioned the dangers of infinite summations. An example of a meaningless quantification involving a logical operator is the (associative) equivalence of an infinite sequence of false values (denoted by $\langle\equiv i : 0 \leq i : \mathsf{false}\rangle$). It is undefined because the sequence of finite quantifications $\langle\equiv i : 0 \leq i < N : \mathsf{false}\rangle$ alternates between true and false and has no limit. How to handle infinite quantifications (other than universal and existential quantifications) is beyond the scope of this text.

14.4.1 The Notation

The quantifier notation extends a binary operator, $\oplus$ say, to an arbitrary bag of values, the bag being defined by a function (the *term*) acting on a set (the *range*). The form of a quantified expression is

$$\langle \oplus\, bv \in type : range : term \rangle$$

where $\oplus$ is the quantifier, bv is the dummy or bound variable and type is its type, range defines a subset of the type of the dummy over which the dummy ranges, and term defines a function on the range. The value of the quantification is the result of applying the operator $\oplus$ to all the values generated by evaluating the term at all instances of the dummy in the range.

Strictly, the type of the dummy should always be explicitly stated because the information can be important (as in, for example, the stronger relation between the less-than and at-most orderings on integers compared with their properties on reals). It is, however, information that is often cumbersome to repeat. For this reason, the information is often omitted and a convention on the naming of dummies (such as i, j and k denote integer values) is adopted. This means that the most common use of the notation is in the form

$$\langle \oplus bv : range : term \rangle .$$

In addition, the range is sometimes omitted (again to avoid unnecessary repetition in calculations). In this case the form of the quantification is

$$\langle \oplus bv :: term \rangle$$

and the accompanying text must state clearly what the range is.

As we have defined it, a quantification only has meaning if the operator $\oplus$ is associative and symmetric.[1] The operator $\oplus$ should also have a unit in order to make quantification over an empty range meaningful. We denote the unit of $\oplus$ by $1_{\oplus}$.

There is often an existing, long-standing, mathematical convention for the choice of the symbol "$\oplus$" corresponding to the operator $\oplus$. If so, we follow that convention. If not we use the same operator symbol, made larger if the printer will allow it. Examples of

---

[1] This assumption can be avoided if an order is specified for enumerating the elements of the range – this is what is done in so-called "list comprehensions" in functional programming languages. The rules on nesting and rearrangement would then no longer apply.

quantifications are as follows:

Summation	$\langle \Sigma \, bv : range \, : \, term \rangle;$
Product	$\langle \Pi \, bv : range \, : \, term \rangle;$
Universal (and)	$\langle \forall \, bv : range : term \rangle;$
Existential (or)	$\langle \exists \, bv : range : term \rangle;$
Minimum	$\langle \Downarrow \, bv : range : term \rangle;$
Maximum	$\langle \Uparrow \, bv : range : term \rangle;$
Equivalence	$\langle \equiv \, bv : range : term \rangle;$
Inequivalence	$\langle \not\equiv bv : range : term \rangle.$

14.4.2 Free and Bound Variables

The notions of "free" and "bound" occurrences of variables were discussed in Section 14.2.2 in the context of summation. The definitions apply to all quantifications, as do the side conditions on the use of rules. (Briefly, capture or release is forbidden, as is repetition of a variable in a list of dummies.) We do not repeat the side conditions below but trust in the reader's understanding of the concepts.

14.4.3 Dummies

The dummies (or bound variables) in a quantification serve to relate the range and term. There are three rules governing their use:

[Dummy Renaming] $\quad [\, \langle \oplus j : R : T \rangle \; = \; \langle \oplus k : R[j := k] : T[j := k] \rangle \,];$ (14.35)

[Nesting] $\quad [\, \langle \oplus j, js : R \wedge S : T \rangle \; = \; \langle \oplus j : R : \langle \oplus js : S : T \rangle \rangle \,];$ (14.36)

[Rearranging] $\quad [\, \langle \oplus j, k : R : T \rangle \; = \; \langle \oplus k, j : R : T \rangle \,].$ (14.37)

14.4.4 Range Part

The range part is a boolean-valued expresssion that determines the set of values over which the dummy ranges. There are four rules, two simplification rules and two splitting rules:

[Empty Range] $\quad [\, \langle \oplus k : \mathsf{false} : T \rangle \; = \; 1_\oplus \,];$ (14.38)

[One-Point] $\quad [\, \langle \oplus k : k = e : T \rangle \; = \; T[k := e] \,];$ (14.39)

[Splitting]
$$[\, \langle \oplus k : P : T \rangle \oplus \langle \oplus k : Q : T \rangle \; = \; \langle \oplus k : P \vee Q : T \rangle \oplus \langle \oplus k : P \wedge Q : T \rangle \,].$$

(14.40)

In the case where $\oplus$ is idempotent, the splitting rule can be simplified to

$$[\ \langle\oplus k : P : T\rangle \oplus \langle\oplus k : Q : T\rangle\ =\ \langle\oplus k : P \vee Q : T\rangle\ ]. \tag{14.41}$$

Furthermore, the right side can be generalised from a disjunction of two propositions P and Q to a disjunction of an arbitrary number (i.e. existential quantification) of propositions. We obtain the following: if $\oplus$ is idempotent,

$$[\text{Splitting}] \quad [\ \langle\oplus j : R : \langle\oplus k : S : T\rangle\rangle\ =\ \langle\oplus k : \langle\exists j : R : S\rangle : T\rangle\ ]. \tag{14.42}$$

14.4.5 Trading

Two trading rules allow information to be traded between the type of the dummy and the range, and between the range and the term part:

$$[\text{Trading}] \quad [\ \langle\oplus k{\in}K : P \wedge Q : T\rangle\ =\ \langle\oplus k \in \{k{\in}K\,|\,P\} : Q : T\rangle\ ]; \tag{14.43}$$

$$[\text{Trading}] \quad [\ \langle\oplus k : P \wedge Q : T\rangle$$
$$=\ \langle\oplus k\ :\ Q\ :\ \text{if } P \to T \ \square\ \neg P \to 1_\oplus\ \text{fi}\rangle\ ]. \tag{14.44}$$

14.4.6 Term Part

We give just one rule pertaining to the term part (see also the discussion of distributivity below):

$$[\text{Rearranging}] \quad [\ \langle\oplus k\ :\ R\ :\ T_0 \oplus T_1\rangle$$
$$=\ \langle\oplus k : R : T_0\rangle \oplus \langle\oplus k : R : T_1\rangle\ ]. \tag{14.45}$$

14.4.7 Distributivity Properties

Distributivity properties are very important in mathematical calculations; they are also very important in computations because they are used to reduce the number of calculations that are performed.

A typical distributivity property is the property that negation distributes through addition:

$$-(x+y)\ =\ (-x)+(-y).$$

The property is used to "factor out" negation, in order to replace subtractions by additions. Similarly, the fact that multiplication distributes through addition,

$$x{\times}(y+z)\ =\ x{\times}y + x{\times}z,$$

is used to reduce the number of multiplications. Another example is the distributivity of addition through minimum:

$$x+(y\downarrow z) = (x+y)\downarrow(x+z).$$

This property is fundamental to finding shortest paths.

Sometimes distributivity properties involve a change in the operator. Multiplication of real numbers is translated into addition, and vice versa, by the rules of logarithms and exponentiation:

$$\ln(x\times y) = \ln x + \ln y,$$

$$e^{x+y} = e^x \times e^y.$$

In words, the logarithm function distributes through multiplication turning it into addition, and exponentiation distributes through addition turning it into multiplication.

It is clear that a distributivity property can be extended from two operands to a finite, non-zero number of operands. We have, for example,

$$a\times(x+y+z) = a\times x + a\times y + a\times z.$$

Extending a distributivity property to *zero* operands amounts to requiring that units be preserved. And, by good fortune, that is indeed the case in all the examples given above. Specifically, we have:

$-0 = 0$ (minus preserves the unit of addition),

$x\times 0 = 0$ (multiplying by x preserves the unit of addition),

$\ln 1 = 0$ (the unit of multiplication becomes the unit of addition),

$e^0 = 1$ (the unit of addition becomes the unit of multiplication).

In addition, we can postulate that minimum has a unit ∞ and that

$x+\infty = \infty$ (addition of x preserves the unit of minimum).

So, in each case, the distributivity property with respect to a binary operator extends to a distributivity property with respect to any finite number of operands, including zero. (The case where there is only one operand is trivial.)

Formally, the general distributivity for quantifications is as follows. Suppose both $\oplus$ and $\otimes$ are associative and symmetric operators, with units $1_\oplus$ and $1_\otimes$, respectively. Suppose f is a function with the properties that

$$f(1_\oplus) = 1_\otimes$$

and, for all x and y,

$$f(x \oplus y) = f(x) \otimes f(y).$$

Then

$$[\text{Distributivity}] \quad \left[\; f(\langle \oplus k : R : T \rangle) \;=\; \langle \otimes k : R : f(T) \rangle \; \right]. \qquad (14.46)$$

An important example of the distributivity law is given by the so-called De Morgan's rules for universal and existential quantification. De Morgan's rules for binary conjunctions and disjunctions were given in Section 13.4. In words, logical negation distributes through disjunction, turning it into conjunction; logical negation also distributes through conjunction, turning it into disjunction. But, since ¬false is true and ¬true is false, the binary rule extends to an arbitrary existential or universal quantification:

$$[\text{De Morgan}] \quad \left[\; \neg \langle \exists k : R : T \rangle \;=\; \langle \forall k : R : \neg T \rangle \; \right]; \qquad (14.47)$$

$$[\text{De Morgan}] \quad \left[\; \neg \langle \forall k : R : T \rangle \;=\; \langle \exists k : R : \neg T \rangle \; \right]. \qquad (14.48)$$

The warning about existence of summations over an infinite range does not apply to universal or existential quantifications. Any universal or existential quantification you care to write down has meaning and the above rules apply.

14.5 EXERCISES

1. **Evaluate the following summations.**
   (a) $\langle \Sigma k \,:\, 1 \le k \le 3 \,:\, k \rangle$
   (b) $\langle \Sigma k \,:\, 0 \le k < 5 \,:\, 1 \rangle$
   (c) $\langle \Sigma i,j \,:\, 0 \le i < j \le 2 \wedge \text{odd}(i) \,:\, i+j \rangle$
   (d) $\langle \Sigma i,j \,:\, 0 \le i < j \le 2 \wedge \text{odd}(i) \wedge \text{odd}(j) \,:\, i+j \rangle$

2. **What is the value of** $\langle \Sigma k : k^2 = 4 : k^2 \rangle$ **in the case where the type of k is**
   (a) a natural number,
   (b) an integer?

3. **Identify all occurrences of free variables in the following expressions.**
   (a) $4 \times i$
   (b) $\langle \Sigma j : 1 \le j \le 3 : 4 \times i \rangle$

(c) $\langle \Sigma j : 1 \leq j \leq 3 : 4 \times j \rangle$

(d) $\langle \Sigma j : 1 \leq j \leq 3 : m \times j \rangle + \langle \Sigma j : 1 \leq j \leq 3 : n \times j \rangle$

(e) $\langle \Sigma j : 1 \leq j \leq 3 : m \times j \rangle + \langle \Sigma k : 1 \leq k \leq 3 : n \times j \rangle$

4. Evaluate the left and right sides of the following equations. Hence, state which are everywhere true and which are sometimes false.

(a) $\langle \Sigma j : 1 \leq j \leq 3 : 4 \times i \rangle = \langle \Sigma k : 1 \leq k \leq 3 : 4 \times i \rangle$

(b) $\langle \Sigma j : 1 \leq j \leq 3 : 4 \times j \rangle = \langle \Sigma k : 1 \leq k \leq 3 : 4 \times j \rangle$

(c) $\langle \Sigma j : 1 \leq j \leq 3 : \langle \Sigma k : k = 0 : 4 \times j \rangle \rangle$
$= \langle \Sigma i : 1 \leq i \leq 3 : \langle \Sigma k : k = 0 : 4 \times i \rangle \rangle$

(d) $\langle \Sigma j : 1 \leq j \leq 3 : \langle \Sigma j : j = 1 : 4 \times j \rangle \rangle$
$= \langle \Sigma k : 1 \leq k \leq 3 : \langle \Sigma j : j = 1 : 4 \times k \rangle \rangle$

5. Derive the trading rule (14.10) from the splitting rule (14.6). You may assume that $\langle \Sigma k : R : 0 \rangle = 0$ for all ranges R.

6. Derive (14.8) from the one-point rule (14.5), the nesting rule (14.2) and the rearrangement rule (14.3). Hint: your derivation should head for using the fact that f is a bijection, that is, that there is a function g such that, for all $j \in J$ and $k \in K$,

$$f(j) = k \equiv j = g(k).$$

Use the one-point rule to introduce a second dummy so that you can exploit this property.

7. Prove the generalised distributivity law

$$\langle \Sigma j : P : S \rangle \times \langle \Sigma k : Q : T \rangle = \langle \Sigma j,k : P \wedge Q : S \times T \rangle.$$

What are the side conditions on using this rule?

8. Derive the rule

$$\langle \oplus k : P : T \rangle = \langle \oplus k : P \wedge Q : T \rangle \oplus \langle \oplus k : P \wedge \neg Q : T \rangle.$$

Use this rule to derive (14.41) from (14.40) in the case where $\oplus$ is idempotent.

9. The translation rule for summations (14.8) requires function f to be a bijection. The rule is applicable to all quantifications, and not just summations.

In the case where the quantifier is idempotent, the rule can be simplified. The translation rule for idempotent quantifiers is as follows. Suppose f is a function from the type of dummy j to the type of dummy k such that

$$\langle \forall k :: \langle \exists j :: k = f(j) \rangle \rangle.$$

Then

$$\langle \oplus k : R : T \rangle \;=\; \langle \oplus j : R[k := f(j)] : T[k := f(j)] \rangle.$$

Prove this rule.

10. The following table shows a number of associative and symmetric binary operators together with their units. For each, give an instance of the distributivity rule (14.46) not already mentioned in the text.

Operator	Unit	Quantifier
$\wedge$	true	$\forall$
$\vee$	false	$\exists$
$+$	0	Σ
$\times$	1	Π
$\downarrow$	∞	$\Downarrow$
$\uparrow$	$-\infty$	$\Uparrow$
$\equiv$	true	$\equiv$
$\not\equiv$	false	$\not\equiv$
$\cup$	ϕ	$\bigcup$
$\cap$	$\mathcal{U}$	$\bigcap$

Chapter

Elements of Number Theory

15

> Number theory aims to catalogue the properties of numbers (natural numbers, integers, rational and real numbers), usually in a way that promotes effective calculation. As such, it has always been a central pillar of algorithmic mathematics. The theory is too extensive for us to cover in any detail here. The chapter is therefore about a few core elements of the theory. Sections 15.1 and 15.2 are about reasoning with the standard ordering of numbers. Sections 15.3 and 15.4 are about a different (partial) ordering on natural numbers, the divides relation.

15.1 INEQUALITIES

Expressions involving the at-most relation (denoted by "$\leq$") or the less-than relation (denoted by "$<$") on numbers are traditionally called *inequalities*. The at-most relation is a so-called *total ordering*; that is, it is an ordering relation (i.e. reflexive, transitive and anti-symmetric) that is *total*:

$$[\text{Total}] \quad [\ x \leq y \ \lor \ y \leq x\ ]. \tag{15.1}$$

Often it is pronounced "less than or equal to" which stresses the fact that it is the reflexive closure of the less-than relation:

$$[\text{Reflexive Closure}] \quad [\ x \leq y \ \equiv \ x < y \ \lor \ x = y\ ]. \tag{15.2}$$

The rule is used when a case analysis on "less than" or "equal to" becomes necessary.

The anti-symmetry of the at-most relation,

$$[\text{Anti-symmetry}] \quad [\ x = y \ \equiv \ x \leq y \ \land \ y \leq x\ ], \tag{15.3}$$

is commonly used to establish equalities (everywhere) between numeric expressions in the same way that the anti-symmetry of the implication relation is used in "if and only if" proofs to establish equalities (everywhere) between boolean expressions. An alternative is the rule of *indirect equality*:

[Indirect Equality] $[\ x = y\ \equiv\ \langle\forall z :: x \leq z \equiv y \leq z\rangle\ ]$ (15.4)

Indirect equality turns an equality between numbers into an equality between boolean expressions, thus encouraging equational reasoning. It is valid with "$\leq$" replaced by any reflexive and anti-symmetric relation. See Sections 15.2 and 15.3 for examples of its use.

The converse of the at-most relation is the at-least relation,

[Converse] $[\ x \leq y\ \equiv\ y \geq x\ ],$ (15.5)

and the converse of the less-than relation is the greater-than relation,

[Converse] $[\ x < y\ \equiv\ y > x\ ],$ (15.6)

The contrapositive of the at-most relation is the greater-than relation:

[Contrapositive] $[\ \neg(x \leq y)\ \equiv\ y > x\ ]$ (15.7)

It follows that the contrapositive of the anti-symmetry rule (15.3) is the inequality rule:

[Inequality] $[\ x \neq y\ \equiv\ x < y\ \vee\ y < x\ ].$ (15.8)

The transitivity of the at-most and less-than relations is commonly used in combination with *monotonicity* properties. In general, we say that a function f from numbers to numbers is *monotonic* with respect to the at-most relation if

$[\ f(x) \leq f(y) \Leftarrow x \leq y\ ].$

Similarly, f is monotonic with respect to the less-than relation if

$[\ f(x) < f(y) \Leftarrow x < y\ ].$

Addition of an arbitrary number is monotonic with respect to both "at most" and "less than":

$[\ x+z \leq y+z \Leftarrow x \leq y\ ]\ \ \wedge\ \ [\ x+z < y+z \Leftarrow x < y\ ].$

Because addition is cancellative ("+z" is cancelled by "−z") the monotonicity is actually stronger:

$$\textbf{[Monotonicity]} \quad [\ x+z \leq y+z \ \equiv \ x \leq y\ ] \tag{15.9}$$

and

$$\textbf{[Monotonicity]} \quad [\ x+z < y+z \ \equiv \ x < y\ ]. \tag{15.10}$$

(Strictly, when the implication in the definition of monotonicity can be replaced by equivales, as here, the property is called an *order isomorphism*.)

Multiplication by a strictly positive number is also monotonic and cancellative, so that we have

$$\textbf{[Monotonicity]} \quad [\ (x \times z \leq y \times z \ \equiv \ x \leq y) \ \Leftarrow \ 0 < z\ ] \tag{15.11}$$

and

$$\textbf{[Monotonicity]} \quad [\ (x \times z < y \times z \ \equiv \ x < y) \ \Leftarrow \ 0 < z\ ]. \tag{15.12}$$

A simple instance of (15.9) is the so-called *anti-monotonicity* of multiplication by −1:

$$[\ x \leq y \ \equiv \ -y \leq -x\ ].$$

(Instantiate z to −(x+y).) Similarly for "less than" instead of "at most". Hence, multiplication by an arbitrary strictly negative number is *anti-monotonic*. The rules are

$$\textbf{[Anti-monotonicity]} \quad [\ (x \times z \leq y \times z \ \equiv \ x \geq y) \ \Leftarrow \ z < 0\ ] \tag{15.13}$$

and

$$\textbf{[Anti-monotonicity]} \quad [\ (x \times z < y \times z \ \equiv \ x > y) \ \Leftarrow \ z < 0\ ]. \tag{15.14}$$

(We leave to the reader the question whether multiplication by zero is monotonic or not with respect to the at-most and/or less-than relations.)

The rules given above are valid whatever the type of numbers: natural, integer, rational or real. For integers, there is an important additional rule that is not obeyed by rational or real numbers in general:

$$\textbf{[Add-One]} \quad [\ m < n \ \equiv \ m+1 \leq n\ ]. \tag{15.15}$$

Note the use of the convention that m and n denote integers and not arbitrary real numbers. The rule has several different but equivalent forms – see the exercises at the end of the chapter – which we use as well.

For precise reasoning about rational numbers (numbers of the form $\frac{m}{n}$ for integers m and n), the first step is often to use the monotonicity of multiplication to replace a given inequality by an inequality between integers. For example, suppose m and n are integers, n is strictly positive, and we want to determine the relation between $\frac{m}{n}$ and $\frac{m+1}{n+1}$. Then, with "?" denoting the unknown relation, we calculate:

$$\frac{m}{n} \; ? \; \frac{m+1}{n+1}$$

$$= \qquad \{ \qquad \text{monotonicity: (15.11) or (15.12) with}$$

$$x,y,z := m, m+1, n \times (n+1)$$

$$(0 < n \times (n+1) \Leftarrow 0 < n) \quad \}$$

$$m \times (n+1) \; ? \; (m+1) \times n$$

$$= \qquad \{ \qquad \text{distributivity, unit} \quad \}$$

$$m \times n + m \; ? \; m \times n + n$$

$$= \qquad \{ \qquad \text{monotonicity: (15.9) or (15.10) with } x,y,z := m, n, m \times n \quad \}$$

$$m \; ? \; n.$$

We conclude that

$$\left[\; (\tfrac{m}{n} \leq \tfrac{m+1}{n+1} \; \equiv \; m \leq n) \; \Leftarrow \; 0 < n \; \right] \; \wedge \; \left[\; (\tfrac{m}{n} < \tfrac{m+1}{n+1} \; \equiv \; m < n) \; \Leftarrow \; 0 < n \; \right].$$

Note how the calculation makes clear which properties are assumed at each step so that we can determine, for any relation ?, whether or not the step is valid.

15.2 MINIMUM AND MAXIMUM

Denoting the maximum function on real numbers by the infix operator $\uparrow$, we have:

[Maximum] $[\; x \uparrow y \leq z \; \equiv \; x \leq z \wedge y \leq z \;]$.   (15.16)

This is a *specification* of maximum rather than a *definition*. (A definition would have the form of an equality with left-hand side $x \uparrow y$.) In words, the maximum of x and y is the smallest z such that x is at most z and y is at most z. (This is not a literal transliteration of the specification but close enough for this discussion.) It is common for functions associated with an ordering relation to be specified by one or more properties rather than have an equational definition. We will see several examples in this chapter. Maximum and minimum are the simplest examples, so this is a good way to start.

Specification (15.16) is a distributivity property: it is the property that the boolean-valued function $(\leq z)$ distributes through maximum, turning it into a conjunction. In this way, properties of maximum are translated into properties of conjunction. Three properties can be deduced very easily from the definition. First, by instantiating z to $x{\uparrow}y$, the left side of the definition becomes true so that

$$[\, x \leq x{\uparrow}y \,] \;\;\wedge\;\; [\, y \leq x{\uparrow}y \,].$$

Second and third, by instantiating z to x and z to y we get, respectively,

$$[\; x{\uparrow}y \leq x \;\equiv\; y \leq x \;]$$

and

$$[\; x{\uparrow}y \leq y \;\equiv\; x \leq y \;].$$

A fourth property can be obtained from the fact that $\leq$ is a total ordering:

$$x{\uparrow}y = x \;\vee\; x{\uparrow}y = y$$
$$=\qquad\{\qquad \text{anti-symmetry of } \leq \;\}$$
$$(x{\uparrow}y \leq x \wedge x \leq x{\uparrow}y) \;\vee\; (x{\uparrow}y \leq y \wedge y \leq x{\uparrow}y)$$
$$=\qquad\{\qquad \text{above, substitution of equals for equals,}$$
$$\text{true is the unit of conjunction} \;\}$$
$$y \leq x \vee x \leq y$$
$$=\qquad\{\qquad \leq \text{ is a total ordering} \;\}$$
$$\text{true.}$$

So maximum is a *choice* function: $x{\uparrow}y$ chooses between x and y.

To derive additional *equalities*, we exploit the rule of indirect equality. Here are two examples. In the first example, we show that maximum is associative because conjunction is associative. We have, for all w,

$$(x{\uparrow}y){\uparrow}z \leq w$$
$$=\qquad\{\qquad \text{definition of max} \;\}$$
$$x{\uparrow}y \leq w \wedge z \leq w$$
$$=\qquad\{\qquad \text{definition of max} \;\}$$
$$(x \leq w \wedge y \leq w) \wedge z \leq w$$
$$=\qquad\{\qquad \wedge \text{ is associative} \;\}$$

$$x \leq w \wedge (y \leq w \wedge z \leq w)$$

=   {   definition of max (applied twice)   }

$$x{\uparrow}(y{\uparrow}z) \leq w.$$

Thus, by indirect equality,

$$[\ (x{\uparrow}y){\uparrow}z\ =\ x{\uparrow}(y{\uparrow}z)\ ].$$

Note how short and straightforward this proof is. In contrast, if maximum is defined by case analysis, it would be necessary to consider six different cases, six being the number of ways to order three values x, y and z. The calculation simply translates properties of maximum into properties of conjunction; because conjunction is associative, so is maximum. Similarly, maximum is symmetric and idempotent because conjunction is symmetric and idempotent.

In the second example, we derive a distributivity property of maximum. We have, for all w,

$$x + (y{\uparrow}z) \leq w$$

=   {   use (15.9) with x,y,z := $y{\uparrow}z, w{-}x, x$ to shunt "x+"

          out of the way in order to be able to apply the definition

          of maximum   }

$$y{\uparrow}z \leq w{-}x$$

=   {   definition of max   }

$$y \leq w{-}x\ \wedge\ z \leq w{-}x$$

=   {   shunt "x+" back in order to be

          able to apply the definition of maximum   }

$$x{+}y \leq w\ \wedge\ x{+}z \leq w$$

=   {   definition of max   }

$$(x{+}y){\uparrow}(x{+}z) \leq w.$$

Thus, by indirect equality,

$$[\ x + (y{\uparrow}z)\ =\ (x{+}y){\uparrow}(x{+}z)\ ].$$

In this calculation, we have used the fact that addition is monotonic and cancellative. Multiplication by a strictly positive number is also monotonic and cancellative, so that multiplication by a strictly positive number distributes through maximum.

Dual to maximum is minimum. It is defined in the same way except that the orderings are turned around:

[**Minimum**] $[\ z \le x{\downarrow}y \ \equiv\ z{\le}x \wedge z{\le}y\ ].$ (15.17)

(In words, the minimum of x and y is the largest z such that z is at most x and y.)

15.3 THE DIVIDES RELATION

The *divides* relation, which we introduced in Section 12.7, is the relation on integers defined to be the converse of the "is a multiple of" relation:

[**Divides Relation**] $[\ m{\backslash}n \ \equiv\ \langle\exists k : k{\in}\mathbb{Z} : n{=}k{\times}m\rangle\ ].$ (15.18)

In words, an integer m *divides* an integer n exactly when there is some integer k such that $n{=}k{\times}m$. Other terminology that is used is "m is a *divisor* of n" or "n is a *multiple* of m". Examples are $1{\backslash}1$ and $2{\backslash}6$.

The divides relation is a partial ordering on the natural numbers. It is reflexive because $[\ n{=}1{\times}n\ ]$ and transitive because, for all n, m, p, j and k, if $n{=}k{\times}m$ and $p{=}j{\times}n$ then $p{=}(j{\times}k){\times}m$. (Note the use of the associativity of multiplication.) It is anti-symmetric because, for all n, m, j and k, if $n{=}k{\times}m$ and $m{=}j{\times}n$ then $n{=}(j{\times}k){\times}n$ and $m{=}(j{\times}k){\times}m$. So, if m and n are natural numbers, either m and n are both 0, or j and k are both 1 and, hence, m and n are equal.

On *integers*, the divides relation is *not* anti-symmetric because, for all m, $m{\backslash}{-}m$ and $-m{\backslash}m$ but m and $-m$ are not necessarily equal. So, on integers, the divides relation is not a partial ordering. (It is called a *pre-ordering*.)

Because 0 is a multiple of any number (specifically, $[\ 0{=}0{\times}m\ ]$), it is divided by every number:

$[\,m{\backslash}0\,].$

(This, of course, includes 0 itself: $0{\backslash}0$.) That is, 0 is the "greatest" element in the divisibility ordering of the natural numbers.

The *greatest common divisor* of two natural numbers is defined just like the minimum of two numbers (see (15.17)):

[**Greatest Common Divisor**] $[\ p{\backslash}(m\,\mathrm{gcd}\,n)\ \equiv\ p{\backslash}m \wedge p{\backslash}n\ ].$ (15.19)

Strictly, (15.19) specifies the greatest common divisor but it is not immediately clear that the specification can be satisfied. We need to give an algorithm to show how to calculate m gcd n for arbitrary m and n. One such algorithm is Euclid's algorithm which is discussed in many books on mathematics.

Dual to the definition of greatest common divisor is the least common multiple (denoted by "lcm"):

[**Least Common Multiple**] $[\ (m \operatorname{lcm} n) \backslash p \ \equiv \ m \backslash p \ \wedge \ n \backslash p\ ]$.   (15.20)

Comparing (15.20) with (15.16), we see that they are exactly the same except that "lcm" replaces "↑" and "\" replaces "≤". So several of the properties of maximum are also enjoyed by least common multiple: associativity, symmetry and idempotence. Other properties of maximum that depend on particular properties of the at-most relation are not enjoyed by least common multiple. For example, addition is not monotonic with respect to the divisibility relation and does not distribute through least common multiple. Multiplication *is* monotonic with respect to the divisibility relation. That is,

[**Monotonicity**] $[\ m \times n \backslash m \times p \ \Leftarrow \ n \backslash p\ ]$,   (15.21)

and the implication can be strengthened to an equality provided that m is non-zero. But the simple calculation we used to show that addition distributes through maximum cannot be copied to show that multiplication distributes through least common multiple; multiplication *does* distribute through least common multiple but the proof is harder. (See the exercises for a hint on how to construct the proof.) Multiplication also distributes through greatest common divisor but the proof involves an analysis of Euclid's algorithm.

15.4 MODULAR ARITHMETIC

Modular arithmetic is about calculating with remainders after performing an integer division. It is necessary, therefore, that we begin the section with a discussion of integer division.

15.4.1 Integer Division

Integer division is an approximation to real division. The integer division of (integer) m by (integer) n is specified to be a solution of the inequation in the unknown k:

$$k \quad :: \quad k \times n \leq m < (k+1) \times n.$$ (15.22)

For example, since

$$[\ m \times n \leq m \times n < (m+1) \times n \ \Leftarrow \ 0 < n\ ],$$

the number m satisfies the specification of the integer division of $m \times n$ by the strictly positive integer n.

Equation (15.22) is a specification and not a definition because it might not be satisfiable and it might have more than one solution. By showing that the inequation has a unique solution, we establish that there is a function from pairs of numbers m and n to their integer division, which we denote by m÷n. This is what we explore in this section.

In fact, (15.22) does not have a solution when n is 0 since it simplifies to

$$k \quad :: \quad 0 \le m < 0.$$

This is obviously not satisfiable! We must conclude that integer division of m by n is undefined when n is 0. That is not surprising. But (15.22) is not satisfiable for any n at most 0. For, if $n < 0$,

$$k \times n \le m < (k+1) \times n$$

=   {   anti-monotonicity: (15.13) and (15.14)   }

$$k \times (-n) \ge -m > (k+1) \times (-n)$$

⇒   {   transitivity   }

$$k \times (-n) > (k+1) \times (-n)$$

=   { $n < 0$, monotonicity: (15.12)   }

$$k > k+1$$

=   {   monotonicity: (15.10)   }

$$0 > 1.$$

We conclude that for $n < 0$, whatever the value of k, the value of $k \times n \le m < (k+1) \times n$ is false; that is, the specification (15.22) cannot be satisfied.

We now consider whether or not (15.22) has at most one solution. Assume $0 < n$ and suppose i and j satisfy (15.22). That is, $i \times n \le m < (i+1) \times n$ and $j \times n \le m < (j+1) \times n$. Then

$$i \times n \le m < (i+1) \times n \;\wedge\; j \times n \le m < (j+1) \times n$$

⇒   {   omitting two conjuncts   }

$$i \times n \le m \;\wedge\; m < (j+1) \times n$$

⇒   {   transitivity   }

$$i \times n < (j+1) \times n$$

=   { $0 < n$, monotonicity: (15.12)   }

$$i < j+1$$

=   {   (15.15)   }

$$i \le j.$$

We conclude, by omitting two conjuncts in the specifications of i and j, that $i \leq j$. Symmetrically, by omitting the other two conjuncts, we conclude that $j \leq i$. By anti-symmetry of the at-most relation, it follows that i and j are equal. That is, (15.22) has at most one solution.

The final task is to show that (15.22) has at least one solution when $0 < n$. To do this, we must give an algorithm that, given m, computes an integer k such that $k \times n \leq m < (k+1) \times n$. Such an algorithm is derived as follows. Let us suppose $0 \leq m$ and $0 < n$. We split the specification of k into two separate conjuncts: $k \times n \leq m$ and $m < (k+1) \times n$. Then, since $0 = 0 \times n$, we can consider an algorithm that initialises k to 0 and then repeatedly increments k while maintaining the invariant $k \times n \leq m$. The algorithm terminates when $m < (k+1) \times n$. An upper bound on the number of iterations is m because $m < (m+1) \times n$ whenever $0 < n$.

$$\{ \ 0 \leq m \ \wedge \ 0 < n \ \}$$

$$k := 0 \ ;$$

$$\{ \ \textbf{Invariant:} \ \ k \times n \leq m$$

$$\quad \textbf{Measure of progress:} \ \ m - k \ \}$$

$$\text{do} \ (k+1) \times n \leq m \ \rightarrow \ k := k+1$$

$$\text{od}$$

$$\{ \ k \times n \leq m < (k+1) \times n \ \}$$

When $m \leq 0$, a similar algorithm can be constructed. The algorithm initialises k to 0 establishing the property $m < (k+1) \times n$. This property is then used as the invariant in an algorithm that repeatedly decrements k until $k \times n \leq m$.

We have now shown that (15.22) has a unique solution whenever $0 < n$. We denote the unique solution by $m \div n$ (pronounced m "div" n). Its *defining* property is

[Integer Division] $[\ (m \div n) \times n \leq m < (m \div n + 1) \times n \ ]$,   (15.23)

with the proviso that $0 < n$.

When $n < 0$ we can always define $m \div n$ to be $(-m) \div (-n)$. Note that $(-m) \div n$ is typically different from $-(m \div n)$. (For example, $(-1) \div 2 = -1 \neq 0 = -(1 \div 2)$.) In fact, integer division is rarely used for negative numbers (in spite of its name); if one does so in a computer program, great care should be taken to check the programming manual for the definition that is used because it may differ from the one given here, it may differ from one language to another and it may even differ from compiler to compiler.

Although we now have an algorithm to compute m÷n, the primary tool for reasoning about integer division remains its specification. For example, we have

$$[(m \times n) \div n = m].$$ (15.24)

The proof consists of the two steps:

$$k \times n \leq m \times n < (k+1) \times n$$

$$= \qquad \{ \qquad \text{monotonicity: (15.11)} \quad \}$$

$$k \leq m < k+1$$

$$= \qquad \{ \qquad \text{(15.15) and anti-symmetry} \quad \}$$

$$k = m$$

followed by instantiating k to (m×n)÷n. Since the first line is then true, (m×n)÷n=m is also true. Note that [0÷n=0] and [m÷1=m] are corollaries of (15.24).

Some properties of integer division are more difficult to identify directly from its specification. A powerful alternative specification of m÷n (for strictly positive n) is the largest integer k such that k times n is at most m. Formally, this is expressed by the property

[Integer Division] $\quad [k \leq m \div n \equiv k \times n \leq m].$ (15.25)

The derivation of (15.25) from (15.23) involves the use of mutual implication:

$$k \leq m \div n$$

$$= \qquad \{ \qquad 0 < n, \text{monotonicity: (15.11)} \quad \}$$

$$k \times n \leq (m \div n) \times n$$

$$\Rightarrow \qquad \{ \qquad \text{(15.23) and transitivity} \quad \}$$

$$k \times n \leq m$$

$$\Rightarrow \qquad \{ \qquad \text{(15.23) and transitivity} \quad \}$$

$$k \times n < (m \div n + 1) \times n$$

$$= \qquad \{ \qquad 0 < n, \text{monotonicity: (15.12)} \quad \}$$

$$k < m \div n + 1$$

$$= \qquad \{ \qquad \text{(15.15)} \quad \}$$

$$k \leq m \div n.$$

Combined with the rule of indirect equality, (15.25) is a simple and effective tool. An example of its use is to prove that

$$[(m \div n) \div p = m \div (n \times p)].$$
(15.26)

Here is the calculation:

$$k \leq (m \div n) \div p$$

$$= \qquad \{ \qquad (15.25) \quad \}$$

$$k \times p \leq m \div n$$

$$= \qquad \{ \qquad (15.25) \quad \}$$

$$k \times p \times n \leq m$$

$$= \qquad \{ \qquad (15.25) \quad \}$$

$$k \leq m \div (n \times p).$$

Note the implicit use of the associativity and symmetry of multiplication.

A second example of the use of (15.25) is to simplify $(j \times n + m) \div n$. We have

$$k \leq (j \times n + m) \div n$$

$$= \qquad \{ \qquad (15.25) \quad \}$$

$$k \times n \leq j \times n + m$$

$$= \qquad \{ \qquad \text{monotonicity: (15.9)} \quad \}$$

$$(k - j) \times n \leq m$$

$$= \qquad \{ \qquad (15.25) \quad \}$$

$$k - j \leq m \div n$$

$$= \qquad \{ \qquad \text{monotonicity: (15.9)} \quad \}$$

$$k \leq j + m \div n.$$

We conclude, by indirect equality, that

$$[(j \times n + m) \div n = j + m \div n].$$
(15.27)

Both (15.26) and (15.27) are relatively difficult to prove without using (15.25).

15.4.2 Remainders and Modulo Arithmetic

The remainder after dividing a natural number m by a strictly positive natural number n is denoted by $m \bmod n$. It is defined by

$$[\text{mod}] \quad [m \bmod n = m - (m \div n) \times n].$$
(15.28)

By combining the definition of integer division (15.23) with the monotonicity of addition (15.9) and (15.10), we get

$$[\textbf{mod}] \quad [\; 0 \le m \bmod n < n \;]. \tag{15.29}$$

Values in the range $0 .. n-1$ are called *modulo-n numbers*.

Counting modulo some number is a very common first step in algorithmic problem solving. If we want to determine whether some number of things is divisible by, say, 3, we count 0, 1, 2, 0, 1, 2, 0, 1, 2, 0, etc. This is a lot easier than counting 0, 1, 2, 3, 4, 5, etc. and then dividing the final value by 3.

Numbers can also be added and multiplied modulo some number. Figure 15.1 shows addition and multiplication modulo 3, respectively.

$\oplus$	0	1	2
0	0	1	2
1	1	2	0
2	2	0	1

$\otimes$	0	1	2
0	0	0	0
1	0	1	2
2	0	2	1

Figure 15.1: Addition and multiplication modulo 3.

For a strictly positive number n, addition modulo n is defined on modulo-n numbers i and j by

$$[\; i \oplus j \;=\; (i+j) \bmod n \;] \;. \tag{15.30}$$

Similarly, multiplication modulo n is defined on modulo-n numbers i and j by

$$[\; i \otimes j \;=\; (i \times j) \bmod n \;]. \tag{15.31}$$

Because (integer) addition is symmetric, it is clear from (15.30) that addition modulo-n is also symmetric. Similarly, multiplication modulo-n is symmetric. Also 0 is a modulo-n number and it is clear from (15.30) and (15.31) that $[\; 0 \oplus j = j \;]$ and $[\; 0 \otimes j = 0 \;]$ (where j ranges over modulo-n numbers). Also, if $1 < n$, the number 1 is a modulo-n number and it is clear from (15.31) that $[\; 1 \otimes j = 1 \;]$.

For arbitrary numbers k and m, we have the distributivity properties

$$[\; (k+m) \bmod n \;=\; (k \bmod n) \oplus (m \bmod n) \;] \tag{15.32}$$

and

$$[\; (k \times m) \bmod n \;=\; (k \bmod n) \otimes (m \bmod n) \;]. \tag{15.33}$$

As a consequence, addition modulo-n and multiplication modulo-n are both associative, and multiplication modulo-n distributes through addition modulo-n.

In summary, for any number n such that $2 < n$, the 5-tuple $(\{i \mid 0 \leq i < n\}, 1, 0, \otimes, \oplus)$ is a semiring where $\otimes$ denotes multiplication modulo n and $\oplus$ denotes addition modulo n.

15.5 EXERCISES

1. Is multiplication by zero monotonic with respect to the at-most relation? Is it monotonic with respect to the less-than relation?

2. Simplify $\frac{1}{x} \leq \frac{1}{y}$ using the rule (15.11). That is, determine a rule of the form

   $$\left[(\tfrac{1}{x} \leq \tfrac{1}{y} \equiv ?) \Leftarrow ?? \right]$$

   where the unknown expressions ? and ?? do not involve division.

3. Simplify the following. State clearly the rules you use in each step of your calculation.
   (a) $n - \frac{1}{2}m \leq m - \frac{1}{2}n$
   (b) $n - m < \frac{1}{2}(m - \frac{1}{2}n)$

4. Prove that

   $$\left[(k \times m + r < j \times m \equiv k < j) \Leftarrow 0 \leq r < m \right].$$

5. Derive (15.13). Use

   $$[\, x \leq y \equiv -y \leq -x \,].$$

6. There are three additional variants of the rule (15.15). For example, one variant is

   $$[\, m \leq n \equiv m < n+1 \,].$$

   Identify all three and show how to derive them from the rules given in Section 15.1.

7. Prove that multiplication distributes through lcm. Use

   $$[\, m \times n \backslash p \equiv m \backslash p \wedge n \backslash p \div m \,]$$

   provided that m is non-zero.

8. Simplify $(10 \times m + n) \bmod 9$ by eliminating the multiplication. Use your answer to calculate $24 \bmod 9$, $243 \bmod 9$ and $2437 \bmod 9$. Formulate an algorithm for calculating $n \bmod 9$ for an arbitrary number n given as a decimal number (i.e. a list ds of digits).

9. Calculate $24 \bmod 3$, $243 \bmod 3$ and $2437 \bmod 3$. Formulate general rules that help simplify the calculation.

10. The unary operator $\ominus$ is defined by, for all integers m,

$$\ominus m = (-m) \bmod n.$$

Note that $\ominus m$ is a modulo-n number for all integers m. In particular, $\ominus m$ is a modulo-n number when m is a modulo-n number. The unary operator $\ominus$ is called *negation modulo* n.

Prove the following properties of negation modulo n. Assume that m ranges over all integers while j and k range over modulo-n numbers.

(a) $[\ominus m = \ominus(m \bmod n)]$

(b) $[j \oplus (\ominus j) = 0]$

(c) $[\ominus j = k \equiv j = \ominus k]$

(d) $[\ominus(j \oplus k) = (\ominus j) \oplus (\ominus k)]$

11. Prove that integer division is monotonic with respect to the at-most relation:

$$[i \div n \leq j \div n \Leftarrow i \leq j].$$

You should assume that $0 < n$. Hint: exploit (15.25).

12. The specification (15.22) of integer division can be described as rounding real division down to the nearest integer. Modify the specification so that real division is rounded up.

13. Prove that

$$[i < (i+j) \div 2 < j \Leftarrow i+1 \neq j \wedge i < j],$$

where "$\div$" denotes integer division. Assume the following properties of integer division. Division of an even number by 2 is exact:

$$[(2 \times i) \div 2 = i].$$

Integer division is monotonic with respect to the at-most relation:

$$[i \div 2 \leq j \div 2 \Leftarrow i \leq j].$$

Take care: integer division is *not* monotonic with respect to the less-than relation. (Note that, if carried out as suggested rather than using, say, (15.25), your proof is valid however integer division is implemented: by rounding real division up, down or towards zero.)

Chapter

Relations, Graphs and **16** Path Algebras

In Section 12.7, we showed how binary relations can be depicted as graphs. In this chapter, we discuss the connection between relations and graphs in more detail. Many algorithmic problems involve finding and/or evaluating paths through a graph. Our goal in this chapter is to show how these problems are represented algebraically so that the solution to such tasks can be calculated.

16.1 PATHS IN A DIRECTED GRAPH

We begin the chapter with a number of formal definitions about graphs and paths in a graph. Informally, the notions we introduce are easy to grasp. So, on a first reading, it is not essential to pay attention to the details of the definitions. The details are essential later, when the definitions are used in earnest.

Definition 16.1 (Directed Graph) A *directed graph* comprises two sets N and E, called the *nodes* and the *edges* of the graph, and two functions from and to, both of which have type E→N.

If e is an edge of a graph and from(e) = m and to(e) = n (where m and n are nodes of the graph), we say that e is an edge *from* node m *to* node n.

We sometimes write statements of the form "let G = (N,E,from,to)" as a shorthand for introducing a graph and giving it the name G.

Very often, the graphs we consider have a finite set of nodes and a finite set of edges. Later, we also consider *labelled* graphs. A labelling of a graph is a function defined on the edges of the graph. The labels (the values taken by the function) may be booleans, in which case the function has type E→Bool, or numbers, in which case the function has type E→N, or indeed any type that is relevant to the problem in hand.

If the sets of nodes and edges are sufficiently small, it can be informative to draw a picture of a graph. Figure 16.1 shows how we depict a labelled edge in a graph from a node called fee to a node called foo with label fum. Note how the arrowhead indicates the values of the functions from and to when applied to the edge. Sometimes, if there is no need to name the nodes, we draw them as small black dots.

Figure 16.1: A labelled edge.

The definition of a graph allows multiple edges with the same from and to nodes. This is an aspect of the definition that we do not exploit. Generally, for any pair of nodes m and n, we assume that there is at most one edge from m to n.

Often we talk about "graphs" instead of "directed" graphs. A directed graph can be thought of as a communication network where all communication is one-way, in the direction indicated by the arrows. Sometimes it is more appropriate to use "undirected" graphs, which can be thought of as communication networks where communication is always two-way and entirely symmetric.

Definition 16.2 (Undirected Graph) An *undirected graph* comprises two sets N and E, called the *nodes* and the *edges* of the graph, and a function endpts with domain E. The function endpts is such that, for each edge e, the value of endpts(e) is a bag of nodes of size 2.

The name "endpts" is short for "end-points". That endpts(e) is a bag of size 2 means that it may have two distinct elements, or just one element repeated twice. In the latter case, the edge is called a *self-loop*. Figure 16.2 depicts an undirected graph with two (unnamed) nodes and two edges, one of which is a self-loop. Just as for directed graphs, although the definition allows the possibility of multiple edges with the same end-points, we generally assume that there is at most one edge between any pair of end-points.

Figure 16.2: An undirected graph with two nodes and two edges.

Clearly, an undirected graph can be converted into a directed graph. An edge e with distinct end-points m and n is converted into two edges e_1 and e_2 with m and n as their from and to nodes but in opposite directions. A self-loop is converted into a single edge where the from and to nodes are equal.[1] We often omit the adjectives "directed" or "undirected" when it is clear from the context which is meant.

Many problems are modelled as searching paths through a graph. Here is the definition of a "path".

Definition 16.3 (Path) Suppose $(N, E, \text{from}, \text{to})$ is a graph and suppose s and t are nodes of the graph. A *path from* s *to* t *of edge-count* k is a sequence of length $2k + 1$ of alternating nodes and edges; the sequence begins with s and ends with t, and each subsequence of the form m, e, n where m and n are nodes and e is an edge has the property that $\text{from}(e) = m \land \text{to}(e) = n$. The nodes s and t are called the *start* and *finish* nodes of the path.

Figure 16.3 depicts a path of edge-count 3 from node start to node finish. Formally, the path is the sequence

start , e1 , n1 , e2 , n2 , e3 , finish.

Figure 16.3: A path of edge-count 3.

It is important to note that the definition of a path allows the edge-count to be 0. Indeed, there is a path of edge-count 0 from every node in a graph to itself: a sequence of length 1 consisting of the node s satisfies the definition of a path from s to itself. Such a path is called an *empty path*. Note also that edge e defines the path

from(e) , e , to(e)

of edge-count 1.

Edges and paths have different types and should not be confused. Even so, it is sometimes convenient not to make the distinction between edges and paths of edge-count 1. However, a self-loop on a node should never be confused with the path of edge-count 0 from the node to itself: a self-loop defines a path of edge-count 1 from the node to itself.

[1] Beware: for some problems it is better to convert a self-loop into two copies of the same directed edge.

Paths are sometimes represented by sequences of nodes, omitting explicit mention of the connecting edges. (We use such a representation in Section 16.4.4.) Paths may also be represented by sequences of edges, omitting explicit mention of the nodes (e.g. where there may be more than one edge connecting a given pair of nodes and the distinction between edges is important.) This is unproblematic except for the case of empty paths, where the representation is ambiguous: the empty sequence of edges does not identify the start/finish node of the path.

Definition 16.4 (Simple Paths and Cycles)   A path in a graph is said to be *simple* if no node is repeated. A path of edge-count at least 1 with the same start and finish nodes is called a *cycle*. A graph is said to be *acyclic* if it has no cycles.

16.2 GRAPHS AND RELATIONS

We first introduced graphs in Section 12.7 as a way of picturing binary relations. We introduced Hasse diagrams in Section 12.7.6 as an economical way of presenting the transitive closure of a relation because it is easy for us to see paths through the graph. In this section, we explore in more detail the correspondence between relations and graphs.

Recall that a binary relation is a function of two arguments that is boolean-valued. Recall also that sets and boolean-valued functions are "isomorphic". That is, a boolean function defines a set (the set of all values for which the value of the function is true) and, vice versa, a set defines a boolean function on values via membership (each value is either a member of the set or not). Applied to relations, this means that a binary relation can be defined to be a set; if the types of its arguments are A and B, a relation is a subset of A×B. In other words, a binary relation on A and B is a set of pairs (a, b) where a is an element of A and b is an element of B. When the sets A and B are very small, this set-oriented view of relations can be easier to work with. This is the case for the examples we present in this section. Our practice is to switch between the two views of relations, choosing the set-oriented or the boolean-valued-function view as appropriate.

The examples of relations in Section 12.7 were all of so-called *homogeneous* relations, that is, relations where the types A and B are the same. Homogeneous relations are of most interest, but let us consider so-called *heterogeneous* relations, that is, relations where A and B may be different.

Let us begin with an example. We start with just two sets: {a,b,c} with three elements and {j,k} with two elements. The cartesian product {a,b,c}×{j,k} has 3×2 (i.e. 6) elements. A relation between {a,b,c} and {j,k} is a subset of {a,b,c}×{j,k}. There are 2^6 (i.e. 64) such relations because there are 2 possibilities for each of the 6 elements of {a,b,c}×{j,k}: each is either an element of or not an element of the relation. Since the number of elements in each relation is at most 6, we can specify each relation just by listing its elements. Indeed, we can draw a picture depicting each relation.

Figure 16.4 depicts one such relation. Viewing relations as sets, it is

$\{(a,j),(b,k),(c,j),(c,k)\}.$

Viewing relations as boolean-valued functions, it is the function that maps the pairs (a,j), (b,k), (c,j) and (c,k) to true and the pairs (a,k) and (b,j) to false. In words, we would say that a is related to j, b is related to k, and c is related to j and k. Figure 16.4 depicts the relation as a graph in which the nodes are the elements of the set $\{a,b,c\} \cup \{j,k\}$ and there is an edge from an element of $\{a,b,c\}$ to an element of $\{j,k\}$ when the pair of elements are related.

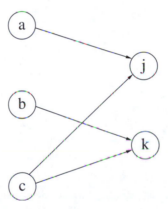

Figure 16.4: Bipartite graph depicting the relation $\{(a,j),(b,k),(c,j),(c,k)\}$.

For arbitrary sets A and B, a subset of A×B is said to be a (heterogeneous) *relation of type* A~B. This defines "~" as a type former which combines cartesian product and power sets; indeed, A~B is an alternative notation for $2^{A \times B}$, the set of subsets of A×B. Figure 16.4 depicts a relation of type $\{a,b,c\} \sim \{j,k\}$.

The graph in Figure 16.4 is called a *bipartite graph* because the nodes of the graph can be split into two disjoint sets such that all edges are from nodes in one of the sets to nodes in the other set. It is bipartite for the simple reason that it models a relation of type A~B for which A and B are disjoint sets. When the sets A and B are not disjoint and we model a heterogeneous relation of type A~B as a graph, we lose type information: we view it as a homogeneous relation on the set A∪B. The distinction is sometimes important – it first becomes important for us when we introduce matrices in Section 16.5 – but often it can be ignored. Nevertheless, for greater clarity our initial examples are all of relations of type A~B where A and B are indeed disjoint.

16.2.1 Relation Composition

In Figure 16.5, the same relation is depicted together with a second relation. The second relation is a relation, $\{(j,y),(j,z),(k,y)\}$, of type $\{j,k\} \sim \{y,z\}$. A relation of type A~B can be *composed* with a relation of type B~C; the result is a relation of type A~C. The result of composing the two relations in Figure 16.5 is depicted in Figure 16.6. Let us explain how the graph in Figure 16.6 is constructed from the two graphs in Figure 16.5. Afterwards we give a precise definition of the composition of two relations.

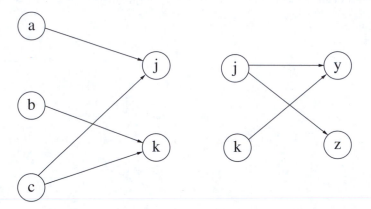

Figure 16.5: Graphs depicting two relations that can be composed.

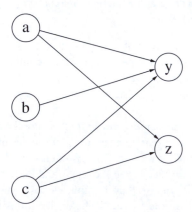

Figure 16.6: Graph depicting the composition of the two relations in Figure 16.5.

Essentially the process is to replace two connecting edges by one edge. For example, in Figure 16.5 there is an edge in the left graph from a to j and an edge in the right graph from j to y; this results in an edge from a to y in Figure 16.6. Similarly, there is an edge from b to y resulting from the two connecting edges from b to k and from k to y. But there is a complication. Note that there is only one edge from c to y but there are two ways that the edge arises: both nodes j and k act as connecting nodes.

An *edge* in the graph shown in Figure 16.6 corresponds to the *existence* of at least one *path* formed by an edge in the left graph of Figure 16.5 followed by an edge in the right graph of Figure 16.5; two such edges form a path if they are connected, that is, they have an intermediate node in common.

Retracing our steps, the two graphs in Figure 16.5 depict two relations, the first of type $\{a,b,c\} \sim \{j,k\}$ and the second of type $\{j,k\} \sim \{y,z\}$. The two relations can be composed and their composition is depicted by the graph in Figure 16.6. Formally, suppose R is a relation of type A~B and S is a relation of type B~C. Then their *composition*, which we denote by R∘S, is the relation of type A~C defined by:

$$[\ (a,c) \in R{\circ}S \ = \ \langle \exists b : b{\in}B : (a,b){\in}R \wedge (b,c){\in}S \rangle \ ].$$ (16.5)

Definition (16.5) views relations as sets of pairs. If we take the view that a relation is a boolean-valued function, we would write a R b instead of $(a,b){\in}R$. In that case, the definition would be formulated as:

$$[\ a \ (R{\circ}S) \ c \ = \ \langle \exists b : b{\in}B : (a \ R \ b) \wedge (b \ S \ c) \rangle \ ].$$ (16.6)

Having introduced a binary operator on relations, it is important to investigate its algebraic properties. Composition is easily shown to be associative. Specifically, if A, B, C and D are types and R, S and T are relations of type A~B, B~C and C~D, R∘(S∘T) and (R∘S)∘T are equal relations of type A~D. The proof is a straightforward calculation. Here is an outline:

      a (R∘(S∘T)) d

=   {   expand the definition of composition twice;

                      apply distributivity of conjunction over disjunction

                      and idempotence of conjunction   }

   ⟨∃b,c : b∈B ∧ c∈C : (a R b) ∧ (b S c) ∧ (c T d)⟩

=   {   same steps but applied to (R∘S)∘T

                      and reversed   }

      a ((R∘S)∘T) d.

The associativity law

[**associativity**] $[R \circ (S \circ T) = (R \circ S) \circ T]$ (16.7)

then follows by the rule of extensionality (two functions are equal if they always return equal values). As a consequence, we may omit parentheses and write simply $R \circ S \circ T$.

Note how relation composition is defined in terms of conjunction and disjunction; it is thus the algebraic properties of these two logical operators that are the key to the properties of composition. Note also how the middle formula of the skeleton calculation above expresses that a and d are related by $R \circ S \circ T$ if there is a path in the graphs for R, S and T beginning with an edge in the graph for R followed by an edge in the graph for S and ending with an edge in the graph for T; associativity of composition captures the property that the order in which the edges are combined to form a path is not significant.

Relation composition is not symmetric. Indeed, for heterogeneous relations it does not usually make sense to swap the order of composition. For homogeneous relations – relations R and S both of type $A \sim A$ for some A – the equality $R \circ S = S \circ R$ makes sense but is sometimes true and sometimes false. Oviously, it is true when R=S. For an example of when it is false, take $A = \{a,b,c\}$, $R = \{(a,b)\}$ and $S = \{(b,c)\}$. Then $R \circ S = \{(a,c)\}$ and $S \circ R = \emptyset$. Thinking in terms of paths in a graph, it is obvious that the order of the edges is important.

Note that we have just used our standard notation "$\emptyset$" for the empty set. Strictly, because relations are typed, we should distinguish between different "types" of empty set, as in $\emptyset_{A \sim A}$. This is not usually done, the context being used to determine which relation is meant. In the context of relations, it is usual to call $\emptyset$ the empty *relation* and sometimes a different symbol is chosen. For reasons explained in Section 16.4, we use the symbol 0 for the empty relation (the type being either evident from the context or left to the reader to infer).

The empty relation (of appropriate type) is the left and right zero of composition. That is, for all relations R,

[**Zero**] $[0 \circ R = 0 = R \circ 0]$.   (16.8)

(Typically, all three occurrences of "0" in this law have different type, but that is not important.)

16.2.2 Union of Relations

Union is defined on all sets and so also on relations, the only proviso being that the relations being combined have the same type. That is, if R and S both have the same type,

A~B say, then R∪S is a relation also of type A~B. The union of relations is symmetric, associative, idempotent and has unit **0** (the empty relation).

The set A×B is a subset of A×B – after all, the two are equal – and so is a relation of type A~B. It is called the *universal relation* of its type because it relates every element of A to every element of B. It is interesting because it is the zero of the union of relations of type A~B: with R ranging over relations of type A~B, we have

$$[(A×B)∪R = A×B].$$

This is a simple consequence of the fact that R is a relation of type A~B is, by definition, R ⊆ A×B.

If we depict relations of type A~B as bipartite graphs, union corresponds to choice: there is an edge in the graph of R∪S from a to b if there is an edge in the graph of R from a to b or there is an edge in the graph of S from a to b. An expression like (R∪S)∘T captures paths formed by a choice of edge in R or S followed by an edge in T. The expression R∘T∪S∘T is similar; it captures paths formed by either an edge in R followed by an edge in T or an edge in S followed by an edge in T. Indeed, the two are equal; composition distributes over union. That is, if R and S both have type A~B and T has type B~C, for some A, B and C, we have

$$\textbf{[Distributivity]}\,[(R∪S)∘T = (R∘T)∪(S∘T)]. \tag{16.9}$$

Similarly, if R has type A~B and S and T have type B~C, for some A, B and C,

$$\textbf{[Distributivity]}\,[R∘(S∪T) = (R∘S)∪(R∘T)]. \tag{16.10}$$

An immediate consequence of distributivity is that composition is monotonic. Specifically, if R has type A~B and S and T have type B~C, for some A, B and C,

$$\textbf{[Monotonicity]}\,[R∘S ⊆ R∘T ⟸ S⊆T], \tag{16.11}$$

and, if S and T have type A~B and R has type B~C, for some A, B and C,

$$\textbf{[Monotonicity]}\,[S∘R ⊆ T∘R ⟸ S⊆T]. \tag{16.12}$$

The following calculation establishes (16.11):

$$R∘S ⊆ R∘T$$
$$= \qquad \{ \qquad \text{definition of } ⊆ \ \}$$
$$(R∘S)∪(R∘T) = R∘T$$

$$= \qquad \{ \qquad \text{distributivity: (16.9)} \quad \}$$

$$R{\circ}(S{\cup}T) = R{\circ}T$$

$$\Leftarrow \qquad \{ \qquad \text{Leibniz} \quad \}$$

$$S{\cup}T = T$$

$$= \qquad \{ \qquad \text{definition of } \subseteq \quad \}$$

$$S \subseteq T.$$

16.2.3 Transitive Closure

In a bipartite graph of type $A{\sim}B$, edges are from nodes in A to nodes in B; in an arbitrary graph, there is no restriction on the edges. Such graphs correspond to *homogeneous relations*, that is, relations of type $A{\sim}A$ for some A. Indeed, every relation R of type $A{\sim}A$ defines a graph with node-set A and an edge from node a to node a' whenever a R a'. Conversely, given a graph (A,E,from,to), we can define a relation R of type $A{\sim}A$ by a R a' exactly when there is an edge from a to a' in E.

In this section, we fix the set A and consider relations of type $A{\sim}A$. This has the enormous advantage that we do not have to continually mention types or type restrictions. Composition and union are well defined on all relations and there is no ambiguity about using 0 to denote the empty relation. The set A does not go away; it becomes an implicit parameter in all definitions.

Our goal in this section is to show that computing the transitive closure of a relation is the same as establishing the existence of paths (of edge-count at least 1) in the graph of the relation.

Recall that a relation R is transitive if, for all x, y and z, whenever $x\,R\,y$ is true, and $y\,R\,z$ is true, it is also the case that $x\,R\,z$ is true. In the following calculation, we express this property in terms of relation composition:

$$R \text{ is transitive}$$

$$= \qquad \{ \qquad \text{definition} \quad \}$$

$$\langle \forall x,y,z \,:\, x\,R\,y \wedge y\,R\,z \,:\, x\,R\,z \rangle$$

$$= \qquad \{ \qquad \text{range splitting} \quad \}$$

$$\langle \forall x,z \,:\, \langle \exists y :: x\,R\,y \wedge y\,R\,z \rangle \,:\, x\,R\,z \rangle$$

$$= \qquad \{ \qquad \text{definition of composition: (16.6)} \quad \}$$

$$\langle \forall x,z \,:\, x\,(R{\circ}R)\,z \,:\, x\,R\,z \rangle \,.$$

Taking the set-oriented view of relations, the universal quantification

$$\langle \forall x,z \, : \, x\,(R{\circ}R)\,z \, : \, x\,R\,z \rangle$$

equivales

$$R{\circ}R \subseteq R.$$

In this way, we have established the so-called *point-free* definition of transitivity:

$$[\; R \text{ is transitive} \;\; \equiv \;\; R{\circ}R \subseteq R \;]. \tag{16.13}$$

(It is called "point-free" because the "points" x, y and z do not appear in the definition.)

Now let us turn to paths in a graph. The occurrence of "$R{\circ}R$" in definition (16.13) suggests that we consider its graphical representation. We determined in Section 16.2.1 that values related by $S{\circ}T$ correspond to nodes that are connected by a path consisting of an edge in the graph of S followed by an edge in the graph of T. Although Section 16.2.1 restricted graphs to bipartite graphs, the restriction was not essential. Indeed, values related by $R{\circ}R$ correspond to paths in the graph of R of edge-count 2.

A generalisation is obvious. Suppose we write R^1 for R, R^2 for $R{\circ}R$, R^3 for $R{\circ}R{\circ}R$, and so on. Then R^k (for all strictly positive[2] natural numbers k) corresponds to paths in the graph of R of edge-count k. This is exemplified in the graphs in Figure 16.7. The top graph depicts a relation R on a set of size 5. The middle graph depicts R^2 and the bottom graph depicts R^3. An edge in the middle graph corresponds to a path in the top graph of edge-count 2 and an edge in the bottom graph corresponds to a path in the top graph of edge-count 3.

Set union expresses a choice among relations and, hence, a choice among edge-counts. For example, the graph of the relation

$$\left\langle \bigcup k : 1 \leq k \leq 3 : R^k \right\rangle$$

expresses a choice of paths in the graph of R with edge-count 1, 2 or 3. The graph of the relation

$$\left\langle \bigcup k : 1 \leq k : R^k \right\rangle \tag{16.14}$$

expresses a choice among all paths of edge-count at least 1 in the graph of R. We show shortly that this is the transitive closure R^+ of R.

---

[2] We have not forgotten 0. The definition of R^0 is introduced later when we consider the reflexive transitive closure of a relation. It does indeed correspond to paths of length 0.

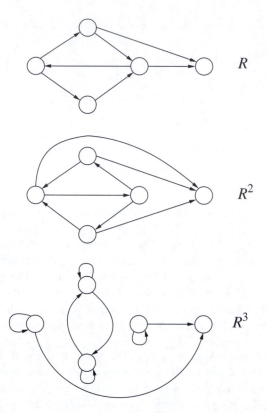

Figure 16.7: First, second and third powers of a relation.

Although (16.14) is a quantification with an infinite range and we have warned that the rules for manipulating quantified expressions do not necessarily apply in such cases, the quantification can always be reduced to a finite range if the domain of the relation R is finite. This is easy to see from the correspondence with paths in a graph. If the number of nodes in a graph is a finite number, n, and there is a path from one node to another in the graph, then there must be a path of edge-count at most n. This is because every path can always be reduced to a simple path by removing proper subpaths that start and finish at the same node; clearly, a simple path comprises at most n edges. (See Definition16.4 for the precise definition of "simple".)

In order to show that (16.14) is indeed the transitive closure R^+ of R, we need a concise definition of transitive closure. A point-free definition is the most concise.

The definition has two clauses. First, R^+ is transitive:

    [Transitivity] $[\ R^+ {\circ} R^+ \subseteq R^+\ ]$.   (16.15)

Second, R^+ is the least relation (in the subset ordering) that includes R and is transitive. Formally:

[Least] $\left[\, \langle \forall S \;:\; S{\circ}S \subseteq S \;:\; R \subseteq S \equiv R^+ \subseteq S \rangle \,\right]$.   (16.16)

Our goal is to establish the law

[Transitive Closure] $\left[\, R^+ = \langle \bigcup k : 1 \leq k : R^k \rangle \right]$.   (16.17)

To do this, we have to show that properties (16.15) and (16.16) are satisfied when R^+ is replaced by $\langle \bigcup k : 1 \leq k : R^k \rangle$. That is, we have to show that

$$\left[\, \langle \bigcup k : 1 \leq k : R^k \rangle \circ \langle \bigcup k : 1 \leq k : R^k \rangle \;\subseteq\; \langle \bigcup k : 1 \leq k : R^k \rangle \right]$$ (16.18)

and

$$\left[\, \langle \forall S \;:\; S{\circ}S \subseteq S \;:\; R \subseteq S \equiv \langle \bigcup k : 1 \leq k : R^k \rangle \subseteq S \rangle \,\right]$$.   (16.19)

We begin with the transitivity requirement:

$$\langle \bigcup k : 1 \leq k : R^k \rangle \circ \langle \bigcup k : 1 \leq k : R^k \rangle$$

$=$ { distributivity: (16.9) and (16.10) }

$$\langle \bigcup i,j \;:\; 1 \leq i \wedge 1 \leq j \;:\; R^i{\circ}R^j \rangle$$

$\subseteq$ { $R^i{\circ}R^j = R^{i+j}$, $1 \leq i \wedge 1 \leq j \Rightarrow 1 \leq i{+}j$ }

$$\langle \bigcup k \;:\; 1 \leq k \;:\; R^k \rangle.$$

This proves (16.18). Now we establish the "least" requirement. We begin with the more complicated side of the equivalence in (16.19) and try to prove it equal to the left side. On the way we discover that a proof by mutual implication is necessary.

$$\langle \bigcup k : 1 \leq k : R^k \rangle \;\subseteq\; S$$

$=$ { definition of set union }

$$\langle \forall k \;:\; 1 \leq k \;:\; R^k \subseteq S \rangle$$

$=$ { principle of mathematical induction }

$$R^1 \subseteq S \wedge \langle \forall k \;:\; 1 \leq k \wedge R^k \subseteq S \;:\; R^{k+1} \subseteq S \rangle$$

$\Leftarrow$ { $\left[R^{k+1} = R{\circ}R^k \right]$,

assumption: $S{\circ}S \subseteq S$, and transitivity of $\subseteq$ }

$$R \subseteq S \wedge \langle \forall k \;:\; 1 \leq k \wedge R^k \subseteq S \;:\; R{\circ}R^k \subseteq S{\circ}S \rangle$$

$\Leftarrow$ {   montonicity: (16.11) and (16.12) }

$R \subseteq S \wedge \langle \forall k : 1 \leq k \wedge R^k \subseteq S : R \subseteq S \wedge R^k \subseteq S \rangle$

$=$ { $\left[R^k \subseteq S \Rightarrow R^k \subseteq S \right]$ and idempotence of $\wedge$ }

$R \subseteq S$

$\Leftarrow$ {   by range splitting on $k = 1$, $\left[R \subseteq \langle \bigcup k : 1 \leq k : R^k \rangle \right]$,

transitivity of $\subseteq$ }

$\langle \bigcup k : 1 \leq k : R^k \rangle \subseteq S$.

Noting that this calculation begins and ends with the right side of (16.19), and the left side is the penultimate expression, we conclude (16.19) by the rule of mutual implication.

16.2.4 Reflexive Transitive Closure

The *reflexive transitive closure* of a (homogeneous) relation R is denoted by R*. It is defined similarly to the transitive closure. In words, it is the least reflexive and transitive relation that includes R.

In order to give it a compact, point-free definition, we need to express reflexivity in a point-free way. Recall that R is reflexive if x R x for all x. Let us define the relation **1** by

$\langle \forall x,y :: x\, \mathbf{1}\, y \equiv x = y \rangle$.

Then we have:

R is reflexive

$=$ {   definition }

$\langle \forall x :: x\, R\, x \rangle$

$=$ {   one-point rule }

$\langle \forall x,y : x = y : x\, R\, y \rangle$

$=$ {   definition of **1**, Leibniz }

$\langle \forall x,y : x\, \mathbf{1}\, y : x\, R\, y \rangle$

$=$ {   definition of subset }

$\mathbf{1} \subseteq R$.

The relation **1** is called the *identity relation* and sometimes denoted by id (or Id). We choose to use the symbol **1** here because the identity relation is the (left and right) unit of composition. That is,

[Unit] $[\, \mathbf{1} \circ R = R = R \circ \mathbf{1} \,]$.   (16.20)

On account of the unit law, it is appropriate to define

$$\left[R^0 = 1 \right];$$

then we have the familiar-looking law of powers

$$\left[R^{m+n} = R^m {\circ} R^n \right]$$

where m and n are arbitrary natural numbers.

We can now give a definition of reflexive transitive closure. First, R^* is reflexive and transitive:

[Reflexivity and Transitivity] $[\ 1 \cup R^* {\circ} R^* \subseteq R^*\ ]$.   (16.21)

Second, R^* is the least relation (in the subset ordering) that includes R and is reflexive and transitive. Formally:

[Least] $\left[\langle \forall S\ :\ 1 \cup S {\circ} S \subseteq S\ :\ R \subseteq S \equiv R^* \subseteq S \rangle \right]$.   (16.22)

The graph of **1** has a self-loop on every node (an edge from every node to itself) and no other edges. For any given graph, it represents the paths of edge-count 0. The graph of the reflexive transitive closure of R has an edge for every path, including paths of edge-count 0, in the graph of R. Formally:

[Reflexive Transitive Closure] $\left[R^* = \left\langle \bigcup k : 0 \leq k : R^k \right\rangle \right]$.   (16.23)

(Note the inclusion of $0 = k$ in the quantified expression.) The proof of this law is almost a repetition of the proof of the law (16.17).

Laws (16.17) and (16.23) are the mathematical basis for the use of Hasse diagrams to depict ordering relations and the use of genealogy trees to depict ancestral relations. More broadly, we exploit these laws every time a graph is used to depict a network of points with connecting lines. The information content of the diagram is kept to a minimum while we rely on our ability to trace paths in order to deduce required information from the graph. Even for problems where the graph is too big to display, the laws form the basis for many search algorithms. The transitive closure and reflexive transitive closure operations on relations/graphs are thus very important concepts.

16.3 FUNCTIONAL AND TOTAL RELATIONS

Functions are relations that relate exactly one output to each and every input value. This section makes this precise.

First, let us note that relations are ambivalent about "input" and "output". That is, given a relation R of type $A \sim B$, we may choose arbitrarily whether we regard A to be the set of "inputs" and B the set of "outputs" or, vice versa, B to be the set of "inputs" and A the set of "outputs". Because it fits better with conventional notations for the composition of relations and functions, we choose to call B the input set and A the output set.

We say that R is *functional* (on B) if, for all x, y in A and for all z in B, if $x \mathbin{R} z$ and $y \mathbin{R} z$ then $x = y$. (In words, R returns at most one "output" for each "input" value.) We also say that R is *total* (on B) if, for all z in B, there is some x in A such that $x \mathbin{R} z$. (In other words, R returns at least one "output" for each "input" value.) We say that the relation R of type $A \sim B$ is a *function* to A from B if R is both functional and total on B. If this is the case, we write $R(z)$ for the unique value in A that is related by R to z.

The converse of relation R of type $A \sim B$, which we denote by $R^{\cup}$, has type $B \sim A$. If $R^{\cup}$ is functional on A, we say that R is *injective*. If $R^{\cup}$ is total on B, we say that R is *surjective*. A relation R of type $A \sim B$ is a *bijective* function if R is a function to A from B and $R^{\cup}$ is a function to B from A. "Bijective function" is commonly abbreviated to "bijection". If there is a bijection of type $A \sim B$, we say that sets A and B are in one-to-one correspondence. For example, the doubling function is a bijection that defines a one-to-one correspondence between the natural numbers and the even natural numbers.

When the definitions of functionality and injectivity, totality and surjectivity are expressed in a point-free fashion, the duality between them becomes very clear. Using the notations $\mathbf{1}_A$ and $\mathbf{1}_B$ for the identity relations on A and B, respectively, we have:

$$[\textbf{Functionality}] \quad \left[\ R \text{ is functional} \ \equiv \ R{\circ}R^{\cup} \subseteq \mathbf{1}_A \ \right]; \tag{16.24}$$

$$[\textbf{Totality}] \quad \left[\ R \text{ is total} \ \equiv \ R^{\cup}{\circ}R \supseteq \mathbf{1}_B \ \right]; \tag{16.25}$$

$$[\textbf{Injectivity}] \quad \left[\ R \text{ is injective} \ \equiv \ R^{\cup}{\circ}R \subseteq \mathbf{1}_B \ \right]; \tag{16.26}$$

$$[\textbf{Surjectivity}] \quad \left[\ R \text{ is surjective} \ \equiv \ R{\circ}R^{\cup} \supseteq \mathbf{1}_A \ \right]; \tag{16.27}$$

$$[\textbf{Bijectivity}] \quad \left[\ R \text{ is a bijection} \ \equiv \ R{\circ}R^{\cup} = \mathbf{1}_A \ \wedge \ R^{\cup}{\circ}R = \mathbf{1}_B \ \right]. \tag{16.28}$$

If f and g are functional relations of type $A \sim B$ and $B \sim C$, respectively, their composition $f{\circ}g$ is a functional relation of type $A \sim C$. We say that functionality is *preserved* by composition. Similarly, totality, injectivity and surjectivity are all preserved by composition. In particular, the composition of a function f of type $B \rightarrow A$ (a total, functional relation of type $A \sim B$) and a function g of type $C \rightarrow B$ (a total, functional relation of type $B \sim C$) is a function $f{\circ}g$ of type $C \rightarrow A$. Given input z, the unique value related to z by $f{\circ}g$ is $f(g(z))$.

16.4 PATH-FINDING PROBLEMS

In this section, we look at different applications of graph theory that can all be described under the general heading of "path-finding problems". At the same time, our goal is to formulate the mathematical structure of such problems. To this end, we introduce product and sum operations on labelled graphs. The definition of "product" and "sum" depends on the application; the mathematical structure binds the applications together.

16.4.1 Counting Paths

In Section 16.2 the focus was on boolean values: whether or not two nodes in a graph are related by the existence of a path connecting them. Suppose now that we would like to determine in how many ways two nodes are connected. Then we need to redefine the way graphs are composed.

To better illustrate the technique, Figure 16.8 shows the same two graphs as in Figure 16.5 but now each edge has been labelled with a number. For example, the edge from c to k in the left graph has label 2. Let us interpret this as meaning that there are in fact two different edges from c to k. Similarly, the label 5 on the edge from c to j means that there are actually five edges from c to j. Where there is no edge (for example, there is no edge from node b to node j in the left graph), we could equally have drawn an edge with label 0. Now suppose we want to determine the number of different paths from each of the nodes a, b and c to each of the nodes y and z in the combined graph. There are six different combinations. Let us consider each combination in turn.

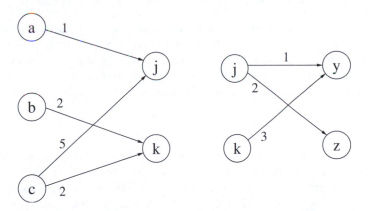

Figure 16.8: Two labelled graphs that can be connected.

From a to y there is just one path, because there is one edge from a to j and one edge from j to y, and j is the only connecting node. From a to z there are 1×2 paths because, again, j is the only connecting node, and there is one edge from a to j and there are two edges from j to z.

From b to y, there are 2×3 paths because a path consists of one of the 2 edges from b to k followed by one of the 3 edges from k to y.

From c to y there is a choice of connecting node. There are 5×1 paths from c to y via the connecting node j; there are also 2×3 paths from c to y via the connecting node k. In total, there are thus $5 \times 1 + 2 \times 3$ paths from c to y. Finally, there are 5×2 paths from c to z.

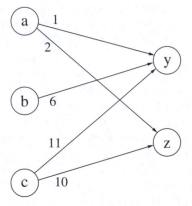

○ **Figure 16.9: Result of counting paths: the standard product.**

Figure 16.9 shows the result of this calculation. Note that 1 (the number of paths from a to y) equals $1 \times 1 + 0 \times 0$, 2 (the number of paths from a to z) equals $1 \times 2 + 0 \times 0$, 6 (the number of paths from b to y) equals $2 \times 3 + 0 \times 0$, and 10 (the number of paths from c to z) equals $5 \times 2 + 0 \times 0$. Moreover, 0 (the number of paths from b to z) equals $0 \times 0 + 0 \times 0$. In this way, there is a systematic method of computing the number of paths for each pair of nodes whereby "+" corresponds to a choice of connecting node and "×" corresponds to combining connecting edges.

Let us fomalise this method. We begin by overloading the notation introduced earlier for describing the types of relations. We say that G is a bipartite graph of type A~B if A∪B is the set of vertices of G and each edge of G is from a node in A to a node in B. If the edges of bipartite graphs G and H are labelled with numbers, and G has type A~B and H has type B~C (for some A, B and C), the *(standard) product* G×H is a bipartite graph of type A~C; writing a G b for the label given to the edge from a to b, the labels of edges of G×H are given by

$$[\, a\,(G{\times}H)\,c \;\; = \;\; \langle \Sigma b : b{\in}B : (a\,G\,b) \times (b\,H\,c) \rangle \,]. \tag{16.29}$$

Note that (16.29) assumes that, for each pair of nodes, no edge connecting them is the same as an edge that does connect them but with label 0. The reason for naming this combination of G and H a "product" will become clear in Section 16.4.5.

16.4.2 Frequencies

Figure 16.10 shows our two example graphs again but this time the edge labels are ratios of the form m/n. Imagine that the nodes of the graphs represent places and the edges represent routes connecting the places. The two graphs might represent different modes of transport. For example, the left graph might represent bicycle routes and the right graph bus routes. A person might complete the first part of a journey by bicycle and then the second part by bus. The labels represent the frequency with which a particular route is chosen. For example, a person starting at c might follow the route to j one time in every three and the route to k twice. Note that, for the labels to make sense in this way, the labels on the edges *from* each node must add up to 1. Indeed, this is the case for node c (since $\frac{1}{3}+\frac{2}{3}=1$). Since there is only one edge from node a, the edge has to be labelled $\frac{1}{1}$. Note, however, that the sum of the edge labels for edges *to* a given node do not have to add up to 1. For example, the edge labels on the edges into node j add up to $\frac{4}{3}$.

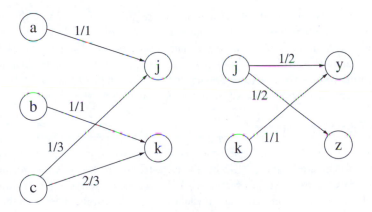

Figure 16.10: Frequency labellings.

A question we might ask is with what frequency a person takes a particular (bicycle followed by bus) route. Since the question is very similar to counting paths, it is not surprising that the method is to add products of frequencies according to the formula (16.29). Let us see how this works for node c.

Referring to Figure 16.10, since 6 is the least common multiple of 2 and 3, we consider 6 trips starting from c. Of these, $6\times\frac{1}{3}$ (i.e. 2) will be made to node j, from where $6\times\frac{1}{3}\times\frac{1}{2}$ will proceed to node y. Simplifying, 1 of the 6 trips will be made from c to y via node j. Similarly, $6\times\frac{2}{3}\times\frac{1}{1}$ (i.e. 4) of the trips will be made from c to y via node k. In total, 1+4 (i.e. 5) out of 6 trips from c will be to y. Also, $6 \times \frac{1}{3} \times \frac{1}{2}$ (i.e. 1) out of 6 trips will be made from c to z. Note that $\frac{5}{6} + \frac{1}{6} = \frac{6}{6}$, meaning that all 6 of the 6 trips are made to either y or z.

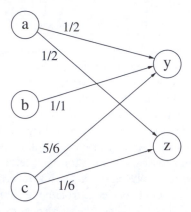

Figure 16.11: Frequency count: the standard product of the graphs in Figure 16.10.

Figure 16.11 shows the result of calculating the frequencies for each of the nodes in the left graph. The formula used to calculate frequencies is precisely the same formula (16.29) used to count paths. As remarked earlier, this is not surprising: if all the labels are ratios of positive integers, and m is the least common multiple of all the denominators (the denominator of $\frac{p}{q}$ is q), then multiplying each label by m gives a count of the number of times the edge is followed in every m times that a path is traversed.

16.4.3 Shortest Distances

Let us return to Figure 16.8. In Section 16.4.1 we viewed the labels on the edges as counts. So, for example, the label 2 on the edge from c to k was taken to mean the existence of two different edges from c to k. Let us now view the labels differently. Suppose the nodes represent places and the labels represent distances between the places. So the label 2 on the edge from c to k means that the two places c and k are connected by a (one-way) path of length 2. The question is: if the paths from a, b and c via j and k to y and z are followed, what is the shortest distance that is travelled?

The analysis is almost the same as for counting paths. From a to y the distance is 1+1 (i.e. 2) because there is one edge from a to j of length 1 and one edge from j to y, also of length 1, and j is the only connecting node. From a to z the distance is 1+2 because, again, j is the only connecting node, and the edge from a to j has length 1 and the edge from j to z has length 2. Similarly, the distance from b to y is 2+3.

As in Section 16.4.1, the interesting case is from c to y because there is a choice of connecting node. The distance from c to y via the connecting node j is 5+2; via the connecting node k, the distance is 2+3. The shortest distance is thus their minimum, $(5+2)\downarrow(2+3)$. That is, the shortest distance from c to y is 5. The result of this calculation is shown in Figure 16.12.

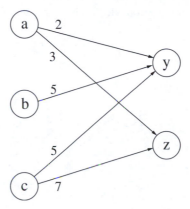

Figure 16.12: Shortest paths: the minimum-distance product of the graphs in Figure 16.8.

Just as we did for counting paths, we can formalise the calculation of shortest distances. Suppose the edges of bipartite graphs G and H are labelled with numbers, and G has type A~B and H has type B~C (for some A, B and C). Then the *(minimum distance) product* G×H is a bipartite graph of type A~C; writing a G b for the label given to the edge from a to b, the labels of edges of G×H are given by

$$[\,a\,(G{\times}H)\,c\ =\ \langle\Downarrow b: b{\in}B: (a\,G\,b)+(b\,H\,c)\rangle\,].\tag{16.30}$$

The formula (16.30) assumes that no edge connecting two nodes is the same as an edge connecting the nodes with label ∞.

16.4.4 All Paths

In the preceding sections, we have considered different aspects of paths consisting of an edge in a graph G followed by an edge in a graph H. Section 16.2.1 was about the existence of a path, Sections 16.4.1 and 16.4.2 were about counting numbers of paths and frequencies, while Section 16.4.3 was about finding the shortest path. For our final path-finding problem, we consider the problem of finding paths.

Figure 16.13 shows our familiar two graphs, but now with edges labelled by sets. The elements of the set are sequences of nodes representing paths. The label {j} on the edge from a to j represents a direct path from a to j; the label {dk,ek} on the edge from b to k represents a choice of paths from b to k, one going through a node d and the other going through a node e; similarly, the label {vz,z} on the edge from j to z represents a choice of paths from j to z, one going through v and the other a direct path. (Imagine that the graphs have been constructed by some earlier analysis of paths through yet simpler graphs.) The start node of a path is deliberately omitted in this representation in order to simplify the definition of product. This has the side-effect that it is impossible to represent empty paths.

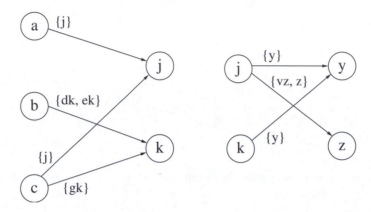

Figure 16.13: Two route graphs.

Figure 16.14 shows the (path) product of the two graphs. As in the previous sections, this product has five edges. The label {jy} on the edge from a to y indicates that there is just one path from a to y, going through the node j. All other edge labels represent a choice of paths. For example, from c to z, there is a choice of two paths, one going through j and then v, and the second going through j directly to z. Note that labelling

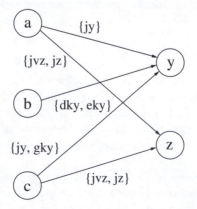

Figure 16.14: All paths: the path product of the graphs in Figure 16.13.

one edge by a finite set is equivalent to there being a number of edges with the same from and to nodes, each of which is labelled by an element of the set.

The formalisation of the product of G and H in this case requires that we first define product operations on paths (represented by sequences of nodes) and on sets of paths. Suppose p and q are two sequences of nodes. The *product* of p and q, denoted pq, is the sequence formed by combining the sequences in the order p followed by q. Now let P and Q be two sets of (node) sequences. We define the product $P \cdot Q$ as follows:

$$[\ P \cdot Q \ = \ \{p, q : p \in P \wedge q \in Q : pq\}\ ].$$
(16.31)

Suppose now the edges of bipartite graphs G and H are labelled with numbers, and G has type A∼B and H has type B∼C (for some A, B and C). Then the *(path) product* G×H is a bipartite graph of type A∼C; writing a G b for the label given to the edge from a to b, the labels of edges of G×H are given by

$$[\ a\ (G{\times}H)\ c \ = \ \langle \bigcup b : b \in B : (a\ G\ b) \cdot (b\ H\ c) \rangle\ ].$$
(16.32)

Formula (16.32) assumes that no edge connecting two nodes is the same as an edge connecting the nodes with label Ø (the empty set).

Of the graph products we have introduced, the path product is the most complicated. It is complicated because it depends on first defining the product of two paths, and then the product of sets of paths. This process is called *extending* the product operation on sequences to sets of sequences. The definition of graph product is also an example of *extending* an operator of one type to an operator on a more complex type.

16.4.5 Semirings and Operations on Graphs

In Section 16.2.1 and Sections 16.4.1 thru 16.4.4, we considered several problems involving combining two bipartite graphs. In Section 16.2.1, the graphs depicted binary relations and the edges were unlabelled. The combination of the graphs depicts the composition of the relations. In Section 16.4.1, edges were labelled with a count and the combined graph depicts the number of paths between pairs of nodes. In Section 16.4.2, edges were labelled with frequencies and the combined graph depicts the frequency with which the final destination was chosen from each starting node. In Section 16.4.3, the labels represented distances and the combined graph depicts shortest distances. Finally, in Section 16.4.4, the labels represent sets of paths and the combined graph also represents sets of paths.

Algebraically there is a commonality among all these problems. Table 16.1 shows how the label of the edge from c to y is computed for four of the problems. (Frequency calculation has been omitted because it is algebraically identical to counting paths. Relation composition is slightly special because the edges are not labelled but it is the existence of an edge that is in question. In algebraic terms, the labels on edges are the booleans.) For relation composition, two connecting edges are combined by conjunction ($\wedge$) and a choice of connecting node is effected by disjunction ($\vee$); for counting paths, the labels of two connecting edges are combined by multiplication ($\times$) and a choice of connecting node is effected by addition ($+$); for shortest paths, the labels of two connecting edges are combined by addition ($+$) and a choice of connecting node is effected by minimisation ($\downarrow$); finally, for finding paths, two connecting edges are combined by the product operation defined in (16.31) and a choice of connecting node is effected by set union ($\cup$).

	c		$\longrightarrow$	y	
	c→j	j→y		c→k	k→y
Relation composition	(true	∧ true)	∨	(true	∧ true)
Counting paths	(5	× 1)	+	(2	× 3)
Shortest path	(5	+ 1)	↓	(2	+ 3)
Routes	({j}	· {y})	∪	({gk}	· {y})

Table 16.1: Computing the label of an edge.

The same process is used when edges are missing. In Table 16.2 we show how the edge labels are combined to determine the label of the edge from b to y in the combined graph. Note that there is no edge from b to j in the left graph. This is modelled by false in the case of relation composition, by 0 in the case of counting paths, by ∞ (infinity) in the case of shortest paths and by $\emptyset$ in the case of paths. Recall that false is the "zero" of conjunction, 0 is the "zero" of multiplication, and ∞ is the "zero" of addition. (That is, [false $\wedge$ x = false], [0$\times$x = 0] and [∞+x = ∞].) It is clear from (16.31) that $\emptyset$ is the "zero" of the product of sets of paths.

	b		$\longrightarrow$	y	
	b→j	j→y		b→k	k→y
Relation composition	(false	∧ true)	∨	(true	∧ true)
Counting paths	(0	× 1)	+	(2	× 3)
Shortest path	(∞	+ 1)	↓	(2	+ 3)
Routes	(∅	· {y})	∪	({dk,ek}	· {y})

Table 16.2: Combining edge labels.

The commonality in the algebraic structure is evident when we summarise the rules for combining edges and combining paths in the four cases. This is done in Table 16.3. The first column shows how the labels on two connecting edges are combined. The second column shows how the labels on two paths connecting the same nodes are combined; the name given to the corresponding quantifier is included in brackets. The third column gives the zero of edge combination (i.e. the label given to a non-existing edge) and the fourth column is the formula for determining the (a, c)th element of the relevant product $G \times H$ of graphs G and H.

	Connecting paths	Choice of path	Zero	$a (G \times H) c$
Relation composition	$\wedge$	$\vee$ $(\exists)$	false	$\langle\ \exists b\ ::\ (a\,G\,b) \wedge (b\,H\,c)\ \rangle$
Standard product	$\times$	$+$ (Σ)	0	$\langle\ \Sigma b\ ::\ (a\,G\,b) \times (b\,H\,c)\ \rangle$
Min. dist. product	$+$	$\Downarrow$ $(\Downarrow)$	∞	$\langle\ \Downarrow b\ ::\ (a\,G\,b) + (b\,H\,c)\ \rangle$
Routes	$\cdot$	$\cup$ $(\bigcup)$	$\emptyset$	$\langle\ \bigcup b\ ::\ (a\,G\,b) \cdot (b\,H\,c)\ \rangle$

Table 16.3: Rules for combining edges and paths.

We recall from Section 12.5.6 that a semiring is a set on which are defined two binary operations $+$ and $\times$. The set includes two elements 0 and 1; the element 0 is the unit of $+$ and the zero of $\times$, the element 1 is the unit of $\times$. In general, if the edges of a bipartite graph G are labelled with the elements of a semiring S, and G has type $A \sim B$, then G is isomorphic to a function of type $A \times B \rightarrow S$. If bipartite graphs G and H are labelled with the elements of a semiring S, and G has type $A \sim B$ and H has type $B \sim C$ (for some A, B and C), the (S) *product* $G \times H$ is a bipartite graph of type $A \sim C$; writing a G b for the label given to the edge from a to b (which by definition is the element 0 in S if no edge exists), the labels of the edges of $G \times H$ are given by

$$[\ a\ (G \times H)\ c\ =\ \langle \Sigma b : b \in B : (a\,G\,b) \times (b\,H\,c) \rangle\ ]. \tag{16.33}$$

If G and H both have the same type (i.e. $A \sim B$ for some A and B), it makes sense to define $G+H$. It is a graph of type $A \sim B$; the definition of the edge labels is

$$[\ a\ (G+H)\ b\ =\ (a\,G\,b) + (a\,H\,b)\ ]. \tag{16.34}$$

Note the overloading of notation in these definitions. On the left side of equality is a new operator which is defined in terms of an existing operator on the right side with exactly the same name ("$\times$" in (16.33) and "$+$" in (16.34)). This takes some getting used to. Possibly harder to get used to is that the names stand for operators in some arbitrary semiring – in the case of shortest paths, "$\times$" stands for addition ("$+$") in normal arithmetic. That can indeed be confusing. The justification for the overloading is the fact that the algebraic properties of the new product and sum operators now look very familiar.

In formal terms, if the edges of a bipartite graph G are labelled with the elements of a semiring S, and G has type $A \sim B$, then G can be identified with a function of type

$A \times B \to \mathcal{S}$. Definitions (16.33) and (16.34) denote application of G to arguments a and b by a G b, and define operators $\times$ and $+$ of type

$$(A \times B \to \mathcal{S}) \times (B \times C \to \mathcal{S}) \quad \to \quad (A \times C \to \mathcal{S})$$

and

$$(A \times B \to \mathcal{S}) \times (A \times C \to \mathcal{S}) \quad \to \quad (A \times C \to \mathcal{S}),$$

respectively. The following theorem records the algebraic properties of these functions.

Theorem 16.35 Graph addition is associative and symmetric. Graph product is associative. Graph product distributes through graph addition. There are graphs **0** and **1** such that **0** is the unit of addition and the zero of product, and **1** is the unit of product.

Formally, suppose $\mathcal{S} = (S, 0, 1, +, \times)$ is a semiring. Then, if G and H are functions of type $A \times B \to \mathcal{S}$, for some A and B, and addition is defined by (16.34), then

$$[\ G+H \ = \ H+G\ ].$$

Also, if G, H and K are functions of type $A \times B \to \mathcal{S}$,

$$[\ (G+H)+K \ = \ G+(H+K)\ ].$$

Defining the function $0_{A \sim B}$ of type $A \times B \to \mathcal{S}$ by

$$[\ a\ 0_{A \sim B}\ b \ = \ 0\ ],$$

we have

$$[\ G+0_{A \sim B} \ = \ G\ ].$$

If G, H and K are functions of type $A \times B \to \mathcal{S}$, $B \times C \to \mathcal{S}$ and $C \times D \to \mathcal{S}$ (for some A, B, C and D) and product is defined by (16.33), then

$$[\ (G \times H) \times K \ = \ G \times (H \times K)\ ].$$

Also, if G is a function of type $A \times B \to \mathcal{S}$ and H and K are functions of type $B \times C \to \mathcal{S}$ (for some A, B and C) then

$$[\ G \times (H+K) \ = \ G \times H + H \times K\ ].$$

If G is a function of type $B \times C \to \mathcal{S}$ (for some B and C) and A is an arbitrary set,

$$[\ 0_{A \sim B} \times G \ = \ 0_{A \sim C}\ ].$$

Finally, defining the function $\mathbf{1}_A$ of type $A \times A \to \mathcal{S}$ by

$$\left[\ a\ \mathbf{1}_A\ a' \ =\ \text{if}\ a = a' \to 1 \ \square\ a \neq a' \to 0\ \text{fi}\ \right],$$

then, if G is function of type $A \times B \to \mathcal{S}$ (for some A and B),

$$\left[\ \mathbf{1}_A \times G\ =\ G\ =\ G \times \mathbf{1}_B\ \right].$$

16.5 MATRICES

Recall that a (bipartite) directed graph is a method of representing a heterogeneous relation of type $A \sim B$. When the types A and B are finite, a relation can also be represented by a boolean *matrix*. For example, the relation depicted in Figure 16.4 can be represented by the following matrix:

$$\begin{bmatrix} \text{true} & \text{false} \\ \text{false} & \text{true} \\ \text{true} & \text{true} \end{bmatrix}.$$

Whereas a bipartite directed graph has a type of the form $A \sim B$, a matrix has a *dimension* of the form $m \times n$ (pronounced "m by n") for some strictly positive integers m and n. The above matrix has dimension 3×2. Matrices are commonly denoted by bold capital letters, like **A** and **B**. It is also common to refer to the *rows* and *columns* of a matrix and to index them by numbers from 1 thru m and 1 thru n, respectively. The element of matrix **A** in row i and column j is often denoted by a_{ij}. Sometimes mathematicians write "let $\mathbf{A} = \left[a_{ij}\right]$" as a shorthand for introducing the name of a matrix and a means of denoting its elements. Formally, a matrix of dimension $m \times n$ with entries in the set S is a function of type

$$\{i \mid 1 \leq i \leq m\} \times \{i \mid 1 \leq i \leq n\}\ \to\ \text{S}.$$

The matrix representation of finite directed graphs is sometimes exploited in computer software since a matrix corresponds to what is called a *two-dimensional array*. (In computer software, array indices commonly begin at 0 and not at 1 because this is known to be less error-prone.)

Labelled bipartite graphs can also be represented by matrices of an appropriate type, provided the graph has a finite number of nodes and a suitable representation can be found for non-existent edges.

The graphs in Figure 16.8 were used to illustrate two different problems. In Section 16.4.1, the labels represented a number of different edges and the problem was to count the number of paths from one node to another in the combined graph. In Section 16.4.3, the labels represented distances and the problem was to determine shortest distances. In both cases, the graphs can be represented as a matrix but the representation of non-existent edges is different.

In the case of counting paths, the left-hand labelled graph in Figure 16.8 is represented by the following matrix, where non-existent edges are represented by 0:

$$\begin{bmatrix} 1 & 0 \\ 0 & 2 \\ 5 & 2 \end{bmatrix}.$$

In the case of determinining shortest paths, the left-hand labelled graph in Figure 16.8 is represented by the following matrix, where non-existent edges are represented by ∞:

$$\begin{bmatrix} 1 & \infty \\ \infty & 2 \\ 5 & 2 \end{bmatrix}.$$

In general, the type of a labelled directed graph has the form $A \times B \to L$, where A and B are the two sets of nodes and L is the type of the labels. (This assumes that non-existent edges can be suitably represented by an element of L.) Corresponding to such a graph is a matrix of type

$$\{i \mid 1 \leq i \leq |A|\} \times \{j \mid 1 \leq j \leq |B|\} \to L.$$

In this way, two-dimensional matrices are graphs except for loss of information about the names of the nodes. Product and addition of matrices is the same as product and addition of graphs.

We conclude this section with an aside. In (engineering) mathematics, matrices are typically assumed to have elements that are real numbers. The standard definition of sum and product of matrices in mathematics corresponds to what we called the "standard" sum and product of graphs in Section 16.4.1. This is how matrix addition and multiplication might be introduced in a conventional mathematics text.

The sum of two $m \times n$ *matrices* **A** *and* **B** *is an* $m \times n$ *matrix:*

$$\mathbf{A} + \mathbf{B} = \begin{bmatrix} a_{ij} \end{bmatrix} + \begin{bmatrix} b_{ij} \end{bmatrix} = \begin{bmatrix} a_{ij} + b_{ij} \end{bmatrix}.$$

The product $\mathbf{C} = \mathbf{AB}$ *of the* $m \times n$ *matrix* **A** *and the* $n \times r$ *matrix* **B** *is an* $m \times r$ *matrix:*

$$c_{ij} = \sum_{k=1}^{n} a_{ik} b_{kj}.$$

Note that i and j are dummies in an implicit universal quantification. The range of i in both definitions is 1 thru m; the range of j in the definition of $\mathbf{A}+\mathbf{B}$ is 1 thru n and in the definition of $\mathbf{AB}$ is 1 thru r. Note also the overloading of "+" and the invisible product operator.

Matrices are used to formulate the solution of simultaneous equations (in standard arithmetic). The method that children learn is called *Gaussian elimination*. Gaussian elimination can, in fact, be formulated in terms of path-finding, but this goes beyond the scope of this text.

16.6 CLOSURE OPERATORS

Just as in Section 16.2 we progressed from heterogeneous relations to homogeneous relations, we now progress from labelled bipartite graphs to labelled graphs with a fixed set of nodes, A. As before, the parameter A is sometimes implicit.

The following theorem is just a special case of Theorem 16.35 (albeit a very important special case).

Theorem 16.36 (Graph Semirings) Suppose $\mathcal{S} = (S, 0, 1, +, \times)$ is a semiring and suppose A is an arbitrary set. Let 0 and 1 denote, respectively, the functions $0_{A \sim A}$ and 1_A defined in Theorem 16.35. Let the addition operator $+$ and the product operator $\times$ on elements of $A \times A \to \mathcal{S}$ be as defined in (16.34) and (16.33). Then, with these definitions, $(A \times A \to \mathcal{S}, 0, 1, +, \times)$ is a semiring.

We call $(A \times A \to \mathcal{S}, 0, 1, +, \times)$ the *semiring of graphs* (with node-set A).

Theorem 16.36 is fundamental to solving many search problems. The problem is modelled as evaluating the paths in a (finite) graph. The semiring $\mathcal{S}$ is used to evaluate paths by dictating how to combine the values of edges – their labels–when forming a path (the product operation of $\mathcal{S}$) and how to choose between paths (the sum operation of $\mathcal{S}$). The particular choice of $\mathcal{S}$ depends on the nature of the problem to be solved; this could be just showing the existence of a path, finding the length of a shortest path, finding the best path in terms of minimising bottlenecks, and so on.

If G and H are two labelled graphs (with the same node-set), the sum G+H evaluates a choice of edges from G or H. The product G×H evaluates paths of edge-count 2 consisting of an edge in G followed by an edge in H. Similarly, if K is also a graph with the same node-set, (G+H)×K evaluates paths of edge-count 2 consisting of first an edge chosen from the graph G or the graph H and followed by an edge in the graph K.

In this way, the product G×G gives a value to paths of edge-count 2 in the graph G, G×G×G gives a value to paths of edge-count 3. Defining G^0 to be 1, G^0 gives a value to paths of edge-count 0. In general, G^k evaluates paths in the graph G of edge-count k and $\langle \Sigma k : 0 \leq k < n : G^k \rangle$ evaluates a choice of all paths in the graph G of edge-count less than n.

Care needs to be taken when extending this argument to arbitrary edge-count. For example, if there is a cycle in a graph (a path of edge-count 1 or more from a node to itself), counting the number of paths – as we did in Section 16.4.1 – will increase without limit as n increases. Another example is when distances (see Section 16.4.3) can be negative: if there is a cycle of negative length on a node, the minimum distance between two nodes can decrease without limit as the maximum edge-count of paths is allowed to increase. The infinite summation $\langle \Sigma k : 0 \leq k : G^k \rangle$ is not always meaningful.

Whenever $\langle \Sigma k : 0 \leq k : G^k \rangle$ is meaningful, it is called the *reflexive transitive closure* of G and denoted by G^*. (Note that the semiring giving meaning to the addition and product operations in this expression is a parameter of the definition.) A semiring that admits the introduction of a reflexive transitive closure operator with certain properties is called a *regular algebra*. (An important example of such a semiring is the semiring of homogeneous relations on a fixed set with addition and product being defined to be set union and relation composition, respectively.) Regular algebra is a fundamental topic in the computing science curriculum, but beyond the scope of this text.

16.7 ACYCLIC GRAPHS

A class of graphs for which the summation $\langle \Sigma k : 0 \leq k : G^k \rangle$ is always meaningful is the class of finite, acyclic graphs. Recall that a graph is acyclic if there are no cycles in the graph. This has the obvious consequence that, if the graph has a finite set of nodes, all paths have edge-count less than the number of nodes in the graph – because no node is repeated on a path. That is, G^* equals $\langle \Sigma k : 0 \leq k < n : G^k \rangle$, where n is the number of nodes in the graph.

One might wonder when acyclicity is relevant. After all, many of the problems discussed in earlier chapters clearly involve undirected graphs, and such graphs always contain cycles!

Of theoretical importance is that the reflexive transitive closure of the relation on nodes defined by an acyclic graph is a partial ordering relation. It is reflexive and transitive by definition. Acyclicity of the graph guarantees that the relation is anti-symmetric.

Acyclicity is relevant to the games discussed in Chapter 4. There we imposed the restriction that all games are guaranteed to terminate, irrespective of how the players choose their moves. In other words, we imposed the restriction that the graph of all moves starting from any initial position has no cycles.

For other problems, it is often interesting to know in how many different ways the problem can be solved. Figure 16.15 shows, on the left, an undirected graph where the problem is to find a path from the start to the finish node.

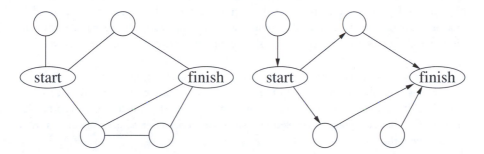

Figure 16.15: An undirected graph and the subgraph determining paths of minimal edge-count to the finish node.

If we ask the question how many paths there are, the answer is "infinitely many". A more sensible question is to ask how many paths there are that use a minimal number of edges. This question is answered by the acyclic, directed graph on the right of Figure 16.15. The reflexive transitive closure of this graph gives all the paths from each node to the finish node of minimal edge-count; the graph makes it clear that there are two paths from start to finish that have minimal edge-count. A very simple example of this sort of analysis is the discussion of the goat–cabbage–wolf problem in Section 3.2.1.

Given a graph G with a finite number of nodes and a designated finish node, it is easy to determine a subgraph of G that defines all paths to the finish node of minimal edge-count. Let the *distance* of a node to the finish node be the edge-count of any path of minimal edge-count from the node to the finish node. The distance of each node to the finish node can be determined by computing in turn the nodes at distance 0, the nodes at distance 1, the nodes at distance 2, etc. The computation starts from the finish node which is the only node at distance 0. The edges of the subgraph are all edges from a node at distance k+1 to a node at distance k, for some k. (The technique of exploring nodes in order of their edge-count distance from the start or finish node is often used in brute-force search.)

16.7.1 Topological Ordering

A common task is to "visit" all the nodes in a finite, acyclic graph collecting some information about the nodes along the way. For example, in a genealogy tree we might want to determine the number of male and/or female descendants of every person recorded in the tree. More formally, suppose that a is a node of the graph, and there are edges e,...,f from a to nodes u,...,v; suppose also that the nodes u,...,v have been assigned values m,...,n, and we want to assign to a a value g(e,...,f,m,...,n) for some function g, which may be different for different nodes. In order to do so, the nodes must be visited in a so-called *topological order*. In the case of determining the number of male descendants in a genealogy tree, each such function g returns a number. For people with no children the function g (of no arguments) is the constant 0. For each person with children, the function g adds together the number of male children and the number of male descendants of each child. A topological search begins with the people with no children and then ascends the tree level-by-level until the entire tree has been visited.

In general, a *topological ordering* of the nodes in an acyclic graph is a linear ordering of the nodes that places node a after node b if there is a non-empty path from a to b in the graph. Formally, we are given a relation R on a finite set N such that R^* is a partial ordering relation. A topological ordering assigns a number ord.a to each element a in N in such a way that

$$\langle \forall a,b \: : \: a{\in}N \wedge b{\in}N \: : \: a \: R^+ \: b \Rightarrow ord.a > ord.b \rangle .$$

(Think of R as the relation on nodes defined by the existence of an edge and R^+ as the relation corresponding to the existence of paths.)

The following algorithm effects a topological search. The algorithm uses a set V to record the elements of N (the nodes) that have been ordered ("visited") and a set NV to record the elements of N that have not been ordered ("not visited"). The number k is initially 0 and is incremented each time a node is ordered.

{ R^* is a partial ordering on the finite set N }

V,NV,k := ∅,N,0 ;

{ **Invariant:**

    V∪NV = N

∧ $\langle \forall a,b \: : \: a{\in}V \wedge b{\in}V \: : \: a \: R^+ \: b \Rightarrow ord.a > ord.b \rangle$

∧ $\langle \forall b \: : \: b{\in}V \: : \: k > ord.b \rangle$

∧ $\langle \forall a,b \: : \: a{\in}V \wedge a \: R \: b \: : \: b{\in}V \rangle$

Measure of progress: |NV| }

do NV ≠ ∅ →   choose a∈NV such that $\langle \forall b \: : \: a \: R \: b \: : \: b{\in}V \rangle$;

                  ord.a , k := k , k+1 ;

                  remove a from NV and add it to V

od

{ V = N ∧ $\langle \forall a,b \: : \: a{\in}N \wedge b{\in}N \: : \: a \: R^+ \: b \Rightarrow ord.a > ord.b \rangle$ }.

The invariant of the algorithm expresses the fact that, at each stage, the subrelation obtained by restricting the domain of R to V has been linearised,

$$\langle \forall a, b \; : \; a{\in}V \wedge b{\in}V \; : \; a \, R^{+} \, b \Rightarrow ord.a > ord.b \rangle ,$$

each element of V having been assigned an order that is less than k,

$$\langle \forall b \; : \; b{\in}V \; : \; k > ord.b \rangle .$$

Also, the set of visited nodes V is "closed" under the relation R:

$$\langle \forall a, b \; : \; a{\in}V \wedge a \, R \, b \; : \; b{\in}V \rangle .$$

At each iteration, an unvisited node a is chosen such that the only edges from a are to nodes that are already visited:

$$\langle \forall b \; : \; a \, R \, b \; : \; b{\in}V \rangle .$$

(For nodes with no outgoing edges, the universal quantification is vacuously true; the first iteration will choose such a node.) The precondition that R^{*} is a partial ordering on N is needed to guarantee that such a choice can always be made. If not, the subset NV is not partially ordered by R^{*}. The chosen node is "visited" by assigning it the number k. The sets V and NV and the number k are updated accordingly. The measure of progress gives a guarantee that the algorithm will always terminate: at each iteration the size of the set NV is reduced by 1; the number of iterations is thus bounded by its initial size, which is |N| which is assumed to be finite.

In practice, the linearisation is not the primary purpose and is left implicit. For example, a topological search might be used to count the number of minimal-edge-count paths to a given node. The count begins with the number 1 for the given node (since there is always one path from each node to itself) and then calculates the number of paths for the remaining nodes in topological order, but without explicitly ordering the nodes. If edges of the graph are labelled with distances, topological search is used to determine the shortest path from all nodes to a given node; the search begins at the given node, which is at distance 0 from itself, and then computes the distance of each of the other nodes from the given node in topological order. In this context, the technique is called *dynamic programming*.

16.8 COMBINATORICS

Combinatorics is about determining the number of "combinations" of things in a way that does not involve counting one by one. For example, if a person has three pairs of shoes, two coats and five hats, we might want to know how many different ways these items of clothing can be combined – without listing all the different possibilities.

16.8.1 Basic Laws

Some basic results of combinatorics were mentioned in Chapter 12: the number of elements in the set A+B (the disjoint sum of A and B) is |A|+|B|, the number of elements in A×B (the cartesian product of A and B) is |A|×|B| and the number of elements in A^B (the set of functions from B to A) is $|A|^{|B|}$.

As an example of the use of the first two of these rules, let us point the way to tackling the nervous-couples project (Exercise 3.3). We show how to calculate formally the number of valid states. Refer back to Section 3.3 for the full statement of the problem and the definition of a state.

First we note that a state is completely characterised by the position of the boat and the positions of the presidents and bodyguards. A state is therefore an element of the cartesian product

BoatPosition × PBconfigurations

where BoatPosition is the two-element set {left,right} and PBconfigurations is a set describing the possible configurations of the presidents and bodyguards on the two banks. The number of valid states is therefore

2 × |PBconfigurations|.

(Note that we are counting valid states and not reachable states. For example, a state where the boat is on one bank and all couples are on the other bank is valid, but not reachable.)

The next step is to note that a configuration of the presidents and bodyguards is characterised by the number of presidents and the number of bodyguards on the left bank. (This is because the number of presidents/bodyguards on the left and right banks adds up to N.) Let us use lP and lB to denote these two quantities. Now, a pair (lP, lB) describes a valid configuration exactly when

$$lB=0 \ \lor \ lB=N \ \lor \ lB=lP. \tag{16.37}$$

(Take care: this is the most error-prone step of the analysis because it is the step when we go from the informal to the formal. We have to formulate precisely the constraint that a president may not be on the same bank as a bodyguard unless their own bodyguard is also present. We also have to formulate precisely what it is we are counting. It is often the case that informal problem descriptions are unclear; the purpose of formalisation is to add clarity. Make sure you agree that (16.37) does indeed characterise the valid configurations.)

From (16.37), we conclude that the number of valid president–bodyguard configurations is

$$| \{ lB, lP : 0 \le lB \le N \land 0 \le lP \le N$$
$$\land (lB=0 \lor lB=N \lor lB=lP) : (lB,lP) \} |. \tag{16.38}$$

In order to simplify this expression, we aim to express the set of president–bodyguard configurations as a disjoint sum. This is done by first rewriting (16.37) as

$$lB=0 \lor lB=N \lor 0 < lB = lP < N.$$

This splits the set of president–bodyguard configurations into three disjoint sets (assuming $N \ne 0$), namely the configurations satisfying $lB=0$, the configurations satisfying $lB=N$ and the configurations satisfying $0 < lB = lP < N$. The number of such configurations is, respectively, $N+1$, $N+1$ and $N-1$.

Combining the number of president–bodyguard configurations with the two positions of the boat, we conclude that the number of valid states is

$$2 \times ((N+1) + (N+1) + (N-1)).$$

That is, there are $6N+2$ valid states. (In the three-couple problem there are thus 20 valid states and in the five-couple problem there are 32 valid states.)

16.8.2 Counting Choices

A typical problem that is not covered by the laws for disjoint sum, cartesian product and function spaces is in how many ways m indistinguishable balls can be coloured using n different colours. Although the problem involves defining a function from balls to colours, it is complicated by the fact that balls are indistinguishable.

Fundamental to such problems is the notion of a "permutation" of a set. A *permutation* of a set A is a total ordering of the elements of A. If A is finite, a permutation of A is specified by saying which element is first, which element is second, which is third, and so on to the last. If A has n elements, there are n ways of choosing the first element. This then leaves $n-1$ elements from which to choose the second element. Thus there are $n \times (n-1)$ ways of choosing the first and second elements. Then there are $n-2$ elements from which to choose the third element, giving $n \times (n-1) \times (n-2)$ ways of choosing the first, second and third elements. And so it goes on until there is just one way of choosing the nth element. We conclude that there are $\langle \Pi k : 0 \le k < n : n-k \rangle$ different permutations of a set of size n. This number is called n "factorial" and denoted by n!. Although the notation is not standard, by analogy with the notations for disjoint sum and cartesian product, we use the notation A! for the set of permutations of A. This allows us to formulate the rule

$$[\quad |A!| \;=\; |A|! \quad].$$

Note that the empty set has 0 elements and $\langle \Pi k : 0 \leq k < 0 : 0-k \rangle$ equals 1. So

$$|\varnothing!| \;=\; 0! \;=\; 1.$$

In general there are

$$\langle \Pi k : 0 \leq k < m : n-k \rangle$$

ways of choosing in order m elements from a set of n elements. This formula is sometimes denoted by $P(n,m)$. Noting that $(n-m)!$ is $\langle \Pi k : m \leq k < n : n-k \rangle$, it is easy to derive the following definition of $P(n,m)$:

$$\left[\quad P(n,m) = \frac{n!}{(n-m)!} \quad \right] \tag{16.39}$$

Now we turn to the problem of determining in how many ways it is possible to choose a subset with m elements from a set of n elements, which we denote (temporarily) by $C(n,m)$. So, for example, if there are six differently coloured balls, in how many ways can we choose four of them? That is, what is the value of $C(6,4)$?

The solution is to consider an algorithm to choose *in order* m elements from a set of n elements. The algorithm has two phases. First we choose a subset with m elements from the set of n elements. This can be done in $C(n,m)$ ways. Next we choose a particular ordering of the m elements in the chosen subset. This can be done in m! ways. Combining the two phases, there are

$$C(n,m) \times m!$$

ways of choosing in order m elements from a set of n elements. But this is what we denoted above by $P(n,m)$. That is,

$$[\quad P(n,m) \;=\; C(n,m) \times m! \quad].$$

With some simple arithmetic combined with (16.39), we conclude that

$$\left[\quad C(n,m) \;=\; \frac{n!}{m! \times (n-m)!} \quad \right]. \tag{16.40}$$

We said above that we would use the notation $C(n,m)$ only temporarily. The reason is that the quantity is considered so important that it deserves a special notation. The notation that is used is $\binom{n}{m}$ and it is called a *binomial coefficient*.[3] The definition (16.40) thus becomes:

$$\text{[Binomial Coefficient]} \qquad \left[\quad \binom{n}{m} = \frac{n!}{m! \times (n-m)!} \quad \right]. \qquad (16.41)$$

As an example, the number of ways of choosing 4 colours from 6 is $\binom{6}{4}$ which equals $\frac{6!}{4! \times 2!}$. This simplifies to $\frac{6 \times 5}{2 \times 1}$ (i.e. 15). Note that

$$\left[\quad \binom{n}{m} = \binom{n}{n-m} \quad \right].$$

The number of ways of choosing a subset of size m is the same as the number of ways of choosing a subset of size n−m. In particular, the number of ways of choosing a subset of size 0 is 1, which is the same as the number of ways of choosing a subset of size n. (A subset of size n is the whole set.) The formula (16.41) remains valid when m equals n or m equals 0 because 0! is defined to be 1. Another special case is that of choosing 1 element from a set of n elements. Formula (16.41) predicts that $\binom{n}{1}$ is n, as expected.

16.8.3 Counting Paths

Many combinatorial problems are solved by so-called *recurrence relations* and, as we have seen in this chapter, relations can be represented by graphs. Combinatorial problems are thus often solved by a process that is equivalent to counting paths in a graph. Some problems have a lot of structure – they involve "recurring" patterns, which enables their solution to be formulated as compact mathematical formulae. Many problems, however, have only limited structural properties. They can still be solved by counting paths in a graph, but their solution cannot be given in the form of a compact mathematical formula; instead their solution involves the use of an efficient algorithm. This section is about two examples, one much more structured than the other.

Recall the ball-colouring problem mentioned above: in how many ways can m indistinguishable balls be coloured using n colours. Suppose the colours are given numbers 1, 2, ..., n. A colouring of the balls defines a function no. such that no.c is the number of balls with colour c. (So no.1 is the number of balls with colour 1, no.2 is the number of balls with colour 2, and so on.) All balls have to be coloured, so it is required that

$$\text{no.1} + \text{no.2} + \ldots + \text{no.m} = \text{n}.$$

---

[3] The name comes from the expansion of the "binomial" $(x+y)^n$ as a sum of products:

$$\left[\quad (x+y)^n = \left\langle \Sigma m : 0 \leq m \leq n : \binom{n}{m} \times x^m \times y^{n-m} \right\rangle \quad \right].$$

The "coefficient" of $x^m \times y^{n-m}$ is thus $\binom{n}{m}$.

The problem is to determine the number of functions no. that have this property. In words, it is the number of different ways of partitioning the number n into m numbers.

One way to solve the problem is to imagine an algorithm to perform the partitioning. Suppose we place all the balls in a line, which we represent by a sequence of bs. For example, if there are seven balls we begin with the sequence

   b b b b b b b.

Now suppose there are three colours. We choose how to colour the balls by inserting vertical lines, representing a partitioning of the balls. For example, the sequence

   b | b b | b b b b

assigns one ball the first colour, two balls the second colour and four balls the third colour. The sequence

   | b b b b b b b |

assigns all balls the second colour and none the first or third colour.

If there are m balls and n colours, the sequence has length m+n−1. It is formed by choosing m positions to place a b, the remaining positions then being filled with the partitioning symbol "|". In this way, we conclude that the total number of colourings is

$$\binom{m+n-1}{m}.$$

A way of visualising the above algorithm is by means of a graph. Figure 16.16 shows the graph for the case where there are five balls and three colours. The arrangement of the balls in a line is shown by the numbers above the graph and the colours are shown by the numbers at the side of the graph. The nodes in the graph are the points where two lines meet. Starting from the top-left corner and traversing a path to the bottom-right corner represents the process of constructing a sequence of bs and partition symbols, symbol by symbol. Horizontal moves correspond to adding a b to the sequence, and vertical moves to adding a partition symbol. At the top-left corner, the position labelled $(5, 3)$, nothing has been done; at the bottom-right corner, the position labelled, $(0, 1)$, the balls have been completely partitioned. At an intermediate node, a position labelled (i, j), the balls to the left of the node have been assigned colours and those to the right have not; i is the number of balls remaining to be coloured and j is the number of colours that are to be used. Choosing to move horizontally from position (i, j) to position $(i-1, j)$ represents adding a b to the sequence, that is, choosing to colour another ball with colour j. Choosing to move vertically from position (i, j) to position $(i, j-1)$ represents choosing

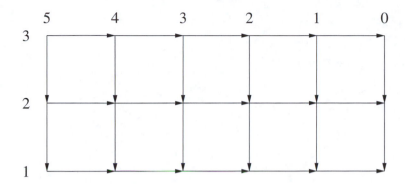

Figure 16.16: Counting ball colourings.

not to give any more balls the colour j. The number of colourings is the number of paths from the top-left node to the bottom-right node.

The number of paths from the top-left to the bottom-right node in an $(m+1) \times (n+1)$ acyclic, rectangular grid is $\binom{m+n}{n}$ (or equally $\binom{m+n}{m}$). This is because each path has edge-count $m+n$ of which m are horizontal edges and n are vertical edges.

Now, from the top-left node of such a graph, each path begins with either a horizontal edge or a vertical edge. This divides the paths into a disjoint sum of paths. Moreover, a path that begins with a horizontal edge is followed by a path from the top-left to the bottom-right node in an $((m-1)+1) \times (n+1)$ rectangular grid; similarly, a path that begins with a vertical edge is followed by a path from the top-left to the bottom-right node in an $(m+1) \times ((n-1)+1)$ rectangular grid. We thus conclude that

$$\left[\quad \binom{m+n}{n} \;=\; \binom{m-1+n}{m-1} + \binom{m+n-1}{n-1} \quad \right]. \tag{16.42}$$

Property (16.42) is an example of what is called a *recurrence relation*. It is a relation between binomial coefficients defined by an equation in which the coefficients "recur" on both the left and right sides. This particular property is called the *addition formula* for binomial coefficients.

The graph in Figure 16.16 has a very regular rectangular-grid structure. Other combinatorial problems are not so well structured but can still be expressed as counting the number of paths in an acyclic graph. For such problems the use of topological search (or a similar algorithm) to compute the number of paths is unavoidable. Let us illustrate this by returning, for the last time, to the nervous-couples problem first introduced in Section 3.1.

Figure 16.17 shows the state-transition diagram for getting three couples across the river. Of the 20 valid states, it shows just the 16 that can be reached from the starting position

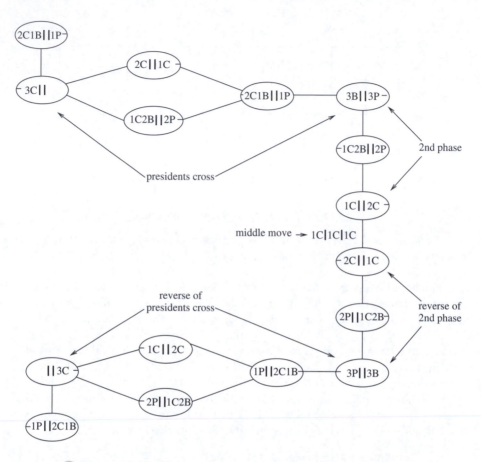

○ **Figure 16.17: Three nervous couples: state-transition diagram.**

of three couples on the left bank. (Four states not shown are valid, but no move is possible to or from each of them.) The notation introduced in Section 3.3.3 is used for indicating the positions of the presidents and their bodyguards; this is supplemented by a short horizontal line to indicate the position of the boat.

The structure of Figure 16.17 reflects the decomposition of the problem discussed in Section 3.3.4. The set of solutions is symmetric about a middle move in which one couple crosses from right to left. Preparatory to this middle move, the presidents first cross and then two additional moves are needed to get to a position where the middle move can be executed. These two additional moves are called the "2nd phase" in Figure 16.17. Following the middle move, the presidents' and 2nd-phase moves are reversed.

It is clear from Figure 16.17 that, if the individual presidents and/or bodyguards are not distinguished, there are just four different ways of getting everyone across with the minimum number of crossings. However, let us suppose we distinguish them all by giving each person a name. How many different ways of getting them across are there now?

It is not necessary and, indeed, it is impractical to redraw the state diagram. It suffices to label each edge with a number that gives the number of different crossings of each type. (Refer back to Section 16.4.1 for further explanation.) In addition we exploit the symmetric structure of the graph.

Figure 16.18 shows three of the five component parts of the state diagram relevant to getting the couples across the river in a minimum number of crossings: getting the presidents across the river, the 2nd phase and the middle crossing. (Symmetry allows us to omit the remaining two component parts.) Arrowheads have been added to show the direction in which the state change occurs. More importantly, the label on each edge gives the number of crossings of that type. For example, there is a label of 3 on the edge from the state 3C || to the state 1C,2B || 2P because there are $\binom{3}{2}$ ways (i.e. 3 ways) of choosing 2 (named) presidents to cross the river. Similarly, the middle crossing has the label 2 because there are 2 ways of choosing a couple from 2 couples to make the crossing.

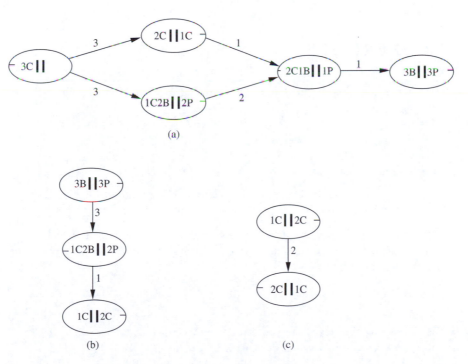

Figure 16.18: Counting crossings: (a) presidents cross; (b) 2nd phase; (c) middle crossing.

We can now use a simple topological search to evaluate the number of paths from start to finish in each of the component graphs. In the 2nd phase, there are 3×1 (i.e. 3) different paths and there are $(3 \times 2 + 3 \times 1) \times 1$ (i.e. 9) paths that get the presidents across. The final step is to combine all the components. The number of ways of getting all the couples across the river when each individual is named is

$9 \times 3 \times 2 \times 3 \times 9.$

That is, there are an astonishing 1458 ways of getting them across!

This example is very suitable for concluding this text because it illustrates a potential pitfall of poor problem-solving technique, namely an unnecessary explosion in the size of the space in which solutions are sought. A crucial first step in algorithmic problem solving is to clearly identify what is relevant and what is not relevant. This is reflected in how the problem is represented formally. Choosing the wrong representation can turn a relatively simple problem into one that is impossible to solve in practice. Even in the cases where a simple problem remains tractable, solutions should be carefully reviewed in order to eliminate unnecessary complexity.

16.9 EXERCISES

1. Draw the graphs corresponding to the following relations. Assume that each has type $\{a,b,c,d\} \times \{u,v,w\}$.
   (a) $\{(a, u), (b, v), (c, w)\}$
   (b) $\{(a, u), (a, v), (a, w), (b, v), (c, w)\}$
   (c) The universal relation.
   (d) The empty relation.

2. Figure 16.19 depicts a homogeneous relation. Let us call the relation R. Construct the first four powers of R (i.e. R^0, R^1, R^2, R^3).

   Suppose you are asked to calculate $\left\langle \bigcup k : 0 \leq k < n : R^k \right\rangle$ for successive values of n (starting from $n = 0$). At some stage, the value does not change. That is, for some value of n,

   $$\left\langle \bigcup k : 0 \leq k < n : R^k \right\rangle = \left\langle \bigcup k : 0 \leq k < n+1 : R^k \right\rangle.$$

   By inspecting the graph, can you determine the smallest number n for which this is the case without actually calculating the value of $\left\langle \bigcup k : 0 \leq k < n : R^k \right\rangle$?

3. Suppose the rightmost node in the graph shown in Figure 16.19 is called the finish node. Construct a graph that depicts all minimal-edge-count paths from

nodes in the graph to the finish node. Do so by identifying which nodes are at (edge-count) distance 0, 1, 2, etc. from the finish node and including those edges in the given graph that are from a node at distance k+1 to a node at distance k for some k.

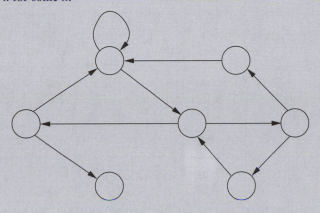

Figure 16.19: A homogeneous relation.

4. A labelled acyclic graph is depicted in Figure 16.20. In the graph, one node has no incoming edges and one node has no outgoing edges. Call these the *start* and *finish* nodes, respectively.

   (a) Suppose the edge labels count the number of edges between a pair of nodes. Use topological search to determine how many different paths there are from the start to the finish node.

   (b) Suppose the edge labels represent distances. Use topological search to determine the length of a shortest path from the start to the finish node.

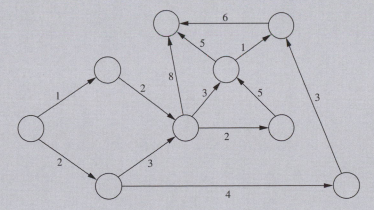

Figure 16.20: An acyclic graph.

5. Consider the graph in Figure 16.20 again. Suppose the edges now represent low bridges, the edge label being the height of the bridge. It is required to drive a load from the start node to the finish node that maximises the height of the lowest bridge on the path. Identify the appropriate product and sum operations on paths and calculate the best path according to this criterion.

6. Consider the graph in Figure 16.20 yet again. Suppose the edges of the graph represent tasks. A node connecting two edges means that one task must be completed before the next task can be begun. (For example, when building a house a task might be to lay the foundations. This task must be completed before the walls can be built.) The label on an edge represents the estimated time to complete the task.

   Suppose the problem is to determine the shortest time to complete all tasks from start to finish, assuming that as many tasks as possible are done simultaneously. For the graph shown in Figure 16.20, calculate the shortest time.

   Hint: formulate the problem as a path-finding problem. Formulate how two connecting paths should be combined (the product operation) and how a choice is made between two paths between the same pair of nodes.

   (In operations research, a graph that represents orderings between tasks and the time to complete each task is called a *Gantt chart*.)

7. The topological search algorithm in Section 16.7.1 assumes that R^* is a partial ordering. How would you modify the algorithm so that it tests whether or not R^* is a partial ordering?

Solutions to Exercises

Solution 2.1 1233 games must be played. Let k be the number of players who have been knocked out, and let g be the number of games that have been played. Initially, k and g are both equal to 0. Every time a game is played, one more player is knocked out. So, k and g are always equal. To decide the tournament, 1234−1 players must be knocked out. Hence, this number of games must be played.

In general, if there are p players, the tournament consists of p−1 games.

Solution 2.4 Introducing variables b and e as before, filling boxes is modelled by the assignment

$$b,e := b+k, e+k-1.$$

The value of $(k-1)\times b - k \times e$ is invariant. Its initial value is $-m$. So, when the process of filling boxes is complete,

$$(k-1)\times b - k \times n = -m. \tag{S.1}$$

Assuming $k \neq 1$ and simplifying, we get that $b = n + \frac{n-m}{k-1}$. For the problem to be well formulated, we require this to be a natural number. That is, we require that n is at least m, k is at least 2 and n−m is a multiple of k−1.

When k is 1, (S.1) simplifies to n=m. That is, the number of empty boxes remains the same. However, the number of boxes cannot be determined.

Solution 2.5 The ball problem is modelled by the choice

$$b,w := b+1,w-2 \quad \square \quad b,w := (b-2)+1,w \quad \square \quad b,w := b-1,w.$$

In order, the assignments model what happens when two white balls, two black balls and two differently coloured balls are taken out of the urn. Clearly, w either remains unchanged or is decreased by 2. Its parity is thus invariant. That is, the colour of the last ball in the urn is white exactly when the number of white balls in the urn is odd.

For the chessboard problem, let b and w be the number of covered black and white squares, respectively. Placing a domino on the board is modelled by the assignment

$$b,w := b+1,w+1.$$

The difference $b-w$ is invariant. Initially it is 0 (since b and w are both 0) and so it remains 0 no matter how many dominoes are placed on the board. But to cover the board completely it must have final value -2 (because the mutilated board has 2 fewer black squares than white squares). This is impossible.

Solution 2.6   f should be symmetric.

Solution 2.7

(a) $m \bmod 3$ is invariant.

(b) $m \bmod (j \gcd k)$ is invariant. We have:

$$(m \bmod (j \gcd k))[m := m+j]$$

$$= \qquad \{ \qquad \text{substitution} \quad \}$$

$$(m+j) \bmod (j \gcd k)$$

$$= \qquad \{ \qquad \text{distributivity of mod through addition} \quad \}$$

$$(m + j \bmod (j \gcd k)) \bmod (j \gcd k)$$

$$= \qquad \{ \qquad j \text{ is a multiple of } j \gcd k, \text{ so } j \bmod (j \gcd k) = 0 \quad \}$$

$$m \bmod (j \gcd k).$$

Similarly, $m \bmod (j \gcd k)$ is an invariant of the assignment $m := m+k$.

(c) Yes, the answer is valid. For arbitrary j, $j \gcd 0 = j$. If k is zero, $m \bmod j$ is invariant, which is what (b) predicts. This is even the case when j is also zero because $m \bmod 0 = m$: if both j and k are zero, the statement is equivalent to skip and m is indeed invariant.

Another extreme case is when $j \gcd k$ equals 1 (that is, j and k are coprime). Since $m \bmod 1 = 0$ whatever the value of m, we deduce that 0 is an invariant of the choice. This is a case when looking for an invariant does not help.

Solution 2.8 $p \bmod 3$ is invariant. This is the only invariant that is dependent on just one of the variables. $n-2 \times m$ is an invariant of the first assignment and $3 \times n - p$ is an invariant of the second assignment. Neither of these is an invariant of the non-deterministic choice but, by combining them,

$$3 \times n - p - 6 \times m$$

is an invariant of the non-deterministic choice. Alternatively, we postulate that $A \times m + B \times n + C \times p$ is an invariant and calculate A, B and C as follows:

$$A \times m + B \times n + C \times p \text{ is an invariant}$$

$$= \quad \{ \quad \text{definition of an invariant, substitution} \quad \}$$

$$A \times m + B \times n + C \times p \;=\; A \times (m+1) + B \times (n+2) + C \times p$$

$$\wedge \;\; A \times m + B \times n + C \times p \;=\; A \times m + B \times (n+1) + C \times (p+3)$$

$$= \quad \{ \quad \text{cancellation} \quad \}$$

$$0 = A + B \times 2 \;\wedge\; 0 = B + C \times 3$$

$$= \quad \{ \quad \text{substitution} \quad \}$$

$$A = C \times 6 \;\wedge\; B = -(C \times 3).$$

Solution 2.9

(a) The only linear combination that is invariant is the constant 0.

(b) Here is how to construct a suitable linear combination of b, d and l:

$$A \times b + B \times d + C \times l \text{ is an invariant}$$

$$= \quad \{ \quad \text{definition of an invariant, substitution} \quad \}$$

$$A \times b + B \times d + C \times l \;=\; A \times (b+3) + B \times (d+1) + C \times l$$

$$\wedge \;\; A \times b + B \times d + C \times l \;=\; A \times (b+1) + B \times d + C \times (l+1)$$

$$= \quad \{ \quad \text{cancellation} \quad \}$$

$$0 = A \times 3 + B \;\wedge\; 0 = A + C$$

$$= \quad \{ \quad \text{substitution} \quad \}$$

$$B = -(A \times 3) \;\wedge\; C = -A$$

$$\Leftarrow \quad \{ \quad \text{substitution} \quad \}$$

$$A = 1 \;\wedge\; B = -3 \;\wedge\; C = -1.$$

The invariant $b + 8 \times l - 3 \times w$ is constructed in the same way.

(c) We obtain two equations in the four unknown coefficients. There are lots of solutions of these equations, including the four determined in (b).

Solution 3.1

{ 5C || }

2C,3B |3P| ; 2C,3B |1P| 2P ; 5B |3P| 2P

;   { 5B || 5P }

5B |2P| 3P ; 2C |3B| 3P

;   { 2C || 3C }

2C |1C| 2C

;   { 3C || 2C }

3P |3B| 2C ; 3P |2P| 5B

;   { 5P || 5B }

2P |3P| 5B ; 2P |1P| 2C,3B ; |3P| 2C,3B

{ || 5C }.

Solution 3.2   We modify the solution to the five-couple problem, effectively by leaving one couple behind on the left bank. We get:

{ 4C || }

1C,3B |3P| ; 1C,3B |1P| 2P ; 4B |2P| 2P

;   { 4B || 4P }

4B |2P| 2P ; 2C |2B| 2P

;   { 2C || 2C }

2C |1C| 1C

;   { 3C || 1C }

3P |3B| 1C ; 3P |1P| 4B

;   { 4P || 4B }

2P |2P| 4B ; 2P |1P| 1C,3B ; |3P| 1C,3B

{ || 4C }.

By reversing left and right, we get the second solution:

{ 4C || }

1C,3B |3P| ; 1C,3B |1P| 2P ; 4B |2P| 2P

; { 4B || 4P }

4B |1P| 3P ; 1C |3B| 3P

; { 1C || 3C }

1C |1C| 2C

; { 2C || 2C }

2P |2B| 2C ; 2P |2P| 4B

; { 4P || 4B }

2P |2P| 4B ; 2P |1P| 1C,3B ; |3P| 1C,3B

{ || 4C }.

Solution 3.4 We exploit left–right symmetry (moving a coin six places to the right is the same as moving a coin six places to the left). We also decompose the problem into first ensuring that there is a coin in the square six places to the right of the starting position (symmetrically, there is a coin in the square six places to the left of the finishing position).

Achieving this first stage is easy. Below we show how it is done. First, six moves are needed to ensure that a coin is added six places to the right of the starting position. (This is shown below using dots to indicate coins on a square. A blank indicates no coin on the square.)

Symmetrically, working from bottom to top, six moves are needed to ensure that a coin is added six places to the left of the finishing position.

Now the goal is to connect these two intermediate states (the bottom state in the top diagram and the top state in the bottom diagram). An appropriate (symmetrical) sequence of states is as follows. (For the reader's convenience, the last and first states in the above figures are repeated as the top and bottom states in the figure below.)

The moves to the first and last rows make the number of coins in the leftmost and rightmost positions equal. Then a small amount of creativity is needed to identify the (symmetrical) moves to the (symmetrical) middle position.

Solution 3.5

```
    1
1   1   1
1   2   1   1
1   2   2   1   1
1   2   2   2   1   1
1   2   2   2   2   1   1
1   1   2   1   2   1   1
1   1   2   2   2   2   1
    1   1   2   2   2   1
        1   1   2   2   1
            1   1   2   1
                1   1   1
                    1
```

(Other solutions exploiting the hint are possible. Non-symmetric solutions are also possible.)

Solution 3.6 It is possible to displace the coin by three places. This is one way of doing it.

```
    1
1   2   1
1   3   2   1
1   3   3   2   1
1   3   3   3   2   1
1   2   2   2   2   1
1   2   3   3   3   1
    1   2   3   3   1
        1   2   3   1
            1   2   1
                1
```

Solution 3.13 Assuming t.1≤t.2≤t.3≤t.4, the minimum crossing time is

$$\text{t.1+t.2+t.4+(t.3+t.1)}\!\downarrow\!(2\times\text{t.2}).$$

For the problem as originally stated, the crossing time is 1+2+10+5↓4 (i.e. 17).

Choosing 1, 2, 2 and 2 minutes as the crossing times, the total time is 8 minutes if person 1 is the only one to return, and 9 minutes if persons 1 and 2 both return.

Solution 3.14 If all the people are individually named, there are

$$\binom{4}{2} \times \binom{2}{1} \times \binom{3}{2} \times \binom{3}{1} \times \binom{2}{2}$$

(i.e. 108) different ways of getting them across.

Solution 3.15 Using five crossings, the shortest time is 8 minutes. (The three slowest cross together.) The shortest time using three crossings is 9 minutes. (It is not possible for the three slowest to cross together if just three crossings are used.)

See Lemma 10.1 in Chapter 10 for a solution to the second part of this exercise.

Solution 3.16 There are three types of square distinguished by touching: the middle square, the four corner squares and the remaining squares, which we call the edge squares. The middle square touches all other squares. The four corner squares each touch the middle square and two other edge squares. The edge squares each touch the middle square, one corner square and two edge squares.

Because the middle square touches all other squares, one of the four colours must be reserved for this square. Because each edge square touches two other edge squares, it is not possible to use the same colour for all the edge squares; two or three colours must be used. Having chosen the colour of the middle square and the edge squares, there is no choice as to how to colour the corner squares since each corner square touches the middle square and two edge squares all of which touch each other and so must be coloured differently. If two colours are used for the edge squares, there is only one way this can be done: each pair of opposite edge squares must be given the same colour. If three colours are used for the edge squares, there is also only one way this can be done: one pair of opposite edges must be given the same colour. There are thus only two ways to colour the board and all four colours must be used.

Solution 4.1

(a) Naming any day in December, other than 31st December, results in losing. This is forced by the opponent naming 30th November (i.e. the last day of November). Similarly, naming any day in November other than 30th November results in losing, because the opponent can then name 30th November. This is forced by the opponent naming 31st October. In general, the winning strategy is to name the last day of the month. The opponent is then forced to name the 1st of the next month. Whether the year is a leap year or not makes no difference.

(b) In December, the losing positions are the odd-numbered days and the winning positions are the even-numbered days. (Take care: the "losing positions" are the days that the *winning* player names. This is in line with the terminology of losing and winning positions.) That is, if the last-named day is an odd-numbered day, the player whose turn it is must name an even-numbered day and will eventually lose.

In particular, the player who names 1st December wins. Any day in November is thus a winning position. In October, like December, the odd-numbered days are losing positions, and any day in September is a winning position. Similarly, in August, the odd-numbered days are losing positions, and any day in July is a winning position.

The pattern changes in June, which has an even number of days. The player who names 1st July loses; consequently, any even-numbered day in June is a losing position. This means that every even-numbered day in May is a winning position; also, every even-numbered day in April is a winning position. This means that 31st March is a losing position. Since March has an odd number of days, the pattern we saw for December and November recurs. Every odd-numbered day in March is a losing position, and every day in February is a winning position. Finally, the odd-numbered days in January are losing positions.

We conclude that the second player is guaranteed to win. The strategy is to name the 1st day of the following month when the last-named day is in November, September, July or February. Otherwise, the strategy is to name the next day of the year.

Again, it does not matter if it is a leap year.

Solution 4.2 The first 11 positions are shown in the top three rows in Table S.1. The pattern repeats in the next 11 positions, shown in the bottom three rows.

Position	0	1	2	3	4	5	6	7	8	9	10
Type	L	L	W	W	L	W	W	W	L	W	W
Move			2	2		5	6	6		5	6

Position	11	12	13	14	15	16	17	18	19	20	21
Type	L	L	W	W	L	W	W	W	L	W	W
Move			2	2		5	6	6		5	6

Table S.1: Winning (W) and losing (L) positions for subtraction set $\{2, 5, 6\}$.

Solution 4.3 The squares that are not positions are the ones at the foot of a ladder or at the head of a snake. Positions that cannot be identified as winning or losing positions are attributable to cycles in the positions; a *cycle* is a sequence of moves that begins and ends at the same position. Labelling of winning and losing positions assumes that every game is guaranteed to terminate no matter how either player moves. If cycles occur this assumption is not valid.

When a game has cycles, the positions are characterised as losing positions, winning positions or stalemate positions. A losing position is one from which every move is to a winning position; a winning position is one from which there is a move to a losing position; and a stalemate position is one from which there is a move to a stalemate position and there are no moves to losing positions.

From a stalemate position the best strategy is to move to a stalemate position since, if there is an alternative of moving to a winning position, this is clearly the wrong thing to do. The opponent will then use the same strategy and the game will continue forever.

Table S.2 shows all positions and the winning move from winning positions. Position 4 is the only stalemate position. From this position, a move to square 6 has the effect of returning the counter to position 4. Any other move from 4 would be to a winning position.

Position	1	2	4	5	7	13	14	16	18	21	22	23	24	25
Type	W	W	S	W	W	L	W	W	L	W	W	W	W	L
Move to square	3	3	6	9	9		18	18		25	25	25	25	

Table S.2: **Snakes and ladders. Winning (W), losing (L) and stalemate (S) positions.**

Solution 4.5 Consider the simple sum game discussed in Section 4.4.1 where the number of matches in the left and right games is at most 1 and 2, respectively. The sum game has 2×3 positions. As we saw in Section 4.4.1, the position $(1, 2)$ is a winning position and the position $(1, 1)$ is a losing position. Also positions 1 and 2 are both winning positions in the individual games. So, if the operator $\oplus$ exists, we would have:

$$\text{true} = \text{winning}(1,2) = \text{winning}(1) \oplus \text{winning}(2) = \text{true} \oplus \text{true}$$

and

$$\text{false} = \text{winning}(1,1) = \text{winning}(1) \oplus \text{winning}(1) = \text{true} \oplus \text{true}.$$

That is, true=false. This is impossible.

If play begins from a position (l, r) satisfying $\text{losing}_G(l) \wedge \text{losing}_H(r)$, the perfect player's strategy is to maintain this property invariant. Starting from such a position, the opponent must either move in the left game, which has the effect of truthifying $\text{winning}_G(l) \wedge \text{losing}_H(r)$, or play in the right game, which has the effect of truthifying $\text{losing}_G(l) \wedge \text{winning}_H(r)$. By playing in the same game as the one chosen by the opponent, the winner can then truthify $\text{losing}_G(l) \wedge \text{losing}_H(r)$ once again.

Solution 4.6

(a) See Table S.3 for the mex numbers up to and including position 10. The mex numbers repeat from here on; that is, the mex number for position m is equal to the mex number for position m mod 11.

Position	0	1	2	3	4	5	6	7	8	9	10
Type	L	L	W	W	L	W	W	W	L	W	W
Mex number	0	0	1	1	0	2	1	3	0	2	1

Table S.3: The mex numbers for subtraction set $\{2, 5, 6\}$.

(b) In the left game, the mex number of position m is m mod 3. Together with the mex numbers for the right game given above, we can complete Table S.4. (Other answers can be given for the winning moves.)

Left game	Right game	"losing" or winning move
10	20	R14
20	20	losing
15	5	R0
6	9	R4
37	43	losing

Table S.4: Winning moves.

Solution 4.7

(a) The losing positions are positions $2^{i+1}-1$, where i is a natural number; all other positions are winning positions.

The proof is in two parts: we show that, for all i, every move from position $2^{i+1}-1$ is to a position n where $2^i-1<n<2^{i+1}-1$; also, from a position n where, for all i, $n\neq 2^{i+1}-1$ we show that we can choose i so that there is a move from n to position 2^i-1.

When i equals 0, $2^{i+1}-1$ equals 1. Position 1 is an end position and thus a losing position. When i is greater than 0, every move from position $2^{i+1}-1$ is to a position n where $n<2^{i+1}-1\leq 2\times n$. But

$$n < 2^{i+1} - 1 \leq 2 \times n$$

$=$ {   meaning of continued equalities   }

$$n < 2^{i+1} - 1 \;\land\; 2^{i+1} - 1 \leq 2 \times n$$

$=$ {   integer inequalities, symmetry of $\land$ }

$$2^{i+1} - 2 < 2 \times n \;\land\; n < 2^{i+1} - 1$$

$=$ {   monotonicity of $2\times$ }

$$2^i - 1 < n \;\land\; n < 2^{i+1} - 1$$

$=$ {   meaning of continued equalities   }

$$2^i - 1 < n < 2^{i+1} - 1.$$

This establishes the first part.

For the second part, suppose that, for all i, $n \neq 2^{i+1} - 1$. Let i be the largest number such that $2^i - 1 < n$. Then, by definition of i, $n \leq 2^{i+1} - 1$. That is, $2^i - 1 < n \leq 2^{i+1} - 1$. But then

there is a move from n to $2^i - 1$

$=$ {   definition of legal moves   }

$$2^i - 1 < n \leq 2 \times (2^i - 1)$$

$=$ {   arithmetic   }

$$2^i - 1 < n \leq 2^{i+1} - 2$$

$=$ {   integer inequalities   }

$$2^i - 1 < n < 2^{i+1} - 1$$

$=$ {   assumption: for all i, $n \neq 2^{i+1} - 1$ }

$$2^i - 1 < n \leq 2^{i+1} - 1$$

$=$ {   definition of i   }

true.

(b)   Position: 1
       Mex number: 0

       Position: 2 3
       Mex number: 1 0

       Position: 4 5 6 7
       Mex number: 2 1 3 0

Position: 8 9 10 11 12 13 14 15
Mex number: 4 2 5   1   6   3   7   0

In general, mex(2×n) equals n and mex(2×n+1) equals mex(n).

(c) See Table S.5.

No. of columns	No. of rows	"losing" or winning move
2	15	C1 (or R11)
4	11	C2 (or R9)
4	14	R9
13	6	losing
21	19	C19 (or R10)

○ Table S.5: Solution to rectangle game.

Solution 5.4

$$\neg true$$

$$=\qquad\{\qquad [\ \neg p \equiv p \equiv false\ ] \text{ with } p := true\ \}$$

$$true \equiv false$$

$$=\qquad\{\qquad [\ true \equiv p \equiv p\ ] \text{ with } p := false\ \}$$

$$false.$$

Solution 5.5

$$\neg\neg p$$

$$=\qquad\{\qquad [\ \neg p \equiv p \equiv false\ ] \text{ with } p := \neg p\ \}$$

$$\neg p \equiv false$$

$$=\qquad\{\qquad [\ \neg p \equiv p \equiv false\ ] \text{ with } p := p$$

$$\text{and symmetry of equivalence}\ \}$$

$$p.$$

Solution 5.7 Let col be the colour of the square, and n be the number of moves. A move is then

$$col,n := \neg col, n+1.$$

An invariant of this assignment is

$$col \equiv even.n.$$

An odd number of moves, 63, is needed, but the colour of the square does not change. So, in order to move the knight as required, a change has to be made to col≡even.n, which is impossible.

Solution 5.8 Suppose the number of couples is n. There are 2n people, including the host, who each shake hands with between 0 and 2n−2 people. If 2n−1 of them – everyone but the host – shake hands with a different number of people, there must be someone who shakes hands with k people for each k between 0 and 2n−2 (inclusive).

If n is 1, the only person other than the host is the host's partner. Since couples do not shake hands, both shake hands 0 times.

Now suppose that n is greater than 1. In this case, there are at least two people other than the host and the host's partner. Consider the two people who shake hands 0 and 2n−2 times. The person who shakes hands 2n−2 times does so with everyone except their partner (and themselves, of course). By the symmetry of the shake-hands relation, it is thus the case that everyone except that person's partner shakes hands with at least one person. It follows that the two people who shake hands 0 and 2n−2 times are husband and wife. Because neither is the host, it also follows that neither is the host's partner.

Now suppose we discount this couple. That is, we consider the party consisting of the other n−1 couples. The number of times each person shakes hands is then reduced by one. So, again, all but the host have shaken hands a distinct number of times.

Repeating this process, we eliminate all the couples one by one until the party has been reduced to just the host and the host's partner. Each time, the number of times the host and the host's partner shake hands is reduced by one. The host and the host's partner must therefore have both shaken hands n−1 times.

Solution 5.10

(a) false

(b) false

(c) false

(d) p

(e) false

(f) q ≢ r

(g) p

(h) true

Solution 5.11 The process of decryption after encryption computes $a \not\equiv (a \not\equiv b)$. But,

$$a \not\equiv (a \not\equiv b)$$

$=$ $\{$ $\not\equiv$ is associative $\}$

$$(a \not\equiv a) \not\equiv b$$

$=$ $\{$ $(a \not\equiv a \equiv \text{false})$ $\}$

$$\text{false} \not\equiv b$$

$=$ $\{$ definition of $\not\equiv$ $\}$

$$\text{false} \equiv \neg b$$

$=$ $\{$ definition of negation: (5.3) $\}$

    b.

Solution 5.12 Let Q be the question. Then, $Q \equiv A \equiv A \not\equiv B$, that is, $Q \equiv \neg B$. In words, ask A whether B is a knave.

Solution 6.1 It is required that any two lines intersect in a single point. If the lines are not straight and they intersect in a segment of a line, inverting the colours of one of the two regions does not guarantee that the colouring of adjacent regions at the boundary of the left and right regions is satisfactory. This is because, along the line segment, the colours of the adjacent regions are not the same before the inversion takes place, contrary to the assertion made above.

The solution remains valid provided every line cuts the surface in two. A line on a ball does this, whereas a line on a doughnut need not.

The number of colourings is always two no matter how many lines there are. This is clearly the case when there are no lines. When there are $n+1$ lines, choose any one of the lines. Cut the paper along the chosen line. Assume inductively that, for each half, there are exactly two colourings. Combining these gives four different ways of colouring the entire sheet of paper. However, two of these are unsatisfactory because the colours of regions adjacent at the chosen line must be different. This leaves exactly two ways of colouring the paper with $n+1$ lines.

Solution 6.2 The base case, $n=0$, is trivial. The triangle has size 1 and 0 buckets are needed to cover the remaining area.

For the induction step, split a triangle with side of length 2^{n+1} into four triangles each of the same size. The topmost triangle of one of these four triangles is covered; by induction, the remainder can be covered with buckets. The remaining three triangles (of size 2^n) have one common corner. Placing a bucket at the corner then leaves three triangles each of size 2^n with one corner covered; by induction, the remainder of the triangles can also be covered by buckets.

Solution 6.3   The base case can be extracted from Figure 6.5: look at the topmost triangle with side of length 3. For the induction step, a triangle with side of length $3(n+1)$ (where $1 \leq n$) is divided into n triangles each with side of length 3 and one triangle with side of length $3n$. This is illustrated for the case where n is 3 in Figure S.1. By induction, all of these triangles can be covered.

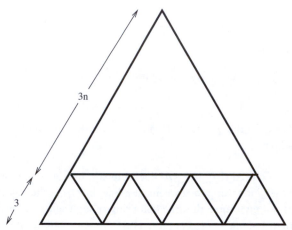

3n

3

Figure S.1: Trapezium problem: sketch of induction step.

Solution 7.1

(a) The base case is when n equals 0. Since $0 \leq m \leq (3^0 - 1)/2$ equivales $0 = m$, the algorithm is to do nothing – there are no coins and, hence, no fake coin.

For the induction step, assume the induction hypothesis. Assume the number of coins m is such that $0 \leq m \leq (3^{n+1} - 1)/2$. If $m \leq (3^n - 1)/2$, the induction hypothesis can be applied directly. So it suffices to consider the case where $(3^n - 1)/2 < m \leq (3^{n+1} - 1)/2$.

Put $(3^n - 1)/2$ coins aside. Place the remaining $m - (3^n - 1)/2$ coins on the balance, using the supplied genuine coin if necessary to make the number even. Note that the number of coins placed on the balance is at most 3^n (since $m \leq (3^{n+1} - 1)/2$ equivales $m - (3^n - 1)/2 \leq 3^n$).

If the balance tips to one side, mark all the coins on the balance either "possibly heavy" or "possibly light" and apply the solution to part (b). If not, apply the induction hypothesis to the $(3^n - 1)/2$ coins that were left aside. The total number of comparisons is then at most $1+n$ as required.

(b) The base case is when n equals 0. Since $1 \leq m \leq 3^0$ equivales $1 = m$, the algorithm is to do nothing – the coin is fake and its marking indicates whether it is lighter or heavier than a genuine coin.

For the induction step, assume the induction hypothesis. Assume the number of coins m is such that $1 \leq m \leq 3^{n+1}$. If $m \leq 3^n$, the induction hypothesis can be applied directly. So it suffices to consider the case where $3^n < m \leq 3^{n+1}$.

In order to be able to apply the induction hypothesis, it is necessary to divide the coins into three groups each of which has size at most 3^n; also, two of the groups – the coins to be placed on the left and right scales of the balance – must have equal size and contain equal numbers of possibly heavy coins. This can be done as described in Section 7.2.3 by placing coins on the scales two at a time, one on the left and one on the right, always choosing two coins with the same marking. The choice can always be made while there are at least three coins from which to choose; by choosing any three coins, at least two of them will have the same marking. The process of placing coins in this way is continued until each scale has its full complement of 3^n coins, or at most two coins remain.

Once this division process has been completed, there are at most 2×3^n coins on the balance and at most 3^n coins left aside. There are two possibilities that have to be considered. One possibility is that 0 coins have been placed on the balance; this is the case where m equals 2. In this case, one of the coins can be compared with the genuine coin; the outcome clearly determines which of the two coins is fake. The other possibility is that the number of coins on the balance is non-zero. If the balance tips to one side, the fake coin is among the coins whose marking is in agreement with the tip; by the way the coins were placed on the balance, this number is exactly half of the total number of coins on the balance. That is, there are at most 3^n of them and the induction hypothesis can be applied to these coins, giving a total of at most $1+n$ comparisons. If the balance does not tip to one side, the coins on the balance are all genuine and the induction hypothesis can be applied to the remaining coins (of which there are at most 3^n). In this way, the total number of comparisons is at most $1+n$ as required.

(c) The basis is when n equals 2 and m equals 3. It is straightforward to determine that 2 comparisons suffice to identify a fake coin (if any). The details are left to the reader. For the induction step, suppose $2 \leq n$ and the number of coins is m, where $3 \leq m < (3^{n+1}-1)/2$. As in parts (a) and (b), it suffices to consider the case where $(3^n-1)/2 \leq m < (3^{n+1}-1)/2$.

Consider two cases: $(3^n-1)/2$ equal to m and $(3^n-1)/2$ different from m. In the first case, compare any two coins. If the scales balance, both are genuine and the solution to part (a) can be applied to find the fake coin (if any) among the remaining $(3^n-1)/2-2$ coins. The total number of comparisons is at most $1+n$.

In the second case, $(3^n-1)/2 < m < (3^{n+1}-1)/2$. Depending on whether $m-(3^n-1)/2$ is even or odd, place $(3^n-1)/2$ or $(3^n-1)/2-1$ coins on the table and divide the remaining coins equally between the scales. If the scales balance, all the coins on the balance are genuine; the solution to part (a) can now be applied to the coins remaining on the table with one of the coins from the balance as the required genuine coin. If the scales tip, the coins on the table are genuine. The coins on the balance can all be marked either "possibly heavy" or "possibly light" and the solution to part (b) applied to them with one of the coins on the table as the required genuine coin. In each case, the total number of comparisons is at most 1+n.

When there are 12 coins, we first note that $(3^2-1)/2<12<(3^3-1)/2$. The algorithm begins by dividing the coins into three groups of 4.

If the scales balance, the algorithm proceeds further with the 4 coins on the table and one of the coins from the balance as the genuine coin. After two further comparisons (details of which are left to the reader) the fake coin, if it exists, is determined.

If the scales do not balance, the 8 coins on the scales are marked appropriately and one of the coins on the table is used as the genuine coin. Six of the 8 marked coins are redistributed on the balance (so that each scale gets 2+1 coins, where the "2" coins are from one side of the balance and the "1" coin is from the other side). After this comparison, either two or three marked coins remain (two if the scales balance, three if the scales do not balance). In the case where two remain, the fake coin can be determined by comparing one of the coins with the genuine coin. In the case where three remain, two with the same marking are compared. This one comparison is sufficient to determine which is the fake coin.

Solution 7.2   When m is 0, there is just one object. This is the unique object and 0 (which equals 2×0) comparisons are needed to discover that fact.

Suppose now that m is greater than 0. Split the 3^m objects into three groups each of 3^{m-1} objects. One of these three groups will have a different weight than the other two, which will be of equal weight. At most 2 comparisons are needed to determine which of the groups it is. Then, by induction, at most a further $2\times(m-1)$ comparisons are required to find the unique object in that group. This gives a total of $2\times(m-1)+2$ (i.e. $2\times m$) comparisons as required by the induction hypothesis.

It is possible to determine whether the unique object is lighter or heavier than the others (although, in the case where there is just one object, the answer is that it is both lighter and heavier than all the rest). It can be decided in the first two comparisons.

Solution 7.3

(a) For n=1, it is clear that 0 comparisons are needed. For the induction step, assume that n−1 comparisons are needed to find the lightest of n objects. To find the lightest of n+1 objects, use n−1 comparisons to find the lightest of n objects, then compare this object with the (n+1)th object. The lightest of the two is the lightest of them all. Also, one extra comparison has been made, making n in total.

(b) For n=2, it is clear that 1 comparison is needed. For the induction step, assume that 2n−3 comparisons are needed to find the lightest and heaviest of n objects. To find the lightest and heaviest of n+1 objects, use 2n−3 comparisons to find the lightest and heaviest of n objects. Call these L and H. Call the (n+1)th object N. The lightest of L and N is the lightest of them all, and the heaviest of H and N is the heaviest of them all. This requires two extra comparisons, making (2n−3)+2, i.e. 2(n+1)−3 in total.

(c) Compare A and C. The lightest of the two is the lightest of the four. Compare B and D. The heaviest of the two is the heaviest of the four.

To weigh four objects, first compare two. Call the lighter one A and the heavier one B. Likewise, compare the remaining two objects and call the lighter one C and the heavier one D. Then proceed as above.

(d) For m=1, it is clear that 1 comparison is needed to find the lightest and heaviest of 2 objects. And $1 = 3 \times 1 - 2$.

Suppose there are 2(m+1) objects. Select and compare any two of the objects. Let the lightest be A and the heaviest B. By induction, we can find the lightest and heaviest of the remaining 2m objects in 3m−2 comparisons. Let these be C and D, respectively. We now have four objects, A, B, C and D, such that A<B and C<D. By part (c), the lightest and heaviest of these four can be found in 2 further comparisons. These are then the lightest and heaviest of all 2(m+1) objects. And the total number of comparisons is 1+(3m−2)+2 which equals 3(m+1)−2.

Solution 7.4

(a) Distinguishing between left and right scales, each widget can be placed on the left scale, on the right scale, or left aside. For a total of n widgets, this gives 3^n different configurations of the balance. One of these is symmetric between left and right – when no widgets are placed on the scales. All the rest are asymmetric between left and right; from the viewpoint of weighing a fudget, this means that the same configuration is counted twice. The total number of different configurations is thus $(3^n-1)/2+1$, which simplifies to $(3^n+1)/2$.

The conclusion is that at most $(3^n+1)/2$ different fudgets can be weighed using at most n widgets.

(b) Take as induction hypothesis that any fudget of weight w, where $0 \le w < (3^n+1)/2$, can be weighed by placing it inside s of the balance, and suitably placing at most n widgets of weights $3^0, 3^1, 3^2, \ldots$, at most one of each weight, on the balance.

The basis is when n equals 0. A fudget of weight 0 can be weighed by placing it on scale s of the balance and 0 widgets (arbitrarily) on the two scales.

For the induction step, it suffices to show that it is possible to weigh fudgets of weight w, where $(3^n+1)/2 \le w < (3^{n+1}+1)/2$, using at most n+1 widgets. Inevitably, the additional widget of weight 3^n will have to be used. A simple calculation shows that

$$\left[(3^n+1)/2 \le w < (3^{n+1}+1)/2 \equiv -(3^n+1)/2 < w - 3^n < (3^n+1)/2 \right].$$

This suggests a case analysis on the sign of $w-3^n$. If $0 \leq w-3^n$, the induction hypothesis prescribes how to weigh a fudget of weight $w-3^n$ by placing it on side s and suitably placing at most n widgets of weights 3^0, 3^1, 3^2, ..., at most one of each weight, on the balance; by adding the widget of weight 3^n on the opposite side of the balance, the fudget of weight w can be weighed. If, conversely, $0 \leq -(w-3^n)$, the induction hypothesis prescribes how to weigh a fudget of weight $-(w-3^n)$ by placing it on side ¬s and suitably placing at most n widgets of weights 3^0, 3^1, 3^2, ..., at most one of each weight, on the balance; by adding the widget of weight 3^n on the opposite side of the balance, the fudget of weight w can be weighed.

Solution 8.1   Formally we have

$$T_0(d)$$

$$= \qquad \{ \qquad \text{definition of T} \quad \}$$

$$\text{length}(H_0(d))$$

$$= \qquad \{ \qquad \text{definition of } H_0(d) \quad \}$$

$$\text{length}([])$$

$$= \qquad \{ \qquad \text{definition of length} \quad \}$$

$$0$$

and

$$T_{n+1}(d)$$

$$= \qquad \{ \qquad \text{definition of T} \quad \}$$

$$\text{length}(H_{n+1}(d))$$

$$= \qquad \{ \qquad \text{definition of } H_{n+1}(d) \quad \}$$

$$\text{length}(H_n(\neg d) \,;\, [\langle n+1, \neg d \rangle] \,;\, H_n(\neg d))$$

$$= \qquad \{ \qquad \text{definition of length} \quad \}$$

$$\text{length}(H_n(\neg d)) + \text{length}([\langle n+1, \neg d \rangle]) + \text{length}(H_n(\neg d))$$

$$= \qquad \{ \qquad \text{definition of T (twice) and length} \quad \}$$

$$T_n(\neg d) + 1 + T_n(\neg d).$$

That is,

$$T_0(d) = 0$$
$$T_{n+1}(d) = 2 \times T_n(\neg d) + 1.$$

If we expand these equations for n=0,1,2,..., just as we did for the equations for H, we discover that $T_0(d)$ is 0, $T_1(d)$ is 1 and $T_2(d)$ is 3 (in each case for all d). This and the form of the equation for $T_{n+1}(d)$ (in particular the repeated multiplication by 2) suggest that $T_n(d)$ is $2^n - 1$. The simple inductive proof is omitted.

Solution 8.2   We begin by considering the permissible states that the puzzle may be in. In any state, the discs on any one pole are in order of decreasing size. So, if we want to specify the state of the puzzle we only need to specify which pole each disc is on. For example, suppose there are five discs and suppose we specify that disc 1 is on pole A, disc 2 is on pole B, discs 3 and 4 are on pole A and disc 5 is on pole B. Then disc 4 must be on the bottom of pole A, disc 3 must be on top of it, and disc 1 must be on top of disc 3. Also, disc 5 must be on the bottom of pole B and disc 2 must be on top of it. No other arrangement of the discs satisfies the rule that no disc is above a disc smaller than itself.

The state of an n-disc puzzle can thus be specified by a sequence of n pole names. The first name in the sequence is the location of disc 1, the second is the location of disc 2, and so on. That is, the kth name in the sequence is the location (pole name) of disc k. Since each disc may be on one of three poles, we conclude that there are 3^n different states in the n-disc problem.

We now consider the transitions between states. We consider first the problem where there are no discs, then the 1-disc problem, then the 2-disc problem, and then we consider the general n-disc problem.

When there are no discs there is exactly one state: the state when there are no discs on any of the poles. This is shown in Figure S.2. (You may have difficulty seeing the figure. It consists of a single dot!)

Figure S.2: State-transition diagram for 0-disc problem.

We now explain how to construct the state-transition diagram for the (n+1)-disc problem, for an arbitrary n, given that we have constructed the diagram for the n-disc problem. (See Figure S.3.) Each state is a sequence of n+1 pole names. The first n names specify the location of the smallest n discs and the (n+1)th specifies the location of the largest disc. Thus, each state in the state-transition diagram for the n-disc problem gives rise to 3 states in the state-transition diagram for the (n+1)-disc problem. That is, a state in the state-transition diagram for the (n+1)-disc problem is specified by a sequence of n pole numbers followed by the pole name A, B or C. We split the permissible moves into two sets: those where the largest disc (the disc numbered n+1) is moved and those where a disc other than the largest disc is moved.

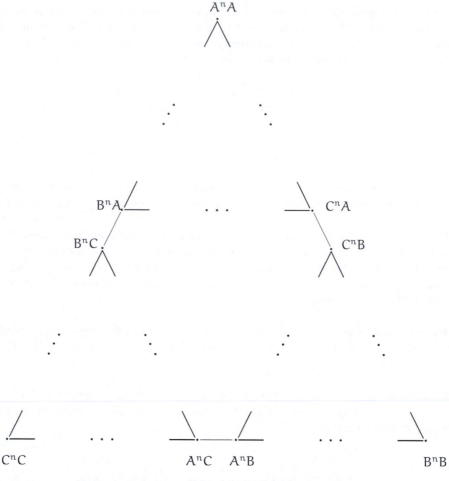

○ **Figure S.3: Construction of the state-transition diagram for the (n + 1)-disc problem.**

Consider first moving a disc other than the largest disc. When doing so, the largest disc may be on pole A, B or C. But its position does not affect the permissibility or otherwise of a move of a smaller disc. That means that every transition from state s to state t in the n-disc problem is also a valid transition from state sp to state tp in the (n+1)-disc problem, where the pole name p is either A, B or C. The first step in the construction of the state-transition diagram for the (n+1)-disc problem given the state-transition diagram for the n-disc problem is to make three copies of the latter. The pth copy is then modified by simply adding p at the end of each sequence of pole numbers labelling the nodes.

Now consider moving the largest disc, the disc numbered n+1. Being the largest disc, it may only be moved if all the other discs are on one and the same pole different than the pole that the largest disc is on. This gives six possibilities for moving disc $n+1$, or three edges in the undirected state-transition diagram: an edge connecting the states A^nB and A^nC, an edge connecting the states B^nC and B^nA and an edge connecting the states C^nA and C^nB. The construction is shown schematically in Figure S.3, the three inner triangles representing the set of all moves that do not move disc $n+1$.

Solution 8.3

(a) Let $C_n(d)$ denote the sequence of discs. The base case, when n equals 0, is the empty sequence.

For the induction step, it is necessary to distinguish two cases: d is clockwise and d is anticlockwise. In the first case, by the inductive hypothesis, it is possible to move the n smallest discs in an anticlockwise direction. By doing so, then moving disc $n+1$ (clockwise) and, finally, moving the n smallest discs again anticlockwise, the goal of moving $n+1$ discs in a clockwise direction is achieved. The second case is harder. The key point is that the largest disc must move twice clockwise in order to displace it one position clockwise. As in the first case, begin by moving the n smallest discs anticlockwise followed by moving disc $n+1$ (clockwise). Then move the n smallest discs clockwise. (This returns the n smallest discs to their original position.) Follow this by moving disc $n+1$ again. Finally, move the n smallest discs anticlockwise. Formally, the complete algorithm is expressed by the following three equations.

$$C_0(d) = []$$
$$C_{n+1}(cw) = C_n(aw); [n+1]; C_n(aw)$$
$$C_{n+1}(aw) = C_n(aw); [n+1]; C_n(cw); [n+1]; C_n(aw)$$

(b) Straightforward generalisation of part (a).

Solution 8.4   Even, because the direction of movement is opposite to that of the smallest disc (which has an odd number).

Solution 8.5   The algorithm is to repeatedly execute the following procedure until it can no longer be executed (i.e. when it is no longer possible to determine k in step 1).

1. Suppose it is possible to move disc k in the direction d', where $k>1$. (Recall that disc 1 is the smallest disc.) Set d to $odd(k) \equiv d'$.

2. Move disc k (in the direction d', of course).

3. Move the smallest disc in the direction d.

The correctness is justified as follows. When step 1 is executed, we know that the first $k-1$ discs are all on the pole in direction $\neg d'$ from disc k. Progress is made if these k smallest discs can be transferred to the same pole. To do this, it is necessary to move the k−1 smallest discs in the direction ¬d'. The direction that disc 1 has to be moved is thus d, where

$$\text{even}(k{-}1) \equiv \neg d' \equiv \text{even}(1) \equiv d.$$

Simplifying, we get that d=(odd(k)≡d'). (In words, the direction that the smallest disc is moved should be the same as the direction that disc k is moved, if k is also odd; otherwise the smallest disc is moved in the opposite direction to disc k.) The correctness of the Tower of Hanoi program then guarantees that this action will initiate a sequence of moves after which all k−1 discs will have been moved onto disc k. During this sequence of moves the smallest disc will continue to move in the same direction. On completion, however, the direction of the smallest disc may or may not be reversed.

The only time that step 1 cannot be executed is when all the discs are on the same pole, as required.

Solution 8.6 The solution is to place the discs in order, starting with the largest and ending with the smallest. Let k denote the number of the discs still to be replaced; so, initially k is N and we are done when k is 0. Each time the value of k is reassigned, we ensure that the k smallest discs are on the same pole.

If the kth disc is on the right pole, decrease k by 1. Otherwise, suppose it needs to be moved in direction d from its current position. Move the smallest k−1 discs in the direction ¬d, then move disc k to its rightful position. Finally, decrease k by 1. Continue this process until k is 0.

Solution 9.4 Clearly, the goal is impossible to reach if the objects are all of the same kind and there is more than one of them. So, as suggested, we assume that there are objects of different kinds. Let m, n and p denote the number of objects of each kind.

The replacement process is modelled by the assignment

$$m,n,p := m{+}1,n{-}1,p{-}1$$

and the two assignments obtained by permuting m, n and p.

Noting that increasing/decreasing by 1 flips the parity of a number, we conclude that an invariant of the assignment is: the numbers are all even or the numbers are all odd. Since the goal is to reach a state in which there are two even numbers (two 0s) and one odd number (one 1), that is, the invariant is false, we conclude that the goal is impossible to reach if the invariant is true in the starting state, that is, if initially all the numbers are even or all the numbers are odd.

Let us assume that initially one kind of object has different parity than the other two. For concreteness, assume that even(m)=even(n)≠even(p). The goal becomes to reduce m and n to 0 and p to 1. As mentioned earlier, we assume also that

¬(m=n=0∧p≠1).

Equivalently, we assume that initially

(m≠0∨n≠0∨p=1)∧(even(m)=even(n)≠even(p)).

This is the invariant of the algorithm.

If m or n is zero, p must be odd and hence non-zero. It follows that if m or n is non-zero, there must be two objects of different kinds. Choosing to increase the number of objects of a kind that occurs least frequently maintains the invariant and reduces the number of objects. This is expressed in the algorithm below.

$$\{ \textbf{Invariant: } (m \neq 0 \vee n \neq 0 \vee p = 1) \wedge (\text{even}(m) = \text{even}(n) \neq \text{even}(p)) $$

Measure of progress: m+n+p }

```
do m≠0∨n≠0  →    if  m≤n↓p  →  m,n,p  :=  m+1,n−1,p−1
                 ☐  n≤p↓m  →  m,n,p  :=  m−1,n+1,p−1
                 ☐  p≤m↓n  →  m,n,p  :=  m−1,n−1,p+1
                 fi
od
{ m=0 ∧ n=0 ∧ p=1 }
```

We need to check that the assignments are valid, that is, no attempt is made to decrease a variable when its value is 0. This is where the invariance of

even(m)=even(n)≠even(p)

is relevant. We also need to check that each assignment truthifies

m≠0∨n≠0∨p=1.

The first two truthify m≠0 and n≠0, respectively. The third assignment truthifies p=1 or, if not, maintains m≠0∧n≠0 (note the conjunction rather than disjunction) because m and n are both at least 2 before the assignment.

Solution 9.6 Suppose the number of tumblers is N. Assume the tumblers are numbered from 0 onwards by their position in the line. An algorithm iteratively ensures that the first k tumblers are upside up, so that the measure of progress is N−k. Initially, k is 0. Each iteration ensures that tumbler k is upside up by, if necessary, turning it and tumbler k+1. If N is odd, the fact that there is always an even number of upside-down tumblers ensures that no attempt is made to turn the non-existent tumbler N on the last iteration. Formally, the algorithm is as follows:

$\{\ \text{even}(\langle \Sigma i : 0 \leq i < N \wedge \text{down}(i) : 1 \rangle)\ \}$

$k := 0;$

$\{$ **Invariant:** $0 \leq k \leq N \wedge \text{even}(\langle \Sigma i : k \leq i < N \wedge \text{down}(i) : 1 \rangle)$

$\wedge\ \langle \forall i : 0 \leq i < k : \text{up}(i) \rangle$

Measure of progress: N−k $\}$

$\text{do } k < N \rightarrow \quad \text{if} \quad \text{down}(k) \rightarrow \{\ 0 \leq k < k+1 < N\ \} \text{ turn tumblers } k \text{ and } k+1$

$\square \quad \text{up}(k) \rightarrow \text{skip}$

$\text{fi} ;$

$k := k+1$

od

$\{\ \langle \forall i : 0 \leq i < N : \text{up}(i) \rangle\ \}$

Solution 9.7 The system invariant is

$$(\text{lB}=\text{lP}) \vee (\text{lB}=0) \vee (\text{lB}=N). \tag{S.2}$$

That is, either there are no single individuals on either bank, or all bodyguards are on one of the two banks. It is a requirement of any solution that this property is an invariant. (If not, either 0<lB<lP or 0<rB<rP. In words, the presidents outnumber the bodyguards on the left bank or on the right bank. In both cases, the solution is invalid.)

Now, we claim that, under the given assumptions on M and N, either

(a) the boat is on the left bank and

$$M < \text{lB}, \tag{S.3}$$

or

(b) the boat is on the right bank and

$$M \leq \text{lB}. \tag{S.4}$$

Property (a) is clearly true initially. (Recall the assumptions about M and N.)

Now, suppose (a) is true and, then, a crossing is made from left to right. Note that lB≠0 both before and after the crossing. (Before the crossing, lB=0 is excluded by the assumption that M<lB. After the crossing, lB=0 is impossible because at most M bodyguards can cross together.) So the invariant (S.2) can be strengthened: the crossing is made starting in a state in which

$$(lB=lP)\lor(lB=N), \tag{S.5}$$

and must result in a state satisfying this property. Otherwise, the crossing is invalid. Note also that a left-to-right crossing causes lB and/or lP to decrease.

We consider two cases before the crossing: lB=N and (lB=lP)∧(lB≠N).

Since at most N/2 bodyguards can cross together, if lB=N before the crossing, at least N/2 bodyguards are left at the left bank. That is, (b) is true after the crossing.

If (lB=lP)∧(lB≠N) before the crossing, the property lB=lP must be maintained by the crossing. (This is because (S.5) must be maintained and the crossing cannot increase lB.) That is, an equal number of presidents and bodyguards must make the crossing. Since only one couple can cross at one time, the value of lB is decreased by at most 1. But (S.3) is assumed to be true before the crossing; consequently, (S.4) is true after the crossing, and the boat is at the right bank. Thus, (b) is true after the crossing.

In both cases, we have established that, after the crossing, (b) is true.

Now suppose (b) is true and a crossing is made from right to left. A right-to-left crossing causes lB and/or lP to increase. Since lB≠0 before the crossing, and lB does not decrease, lB≠0 after the crossing.

Again, we consider two cases: this time, no bodyguards cross, and some bodyguards cross.

If bodyguards cross, the act of crossing increases lB; so after the crossing M<lB and (of course) the boat is at the left bank. Thus, (a) is true after the crossing.

If only presidents cross, it must be the case that lB=N (because (S.5) must be maintained and, if only presidents cross, it is impossible to maintain that lB=lP). That is, lB is unchanged, and M<lB both before and after the crossing. After the crossing, the boat is, of course, at the left bank. Thus, (a) is true after the crossing.

In both cases, we have established that (a) is true after the crossing.

In summary, property (a) is true initially. Also, if (a) is true and a left-to-right crossing is made, (b) is truthified; vice versa, if (b) is true and a right-to-left crossing is made, (a) is truthified. So, at all times, either (a) or (b) is true. That is, it can never be the case that all bodyguards are at the right bank.

Solution 10.15   Binary search is used to determine when the difference between successive values of the funtion OT changes from being negative to being positive. The search is encoded as follows:

$$\{\ 2 \le N\ \}$$

$$i, j\ :=\ 1, N \div 2\ ;$$

$$\{\ \textbf{Invariant:}$$

$$1 \le i \le j \le N \div 2$$

$$\wedge\ \langle \forall k\ :\ 1 \le k < i\ :\ OT.(k+1) - OT.k\ \le\ 0 \rangle$$

$$\wedge\ \langle \forall k\ :\ j \le k < N \div 2\ :\ 0 \le OT.(k+1) - OT.k \rangle\ \}$$

$$do\ i < j\ \rightarrow\quad m := (i+j) \div 2\ ;$$

$$\text{if}\quad 2 \times t.2\ \le\ t.1 + t.(N-2m+1)\ \rightarrow\ i := m$$

$$\square\quad 2 \times t.2\ \ge\ t.1 + t.(N-2m+1)\ \rightarrow\ j := m$$

$$\text{fi}$$

$$od$$

$$\{\quad 1 \le j \le N \div 2$$

$$\wedge\ \langle \forall k\ :\ 1 \le k < j\ :\ OT.(k+1) - OT.k\ \le\ 0 \rangle$$

$$\wedge\ \langle \forall k\ :\ j \le k < N \div 2\ :\ 0 \le OT.(k+1) - OT.k \rangle\ \}.$$

On termination, j is the multiplicity of {1,2} in an optimal regular bag and OT.j is the required optimal time. Corollary 10.12 specifies the composition of the hard trips and Lemma 10.10 specifies how they are scheduled. The remaining $N-2j+2$ people are then scheduled to cross in $N-2j+1$ firm trips as described above.

Solution 10.16

(a) In any state, there are two possible values for the position of each person, and two possible values for the position of the torch. Now, there are 2^{N+1} functions from a set of size $N+1$ to a position. However, if all people are in one position, the torch must be in the same position; this disallows two such functions. Also disallowed are functions that assign the same position to the torch and exactly one person; there are $2 \times N$ such functions. The total number of states is thus

$$2^{N+1} - (2 + 2 \times N).$$

For N equal to 2, 3, 4, 5 and 6, the number of different states is 2, 8, 22, 52, and 114.

(b) If there are k people at the start, there are $\frac{1}{2} \times k \times (k-1)$ ways of choosing the two people to cross. The number k ranges from N down to 2. Thus the number of different ways of composing the forward trips is

$$\left\langle \prod k : N \geq k \geq 2 : \tfrac{1}{2} \times k \times (k-1) \right\rangle.$$

If there are k people at the finish, there are k ways of choosing who is to return. The number k ranges from 2 up to $N-1$. So there are

$$\left\langle \prod k : 1 \leq k \leq N-1 : k \right\rangle$$

ways of composing the return trips. The total number of different ways of getting N people across the bridge is the product of these two formulae. This simplifies to

$$\frac{N! \times (N-1)! \times (N-1)!}{2^{N-1}}.$$

For N equal to 2, 3, 4, 5 and 6, the number of different ways of getting the people across is 1, 6, 108, 4320 and 324 000.

The number of states grows exponentially, the number of different ways grows like the factorial function.

Solution 11.1

(a) The number of moves that have to be made equals the number of squares. After an odd number of moves, the colour of the current square is different from the colour of the starting square. So, after an odd number of moves, it is impossible to return to the starting square.

(b) It's easy to see that a straight-move circuit of a 2×1 board is possible – starting at one of the squares, move to the other square and then move back again – , but, otherwise, no straight-move circuit is possible. If m is greater than 1, at least one square is two moves from the starting square; it is impossible to visit such a square and return to the starting square without visiting the in-between square more than once.

(c) See (b) for a circuit of a 2×1 board. For n greater than 1, a straight-move circuit of a $2 \times n$ board is completed by starting at a corner, moving one-by-one to all the squares in the same row, then returning via the second row.

Solution 11.2   For the 3×3 board, a circuit can be constructed exactly when the omitted square is not adjacent to a corner square. If the squares of the board are coloured black and white as for a chessboard, these are the squares that have a different colour to the corner squares. For larger boards, the same rule applies. Suppose the corner squares are coloured black. (All four corners have the same colour because it is assumed that the board has odd size.) Then the number of black squares exceeds the number of white squares by one. Any circuit comprises an alternating sequence of black and white squares of which the number of black squares equals the number of white squares. If a white square is omitted it is impossible to construct a circuit of all the remaining squares because the number of remaining black squares is greater than the number of remaining white squares.

Suppose the omitted square is black and its coordinates are (m, n). (It doesn't matter whether numbering starts at zero or one or which corner is taken as the origin.) Then $\text{even}(m) = \text{even}(n)$.

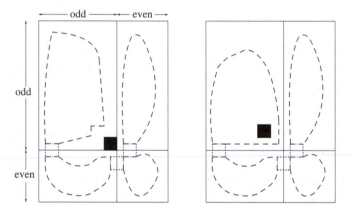

⬭ **Figure S.4: Construction of a straight-move circuit omitting one square.**

The construction is to split the board into four rectangular boards in such a way that the to-be-omitted square is at a corner of a board with an odd number of squares as shown in Figure S.4. (The to-be-omitted square may thus be the corner square, as shown in the left figure, or one space in from the corner, as shown in the right figure.) The odd-sized board must be at least 3×3 but smaller than the entire board. (This is always possible if the to-be-omitted square is at position (m, n) and $\text{even}(m) = \text{even}(n)$.) The other three boards each have an even number of squares, and at least one of them has at least one square. Construct circuits of these three boards, and – inductively, with the 3×3 board as the base case – a circuit of the board with the omitted square. Then, connect the circuits together as shown in Figure S.4: the left figure is the case that the distance of the to-be-omitted square from each corner is odd, and the right figure is the case that the distance is even. In the inductive step, moves within a board are replaced by moves between boards as indicated in the figure.

(The crucial fact is that the replaced lines must exist because any circuit can only enter and leave each corner square in exactly one way.)

Solution 11.6 See Table S.6.

;	n	v	h	c
n	n	v	h	c
v	v	n	c	h
h	h	c	n	v
c	c	h	v	n

Table S.6: **Sequential composition of flip operations.**

Property (11.7) is verified by observing that the table is symmetric about the top-left to bottom-right diagonal. Verification of the associativity property is much more tedious. The case that x, y or z is n can be dealt with simply. This leaves 27 other cases to consider. This is an example of a "tedious, but straightforward" proof!

Solution 11.9 See Table S.7.

;	n	r	a	c
n	n	r	a	c
r	r	c	n	a
a	a	n	c	r
c	c	a	r	n

Table S.7: **Sequential composition of rotation operations.**

Solution 11.10 See Figure S.5.

The parallel moves used to connect circuits of different colours are indicated by dotted lines depicting the straight moves, and solid black lines, depicting the diagonal moves.

Note how the choice of parallel moves constrains the choice of a circuit of the striped squares. In contrast, there is complete freedom in choosing circuits of the white and shaded-and-striped squares. There is some freedom in choosing a circuit of the shaded squares, but not complete freedom. In this way, a substantial number of circuits can be found all based on the same set of combining parallel moves. In the circuit shown, the "shaded", "white" and "shaded-and-striped" circuits were constructed by "copying" the striped circuit.

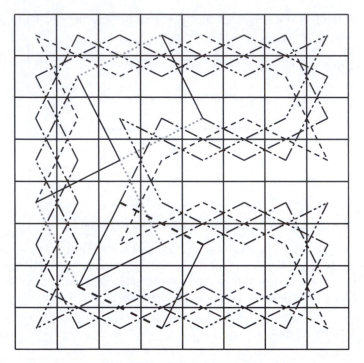

Figure S.5: A knight's circuit. The circuit is formed from the solid and dashed lines. The two pairs of parallel dotted lines depict straight moves that are replaced. The diagonal moves that replace them are depicted by solid black lines.

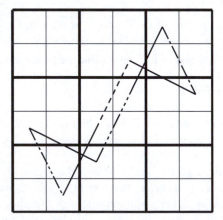

Figure S.6: Details of how the four straight-move circuits are combined; the straight moves indicated by dotted lines are replaced by diagonal moves indicated by solid black lines.

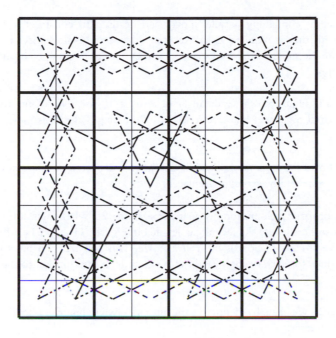

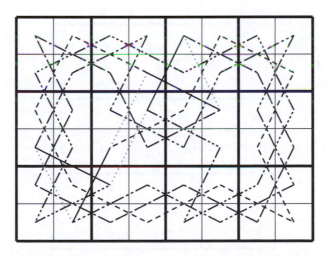

Figure S.7: Knight's circuit of an 8×6 and an 8×8 board. (Dotted lines are not part of the circuit; these are the moves that are replaced by diagonal moves, as detailed in Figure S.6.)

The same set of combining parallel moves can be used to construct a circuit of an 8×6 board; all that is required is to "shorten" the straight-move circuits in order to accommodate the smaller board. (But note that they cannot be used to construct a circuit of a 6×8 board.)

Solution 11.11 Figure S.6 shows details of how the straight-move circuits are combined. Moves indicated by dotted lines are replaced by the diagonal moves indicated by solid black lines.

Figure S.7 shows the circuits obtained in this way. The dotted lines are not part of the circuit; these are the moves that are replaced.

In order to construct a circuit for any board of size 4m×2n, where m is at least 2 and n is at least 3, it suffices to use the technique detailed in Figures 11.2 and 11.3 for extending straight-move circuits to boards of arbitrary size. This construction has to be applied four times, once for each of the straight-move circuits in the solution to the 8×6-board problem.

Solution 11.12 We begin by identifying the moves shown in Figure 11.15. See Figure S.8. (Note the symmetry.)

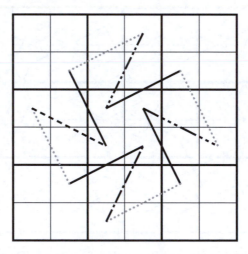

Figure S.8: Details of combining circuits. Diagonal moves are shown in black. Straight moves are coloured. The dotted lines represent the moves that are replaced. Solid lines represent the moves that replace them.

Now it is easy to fill in the straight-move circuits around the remaining squares. See Figure S.9.

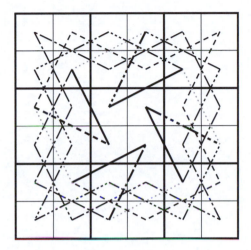

Figure S.9: Knight's circuit of a 6×6 board. (The dotted lines do not form part of the circuit as detailed in Figure S.8.)

For the general problem, it is easy to extend the straight-move circuits.

References

[Bac08] Roland Backhouse. The capacity-C torch problem. In Philippe Audebaud and Christine Paulin-Mohring (eds), *Mathematics of Program Construction, 9th International Conference, MPC2008, Marseille, France, Lecture Notes in Computer Science* 5133, pp. 57–78. Springer, 2008.

[BCaF10] Roland Backhouse, Wei Chen, and João Ferreira. The algorithmics of solitaire-like games. In Claude Bolduc, Jules Desharnais, and Béchir Ktari (eds), *Proceedings of 10th International Conference on Mathematics of Program Construction, Lecture Notes in Computer Science* 6120, pp. 1–18. Springer, 2010.

[BCG82] Elwyn R. Berlekamp, John H. Conway, and Richard K. Guy. *Winning Ways*, vols I and II. Academic Press, 1982.

[BF01] Roland Backhouse and Maarten Fokkinga. The associativity of equivalence and the Towers of Hanoi problem. *Information Processing Letters*, 77: 71–76, 2001.

[BL80] P. Buneman and L. Levy. The Towers of Hanoi problem. *Information Processing Letters*, **10**: 243–244, 1980.

[Dij76] Edsger W. Dijkstra. *A Discipline of Programming*. Prentice Hall, 1976.

[Dij90] Edsger W. Dijkstra. EWD1083: The balance and the coins. http://www.cs.utexas.edu/users/EWD/ewd10xx/EWD1083.PDF, September 1990.

[Dij92] Edsger W. Dijkstra. EWD1135: The knight's tour. http://www.cs.utexas.edu/users/EWD/ewd11xx/EWD1131.PDF, September 1992.

[Dij97] Edsger W. Dijkstra. EWD1260: The marked coins and the scale. http://www.cs.utexas.edu/users/EWD/ewd12xx/EWD1260.PDF, March 1997.

[DS90] Edsger W. Dijkstra and Carel S. Scholten. *Predicate Calculus and Program Semantics*. Springer-Verlag, 1990.

[DW00] John P. D'Angelo and Douglas B. West. *Mathematical Thinking. Problem-Solving and Proofs*. Prentice Hall, 2000.

[Fer10] João Ferreira. Principles of algorithmic problem solving. PhD thesis, School of Computer Science, University of Nottingham, 2010.

[Gar08] Martin Gardner. *Hexaflexagons, Probability Paradoxes and the Tower of Hanoi: Martin Gardner's First Book of Mathematical Puzzles and Games*. Cambridge University Press, 2008.

[Gri81] David Gries. *The Science of Programming*. Springer, 1981.

[GS93] David Gries and Fred B. Schneider. *A Logical Approach to Discrete Math*. Springer, 1993.

[Lei69] Gottfried Wilhelm Leibniz. *Philosophical Papers and Letters, A Selection Translated and Edited, with an Introduction by Leroy E. Loemker*, chapter A Study in the Logical Calculus, pages 371–382. D.Reidel Publishing Company, Dordrecht-Holland, 1969.

[Hon97] Ross Honsberger. *In Pólya's Footsteps: Miscellaneous Problems and Essays, Dolciani Mathematical Expositions* 19. Mathematical Association of America, October 1997.

[Knu68] Donald E. Knuth. *The Art of Computer Programming*, Vol. I: *Fundamental Algorithms*. Addison-Wesley, 1968.

[Knu69] Donald E. Knuth. *The Art of Computer Programming*, Vol. II: *Seminumerical Algorithms*. Addison-Wesley, 1969.

[Lev03] Anany Levitin. *Introduction to The Design and Analysis of Algorithms*. Addison-Wesley, 2003.

[MM08] Zbigniew Michalewicz and Matthew Michalewicz. *Puzzle-Based Learning: An Introduction to Critical Thinking, Mathematics and Problem-Solving*. Hybrid Publishers, 2008.

[Rot02] Günter Rote. Crossing the bridge at night. *Bulletin of the European Association for Theoretical Computer Science*, 78: 241–246, 2002.

[Smu78] Raymond Smullyan. *What Is the Name of This Book?* Prentice Hall, 1978.

[Ste97] Ian Stewart. *The Magical Maze*. Weidenfield and Nicolson, 1997.

[Tar56] Alfred Tarski. *Logic, Semantics, Metamathematics: Papers from 1923 to 1938*, translated by J. H. Woodger. Oxford University Press, 1956.

[vG90] A. J. M. van Gasteren. *On the Shape of Mathematical Arguments*, *Lecture Notes in Computer Science* 445. Springer, 1990.

[Wil87] J. G. Wiltink. A deficiency of natural deduction. *Information Processing Letters*, **25**: 233–234, 1987.

Index